D1310781

HEROES AND HEROINES

of Greece and Rome

DISCARDED

 **Marshall Cavendish**
Reference

New York

LIBRARY
CALDWELL COMMUNITY COLLEGE
HUDSON, NC

Copyright © 2012 Marshall Cavendish Corporation

11-12 MC 52.84

Published by Marshall Cavendish Reference

An imprint of Marshall Cavendish Corporation

All rights reserved.

No part of this publication may be reproduced, stored in a retrieval system or transmitted, in any form or by any means, electronic, mechanical, photocopying, recording, or otherwise, without the prior permission of the copyright owner. Request for permission should be addressed to Permissions, Marshall Cavendish Corporation, 99 White Plains Road, Tarrytown, NY 10591.
Tel: (914) 332-8888, fax: (914) 332-1888.

Website: www.marshallcavendish.us

11-12

This publication represents the opinions and views of the authors based on personal experience, knowledge, and research. The information in this book serves as a general guide only. The authors and publisher have used their best efforts in preparing this book and disclaim liability rising directly and indirectly from the use and application of this book.

Other Marshall Cavendish Offices:

Marshall Cavendish International (Asia) Private Limited, 1 New Industrial Road, Singapore 536196 • Marshall Cavendish International (Thailand) Co Ltd. 253 Asoke, 12th Flr, Sukhumvit 21 Road, Klongtoey Nua, Wattana, Bangkok 10110, Thailand • Marshall Cavendish (Malaysia) Sdn Bhd, Times Subang, Lot 46, Subang Hi-Tech Industrial Park, Batu Tiga, 40000 Shah Alam, Selangor Darul Ehsan, Malaysia

Marshall Cavendish is a trademark of Times Publishing Limited

All websites were available and accurate when this book was sent to press.

Library of Congress Cataloging-in-Publication Data

Heroes and heroines of Greece and Rome.
     p. cm.
  Includes bibliographical references and index.
  ISBN 978-0-7614-7952-9 (alk. paper)
1. Heroes--Greece. 2. Heroes--Rome. 3. Women heroes--Greece. 4. Women heroes--Rome. 5. Mythology, Greek. 6. Mythology, Roman.
  BL795.H46H45 2012
  398.20938'02--dc22

                                                        2011006781

Printed in Malaysia

15 14 13 12 11 1 2 3 4 5

Marshall Cavendish
Publisher: Paul Bernabeo
Project Editor: Brian Kinsey
Production Manager: Michael Esposito
Indexer: Cynthia Crippen, AEIOU, Inc.

CONTENTS

CONTENTS

INTRODUCTION

Heroes and heroines come in all shapes, sizes, and ages. However, strictly speaking, heroes and heroines in Greek and Roman mythology all had one thing in common: they were mortals. These individuals could be good, but that was not necessarily the case. Sometimes they obtained their status because of actions rather than virtue. For example, Agamemnon was portrayed as a brave hero of the Trojan War even though he sacrificed his daughter Iphigeneia to the gods in exchange for winds to carry the Greek fleet to Troy.

The idea of a person being a hero or heroine was also related to the individual's continued influential presence after death (one meaning of the Greek word *heros* is "ghost"). One way in which individuals could live on was to be memorialized in unforgettable tales of their deeds. That is why many of the characters in Homer's *Iliad* and *Odyssey*, including Agamemnon, are called heroes.

The ability to live on gave heroes and heroines a special position in the order of the world. Immortal gods and goddesses lived forever, and mere mortals died, but heroes and heroines could do either—making them the intermediaries between the immortals and the mortals. The heroes and heroines generally seemed more approachable than the immortal gods and goddesses, so people would turn to their heroes and heroines in times of need. Some heroes and heroines were considered to have oracular powers or curative powers, and their physical remains and possessions were believed to provide protection and power. Therefore, many heroes and heroines, including Agamemnon and Odysseus, became the objects of cult worship.

Also present in the world of the mortal heroes and heroines, as apposed to the world of the immortal gods and goddesses, are the demigods (children of gods and mortals), nymphs, sorceresses, and partially human creatures, such as satyrs. Because of their parentage, demigods form a distinct, if overlapping, group where heroes and heroines are concerned. For example, Perseus was the son of the god Zeus and the mortal Danae, so he is not a hero by the strictest definition of the term in relation to mythology, but he did perform heroic acts, including slaying the monster Medusa, which leads many people to think of him as a hero. The same ambiguity characterizes other demigods who fall into this middle territory between the immortals and the mortals.

The 94 articles in *Heroes and Heroines of Greece and Rome* represent the most well-known heroes and heroines from those two civilizations, as well as the overlapping demigods, nymphs, sorceresses, and other creatures that inhabited the mortal world and figured prominently in the myths of the heroes and heroines. The abundant illustrations in this volume represent many centuries of artistic interpretations of these famous beings and their mythologies. Each article includes a bibliography and a selection of cross-references to related articles. At the end of the volume is a detailed pronunciation guide, a list of the major figures in the world of heroes and heroines, resources for further study, and an index.

Although these articles should also appeal to the general reader, they were written with high school students in mind, especially those who may find themselves in classes ranging from history and literature to art and music, where mythology plays a part. These articles illumine subjects that continue to reemerge in modern culture.

Additional information about Greek and Roman mythology is available in the single-volume *Gods and Goddesses of Greece and Rome*, the 11-volume set *Gods, Goddesses, and Mythology*, and the online *Gods, Goddesses, and Mythology* database at www.marshallcavendishdigital.com.

CONTRIBUTORS

Laurel Bowman
University of Victoria, Canada

Anthony Bulloch
University of California, Berkeley

Andrew Campbell
London, UK

Alys Caviness
Noblesville, Indiana

Kathryn Chew
California State University, Long Beach

Anna Claybourne
Edinburgh, UK

Peter Connor
London, UK

Barbara Gardner
Mendocino, California

Lyn Green
Toronto, Canada

Daniel P. Harmon
University of Washington

Karelisa Hartigan
University of Florida

Kathleen Jenks
Hartford, Michigan

Deborah Lyons
Johns Hopkins University

Jim Marks
Spokane, Washington

James M. Redfield
University of Chicago

Carl Ruck
Boston University

Feyo Schuddeboom
Hilversum, Netherlands

Brian Seilstad
Lutherville, Maryland

Kirk Summers
University of Alabama

Deborah Thomas
Anderson, South Carolina

ACHILLES

According to Homer's *Iliad*, Achilles was the Greeks' best fighter in the Trojan War, famed for his strength and courage. The story of Achilles is dominated by prophecies about the future, and by desperate attempts to avoid fate—common themes in Greek mythology. As in other tales, the prophecies come true: despite the efforts of his mother, Achilles dies at Troy while still a young man.

Achilles was the son of the sea goddess Thetis and the mortal Peleus, king of Phthia. Long before his birth, the earth goddess Themis predicted that Thetis would give birth to a son who would be more powerful than his father. Zeus, king of the gods, and his brother, the sea god Poseidon, had both wanted to marry Thetis, but the prophecy put them off, since neither wanted to be overthrown. Instead, Themis said that Thetis should marry a mortal, Peleus, so that her son would be half mortal and thus no threat to the gods. Other versions say that Zeus's wife, Hera, helped to raise Thetis, and the sea goddess refused Zeus's advances out of loyalty to her.

Several events occurred at the wedding of Peleus and Thetis that would have a bearing on Achilles' life. For a wedding gift, the gods gave the happy couple the enchanted horses Xanthus and Balius, which would later pull Achilles' chariot. More significant, during the wedding ceremony, Eris, goddess of discord, threw a golden apple among the guests. The apple was inscribed with the words *For the fairest*, and was claimed by three goddesses: Hera; Athena, goddess of arts and war; and the love goddess Aphrodite. Zeus asked the mortal Paris, son of King Priam of Troy, to judge the victor. Paris chose Aphrodite in return for the goddess's promise to help him win the most beautiful woman alive—Helen, daughter of Zeus and the mortal Leda.

Achilles' younger years

Another of Themis's prophecies regarding Achilles was that he would die in battle. When Achilles was born, Thetis tried to protect her beloved son from his fate. According to one version of the story, she dipped him in the magical Styx River in the underworld in order to make him immortal, but she held onto her son by the heel, which became the one vulnerable point on his body. In other versions, Thetis tried to protect Achilles by applying ambrosia (the ointment of the gods) to his body by day and putting him in the embers of fire by night to burn away his mortality. Peleus, however, was alarmed by his wife's behavior and prevented her from continuing her treatment of Achilles. His intervention irritated Thetis, who left her husband but continued to watch over her son.

Peleus sent Achilles to be educated by Cheiron, a centaur (a human with the body of a horse) famed for his wisdom and kindness. Cheiron trained the boy to use weapons and taught him many other skills, including healing and playing the lyre (see box, page 9). However, as Achilles grew older, he became unruly, stealing things and vandalizing the other centaurs' homes, and Cheiron despaired of his disobedience. After his time with Cheiron, Achilles returned to live with Peleus. His new tutor was Phoenix, whom Peleus had made king of the Dolopians. During his time with Phoenix, Achilles became acquainted with the youth Patroclus. Peleus made Patroclus his son's attendant, and the two became lifelong companions.

Sent away to hide

When Achilles was nine, the seer Calchas said that the great war that was to take place at Troy could only be won if the Greeks had Achilles fighting on their side. This prophecy terrified Thetis, who dreaded her son's death in battle. Hoping to save him from the war, she disguised Achilles as a girl named Pyrrha and took him to live in secret at the court of King Lycomedes on the island of Scyros. She told Lycomedes that Pyrrha was Achilles' sister, and the king believed her. In another version of events, Thetis sent her son to Scyros before Calchas's prophecy, and it was only after the seer gave his prediction that she insisted Achilles hide from the Greeks by pretending to be Pyrrha. At first Achilles was mortified at having to dress as a girl, but he

Above: Thetis is depicted in this painting dipping her son Achilles in the River Styx, by Flemish artist Peter Paul Rubens (1577–1640).

soon realized it was a good way to get close to Lycomedes' daughter, Deidamia. The two fell in love, and by the time Achilles left Scyros, at age 15, Deidamia had given birth to their son, Neoptolemus.

The outbreak of war

Paris sparked off the Trojan War when, aided by Aphrodite, he ran away with Helen, who was married to King Menelaus of Sparta. Many other Greek leaders who had originally hoped to marry Helen themselves had sworn an oath to her stepfather Tyndareos that they would fight anyone who tried to harm her marriage to Menelaus. They now were obliged to go to Troy to help Menelaus win back his wife. Achilles himself had not taken the oath, but because of Calchas's prophecy, the Greeks needed him to go to Troy, too. Odysseus, king of Ithaca, having heard where Achilles was, went to Scyros to collect him. He tricked Achilles out of his disguise by lining up a row of ornaments together with a spear and a shield. Odysseus then played a war trumpet, which caused Achilles instinctively to reach for the weapons, revealing himself as a trained soldier.

Achilles eagerly responded to Odysseus's request that he join the Greeks in their war against Troy. Still only 15, he became the leader of the Myrmidons, an army of soldiers from Phthia, who took 50 ships to Troy. His closest friend, Patroclus, also went with him to the war. Events before the Greeks landed at Troy demonstrated both Achilles' valor and his hotheadedness. He attempted to save the life of Iphigeneia, daughter of the Greek leader Agamemnon, when Agamemnon was poised to sacrifice her to ensure favorable winds for the Greek ships. Iphigeneia, however, offered herself for sacrifice anyway, and the Greeks set sail, landing not in Troy but, by accident, in Mysia, where Achilles acted honorably for a second time. On Mysia, an army led by King Telephus attacked the Greeks and drove them back to their ships. Achilles, however, stood firm and inflicted a serious wound on Telephus. An oracle told Telephus that his wound could only be cured by the one who had caused it. He raced after the Greeks. Odysseus, guessing that the cause of the wound was Achilles' spear, advised Achilles to rub rust from the weapon into the king's body. In thanks, Telephus showed the Greeks the way to Troy. As their journey continued, however, the Greeks stopped at the island of Tenedos, where Achilles fell for Hemithea, the sister of King Tenes. Tenes tried to keep Achilles away from her, and in a fit of anger the young Greek killed him. This murder caused even more grief for Thetis, for it had been said that whoever killed Tenes would in turn be killed by his father, the sun god Apollo.

During the ten-year siege of Troy, the Greeks raided other settlements in the area for supplies, or attacked them because they supported the Trojans. Achilles and his men sacked the island of Lesbos and captured 12 nearby cities. The warrior also killed countless Trojans and their supporters, including King Priam's son Troilus, and Cycnus, a son of Poseidon, whose body could withstand the blows of any weapons. Achilles killed Cycnus by strangling him with the straps of his own helmet. Besides fighting, Achilles managed to develop passionate feelings for Polyxena, a daughter of King Priam, even though she was a Trojan. He also kept a slave girl, Briseis, in his camp. He had captured her in Lyrnessus, one of the cities he had raided.

The Centaur Cheiron

A centaur was a creature that was human from the waist up, but with the body and legs of a horse. The centaurs, who were said to have been born out of a cloud, lived in the mountains of Thessaly in central Greece. They were mostly drunken and violent creatures, but one of them, Cheiron, was not like the rest. He was the son of Cronus, the ruler of the Titans, and he was renowned for his gentleness and wisdom. Cheiron was a master of healing. He knew all about medicinal herbs and potions—Asclepius, god of healing, gained his knowledge of medicine from Cheiron. Besides helping to raise Achilles, the great centaur also taught Jason, Actaeon, Patroclus, and Peleus, Achilles' father, among others. Cheiron's life ended after the hero Heracles accidentally shot him with a poisoned arrow. He was badly hurt and longed to die, but he could not because he was immortal. However, the Titan Prometheus offered to become immortal in his place, and Cheiron was finally allowed to die.

Left: A Roman fresco from c. 100 BCE–70 CE depicts the kindly centaur Cheiron teaching Achilles how to play the lyre.

Right: This illustration from a c. sixth-century-BCE kylix (wide-bowled Greek cup) depicts Achilles (right) bandaging the arm of his friend Patroclus.

The fatal argument

In the 10th year of the war, Achilles had a huge quarrel with Agamemnon that involved the youth's slave girl, Briseis, and the commander's slave girl, Chryseis. Achilles and other Greek warriors pleaded with Agamemnon to restore Chryseis to her father, a priest of the sun god Apollo, to save the Greeks from a plague sent by the angry god. Agamemnon did as the other soldiers asked, but he replaced his slave girl with Achilles'. Achilles was so furious that he withdrew from the battle, refusing to fight or to let his men fight. His decision was disastrous for the Greeks. Without Achilles and his armies, they soon lost ground to the Trojans, who eventually reached the Greeks' ships and began to set fire to them. The success of the Trojans was mainly the work of Zeus, whom Thetis had begged to help teach Agamemnon a lesson for upsetting her son. Thetis's wish was granted: Agamemnon soon tried to make amends to Achilles. He sent an embassy of three men to Achilles' tent—Odysseus, Achilles' old tutor Phoenix, and the warrior Ajax—who relayed Agamemnon's offer to return Briseis, along with gifts of land and riches, if Achilles would fight again. However, Achilles would still not relent.

In the end, what changed Achilles' mind was a tragedy. His companion Patroclus offered to go into battle wearing Achilles' armor and pretending to be him. He hoped this would encourage the Greek forces and scare the Trojans. Achilles agreed to the plan. Although Patroclus was successful at first, he chased the Trojans too far and was killed by the Trojan commander Hector. Now Achilles, spurred on by grief and the desire for revenge, deeply regretted his behavior. He wanted nothing more than to kill Hector—even if it cost him his life. Thetis finally began to come to terms with Achilles' fate and helped him by arranging for Hephaestus, god of fire and metalworking, to make new armor for her son.

Achilles reentered the battle against the Trojans, killing dozens of them. He drove the Trojans back inside their city walls, but Hector turned to meet him at the city gates.

Above: The Death of Hector and the Triumph of Achilles, *by 19th-century Italian artist Antonio Calliani, is painted on the ceiling of the royal palace in Caserta, Italy. The painting depicts Achilles in his chariot, drawn by his immortal horses, Xanthus and Balius.*

Helped by Athena, Achilles killed Hector with a spear wound to his neck, but he was still angry. For the next nine days he dragged Hector's body around the battlefield. Only later, when he had finally calmed down, did he allow Hector's father, King Priam, to take the body back to Troy for a dignified funeral. In his epic the *Iliad*, Greek poet Homer (c. ninth–eighth century BCE) describes a poignant reconciliation between the Trojan king and the Greek warrior: Priam goes to the Greek camp to beg for his son's body, and Achilles is reminded not only of his own father but of the grief he himself has felt for the loss of Patroclus. The two men weep, then share food together, before Achilles hands over Hector's body to Priam.

The death of Achilles

Achilles himself was not to live much longer. His killer was Paris, brother of Hector and Troilus, and whose affair with Helen had ignited the whole war. In some versions, Achilles was killed in battle, although in others it happened while he was trying to make negotiations to marry Polyxena. Either way, Paris aimed an arrow at him, and Apollo, who supported the Trojans, directed its flight so that it killed Achilles. In one account the arrow landed in the hero's heel, the only vulnerable point on his body.

Because Achilles had a divine mother and a human father, ancient writers were divided as to whether he was immortal or subject to death. In some versions of the tale, Achilles ended up with other mortals, including Agamemnon, in the land of the dead. In Homer's epic the *Odyssey*, which concerns itself with events after the fall of Troy, Odysseus meets Achilles' spirit in the underworld. The spirit is inconsolable: though Odysseus tells him that he holds much authority among the dead, Achilles replies that he would rather be alive and have no power than to be recognized as a leader in the underworld. However, other sources state that, after his death, Achilles became immortal and went to live on an island in the Black Sea.

Achilles' place in mythology

Although the details of his story are unique, Achilles was a familiar character in mythology and folklore—a hero with a weakness. His story draws parallels with other legendary characters, such as Balder, the Norse god of beauty, who was killed by the one thing in the world to which he was vulnerable (mistletoe); and Hindu prince Arjuna, whose hesitation before a battle led the god Krishna to deliver a speech on the right course of action in warfare. Some scholars regard Achilles' weakness as his heel; others regard it as his behavior—for instance, his unruly conduct while under Cheiron's tutelage and his withdrawal after Agamemnon took his slave girl. According to this argument, the Greeks admired Achilles' skill in battle, but they did not approve of the way he was constantly at the mercy of his emotions. Hector, by contrast, with his high morals and steely self-control, was much closer to the Greek ideal of a perfect soldier.

Sources

The most famous work about Achilles is Homer's epic poem the *Iliad*, which focuses on the quarrel between Agamemnon and Achilles. However, the *Iliad* says little about Achilles' early life or his death. These and other details were elaborated by later writers, including Greek poet Pindar (c. 522–c. 438 BCE), Greek dramatists Euripides (c. 486–c. 406 BCE) and Apollodorus (third century BCE), and Roman poet Ovid (43 BCE–17 CE). Roman poet Statius (45–96 CE) began a long poem on the life of Achilles called *Achilleid*. He finished only a small part of it, although he was the first to include the story of Achilles' heel. In Hindu mythology the god Krishna was also killed by an arrow in his heel, his one vulnerable spot. It is possible that this element of the story was somehow copied from the Hindu legend, or that Statius's version influenced the Indian story.

Like other Trojan War heroes, the mythical Achilles may have been based on someone real who lived in the 12th or 13th century BCE. Archaeologists believe that it was during this period that the historical events thought to lie behind the Trojan War took place. Over time, tales of a great warrior who died at Troy could easily have been embellished into the story of a half-divine hero. Alexander the Great (356–323 BCE), the conqueror of ancient Greece and the Persian Empire, appeared to believe that Achilles was a real figure: he claimed that Achilles was his ancestor, and he saw him as a role model.

Achilles in the modern world

Today, Achilles is remembered as a great warrior. His story has inspired many paintings, songs, poems, and modern retellings, such as the novel *Achilles* (2002) by Elizabeth Cook. Achilles also features in numerous plays, children's books, and films that deal with the subject of the Trojan War, including the Hollywood movie *Troy* (2004), in which Achilles is played by the actor Brad Pitt. Most of all, people remember the Greek hero's story in the phrase *Achilles' heel*, which means a weak point in an otherwise strong person or organization. The hero also inspired the medical term *Achilles' tendon*, which refers to the strong tendon that runs down the back of the heel, connecting the leg muscles to the foot. If this tendon is damaged, it is impossible to run.

ANNA CLAYBOURNE

Bibliography

Homer, and Robert Fagles, trans. *The Iliad*. New York: Penguin, 2009.

Ovid, and A. D. Melville, trans. *Metamorphoses*. New York: Oxford University Press, 2008.

SEE ALSO: Agamemnon; Ajax; Hector; Iphigeneia; Odysseus; Paris; Patroclus; Peleus; Priam.

Right: This statue of the dying Achilles, by German sculptor Ernst Herter (1846–1917), echoes the classical Greek style and is an exhibit in the Achilleion Palace, Corfu.

ACTAEON

Actaeon was taught to be an excellent hunter by the wise and benevolent centaur Cheiron. Actaeon's story is famous, however, not because he was a renowned hunter, but because he ended up as a hunted stag, killed by his own dogs.

Actaeon's father was Aristaeus, son of the god Apollo, and his mother was Autonoe, daughter of Cadmus, the first king of Thebes. There are four main versions of the Actaeon myth. The most famous one is found in *Metamorphoses*, a collection of tales and myths—

many dealing with transformations of humans into plants or animals—by Roman poet Ovid (43 BCE–17 CE). According to Ovid, Actaeon was hunting in the woods one day when he stumbled upon Artemis, goddess of hunting, and her nymphs, bathing in a hidden spring on Mount Cithaeron. Artemis valued her virginity and the chastity of her attendants very highly, so when she caught Actaeon looking on her naked body she flew into a rage. The vengeful goddess sprinkled a handful of water over Actaeon, transforming him into a stag. He was then chased by his own hunting dogs, until they caught him and tore his body to pieces. Following his death, the hunter's dogs howled continuously for their lost master. Their cries caused Cheiron to take pity on the dogs: he made a statue of his former pupil that was so lifelike the dogs believed it was really their master and stopped howling.

Above: Diana and Actaeon, *by Italian artist Giovanni Battista Tiepolo (1696–1770), depicts Actaeon and his hunting dogs at the entrance to the hidden spring where Artemis (the Roman Diana) and her attendants are bathing.*

Above: Statues depicting Actaeon under attack from his own hunting dogs decorate the 18th-century royal palace of Caserta, southern Italy.

In the second of the four most popular versions of the story, Zeus, king of the gods, killed Actaeon for courting his aunt Semele, whom Zeus wished to keep to himself. In a third version, Actaeon incurred the wrath of Artemis by declaring that his skill at hunting was greater than hers. In the fourth version, he audaciously proposed to make Artemis his wife. The result of the last two accounts was the same as the first one: the goddess turned Actaeon into a stag, which was then hunted and killed.

Actaeon in art

Although the events leading to his death were popular in antiquity, the earliest depictions of Actaeon portray him hunting. One such example is in a sculpted frieze near the top of the fifth-century-BCE temple of Hera, the wife of Zeus, in the Greek city of Selinus (modern-day Selinunte) on the island of Sicily. However, during the same century, images of Actaeon's transformation into a stag began to appear on Greek vases.

In Roman art Actaeon is a favorite motif in mosaics as well as in the wall paintings of Pompeii, the city destroyed by a volcanic eruption in 79 CE. Representations of the unfortunate hunter are often found in the vicinity of water fountains, since the water sprinkled by Artemis transformed him into a stag. Actaeon is also a popular character in later art. In most instances, he appears to be startled by the unexpected sight of the nude goddess and her nymphs. In a number of cases, however, he seems to delight in spying on the naked women, as paintings by Italian artists Paolo Veronese (1528–1588) and Domenichino (1581–1641) demonstrate. Of the many paintings of Actaeon, some of the most noteworthy—all by Italian artists—include a fresco by the architect and painter Baldassare Peruzzi (1481–1536) in the Villa Farnesina, Rome; two paintings by Titian (c. 1489–1576); and one painting by Giovanni Battista Tiepolo (1696–1770).

Dutch artist Rembrandt (1606–1669) also painted a famous picture of Actaeon, but his version included Callisto. Callisto was one of Artemis's attendants who had vowed to remain a virgin and devote her life to the service of the goddess. Zeus, however, appeared to her in the shape of Artemis, seduced her, and left her pregnant. When Artemis went bathing with her nymphs, and Callisto had to take off her clothes, her shameful pregnancy was revealed to the virgin goddess. According to some versions, Artemis became irate, transformed Callisto into a bear, and sent hunting dogs to pursue her. Callisto was saved by Zeus, who lifted her up to the stars, where she became the Big Bear (Ursa Major) constellation.

FEYO SCHUDDEBOOM

Bibliography

Hesiod, and M. L. West, trans. *Theogony* and *Works and Days.* New York: Oxford University Press, 2008.

Howatson, M. C. *The Oxford Companion to Classical Literature.* New York: Oxford University Press, 2005.

Ovid, and A. D. Melville, trans. *Metamorphoses.* New York: Oxford University Press, 2008.

SEE ALSO: Achilles; Callisto.

ADONIS

In Greek mythology, Adonis was the personification of male beauty. Although a mortal by birth, after he was killed he was deified and worshiped as a god of death and rebirth, especially in relation to the seasons of the year.

In the most widely known version of the myth, Adonis was the son of Theias, king of Assyria. The goddess Aphrodite had driven the king's daughter Myrrha, or Smyrna, into an incestuous love for her father. Myrrha went to the king's bed in the dark, concealing her identity, and Adonis was conceived as a result. Theias was horrified at what he had inadvertently done and wanted to kill his daughter. However, Aphrodite was overcome with guilt about her involvement in the deceit, so she mercifully changed the girl into a tree that afterward bore her name: the myrrh.

Adonis was miraculously born from the tree that his mother had become. He was incredibly beautiful, and Aphrodite fell in love with him at first sight. She saved Adonis from Theias by placing the child in a carved chest and putting him in the care of Persephone, the goddess of the underworld. However, Persephone, too, was smitten by the beautiful boy—an attachment that never ended. She refused to give him back to Aphrodite, and the two goddesses had a furious quarrel. Zeus was called on to judge their rival claims. He ruled that the boy must spend one third of the year on earth with Aphrodite, one third of the year in the underworld with Persephone, and the other third in any manner he chose. Adonis spent his free time hunting.

The fatal hunt

Aphrodite had warned Adonis against hunting, but he was a headstrong young man who paid her no heed. Instead, when his dogs had cornered a wild boar, he hurled his spear at the animal, hitting it in the side and maddening it

to the point of attack. The boar dislodged the spear with its snout and pursued the fleeing Adonis. When the animal caught up with the young man, it buried one of its tusks in his groin. As Adonis lay bleeding to death, Aphrodite heard his pitiful moans and turned her swan-drawn chariot in their direction. She took up his mutilated body in her arms and declared that every year a memorial ceremony would be held to honor her beloved, and that his blood would be turned into the flowers of spring. The anemone bloomed at her command; it was a short-lived flower that was almost as beautiful as Adonis himself.

Variations

The above is the most familiar account of the Adonis myth. However, the story is complicated, and there are numerous different versions. Even the parentage of Adonis is not always the same. According to the poet Hesiod (fl. 800 BCE), Adonis was the son of Phoenix and Aephesiboea; Apollodorus, a Greek mythographer of the third century BCE, names the boy's parents as Cinyras and Metharme.

Some accounts say that, after Aphrodite had changed Myrrha into a tree, Theias fired an arrow at the trunk, which burst open, allowing Adonis to emerge. Yet another version states that Adonis sprang from the tree after it had been gored by a wild boar—thus bringing together the cause of his birth and his death. In one story, Zeus does not adjudicate between Aphrodite and Persephone, but delegates the task to Calliope, the muse of poetry.

The story of Adonis has different endings, too. In one version, Aphrodite was so distraught by her lover's death that she went to Persephone and begged to be allowed to bring Adonis back from the dead for half the year. Touched by her appeal, the goddess of the underworld relented.

Significance and origins of the myth

Adonis was not invented by the Greeks but adopted by them from ancient vegetation myths of western Asia. His story first appeared in texts of the 14th century BCE written in Ugaritic, an extinct language of northern Syria. The name itself is a variation of *adonai*, a Hebrew word meaning "lord" that is one of the names of Jehovah in the Old Testament of the Bible.

Adonis and Aphrodite are thought to have originally been a single entity—the male and female forms of a single deity. Almost as soon as they had been separated into two different deities, however, they were reunited in legend as

Above: This painting by Titian (c. 1489–1576) shows Venus (the Roman equivalent of the Greek Aphrodite) embracing Adonis.

lovers. This embellishment is similar to—and almost certainly derived from—the story of Astarte, the Phoenician fertility goddess who also had a lover named Adonis. Among other earlier examples of a union between a god and a goddess of vegetation is the marriage of Tammuz and Ishtar in ancient Babylonian mythology. After their wedding, Tammuz was cut down like wheat in the fields. The inconsolable Ishtar sought him out in the underworld and persuaded the goddess of death to return him for half the year.

In Greek mythology, the closest equivalent to the story of Adonis comes from Phrygia, Asia Minor (part of modern Turkey). It concerns Attis, a beautiful shepherd boy, and the mother goddess Cybele. Mad with love, Attis pursued Cybele, who repelled all his advances. In despair, he emasculated himself, and plants grew where he bled. In another version of the legend, Zeus sent a boar that gored him to death. After his resurrection, Attis finally wed the

repentant Cybele. The ceremony was later imitated by cultists as a way of giving thanks for the harvest in the fall and praying for the renewal of vegetation in the spring.

Supporting archaeological evidence

Adonis was adopted by the Greeks from the Phoenician civilization of the eastern Mediterranean. This has been established by archaeological excavations at Byblos, an ancient town in modern Lebanon. The nearby Adonis River runs red every year during the spring floods. This effect—which is caused by particles of red hematite that break from the river's bedrock—was said to be the blood of Adonis. Near Byblos was a temple to Astarte that was destroyed in the fourth century CE by Constantine (c. 280–337 CE), the first Christian emperor of Rome. The sanctuary was surrounded by high cliffs, and from a grotto within, it poured a stream that cascaded into a gorge. It was in this gorge that Adonis was said to have died.

Byblos was only a small town when Egypt's Old Kingdom flourished (c. 2575–c. 2130 BCE). It was noted for its sea trade, especially in wood. From the surrounding forests the Phoenicians built ships that plied the Mediterranean and spread their influence throughout North Africa, including Egypt, and southern Europe, including Greece. The chief deity of Byblos was the goddess Baalat: she looked much like the Egyptian cow goddess Hathor, with a disk between her two horns. Baalat's name was kept secret from the uninitiated, lest enemies gained knowledge of it and used it to invoke the deity against the Phoenicians themselves. Her generic name corresponded to the baal, or "lord," of Phoenician villages. One form taken by this divinity was that which became known to the Greeks as Adonis. In another manifestation, baal was Hay-Tau, one of the earliest Phoenician deities, a god of forest vegetation who took the form of a tree, in particular the myrrh tree. He replaced the earlier vegetation gods Aleyin and Mot, whose names appear in Ugaritic texts. The Egyptians conflated Hay-Tau with their own

Left: This marble statue, entitled The Death of Adonis, *was sculpted by Giuseppe Mazzuoli (1644–1725).*

Osiris, who had also been imprisoned in a tree, and whose grieving wife sought him everywhere, just as Aphrodite sought Adonis.

Sacrifice and worship

In prehistoric times, Adonis was worshiped at the Adonia festival, where his effigy was mourned and then thrown into the water. From the fifth century BCE, Athenians kept "Adonis gardens" in which they grew plants that could be forced to early growth and then died young, as a parallel to the story of Adonis himself. The ceremony performed at Athens in honor of Adonis featured throwing plants and statues into the sea or into fountains in a form of sacrifice that was intended to increase the harvest.

These rites of Adonis were based on rites for the dead, which go back to prehistoric times when dead ancestors were worshiped in caves and underground stone temples. Women tore their clothes and wept, calling "My lord, my lord" as they paraded through the streets. House fronts bore images of Adonis made of wax or terra-cotta. Dirges were played to the accompaniment of short flutes called giggros. Baskets of quick-growing plants, such as fennel, barley, and lettuce, were set out to denote the transient life of the vegetation god. They wither fast because they have small root systems and are burned by the hot summer sun. Originally, the legend had it that Aphrodite laid the body of her dead Adonis on a bed of lettuce. In later Roman accounts he was mourned by Venus, who placed his body on an imperial bed of silver draped with purple.

The Greeks believed that the spirit of Adonis was present in swine, which were consequently sacrificed to him. Thus victim became conflated with killer, a reflection of the fact that life and death are part of the same continuum. In the rites for Aphrodite, references to swine are accompanied by references to Adonis.

Like Aphrodite, Adonis is linked to the myrrh tree, and its oil was used at his festival. Myrrh was also an embalming oil and was given to the infant Jesus by the Magi from the East as a symbol of his mortality—a reminder that he was doomed to die.

BARBARA GARDNER

Bibliography

Hesiod, and M. L. West, trans. *Theogony* and *Works and Days.* New York: Oxford University Press, 2008.

Howatson, M. C. *The Oxford Companion to Classical Literature.* New York: Oxford University Press, 2005.

SEE ALSO: Myrrha.

AENEAS

Aeneas was a hero of ancient Greek and Roman mythology. A Trojan prince, he was the son of a mortal, Anchises, and the Greek goddess Aphrodite (the Roman Venus). Aeneas was the legendary ancestor of the Roman race.

Although Troy was in Asia Minor (part of modern Turkey), it was thoroughly Hellenized, or influenced by Greek culture, through extensive trade with Greek colonies in the area. Thus, although the mythical Trojans were thought of as non-Greek, they intermarried with Greeks, practiced Greek customs, spoke Greek, and worshiped Greek gods, even tracing their royal line to the chief Greek deity, Zeus. The Trojan Aeneas was reckoned to be the offspring of the Greek goddess Aphrodite. The main source of stories about Aeneas is now the *Aeneid,* by Roman poet Virgil (70–19 BCE), but there were numerous legends about the hero long before in the Greek world.

Aphrodite did not take Anchises as a lover by choice. The match was forced on her by Zeus (the Roman Jupiter) as a punishment: he blamed her for using her power as the goddess of love to make him mate with mortal women. Aphrodite was ashamed of her liaison. She forbade Anchises to speak of it, but she vowed that their son would be a great hero. After Aeneas was born, he was cared for by some nymphs, who raised him until he was old enough to become a warrior.

Aeneas came of age on the eve of the Trojan War. Ancient Greeks and Romans believed that this conflict took place in the distant past, and that the cultural and political map of their own world was a consequence of the clash between the Greek "west" and the Trojan "east." According to this view, Aeneas, and other heroes, including Achilles and Odysseus, are transitional figures who stand at the brink of a monumental shift in human affairs. After the

The Romanization of Aeneas

Although the Romans mythologized their Trojan origins, they did not invent them. By the sixth century BCE, before Rome emerged as a major power, Greeks already identified peoples they encountered in Italy with descendants of Aeneas and other veterans of the Trojan War. As Roman power expanded, Greeks also made use of the link between Troy and Italy. Thus, for example, the Greek king Pyrrhus of Epirus in the third century BCE declared himself a descendant of Achilles and justified his invasion of Italy as Greek opposition to the "new Troy" at Rome.

It is possible that Aeneas was worshiped as a hero or god in Italy as early as the fourth century BCE. By this time he may already have been considered an ancestor of the Roman people in general. Thus Aeneas's remains were supposedly interred at a local shrine, and the half of him that was divine was worshiped by the Romans as Jupiter Indiges ("Jupiter the native").

Partly because of his status as a sort of non-Greek Greek, the figure of Aeneas helped Greeks and Romans to articulate their complex relationship. The Romans were greatly influenced by Greece, which they came to rule in the second century BCE. The link between Aeneas and Rome allowed the Roman rule of Greece to be seen as a kind of payback for the supposed destruction of Troy by the Greeks in the distant past.

Trojan War, no longer would semidivine heroes such as Aeneas and Achilles decide the fate of nations, nor would the world be populated by the monsters and witches encountered by Aeneas and Odysseus.

The Trojan War was generally represented as Greek retaliation for Trojan aggression. With the help of the goddess Aphrodite, Paris, son of the Trojan king Priam, sailed to Greece, abducted Helen, wife of the Spartan king Menelaus, and brought her back to Troy to be his own bride. Aeneas accompanied Paris on this voyage, although he seems not to have been told in advance that their mission was to steal another man's wife. Menelaus was outraged, and with his brother Agamemnon, king of Mycenae, raised an army to invade Troy and rescue Helen. The Greeks sailed to Troy and besieged the city, which Aeneas helped defend as leader of a group of Trojan allies known as the Dardanians. He was one of

Left: The Flight from Troy *by Gian Lorenzo Bernini (1598–1680) depicts Aeneas leaving the ruined city with his father, Anchises, on his shoulders.*

Troy's most valiant defenders, although he was forced to flee from the Greek warrior Achilles and escaped death in battle on more than one occasion only through the intervention of the gods.

Although Aeneas and Priam were on the same side, there was friction between them. Their mutual dislike was attributed variously to Priam's disregard for Aeneas's contribution to the war effort, Aeneas's recommendation that the Trojans make a truce with the Greeks, and the historic rivalry between their two branches of the Trojan royal family. In any case, when the Greeks at last captured Troy, Aeneas, unlike most Trojan warriors, either escaped or was allowed to leave. The hero, with his aged father Anchises on his shoulders and his young son Ascanius (also called Julus) at his side, led a band of survivors from the ruined city; amid the confusion, however, he lost his Trojan wife, Creusa.

Aeneas, Achilles, and Odysseus

Comparisons between the legendary role of Aeneas and the exploits of Achilles and Odysseus provide some useful insights into what the Romans saw as the heroic nature of the founder of their society.

Aeneas was a capable warrior, but not the greatest at Troy. He was overshadowed by Achilles, who, like him, was the son of a goddess and a mortal man. Aeneas's hostility toward Priam paralleled that of Achilles toward Agamemnon. Yet in other ways Aeneas was greater than Achilles: he placed his people's welfare before his own interests, while Achilles was willing to let his fellow Greeks perish over a point of pride. Aeneas survived the Trojan War to establish a new royal family; Achilles died at Troy, and in most accounts founded no royal line.

Although Odysseus was a great fighter, like Aeneas his reputation rested more on his ability to preserve the cohesion of the community, as, for example, when he faced down the troublemaker Thersites or helped to mediate between Achilles and Agamemnon. Also like Aeneas, Odysseus wandered far after the Trojan War, visited the underworld, and fought again once he reached his destination. Yet whereas Odysseus had to kill many fellow citizens on his return in order to establish his power, Aeneas sacrificed himself for his people, dying either during or shortly after the battles that secured the Trojans' position in Italy.

Thus Aeneas occupied the middle ground between the two main Greek heroes. Like Achilles, he came into conflict with authority; like Odysseus, his focus was on the preservation of his people. Whereas Achilles died during the Trojan War, and Odysseus long survived it, Aeneas lived only long enough to see his people safe and their future secure.

Mediterranean wanderings

The fugitive Trojans then wandered for years in search of a new home. As during the war, they were aided by Aphrodite and opposed by Hera (the Roman Juno), the wife of Zeus, who bore a grudge against Troy both because of her attachment to the Greeks and because of wrongs supposedly done to her by members of the Trojan royal family. During these wanderings the Trojans suffered—and some even died as a result of—storms and sickness, failed in a number of attempts to found a new city, and encountered other survivors of the Trojan War, all of whom were seemingly unable to escape from its aftermath.

Local shrines and myths commemorating various supposed stopping points in the Trojans' wanderings are found throughout the Mediterranean region. According to the stories, the Trojans first tried to found a new city, called Aenea, in Thrace, but were warned off by dreadful portents. Setting sail again, they put in at the island of Delos; there they were told by the oracle of Apollo that they should proceed to their "first mother." Anchises concluded that this must mean the island of Crete, original home of one branch of the Trojan royal family. Proceeding there, the Trojans attempted to found a city called Pergamea, one of the names for old Troy. However, when the Trojans were afflicted by a plague, they realized that "first mother" must refer to a different branch of the royal family that had originated in Italy.

Proceeding west, the Trojans stopped at the islands of the Harpies, where they encountered the same hideous flying creatures that had plagued Jason and the Argonauts. Sailing on, they put in at Actium on the west coast of Greece, where they held games in honor of Apollo. The next leg of their journey took them to Buthrotum in northwest Greece, where they met the seer Helenus, Priam's sole surviving son. Helenus provided Aeneas with information about the remainder of his journey. Sailing on to Sicily, the Trojans outwitted the Cyclopes and avoided the monster Scylla and the whirlpool Charybdis that had caused problems for Odysseus. They next stopped at Drepanum,

Below: This painting by Gerard de Lairesse (1640–1711) depicts Aeneas with Dido on the throne in Carthage.

Above: This painting, entitled Aeneas in the Underworld, *is by Flemish artist Peter Paul Rubens (1577–1640).*

Aeneas, Virgil, and Augustus

When in the first century BCE Julius Caesar, and later his nephew Octavian (Augustus), ruled Rome, Aeneas emerged as the quintessential Roman hero, in part because the imperial family, the Julii, claimed descent from Aeneas's son Julus. One of the great Roman statesmen of the reign of Augustus, Gaius Maecenas (c. 70–8 BCE), was an outstanding patron of literature who encouraged the poets Virgil (70–19 BCE), Horace (65–8 BCE), and Propertius (c. 50–c. 15 BCE) to weave patriotic themes into their work.

Augustus wanted an epic poem celebrating Rome's empire and his own government, not as propaganda, but as a heartfelt expression of the Roman values that he believed himself to embody. Poets were reluctant to take on this delicate task. Virgil at last agreed to do so, however, and wrote the *Aeneid*.

Rather than listing Augustus's accomplishments, Virgil turned to a mythical past in which the seeds of the Julii and of Rome itself were merged. Characteristics that distinguish Virgil's Aeneas from Homeric heroes— selfless devotion to his people, compassion for his opponents, and unquestioning deference to the gods— align him with the image that Augustus tried to project. So, for example, Aeneas first appears in the *Aeneid* not as a triumphant warrior, but as a leader deeply distressed by his people's plight. In another episode, Aeneas rescues a Greek whom Odysseus abandoned to the Cyclopes. Thus Virgil's achievement was to fuse the themes of the two major Greek epics, the *Iliad* and *Odyssey*, into a uniquely Roman vision of the past.

where Anchises died, apparently of old age. As they sailed on to mainland Italy, the goddess Juno sent a storm that wrecked many Trojan ships and drove the rest across the Mediterranean to Carthage on the coast of modern Tunisia.

In North Africa the Trojans were invited to join a colony of Phoenicians ruled by queen Dido. Aeneas fell in love with Dido, but the gods told him that the destiny of his people was to merge not with the Phoenicians but with Italians. So Aeneas reluctantly sailed away. He snuck away in the dead of night; when Dido found out that he had gone, she angrily swore that there would be unending conflict between the Carthaginians and the future Romans, and then killed herself.

The Trojans sailed back to Italy. Returning first to Sicily, they held funeral games for Anchises. According to another tradition, Anchises was buried on Mount Anchisia in Arcadia near a sanctuary of Aphrodite. After the games the Trojan women, tired of wandering, set fire to the ships, but Aeneas prayed to Zeus, who sent rain so that only four of

the vessels were destroyed. Proceeding to Cumae (near modern Naples) on the Italian mainland, Aeneas consulted the Sibyl, a prophetess who conducted him to the underworld, having first instructed him to fetch a golden bough from a sacred forest. In the underworld Aeneas encountered the ghosts of his former allies and enemies, as well as the shade of his father, who instructed him about the future and showed him famous Romans to come. Guided by Anchises' instructions and by divine portents, the Trojans pressed on until they found the mouth of the Tiber River.

Approaching journey's end

Although they had reached their promised land, the Trojans' ordeals were not over. Aeneas attempted to form a pact with the inhabitants of the Tiber region, the Latins, whose king Latinus was himself of Greek descent. Latinus at first agreed to the alliance, and promised his daughter Lavinia to Aeneas. However, she was already pledged to

21

Above: This oil painting by Italian artist Pietro da Cortona (1596–1669) is entitled Aeneas with King Evander and Pallas.

Turnus, prince of the Rutulians, and he, goaded by Juno, threatened war. Aeneas then found an ally in Evander, king of another Italian colony of Greeks—Arcadians who had settled near the future site of Rome.

War broke out. On one side Turnus led a coalition of Latins, Rutulians, and Etruscans under the tyrant Mezentius. Against them were Aeneas's Trojans and their allies, including Evander's Arcadians, and another group of Etruscans under King Tarchon. Many on both sides died, including Evander's son Pallas and the brave young Trojans Nisus and Euryalus, as well as Mezentius and Camilla, a female warrior who fought for the Latins. In the course of the battle, Turnus tried to set fire to the Greek ships. However, Juno, upset because the ships were made of wood from her forests, appealed to Jupiter, who decreed that the ships be transformed into sea nymphs.

The death of a hero

Incensed by the death of Pallas, Aeneas killed Turnus in battle. With their champion dead, the Latin coalition sued for peace. Juno at last accepted the Trojans' presence along the Tiber, her only remaining condition being that they should no longer bear the name of the city she despised. Aeneas married Lavinia, who had been betrothed to Turnus. In some accounts she was the mother of Julus; she was perhaps also the mother of Aeneas's daughter Ilia. Aeneas proceeded to rule a Trojan-Italian people from a new city named Lavinium, near the future site of Rome (which was established later by Aeneas's descendants Romulus and Remus).

Aeneas died only three years after arriving in Italy. In some accounts, he died in battle; in others, he simply vanished after his victory. After his death, Aphrodite appealed successfully to the other gods to make her son immortal like other heroes, such as Heracles.

JIM MARKS

Bibliography
Homer, and Robert Fagles, trans. *The Odyssey*. New York: Penguin, 2009.
Virgil, and Robert Fagles, trans. *The Aeneid*. New York: Penguin, 2009.

SEE ALSO: Achilles; Agamemnon; Cyclopes; Helen; Heracles; Jason; Menelaus; Odysseus; Paris; Priam; Romulus and Remus.

AGAMEMNON

The legendary leader of the Greek forces during the Trojan War, Agamemnon was one of the principal characters of the epic conflict. The story of his murder after he returned home was also one of the most famous episodes in Greek literature.

According to the *Iliad* by Homer (c. ninth–eighth century BCE) and the *Oresteia* by Aeschylus (525–456 BCE), Agamemnon was the king of Mycenae, an ancient city-state in the Peloponnese in southern Greece. His father, King Atreus, had feuded with his brother, Thyestes. Aegisthus, the son of Thyestes, killed Atreus, and Thyestes took over the throne of Mycenae, banishing Agamemnon and his brother Menelaus. Eventually, with the help of Tyndareos, king of Sparta, they returned and drove Thyestes out. Agamemnon became king, while Menelaus married Tyndareos's daughter Helen and succeeded to the throne of Sparta when Tyndareos died.

Agamemnon married Clytemnestra against her will. In some versions, he even killed her first husband and baby so that he could marry her. This set the tone for their marriage: Clytemnestra always hated Agamemnon. They had at least three daughters: Iphigeneia, Electra, and Chrysothemis, and a son: Orestes. Agamemnon also had children with other women, including Cassandra and Chryseis.

Left: This gold effigy, discovered in an ancient royal burial site in Mycenae, has been named the Mask of Agamemnon, although there is no proof that it was actually made for him or on his orders.

Many modern historians believe that Agamemnon really did exist, although they accept that most of the stories about him are probably fiction. In 1876, famous archaeologist Heinrich Schliemann uncovered the remains of a great civilization at Mycenae, including royal tombs containing bodies with finely detailed gold masks laid over their faces (see box). Although there is no evidence that any of the tombs belonged to Agamemnon, the discovery suggested that the mythical hero was almost certainly based on a real Mycenaean king.

As with so many other Greek heroes, Agamemnon's story revolves around the Trojan War. The conflict started when Paris, a prince of Troy, in what is now Turkey, ran away with Menelaus's wife, Helen. Menelaus asked his brother Agamemnon to help him win Helen back. Many of the Greek kings and princes who had wanted to marry Helen themselves had sworn an oath to her father, Tyndareos, that they would fight anyone who threatened her marriage to Menelaus. Agamemnon rounded up these former suitors, who included Odysseus, Patroclus, and Diomedes, and gathered them and their armies at Aulis, ready to sail for Troy under his command.

The adventure did not start well, however, because the goddess Artemis was angry with Agamemnon: he had boasted that he was better than her at archery, and she refused to give the Greeks a fair wind. Calchas, a prophet, told Agamemnon that, to appease Artemis, he would have to sacrifice his daughter Iphigeneia. Menelaus persuaded the reluctant Agamemnon to do this, and he sent for Iphigeneia, pretending that he wanted her to marry Achilles. When she arrived with her mother, Agamemnon killed her on the sacrificial altar. According to some versions, Artemis saved Iphigeneia's life by spiriting her away from the altar and replacing her with a deer. Either way, however, Clytemnestra lost her daughter and was heartbroken and furious. Clytemnestra returned to Mycenae, while Agamemnon and the Greek forces sailed for Troy.

Agamemnon at Troy

At Troy, Agamemnon commanded the Greek forces throughout the war, which lasted 10 years. He was a forceful and experienced leader, but he sometimes lacked the ability to make firm decisions, and some of the other Greeks resented his luxurious lifestyle.

In the final year of the war, Agamemnon was forced to give up Chryseis, a slave girl he had captured, to the god Apollo. To replace her, he took Briseis, a girl belonging to Achilles, the Greeks' finest and strongest warrior. Achilles

Schliemann's Discoveries

Heinrich Schliemann (1822–1890) was a wealthy German businessman who retired early, at age 36, to focus on his hobby, archaeology. Although he was only an amateur, he made some of the most important discoveries ever about the ancient world. From 1870 to 1890 he worked on the excavation of Troy, in modern Turkey, revealing that the city had been rebuilt many times, and that it had been at the center of a large-scale war during the 12th or 13th century BCE.

In 1876 he began work at Mycenae, hoping to discover the remains of Agamemnon. The tombs and ruins he found there were full of treasures, including gold burial masks. Schliemann excitedly proclaimed, "I have looked upon the face of Agamemnon!" Later archaeologists, however, determined that the tombs were far older than the 13th century BCE, the earliest estimated period of the Trojan War. Nevertheless, Schliemann's work provided huge amounts of information about the Mycenaean civilization.

Above: German archaeologist Heinrich Schliemann made many important discoveries concerning Mycenaean culture.

Above: Archaeologists believe that this ancient graveyard was the burial site of kings and other members of Mycenaean royalty.

was very upset and angry. He sulked and refused to fight, and because of this the Greeks were almost defeated. They won the war only after Achilles rejoined the fighting following the death of his closest friend, Patroclus. Odysseus's plan for getting past the impenetrable walls of Troy also helped. Odysseus's idea was that a small group of warriors would hide inside a wooden horse made to appear like a gift to the Trojans. Once inside the city, the warriors would emerge from hiding and open the gates to the city, allowing the rest of the Greeks to enter.

Victory and homecoming

Odysseus's plan worked and the Greeks overran Troy and captured many prisoners. Agamemnon himself took Cassandra, daughter of King Priam of Troy, as his mistress, and sailed home. However, during his absence from Mycenae, his wife, Clytemnestra, had taken a lover, Aegisthus, the cousin who had killed Agamemnon's father.

Aegisthus was living as king of Mycenae, and he and Clytemnestra were plotting against Agamemnon—to the horror of Agamemnon's devoted daughter Electra. After Agamemnon returned to his palace with Cassandra, Aegisthus (and in some versions, Clytemnestra) murdered them both (see box, page 26).

After Agamemnon's death, his son, Orestes, who until then had been in exile, came home to avenge his father. Urged on by Apollo and with Electra's help, Orestes killed Aegisthus and Clytemnestra, despite his mother's plea for mercy. Orestes was himself punished for these crimes. He was tormented by the Furies, who were encouraged by Clytemnestra's ghost, until he was absolved of further punishment by the goddess Athena and a panel of Athenian citizens who sat in judgment of his vengeful deeds.

Agamemnon's soul lived on in Hades, land of the dead. In Homer's *Odyssey*, Odysseus visits Hades and meets the hero. Agamemnon explains how he died, and warns Odysseus to take care when returning to his own palace.

The story of Agamemnon is a classic case of a revenge feud. One person is killed; in revenge, another person is

How Did Agamemnon Die?

There are various descriptions of how Agamemnon died and who exactly killed him. In the *Odyssey*, when the spirit of Agamemnon speaks to Odysseus, he tells him it was Aegisthus who killed him, after tricking him by inviting him to a feast. In Aeschylus's *Agamemnon*, however, Clytemnestra says that she was the killer, and in another of Aeschylus's works the god Apollo describes how Clytemnestra threw a cloak over Agamemnon as he climbed out of the bath, then stabbed him. In *Electra*, a play by Sophocles (c. 496–406 BCE), Electra remembers how Clytemnestra and Aegisthus together killed her father by hitting him on the head with an ax. According to Athenian writer Apollodorus (fl. 140 BCE), Clytemnestra tricked Agamemnon by giving him a specially altered shirt that had no neck or armholes. He tried to put it on, and while he was struggling inside it, Aegisthus killed him. However, all the accounts agree that Clytemnestra or Aegisthus or both were responsible for Agamemnon's death.

Left: This clay relief sculpture depicts the murder of Agamemnon (center) by Clytemnestra and Aegisthus. The relief was discovered on the island of Crete and dates from around the seventh century BCE.

murdered, and this second murder inspires yet another killing, and so on. In some ancient societies, such as the Viking culture, people had a legal right to commit revenge killings, but the problem remained of how to break the cycle of violence. The Greeks viewed revenge killings with some sympathy, but they placed a higher value on peace, justice, and harmony. In Greek mythology, revenge tragedies usually ended when the gods intervened to stop them.

Agamemnon in literature

Agamemnon's adventures during the Trojan War are retold in Homer's epic poem the *Iliad*. The story of his murder is recounted in several ancient Greek plays, particularly the *Oresteia* by Aeschylus. *Agamemnon*, the first play in this trilogy, tells of the king's death, while the other two— *Choephoroe* (*Libation Bearers*) and *Eumenides* (*The Furies*)— focus on the tribulations of Orestes. Agamemnon and his family also appear in works by many other ancient writers, including Pindar, Euripides, and Sophocles.

As both a great leader and a tragic figure, Agamemnon has inspired many works of art and literature since ancient times. For example, in the 20th century, novelist Barry Unsworth retold Agamemnon's story in his book *The Songs of the Kings*; British playwright Steven Berkoff wrote a modern version of Aeschylus's *Agamemnon*; and Irish poet W. B. Yeats (1865–1939) mentioned Agamemnon in his poem "Leda and the Swan."

ANNA CLAYBOURNE

Bibliography
Graves, Robert. *The Greek Myths*. New York: Penguin, 1993.
Homer, and Robert Fagles, trans. *The Iliad*. New York: Penguin, 2009.
Homer, and Robert Fagles, trans. *The Odyssey*. New York: Penguin, 2009.
Howatson, M. C. *The Oxford Companion to Classical Literature*. New York: Oxford University Press, 2005.

SEE ALSO: Achilles; Cassandra; Clytemnestra; Electra; Orestes.

AJAX

Ajax (in Greek, Aias) was the name of
two warriors who fought in the Trojan
War. The name usually refers to the
character known as the Great Ajax,
who came from the island of Salamis
near Athens. He was the son of
Telamon and is more precisely called
Telamonian Ajax. The other character
was the son of Oileus, king of Locris
in central Greece. This Ajax is known
as the Lesser or Locrian Ajax.

The reason the two Ajaxes came to be at Troy was
that both had been suitors for the hand in
marriage of Helen, who ultimately chose to marry
Menelaus, son of the king of Mycenae. Tyndareos, king of
Sparta and Helen's stepfather, made each of Helen's many
suitors promise to defend her marriage if it were ever
threatened. As a result, when Paris of Troy abducted Helen,
the suitors were forced to wage war against the Trojans to
recapture Menelaus's wife and uphold his honor.

The Great Ajax
In his epic poem the *Iliad*, Greek poet Homer (c. ninth–
eighth century BCE) portrayed the Great Ajax as an
enormous man who was the defender of the Greeks. Other
Greek heroes such as Achilles and Odysseus were famous
for their offensive weapons—the spear and the bow,
respectively. Ajax was famous for his shield, a protective
device. It was so large that it could shelter not only himself
but also his half brother, Teucer. Ajax did his greatest
fighting when in retreat. Homer described him as being
driven slowly from the battle "like a donkey beaten out of

Left: Ajax by the Sea *by Italian artist Francesco Sabatelli
(1803–1829). The painting depicts the Locrian Ajax clinging to a rock
after his raping of a suppliant caused the goddess Athena to sink the
Greeks' ships.*

27

a field with sticks." Ajax may have been defeated at times, but he never ceased to resist. In further contrast to other Greek heroes in the Trojan War, Ajax was not aided by an Olympian deity. Athena, goddess of war and arts, supported Odysseus; the sea goddess Thetis, together with Zeus's wife, Hera, aided Achilles. Ajax, however, fought alone.

When Achilles refused to fight the Trojans because of an argument with Agamemnon, the Greek commander, the Greeks chose Ajax to battle the Trojan champion Hector in single combat. Although Ajax had the upper hand at some points during the duel, both fighters were well matched for strength. They eventually exchanged gifts since neither of them could win, and Hector died in a later battle at the hands of Achilles. Later, Ajax carried the corpse of the dead Achilles from the battlefield—a scene that was often depicted in Greek art. Although honorable in battle, Ajax showed another side to his character when the Greeks gave Achilles' armor to Odysseus instead of to Ajax. Ajax felt so cheated and betrayed that he went insane. He attacked the army's flocks and herds under the delusion that he was murdering the leading Greeks. When he recovered his wits, he was so ashamed that he killed himself by falling on his own sword. His death was another popular theme in Greek art and was depicted in the play *Ajax* by Greek dramatist Sophocles (c. 496–406 BCE).

Honoring the Great Ajax

According to some sources, particularly Greek poet Pindar (c. 522–c. 438 BCE), the Great Ajax was the first cousin of Achilles, since both men were grandsons of Aeacus, the first king of the island of Aegina. In historical times, Ajax's tomb was believed to have been at Troy; he was worshiped at Byzantium (modern Istanbul in Turkey) and had a hero shrine on Salamis. There is also a record of the Greeks praying to him before the Battle of Salamis in 480 BCE, when the Greek navy faced the mighty Persian fleet off the coast of the island. During the Greeks' famous victory, they captured a Persian trireme (a ship with three banks of oars), which they dedicated to Ajax.

The Greeks held games on the island in Ajax's honor, and when the Athenian tribes were reorganized at the end of the sixth century BCE, one of the new tribes, the Aiantis, was dedicated to Ajax.

In addition, the powerful Athenian Philaidai dynasty claimed descent from Ajax. Philaidai family members included the general Miltiades (c. 554–489 BCE), who led the Greek army to victory over the Persians in the Battle of Marathon, and the historian Thucydides (d. c. 401 BCE), who wrote the *History of the Peloponnesian War* about the conflict between Athens and Sparta.

The Lesser Ajax

In the *Iliad*, Homer described how the Lesser Ajax fought alongside the Great Ajax, but other writers occasionally mistook one Ajax for another or assimilated both their characters. Sometimes they were even referred to together as "the two Ajaxes." They were, however, very different. The Lesser Ajax was smaller than the Great Ajax and far more swift-footed: he would have won the footrace in the

Below: The back of an Etruscan mirror from ancient Italy (c. 480–470 BCE) depicts the Great Ajax fastening his sword with the help of the sea goddess Thetis, left, the mother of Achilles.

funeral games of Patroclus, Achilles' companion, had Athena not intervened. The goddess made him slip on a cow pie, and when he staggered in with a mouthful of manure, all the Greeks laughed at him. It appears that Athena's action was inspired by the Lesser Ajax's arrogance, another quality that distinguished him from the Great Ajax.

The most famous incident involving the Lesser Ajax occurred during the sacking of Troy, when he seized Cassandra, daughter of the Trojan king, Priam. Ajax pulled the girl away from the statue of Athena, which she was holding, and raped her, thus offending the goddess. The Greeks sentenced Ajax to death, but he took sanctuary in the Temple of Athena. The Greeks could not avenge the wrong against Athena without violating her sanctuary, and so they allowed Ajax to return home with them.

Below: A fifth-century-BCE Greek lekythos *(oil flask) depicting the dispute over Achilles' armor. Odysseus and the Great Ajax were the main rivals in this contest; when Ajax lost, he became mad with rage.*

However, Athena was still angry and sent a great storm that sank many of the Greek ships on their journey back from Troy. Among those shipwrecked was the Lesser Ajax, who grasped a rock to prevent himself from drowning. Homer says that he would have lived "in spite of the anger of Athena" had he not boasted that he had saved himself in defiance of the gods. His boast caused the sea god Poseidon to split the rock and drown him.

The epic story of the Lesser Ajax and Cassandra lay behind one of the most unusual ancient Greek rituals. Every year, in penance for the crime of Ajax, the inhabitants of Locris sent two maidens across the Aegean Sea to serve Athena in her temple in Ilion, the Greek city that claimed to be the successor to the legendary Troy. The maidens, who came from the best families, were escorted by Locrian men. They landed on the shore of Ilion (in modern northwest Turkey) at night, where they encountered men from Ilion, armed with swords. However, as one source explains, there was no record of any maiden ever having been killed. It seems that they were greeted with a show of force and then made their way into the city. Once in Ilion their jewelry and fine clothing were taken from them, and they were forced to serve Athena for a year, until two new maidens arrived from Locris to replace them.

The Lesser Ajax was also the hero of the western Locrians, who lived in southern Italy. In the sixth century BCE, the western Locrians defeated the superior forces of the city of Croton in a battle at the Sagra River. According to one of the many colorful stories told about this event, the Locrians left a gap in their battle line in honor of Ajax; when the commander of the Croton forces attacked this spot he received an incurable wound. An oracle told the commander that the wound could only be healed by the one who had made it. He therefore went in search of the Lesser Ajax and found him on the White Island, a ghostly place in the Black Sea. The commander came back healed and told that he had seen both Ajaxes living on the island, beside other heroes such as Achilles and Helen, who were married.

JAMES M. REDFIELD

Bibliography
Homer, and Robert Fagles, trans. *The Iliad*. New York: Penguin, 2009.
Homer, and Robert Fagles, trans. *The Odyssey*. New York: Penguin, 2009.

SEE ALSO: Achilles; Cassandra; Hector; Odysseus.

ALCESTIS

Alcestis occupies an important position in Greek mythology as the paragon of the loyal wife, who volunteered to die in place of her husband, Admetus, and as a loving and devoted daughter, who refused to shed her father's blood.

Alcestis, whose name means "might of the home," was a daughter of Pelias, king of Iolcus—the same Pelias who sent his nephew Jason to retrieve the Golden Fleece. The most famous version of her myth is retold in *Alcestis*, a play by Greek dramatist Euripides (c. 486–c. 406 BCE). Alcestis was the most beautiful of Pelias's three daughters and received many offers of marriage from princes and kings. Pelias knew that an outright refusal of any of these powerful suitors might threaten his position, so he devised a task that a suitor had to complete before marrying his daughter. The challenge was to harness a wild boar and a lion to a chariot and ride it around a racetrack. These two animals were symbols of different halves of the year in ancient Greece. Their inclusion in the myth has been interpreted as representing the peaceful division of a kingdom through marriage.

King Admetus of Pherae had one advantage over Alcestis's other suitors: his aid was the god Apollo, who was serving a punishment imposed on him by Zeus, whom he had angered. With Apollo's help, Admetus completed Pelias's task and married Alcestis. Before long, however, Admetus fell ill and seemed destined to die. Once again Apollo came to his aid. The god interceded with the three Fates, or Moirai—Clotho, Lachesis, and Atropos—and persuaded them to spare Admetus's life on the condition that someone else would die in his place. Admetus thought little of the implications of this arrangement and agreed to it at once. However, neither his friends nor his parents would countenance sacrificing their lives for him. Only Alcestis offered herself as the substitute. When Thanatos, god of death, arrived to take Alcestis away, he was thwarted by the Greek hero Heracles. Armed with a club made from a wild olive branch—a plant used in ancient Greece to cast out

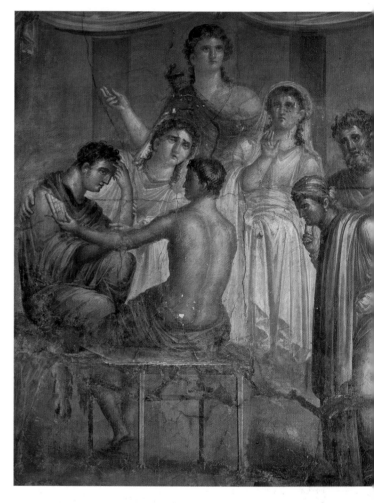

Above: *This Roman fresco depicts Admetus (far left) being comforted by his wife, Alcestis, before she dies in his place.*

evil—Heracles forced Thanatos to surrender Alcestis to her husband, restoring her to life and happiness.

Alternative version

Another version of the Alcestis myth is that Admetus angered the goddess Artemis by forgetting to make the customary sacrifice to her before his marriage. Apollo interceded on Admetus's behalf: a sacrifice was quickly made, and Artemis forgave Admetus, even promising that his life would be spared on the condition that one of his family die instead of him. In this telling, all choice in the matter is taken out of Admetus's hands. Admetus duly falls ill and, when his parents refuse to die for him, Alcestis

Right: French artist Jean Francois Pierre Peyron (1744–1814) painted this version of Alcestis's death in 1794. The melancholy scene depicts the moment of Alcestis's sacrifice rather than her resurrection.

Alcestis in Art and Literature

The myth of Alcestis's death and resurrection have inspired many artists and writers over the centuries. Alcestis appears on a number of reliefs and vase paintings that survive from ancient Greece. For example, in a relief from a temple made in about 356 BCE to Artemis, the goddess of the hunt, Alcestis is shown between Thanatos and Hermes, the messenger of the Olympian gods.

Alcestis's appearances are even more numerous in literature. For instance, Euripides' *Alcestis* portrays its heroine as an example of female courage; by contrast the dramatist shows her husband, Admetus, as shortsighted and morally weak. The Greek philosopher Plato (c. 428–c. 348 BCE) mentions Alcestis in *Symposium*, one of his influential dialogues, or philosophical exchanges. According to Plato's book, Alcestis's sacrifice shows that love strives to achieve the greatest good. Several hundred years later, Roman poet Ovid (43 BCE–17 CE) makes a similar point in his work *The Art of Love*. Ovid proposes that, while not all women in Greek mythology were good, Alcestis is a shining example of virtue. The Alcestis myth also inspired poets in later ages, including Englishman John Milton (1608–1674), German Rainer Maria Rilke (1875–1926), and American James Russell Lowell (1819–1891).

poisons herself and goes to the underworld. However, Persephone, queen of the underworld, refuses to let Alcestis remain in her kingdom because she believes that it is wrong for a wife to die instead of her husband.

The truly devoted daughter

In essence the two versions tell the same story: Alcestis alone is willing to die for her husband, and because of the purity of her action, she returns to life. She represents the Greek ideal of wifely love and devotion. Her goodness is further revealed in a myth involving the sorceress Medea, who offers to kill Pelias on behalf of her lover, Jason. Medea convinces the aged Pelias that she can restore his youth if first his daughters cut his body up into pieces. Unlike her two sisters, Alcestis refuses to butcher her father. Her instinct is proved right, for Medea's plan kills Pelias.

ANDREW CAMPBELL

Bibliography

Euripides, and P. Burian and A. Shapiro, eds. *The Complete Euripides.* New York: Oxford University Press, 2009–2010.
Graves, Robert. *The Greek Myths.* New York: Penguin, 1993.
Pomeroy, Sarah B. *Goddesses, Whores, Wives, and Slaves: Women in Classical Antiquity.* New York: Schocken Books, 1995.

SEE ALSO: Heracles.

AMAZONS

Although stories of female warriors existed in many cultures, the ancient Greek legends of the Amazons are the best known today. The Amazons, a mythological race of fighters and hunters, are still the subject of much discussion. While some scholars regard them as a purely mythical people, others think that there may have been a historical basis for the band of female warriors.

There are two distinct but overlapping classical sources on which our understanding of the Amazons is based. One is the works of ancient Greek and Roman poets and dramatists who wrote down myths. The other is accounts by those classical authors whom modern scholars regard as historians, since they shared a curiosity about events and an ability to view sources in a critical light. The diversity of sources explains the varying accounts of the Amazons' origins.

Different classical origins

According to some accounts, the Amazons lived in the ancient west Asian country of Scythis, north of the Black Sea. However, in "Aethiopis," an obscure poem about the Trojan War, the unknown author says that the female warriors came from Thrace, which is in modern Turkey and Bulgaria. Greek historian Herodotus (c. 484–425 BCE), on the other hand, wrote that the Amazons' capital was Themiscrya, on the banks of the Thermodon River in modern Turkey. Finally, historian Diodorus Siculus, also known as Diodorus of Sicily (90–21 BCE), claimed that the Amazon homeland was off western Libya, on an island

Right: This Roman statue of an Amazon was based on a Greek original from the fifth century BCE.

called Hespera near Mount Atlas. Different accounts also describe Amazon raids in Scythia, Thrace, along the coast of west Asia, on the islands of the Aegean Sea, and even as far afield as Arabia, Syria, and Egypt. These raids were not merely for loot. The Amazons were said to have founded many cities in west Asia and throughout the Mediterranean region, including Smyrna, Ephesus, Sinope, and Paphos.

Surviving and fighting

According to Greek geographer Strabo (c. 64 BCE–23 CE), no men were permitted to live in the land of the Amazons. However, in order to ensure the survival of their race, once a year the Amazons visited a nearby tribe, called the Gargareans, to mate with the men. Amazonian mothers kept the female babies born after these visits—they raised and trained them to be successful in war, hunting, and other professions. The Amazons' male children were either put to death or sent back to the Gargareans.

Ancient and modern authors have tried to explain the word *Amazon* in various ways. Some ancient writers claimed that it meant "without breast," because the women supposedly cut off their right breasts so that they could

Above: This painting, titled The Amazon and Her Children, *by German-born American artist Emanuel Gottlieb Leutze (1816–1868), depicts an Amazon mother teaching her young daughters how to wrestle.*

draw their bows more easily when hunting or fighting. However, all surviving Greek artwork featuring the Amazons depict them with two breasts, although the right one is frequently exposed. Other writers have suggested that the name means "not touching men," or that it came from the word for moon, *maza*, spoken by the people of Circassia in the northwest Caucasus. Several accounts connect the Amazons to a moon goddess figure similar to the Greek deity Artemis. Some modern scholars favor the tradition that the Amazons lived in north Africa—they point out that the Berber peoples of present-day north Africa call themselves the Amazigh. However, *Amazons* was not the only name used for the tribes of female warriors in ancient myths and documents. For example, in the *Iliad* by the Greek poet Homer (c. ninth–eighth century BCE), the Amazons were referred to as Antianeira, or "those who fight like men." Similarly, Herodotus called them Androktones, which means "killers of men."

Although they mainly fought on horseback with bows and arrows, the Amazons also used swords, double-sided axes, and distinctive crescent-shaped shields. In Greek art they are sometimes depicted wearing specialized clothing, which included pants. The most famous classical depictions of the Amazons are the marble carvings from the Parthenon in Athens, which was built in the mid-fifth century BCE.

Amazons in Greek myth

The Amazons appear in several Greek myths. For example, in the story of Jason and the Argonauts, related by Greek poet Apollonius of Rhodes (third century BCE), the king of the gods, Zeus, sent a strong northwest wind so that the Argonauts' ship, the *Argo*, would not land on the Amazonian shore. The *Iliad* contains the story of the hero Bellerophon, whom Iobates, the king of Lycia, sends to single-handedly fight the Amazons. Iobates hopes that Bellerophon would die during the battle; instead, the hero defeats the female warriors.

Another Greek hero who encountered the Amazons was Heracles. One of Heracles' 12 labors was to obtain the girdle, or belt, of the Amazon queen Hippolyte. In some versions of the story, Hippolyte gave the girdle to Heracles as a gift of love. However, in other versions, the Greek hero tried to steal it. In either case, fighting ensued after the goddess Hera, Heracles' enemy, appeared in disguise and told the Amazons that he had possession of the queen's girdle. In some accounts a great battle was fought, in which Heracles killed many Amazons. In other tellings, Heracles kidnapped Melanippe, Hippolyte's sister, returning her in exchange for the girdle.

Antiope and Theseus

Heracles was accompanied on this labor by the Athenian hero Theseus, who carried off the Amazon princess Antiope. Most Greek sources described Antiope as a sister of Hippolyte and Melanippe — although one writer called her the daughter of Hippolyte—and mention that she ruled the Amazons with her two sisters. In one version of the story, Theseus abducted her forcibly, while another version says that Heracles gave her to his friend as a gift. Theseus returned with the woman to Athens, which led to an invasion of the city by the Amazons. Yet by the time the female warriors reached Athens, Antiope had fallen in love with Theseus and given birth to a son by him called Hippolytus. The Amazons besieged Athens for three months but were eventually defeated. Some accounts relate how Antiope, while fighting alongside Theseus, was killed by the

Left: Discovered in Italy, this Greek amphora from the sixth century BCE depicts Achilles using his spear to kill Penthesileia, queen of the Amazons. The artwork is attributed to Exekias, considered the most accomplished amphora painter in the ancient world.

Above: This first- or second-century-BCE carved ivory scabbard tip has an image of a battle between the Greeks and the Amazons.

Camilla, an Italian Amazon

Virgil's *Aeneid*, the Roman poet's account of the voyages of the Trojan refugee and founder of Rome, Aeneas, includes a description of a woman who looked and acted very much like an Amazon. According to Virgil, when Aeneas and his men finally arrived in Italy, they were challenged to battle by a local king, Turnus, whose advances toward Lavinia, the daughter of another king, had been rejected in favor of Aeneas. The virgin warrior Camilla joined forces with Turnus against Aeneas. Virgil related how Camilla was brought up in the wild by her father, Metabus, exiled king of the Volsci tribe. Metabus had taught his daughter how to hunt and fight and dedicated her to Diana, goddess of hunting. In battle against Aeneas, Camilla led a band of female warriors and rode with one breast exposed. She killed many men before dying herself, pierced by a spear belonging to an Etruscan named Arruns. After her death, Diana sent down the nymph Opis to kill Arruns and reclaim Camilla's body.

Amazon Molpadia. In other accounts, Antiope survived the battle only to feel betrayed when Theseus later married Phaedra, the daughter of King Minos of Crete. Flanked by other Amazons, Antiope attempted to thwart the couple's wedding celebrations but was killed by either Theseus or one of his men, or accidentally at the hands of another Amazon.

Amazons and the Trojan War

The epics about the Trojan War contain many references to the Amazons. The *Iliad*, for example, tells how the Amazons came to the aid of the Trojans during their war against the Greeks. Several classical authors, including Roman poet Virgil (70–19 BCE), described how the Amazon queen Penthesileia led her warriors against the Greeks. Penthesileia was the daughter of another Amazon queen, Otrere, and the war god Ares. She became queen when she accidentally killed Antiope with a spear. In some accounts, the death occurred during the battle at the wedding of Theseus and Phaedra; in other versions, it happened when both Amazons were hunting deer. The crime of killing a queen and a fellow Amazon was a serious one, and it was claimed that Penthesileia's support for Troy came in return for the purification of her sin by the Trojan king, Priam.

An Egyptian Amazon Story

An Egyptian story, written down by scribes on papyrus during the time of the Roman Empire, features an Amazon queen who falls in love. Although incomplete, it relates how a prince named Padikhonsu invaded the land of the Amazons, which it describes as being in Khor (modern Syria and northern Iraq). The Amazon queen, Serpot, took to the field against Padikhonsu and his Assyrian allies and came close to defeating them. The prince then challenged the queen to single combat. Serpot agreed, and the two began to fight. After a whole day's battle, the warriors had begun to fall in love with each other.

This Egyptian story shares many features with the tale of Penthesileia and Achilles, but although the papyrus breaks off before the end, it does not appear that the Egyptian tale was intended to have an unhappy ending: together Padikhonsu and Serpot fight off an invasion of the Amazons' territory by an army from India.

In battles against the Greeks, Penthesileia, who was a superb and skilled fighter, killed many warriors, including a healer named Machaon. However, she was no match for the Greek hero Achilles. According to legend, Achilles killed the Amazon queen in a fierce battle and then set about the customary practice of taking her weapons, only to fall in love with the beautiful face of his dead opponent (see box). He immediately regretted fighting her. Thersites, another Greek warrior, mocked him for loving his defeated enemy, so Achilles, always quick to anger, killed Thersites too. Of all the Greeks, only Diomedes mourned for Thersites. He angrily took Penthesileia's body and tossed it into a river, which meant that neither side could give her a proper burial.

One story tells how, after the Trojan War, the Amazons undertook an expedition against the island of Leuke, at the mouth of the Danube River. Leuke was the place where Achilles' mother, the sea nymph Thetis, had deposited the ashes of her son after his death at the hands of Paris and the sun god Apollo. When the Amazons arrived on the island, they saw the ghost of the dead hero. Their horses were so terrified at the sight that the invaders were forced to retreat.

The Amazon queen Myrina

In his work *Bibliotheca historica* (Library of History), Diodorus Siculus wrote that the Amazons came from Libya in north Africa. Diodorus's account is set in the time of myth. He wrote that the warriors' most famous queen was

Myrina, who lived before the hero Perseus saved the Ethiopian princess Andromeda from a sea monster. Myrina led her warriors to a great number of victories, including one against the mythical island of Atlantis. Myrina led a large army of 30,000 foot-soldiers and 3,000 cavalry against the Atlanteans. Diodorus claimed that the Amazon cavalry used tactics similar to those employed by the Parthians of west Asia, who fought the Roman general Crassus (c. 115–53 BCE), firing arrows as they rode away from their enemies. The Atlanteans eventually surrendered to Myrina after she had captured and destroyed one of their cities, enslaving and carrying away the women and the children.

It was during the reign of Myrina that the Amazons encountered another race of female warriors known as the Gorgons. The Amazons and their defeated neighbors, the Atlanteans, were at peace with each other, but Atlantis was raided repeatedly by the Gorgons, who lived nearby. In Greek myth, the Gorgons were monsters with snakes instead of hair and faces so fearsome that looking directly at them could turn a mortal into stone. Diodorus scoffed at these stories of monsters and claimed that, like the Amazons, the Gorgons were nothing more than fierce tribal women who were skilled in warfare. Myrina's large army went to the aid of Atlantis and defeated the Gorgons, capturing more than 3,000 Gorgon warriors. The captive Gorgons began a rebellion but were put down by the Amazons, who killed every remaining prisoner.

Myrina was said to have conquered most of Libya, from where she led her army east toward Egypt. When she reached Egypt, she befriended the king before going on to defeat the Bedouin and Syrian peoples and conquering some of west Asia. Although the people of Cilicia (part of modern Turkey) were not defeated, they were willing to accept her rule. The Amazons also captured the island of Lesbos in the Aegean Sea, where Myrina founded the city of Mitylene, named for her sister. While sailing across the Aegean, Myrina got caught in a storm. The queen prayed to the Mother Goddess to save her and was guided to a deserted island, which she named Samothrace. Myrina's good fortune, however, did not last forever: she died in battle against the Thracians and Scythians, led by the Thracian Mopsos. Without their great leader, the Amazons lost a series of battles to Mopsos. Eventually their empire collapsed and they withdrew back to Libya.

The Amazons and historical figures

While most stories about the Amazons locate them alongside mythical and legendary characters, other accounts include references to historical figures, such as Alexander

Above: Wounded Amazon *by German artist Franz van Stuck (1863–1928). Van Stuck, who was part of the symbolist movement, often used characters from classical mythology in his paintings.*

the Great (356–323 BCE). One source tells how Alexander, who conquered almost all the territory from the western Mediterranean to India before his death at the age of 33, met the Amazon queen Thalestris. According to the story, the queen brought 300 other Amazon women to Alexander, hoping to breed a whole race of children as strong and intelligent as him. In another account, the great Roman general Pompey (106–48 BCE) is said to have found Amazon warriors in the army belonging to Mithradates, king of Pontus.

The mention of Amazons alongside historical figures such as Alexander and Pompey, as well as the fact that they are discussed by classical historians from Herodotus to Diodorus, has led some scholars to argue that they may have existed. Among different historical opinions, some of which claim that the female warriors were entirely the creation of ancient poets, is the argument that the idea of a warlike group of women was based on the practices adopted by women in some cultures in west Asia— practices that the Greeks may have regarded as "masculine."

LYN GREEN

Bibliography

Davis-Kimball, Jeannine, with Mona Behan. *Warrior Women: An Archaeologist's Search for History's Hidden Heroines.* New York: Warner Books, 2003.

Homer, and Robert Fagles, trans. *The Iliad* and *The Odyssey.* New York: Penguin, 2009.

SEE ALSO: Achilles; Bellerophon; Gorgons; Heracles; Hippolyte; Jason; Theseus.

ANDROMEDA

Andromeda plays a significant role in the Perseus legend in Greek mythology. Her father was Cepheus, king of Ethiopia, and her mother Cassiopeia, whose beauty was renowned throughout Greece and beyond.

Andromeda turned out to be every bit as beautiful as her mother. Cassiopeia, who had always been vain about her own appearance, was inordinately proud of her daughter's good looks. One day the notoriously jealous goddess Hera overheard Cassiopeia boasting that she and her daughter were more beautiful than any of the Nereids, the sea nymphs who were daughters of the sea god Poseidon. Greek mythology is full of stories of the gods punishing the sin of hubris, or pride, in humans, and Cassiopeia was destined to become a leading example.

Hera and the Nereids complained to Poseidon, who sent a flood to ravage Ethiopia. He also sent a dreadful female sea monster to haunt the coast of the country. The creature wreaked havoc and had an appetite for human flesh that seemed insatiable.

Cepheus, at his wits' end, consulted an oracle, who told him that the way to get rid of the sea monster forever was to sacrifice his daughter Andromeda to it. Cepheus protested to the gods, but they were adamant that this was the only way to atone for Cassiopeia's effrontery.

Enter the hero
Andromeda was chained to a rock facing the sea, naked except for her jewels, as the gods had instructed. While she lay there, nervously awaiting her fate, she saw a young man fly past, propelled through the air by a pair of winged sandals.

This was Perseus, the hero who had just killed the Gorgon Medusa with a magic sickle and was returning to Argos with the monster's head in a bag. The bag, the sickle, the winged sandals, and a helmet that conferred invisibility on the wearer had been given to him by the

Above: This oil painting from 1630 by Dutch artist Joachim Wtewael (1566–1638) is entitled Perseus Frees Andromeda.

gods to help him to kill the Gorgon, whose horrible looks turned anyone who looked at her to stone.

Perseus was astonished to see a beautiful naked woman chained to a rock. As he descended from the sky to take a closer look, he saw Andromeda's parents watching in despair from the shore. They promised him that he could marry Andromeda if he managed to rescue her from the monster. No sooner had they finished speaking than the monster emerged from the sea and moved toward Andromeda with its mouth wide open, making as if to swallow her whole.

Perseus instantly rose into the air, and with a single stroke of his magic sickle, he cut off the monster's head. He then released Andromeda from her chains and led her back to her delighted parents. Finally, he sacrificed to all the gods as an act of penance for having denied them their vengeance. Poseidon later turned the dead body of the monster into the sea's first coral.

PERSEUS

CASSIOPEIA

TRIANGULUM

TAURUS

ANDROMEDA

ARIES

Above: This painting by James Thornhill (1676–1734) depicts Perseus and Andromeda after they have been turned into constellations.

Andromeda was deeply impressed by the bravery of Perseus and fell in love with him. She urged her parents to let her marry him right away. They reluctantly agreed, but Cassiopeia then secretly told the whole story to Agenor, who had previously been betrothed to Andromeda, but who had done nothing to help her while she was in mortal peril. On the day of the wedding, Agenor arrived uninvited with a group of friends, disrupting the ceremony and demanding that Andromeda be released from the bargain with Perseus. Cepheus and Cassiopeia took Agenor's side, because he was the son of a powerful neighboring king. When Perseus refused to call a halt to the wedding, Agenor tried to carry Andromeda away by force, while his friends lashed out at Perseus with their weapons.

Justice is done

Perseus had anticipated Cassiopeia's treachery, and had therefore brought with him the magic bag containing Medusa's head. He took it out and used it to turn Agenor and his friends to stone. He also transformed Cepheus and Cassiopeia, so that Cassiopeia was punished for her sin of pride.

The gods decided to make an example of Cepheus and Cassiopeia. They set them among the stars as constellations as a warning to the impious. At some times of the year, Cassiopeia's constellation turns upside down—in order, the Greeks said, to punish her further.

As for Andromeda, Perseus flew back to Argos with her in his arms. He then won his kingdom back from his uncle, who had usurped the throne in his absence, and had many further adventures. Perseus and Andromeda eventually became king and queen of Tiryns, an ancient city on the Peloponnese peninsula, and their children ruled over it after them.

When they died, Andromeda and Perseus were also set up in the sky as stars, but in their case this was an honor, not an awful warning. One of the Andromeda constellation's best-known features is the Andromeda nebula, the closest galaxy to our own.

PETER CONNOR

Bibliography

Bulfinch, Thomas. *Bulfinch's Mythology.* New York: Barnes & Noble, 2006.

Howatson, M. C. *The Oxford Companion to Classical Literature.* New York: Oxford University Press, 2005.

SEE ALSO: Gorgons; Perseus.

ANTIGONE

Antigone was one of four children born from the incestuous relationship between Oedipus, king of Thebes, and his mother, Jocasta. In Greek myth and drama, Antigone's chief virtue was loyalty: she guided her father after he blinded and exiled himself; and, in burying her brother Polyneices, she chose family duty and the laws of the gods over the laws of the state.

When King Oedipus went into exile, Antigone accompanied him to Colonus in Attica. Her two brothers, Eteocles and Polyneices, stayed behind in Thebes under the regency of their uncle, Creon. When Oedipus died, Antigone returned to Thebes to live with her brothers and uncle, as well as her sister Ismene. By then, the brothers had come of age and vied for the throne of Thebes. They decided to take turns ruling the city: one year Eteocles would rule, the next year Polyneices, and so on. At the end of the first year, however, Eteocles made no show of yielding the kingdom to his brother. Polyneices was forced into exile and took refuge with Adrastus, king of Argos, whose daughter Argeia he married. Adrastus helped Polyneices assemble a huge army with seven leaders to attack Thebes—the army became known as the Seven Against Thebes.

Deaths in the family

The Seven failed dismally, but not before the two sons of Oedipus faced one another in battle and killed each other. As a consequence Creon, their uncle, became king. He gave an ornate funeral for Eteocles, but forbade the burial of Polyneices, whom he felt had betrayed his people by fighting against his own city. This was a very grave punishment: the ancient Greeks believed that without burial, a human soul could not enter the underworld and instead would flutter ceaselessly above the earth.

Antigone could not accept Creon's treatment of her brother, and with a handful of dirt she gave him a symbolic burial. She asked Ismene to help her, but her sister was too afraid. Antigone's action was a direct violation of the king's orders, and Creon sentenced her to death. He locked her up in a tomb chamber and had its entrance sealed. The old prophet Tiresias, however, warned the king that he would be cursed for killing Antigone. Eventually, Creon changed his mind. He allowed a proper burial for Polyneices and opened the entrance to Antigone's tomb, but it was too late: to avoid death by starvation, Antigone had hanged herself. Creon's son Haemon, who was engaged to marry Antigone, killed himself over his beloved's dead body. His death led Creon's wife, Eurydice, to commit suicide, too. Only Creon himself was left to live out the curse that Tiresias had prophesied.

Antigone in literature and art

The most famous version of Antigone's story is the play *Antigone* by Greek dramatist Sophocles (c. 496–406 BCE). Sophocles' tragedy demonstrates Antigone's qualities of piety and heroism. In burying her brother, she follows the laws of the gods in direct violation of the command of the king. She is aware that there will be serious consequences, but in her mind she has no other option but to act. For her, religious beliefs and family duty take precedence over the laws of the city; the burial of her brother is more important than her uncle's command. She does what is right in spite of the consequences to herself.

Antigone features in two other tragedies by Sophocles. In *Oedipus the King*, she and her sister Ismene appear at the end of the play to be with their father, who has torn out his eyes after learning that he has unwittingly killed his father Laius, and married his own mother. In the sequel to this play, *Oedipus at Colonus* Antigone is portrayed as a faithful daughter who guides her blind father from place to place during his exile.

Antigone has continued to be an important character in more modern times. Inspired by Sophocles' *Antigone*, German philosopher Georg Wilhelm Friedrich Hegel (1770–1831) wrote several treatises about ethics, the individual, and the state. The first modern production of *Antigone* was performed with music by German composer

Left: Oedipus and Antigone at Colonus *by Johann Peter Krafft (1780–1856). Ever loyal to her family, Antigone led her blind father, Oedipus, to Colonus in Attica, where the king knew from a prophecy he would die.*

Felix Mendelssohn in Potsdam, Germany, in 1841—a production that marked the beginning of the revival of Greek plays in western Europe.

Among the many interpretations of the Antigone theme, there is one that deserves special mention. In 1944, during the German occupation of France in World War II, French dramatist Jean Anouilh (1910–1987) wrote another play called *Antigone*. Anouilh's drama portrays Creon as a reasonable ruler, while Antigone is hysterical and unwilling to compromise. Yet despite these qualities, Antigone's attitude is very understandable: her brothers have killed one another, Creon has first refused to honor one of his nephews, and then sentenced one of his nieces to death. Under such circumstances, there is no place for reason.

The play suggests that Antigone's rebellion against her uncle and life itself is the only choice left to her. The tragic end to the drama comes when Creon realizes that, despite all his power, he cannot stop his niece, son, and wife from destroying themselves.

FEYO SCHUDDEBOOM

Bibliography

Graves, Robert. *The Greek Myths.* New York: Penguin, 1993.
Sophocles, and Ruth Fainlight and Robert J. Littman, trans. *The Theban Plays.* Baltimore, MD: Johns Hopkins University Press, 2009.

SEE ALSO: Oedipus.

ARACHNE

The story of Arachne, a woman turned into a spider by the goddess Athena, was a warning to ancient Greeks to respect their deities.

Arachne was the daughter of Idmon, who in some accounts was an aristocrat, in others a dyer. They lived in the ancient Greek city of Colophon in Lydia (part of modern Turkey). The region was famous for its textiles, and Arachne grew up to be a superb weaver of tapestries. She resented any suggestions that she owed her talents to Athena, the goddess of weavers. Arachne's arrogance so displeased Athena that the goddess disguised herself as an old woman and warned the girl to recognize Athena's superiority. Arachne refused to do so, however, and told the crone that she would challenge Athena to a weaving contest. On hearing this, Athena revealed herself to Arachne, and the two immediately set to work on different tapestries. Athena's embroidery pictured her own triumphant exploits and detailed the fates of other mortals who had dared to challenge the gods. Arachne's work

satirized the gods, in particular the lust for mortal women displayed by Poseidon, Apollo, Dionysus, and most of all by Zeus, who often deceived his victims before seducing them. Angered by Arachne's temerity as well as her skill, Athena touched the girl's forehead, causing her to feel such guilt that she hanged herself. Shocked by this turn of events, Athena sprinkled aconite (another name for the highly poisonous monkshood plant) on Arachne's body, transforming her into a spider.

Sources and interpretations

The best-known source for the myth of Arachne was written by Roman poet Ovid (43 BCE–17 CE) in his *Metamorphoses*, a work that contains numerous different accounts of mythical characters whose lives were transformed by the gods. In Ovid's version it is clear that Arachne's problem was one of pride or hubris, an exaggerated belief in one's own abilities. Yet in other versions the theme is more one of Athena's envy of a mortal whose skills are at least comparable with—and possibly even greater than—her own. In one version of

Below: This painting of Athena's contest with Arachne is the work of Venetian artist Tintoretto (c. 1518–1594).

Arachne in Art

Two of the 100 surviving works by Diego Velázquez (1599–1660) show the Spanish painter's fascination with the legend of Arachne. One is a portrait of the woman herself. The other, dated 1657–1658, is entitled *Las Hilanderas* ("The Women Weavers") in Spanish and *The Fable of Arachne* in English. The foreground of this fascinating canvas depicts Arachne in the process of weaving her fatal tapestry. This part of the painting is a partial copy of an earlier masterpiece, *The Rape of Europa* by Titian (c. 1489–1576). The women with Arachne in the foreground are mysterious and unidentified; in the background, Athena is wearing an armored helmet—a reminder that she was the goddess of war, as well as of the arts. Velázquez's masterpiece now hangs in the Prado Museum in Madrid, Spain.

Below: This detail from a painting by Diego Velázquez shows Arachne busily weaving the tapestry that will cost her her life.

the legend, Athena became so jealous of Arachne's tapestry that she tore it in two, causing Arachne to hang herself in terror.

The Arachne myth can be interpreted on a variety of levels. It is a story of the dangers of pride or envy, but also of the consequences of failing to respect the gods. It also attempts to explain a natural phenomenon—spiders' ability to weave their webs. After her transformation, Arachne hid from Athena by weaving the rope on which she hanged herself into an intricate web. Finally, the story can be interpreted in the light of economic rivalry between the city of Athens and the region of Lydia. Historical and archaeological evidence suggests that, in the second millennium BCE, Lydia was the largest exporter of dyed woolen cloth in the Mediterranean. In this reading of the story, Athena is Athens, while Arachne symbolizes her native Lydia.

ANDREW CAMPBELL

Bibliography

Howatson, M. C. *The Oxford Companion to Classical Literature.* New York: Oxford University Press, 2005.

Ovid, and A. D. Melville, trans. *Metamorphoses.* New York: Oxford University Press, 2008.

Warner, Rex. *Men and Gods: Myths and Legends of the Ancient Greeks.* New York: New York Review Books, 2008.

ARIADNE

The daughter of King Minos of Crete and his wife Pasiphae, Ariadne played a crucial role in the slaying of the Minotaur by the Athenian hero Theseus. However, despite promising to marry her, Theseus later abandoned Ariadne on the island of Naxos.

Theseus arrived in Crete as one of the 14 young people sent every year from Athens, as reparation for the murder of a Cretan prince. They were all sacrificed to the Minotaur. This monstrous creature, half bull and half man, was the result of Pasiphae's unnatural coupling with the white bull of Poseidon. He was kept hidden in a palace of winding corridors and hidden rooms, the Labyrinth, built by the inventor and architect Daedalus. None of the young sacrificial victims had managed to kill the Minotaur or escape the Labyrinth.

Right: This carving on a fragment of a sarcophagus depicts Ariadne as a Cretan goddess of fertility. She is shown with Bacchus, the Greek god of wine and abundance, who fell in love with her.

Ariadne's plan

Ariadne caught sight of Theseus on his arrival in Crete and immediately fell in love with him. She promised to supply him with a way to escape from the Labyrinth if he agreed to marry her and take her back to Athens with him. Theseus agreed and Ariadne gave him a ball of twine (or, in some versions, golden thread) that Daedalus had previously given to her. By tying one end of the thread to the doorway at the entrance to the maze and then unraveling the ball as he went, Theseus was able to retrace his steps once he had slain the Minotaur.

When he emerged, Ariadne guided Theseus and the other surviving Athenians to the harbor, where they boarded his ship and fled toward Athens. At this point, the various versions of the myth diverge. In the most widespread version, the Athenian ship arrived at the island of Naxos and Ariadne fell asleep on the shore. Theseus embarked with his companions and abandoned her there. Ariadne awoke to find herself alone and deserted by her lover, for whom she had sacrificed family and homeland. However, Dionysus (Bacchus), the god of wine, had fallen in love with her and descended from heaven to carry her away to be his bride.

Variations in the legend

Another version of the myth says that Dionysus himself ordered Theseus to leave Ariadne, since the god had chosen her as his bride. Other variations tell that Ariadne was so distraught on waking and finding herself abandoned that she hanged herself. In yet another version of the myth, Theseus and the pregnant Ariadne were driven by a storm to Cyprus, where she died in childbirth.

Historical context and links

The story of Ariadne and Theseus illustrates the process whereby Athens freed itself from Crete, which, until about 1200 BCE, was a the leading power in the Mediterranean world. The Athenian Theseus puts an end to Cretan demands for reparations and gains a princess as his bride.

Ariadne herself, whose name means "most pure" or "most pleasing," was at one time worshiped as a fertility goddess in Crete and the eastern Mediterranean. Her union with Dionysus, the god of not only wine but also dance, excess, and abundance, seems to be a link between earlier Eastern and later Greek divinities of renewal and growth. A circular fertility dance led by Theseus is described in Callimachus's *Hymn to Delos,* written in the third century BCE, and Ariadne herself may well have led such a dance in Crete, on a labyrinthine-patterned floor constructed for this purpose by Daedalus.

The image of the solitary and inconsolable Ariadne was a popular theme in the visual art and poetry of antiquity, and she has remained a symbol of loss and abandonment in Western art. The Renaissance Italian artists Titian and Guido Reni both painted her, as did the French artist Jean-Baptiste Regnault at the start of the 19th century. In the early 20th century, Ariadne was the subject of an opera, *Ariadne on Naxos,* by German composer Richard Strauss. More recently, because of Ariadne's part in overcoming the horrors of the Labyrinth, her name has been used by a variety of projects related to information retrieval on the Internet.

PETER CONNOR

Bibliography

Bulfinch, Thomas. *Bulfinch's Mythology.* New York: Barnes & Noble, 2006.
Graves, Robert. *The Greek Myths.* New York: Penguin, 1993.

SEE ALSO: Daedalus; Minos; Pasiphae; Theseus.

Above: A romantic vision of Ariadne imploring Theseus to marry her, painted by Jean-Baptiste Regnault (1754–1829). Theseus holds the ball of yarn aloft, like a trophy, before entering the Minotaur's Labyrinth.

ATALANTA

In Greek mythology Atalanta was beautiful, strong, and the fastest runner of the mortals. She traveled with Jason and his Argonauts on the search for the Golden Fleece, but she is most famous for her adventures after the quest, including the Calydonian boar hunt, the race with Hippomenes, and for misbehaving in a temple of Zeus.

Right: Even in marble, Atalanta looks strong and athletic. This statue dates from the fourth or third century BCE.

A talanta's mythical origins are not certain: some tales say that she was the daughter of Schoeneus of Boeotia, others that Iasus of Arcadia was her father; and there are hints that her mother may have been an attendant of Artemis, the Greek goddess of the hunt. Whoever her parents were, legend tells of a dramatic childhood. When Atalanta was newly born, her father was so disappointed in not having a son that he abandoned the infant in the forest, where she was rescued and nurtured by a bear. Some time later hunters found the bear suckling the baby, and they took her to raise as their own. Atalanta grew up to be a fine archer and hunter.

Some scholars argue that for the ancient Greeks the myth of Atalanta highlights prejudice in favoring sons over daughters. At the same time Atalanta's fictional story fits into a pattern seen in the lives of many mythical heroes. For example, Paris, Oedipus, and Orestes were all abandoned or rejected when young, but legends tell how they survived, succeeded, and fulfilled the fears or desires that prompted their parents to abandon them. Atalanta not only became as strong and successful as any son her father could have wished for, she went on to deny her femininity by rejecting the idea of marriage. She was also the prototype for other female warriors, such as Camilla, who is featured in Book 11 of the *Aeneid* by the Roman poet Virgil (70–19 BCE).

In terms of the chronology of Greek mythology, Atalanta belonged to the generation before the Trojan War, and she participated in the two major heroic expeditions of her fictional time: the quest for the Golden Fleece with the Argonauts and the Calydonian boar hunt. In one account, however, Jason, the Greek hero who led the Argonauts, dissuaded Atalanta from joining the quest because he feared that a woman's presence would spark conflict among his men.

The boar hunt

After the Golden Fleece adventure, Atalanta played a more important role in the Calydonian boar hunt. When King Oeneus of Calydon offended Artemis by failing to offer her a sacrifice, the goddess sent a terrible boar to ravage Calydon. Oeneus's son Meleager, who had been one of the youngest Argonauts, summoned all his erstwhile companions, including Atalanta, to help him destroy the boar. During the hunt Atalanta took first blood from the boar by shooting an arrow into its head. Although the wound did not kill the beast, it made it easy for the others to finish off the boar, with Meleager delivering the final deathblow. Meleager awarded the prize of the boar's skin to Atalanta. This angered the rest of the hunters, especially Meleager's maternal uncles, Plexippus and Toxeus, because they did not believe such an honor should go to a woman. In the ensuing dispute Meleager killed both his uncles. This proved Meleager's undoing.

Meleager had been cursed at his birth by the Fates— three women who controlled destiny. The Fates had

Meanwhile, Aphrodite, the goddess of love, had grown tired of Atalanta's deadly game, and she gave Hippomenes three golden apples from the garden of the Hesperides, maidens who guarded a magical tree. During the race Hippomenes distracted Atalanta by rolling each apple just far enough ahead of her that she would stop to pick it up. By doing this three times, Atalanta slowed enough for Hippomenes to win the race.

Atalanta kept to her word and married Hippomenes. The couple grew to love each other and all seemed well. Then one day Aphrodite, who had grown enraged because Hippomenes had failed to thank her properly for the golden apples, cast a spell on the newlyweds, causing them to make love in the temple of Zeus. The king of the gods saw the couple in his temple and as a punishment turned Hippomenes into a lion and Atalanta into a lioness. Another version has it that the couple were caught in the temple of Cybele (Rhea), mother of the gods. She then turned the lovers into lions and hitched them to her chariot to serve her forever.

appeared to Meleager's mother, Althaea, and predicted that her son would live only as long as the log that was burning in the fireplace remained intact. Althaea had immediately pulled the log from the fireplace and guarded it to protect Meleager. When Althaea heard that her son had slain her own brothers, she angrily threw the fateful log into the fire, causing Meleager to die.

The race

According to legend, Atalanta's success in the Calydonian boar hunt prompted a reconciliation with her father, Schoeneus or Iasus. Like all fathers of ancient Greece, real or fictional, Schoeneus or Iasus had a social responsibility to find his daughter a husband. Yet Atalanta spurned wedlock, possibly because she had been warned against it by an oracle, or fortune-teller. The gods rarely tolerated women who refused to marry, so to appease the gods and her father, she agreed to marry on one condition. The man she married would first have to beat her in a footrace, but the losers would be killed.

Atalanta, who was the fastest mortal on earth, always won the races, even when she gave her opponents a head start. The death toll of failed suitors mounted. Finally Hippomenes (or Melanion in some versions), who was in love with the beautiful Atalanta, took up the challenge.

Atalanta in art

The stories about Atalanta have inspired several artistic masterpieces. Peter Paul Rubens (1577–1640) painted *Meleager and Atalanta* around 1635: it depicts Meleager offering the trophy of the boar's head to Atalanta. Rubens completed *The Hunt of Meleager and Atalanta* some years earlier. This artwork shows Atalanta at the moment just after she shot the arrow into the boar, while Meleager stabs the beast with a spear. Today the painting is housed in the Kunsthistorisches Museum in Vienna, Austria.

Guido Reni (1575–1642) painted Atalanta and Hippomenes around 1612. In Reni's painting the two runners are almost nude. Hippomenes, who is ahead of Atalanta, has just thrown another golden apple and Atalanta stoops to pick it up. Since the late 19th century the painting has hung in Madrid's Prado Museum.

KATHRYN CHEW

Bibliography
Bulfinch, Thomas. *Bulfinch's Mythology.* New York: Barnes & Noble, 2006.
Howatson, M. C. *The Oxford Companion to Classical Literature.* New York: Oxford University Press, 2005.

SEE ALSO: Jason.

ATREUS

Atreus and his extended family featured heavily in Greek drama and mythology. The family was collectively known as the House of Atreus, and its story revolves around themes of jealousy, revenge, sex, and power. The focus of the family battles and intrigue tended to be the throne of Mycenae, which both Atreus and his brother Thyestes occupied at different times.

Below: The cliffs of north Zákinthos, an island west of the Peloponnese Peninsula. The Peloponnese was named for Pelops and was the battleground for the power struggle between Atreus and his brother.

Like a modern soap opera, the rivalry between Atreus and his brother Thyestes lasted many years and included plots of intrigue, murder, incest, and adultery. It also blighted the lives of the two kings' children and grandchildren. Atreus and Thyestes were sons of Pelops and Hippodameia (also spelled Hippodamia), and it was with them that the dramatic story began. Pelops, for whom the Peloponnese (or Peloponnesus) was named, was the son of Tantalus, king of Sipylus, and Hippodameia was the daughter of Oenomaus, king of Pisa in Elis.

Before Pelops could marry Hippodameia he first had to face Oenomaus in a chariot race. If Oenomaus won the race, then Pelops would be killed but if Pelops won, then he could marry Hippodameia. To ensure victory Pelops bribed Oenomaus's charioteer, Myrtilus, to sabotage his master's chariot. Oenomaus was killed and Pelops won the right to marry Hippodameia. After the race, however, Myrtilus demanded his payment: Pelops had promised him a night

The House of Atreus

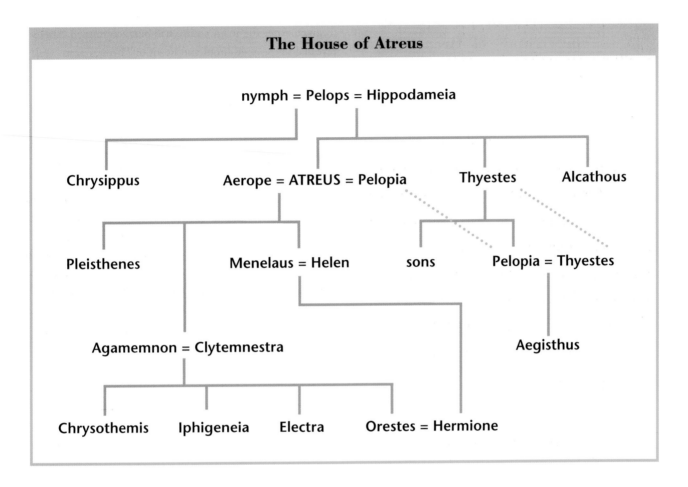

nymph = Pelops = Hippodameia

Chrysippus

Aerope = ATREUS = Pelopia

Thyestes

Alcathous

Pleisthenes

Menelaus = Helen

sons

Pelopia = Thyestes

Agamemnon = Clytemnestra

Aegisthus

Chrysothemis   Iphigeneia   Electra   Orestes = Hermione

with Hippodameia. Instead Pelops killed Myrtilus, who, before he died, cursed Pelops and his children. According to some versions of the story of the House of Atreus, it was Myrtilus's curse that began the troubles for the family.

The throne of Mycenae

The House of Atreus was one of the major dynasties to feature in the plays and stories of the dramatists of ancient Greece. Traditionally the descendants of Pelops were associated with the settlement and political development of large areas of the northern and central Peloponnese Peninsula. Several of Atreus's brothers (not all of whom are shown in the family tree, above), for example, were believed to have ruled important cities in the eastern area of the Peloponnese, including Troezen, Sicyon, and Epidaurus. Atreus and Thyestes were closely linked to the Argolid, the eastern Peloponnesian Plain that includes the historical cities of Argos, Mycenae, Tiryns, and Nauplion. The sons of Pelops came to the Argolid after they were expelled by their father for murdering Chrysippus, Pelops's son by a nymph whom he had married before Hippodameia. As the oldest son, Chrysippus was heir to Pelops's kingdom. (In another version, Chrysippus committed suicide, after he was abducted and raped by another man, Laius.)

Atreus and Thyestes settled near Mycenae, which was ruled by Perseus's grandson Eurystheus. Eurystheus's father had married one of Pelops's daughters, so Eurystheus was the nephew of the two brothers. When Eurystheus died, an oracle prophesied that one of the two sons of Pelops would inherit the throne.

Atreus, who was the older brother, had the stronger claim to the Mycenaean throne, but Thyestes proposed that whoever possessed a certain golden lambskin should become king. The prized lamb had been given to Atreus as a cursed gift by either the god Hermes, father of Myrtilus, or by the goddess Artemis as a test to see if Atreus would willingly sacrifice it to her. Atreus, assuming the lambskin was still safely locked away, agreed. Unknown to Atreus, however, Thyestes had earlier seduced Atreus's wife, Aerope, and persuaded her to give him the golden lambskin. When Thyestes presented the prize, he became king. Atreus, realizing he had been tricked, convinced Zeus to help him win the throne. Zeus made the sun move backward in the sky. The Mycenaeans recognized this as a sign that identified Thyestes as a usurper.

Not satisfied with having become king, Atreus wanted revenge for Thyestes' seduction of Aerope. He threw a banquet in his brother's honor, and all seemed to have been

The Treasury of Atreus

Atreus's name was given to the most famous piece of architecture to survive from the Mycenaean civilization, the Treasury of Atreus. The structure was originally a tomb that would have included valuable grave goods, but it was plundered thousands of years ago. No one knows the name of the king who was buried there. Archaeologists believe that the tomb was built between 1300 and 1200 BCE. It was carved into a hillside and was made of rectangular blocks of stone stacked in 33 rows. It is an example of a *tholos*, or beehive tomb, so called because the shape of its dome resembles a beehive. Inside the tomb the rotunda is 44 feet (13.5 m) high and 48 feet (14.6 m) wide. The pathway leading up to the doorway of the tomb is 115 feet (35 m) long, flanked by high walls. The facade was originally richly decorated, and some of the reliefs survive in museums around the world, such as in Athens, Berlin, and London.

Below: The Treasury of Atreus was the tomb of a Mycenaean ruler whose identity is unknown. The triangle above the doorway is typical of ancient Mycenaean architecture.

forgiven. After the main course had been consumed, Atreus revealed the severed limbs and heads of Thyestes' sons cooked in a stew. Thyestes realized he had already eaten the flesh of his sons. Following the gruesome banquet, Atreus banished Thyestes from Mycenae. According to some versions of the legend, it was Thyestes, not Myrtilus, who then placed a curse on the House of Atreus.

Thyestes' revenge

While in exile, Thyestes learned from the Delphic oracle that to avenge himself he had to have a son by his own daughter, Pelopia. One night he disguised himself and slept with his daughter, who did not know his true identity. Another version of the story tells that Thyestes raped a priestess whom he spied bathing in Sicyon after she had conducted nocturnal rites to Athena. Unknown to him, the priestess was actually Pelopia, and he left without either father or daughter realizing the other's identity.

Meanwhile, Atreus had killed Aerope for her infidelity, but not before she had given birth to his sons Agamemnon and Menelaus. Soon afterward, on a visit to Sicyon, Atreus

fell in love with and married Pelopia, whom he assumed was a Sicyon princess, the daughter of King Thesprotus. Several months later Pelopia gave birth to a son, Aegisthus; unknown to Atreus, the infant was Thyestes' son, not his.

Years later Atreus sent Aegisthus on a mission to assassinate Thyestes, whom Atreus had captured and imprisoned in Mycenae. As Aegisthus approached, Thyestes recognized the sword the young man was carrying as his own. At the time of the rape, Pelopia had stolen Thyestes' sword from its scabbard and had later given it to Aegisthus. Instead of killing Thyestes, Aegisthus murdered Atreus and made his real father king of Mycenae.

In a different version of the story, another one of Atreus's sons was Pleisthenes, who was sometimes spoken of as the father of Agamemnon and Menelaus, making them actually the grandsons of Atreus. When Thyestes went into exile after his attempt to acquire the throne of Mycenae, he took Pleisthenes with him, pretending that he was his own son, not the son of Atreus, who was also ignorant of his paternity. Later Thyestes sent Pleisthenes back to Mycenae with instructions to kill Atreus, which induced Atreus to have Pleisthenes killed, thus unwittingly murdering his own son.

Agamemnon's death

When Agamemnon grew up, he overthrew Thyestes and became king of Mycenae. He then killed Tantalus, one of Thyestes' sons, and married Tantalus's widow Clytemnestra, the sister of Helen. Agamemnon and Clytemnestra had three daughters, Chrysothemis, Iphigeneia, and Electra, and a son, Orestes. Meanwhile Menelaus had become king of Sparta and had taken Helen as his wife.

Right: This Greek amphora was made sometime between 340 and 330 BCE. The artwork illustrates the story of Atreus, including on the top row the murdered king on his throne.

While Agamemnon and Menelaus were leading the Greek forces during the Trojan War, Aegisthus became Clytemnestra's lover. When, after 10 years, Agamemnon returned to Mycenae, the lovers murdered him. Later the lovers were killed by Orestes. After a long period of insanity, Orestes himself became king of Argos and Sparta.

Sources and dramatizations

Classical scholars believe that the major sources for the epic story of the brothers Atreus and Thyestes, the unfaithful Aerope, and the young Pelopia were two lost plays by Sophocles, a fifth-century-BCE Greek dramatist, and that the dramatic life of the rivalry between Atreus and Thyestes was a popular subject on the Athenian stage from the fifth century BCE onward. However, none of the plays that survive by the other major dramatists of ancient Greece —for instance, Aeschylus and Euripides—deals directly with either brother.

Yet some important surviving works do tell the story of the younger generation of the House of Atreus. The main examples are Aeschylus's *Agamemnon* and Euripides' *Electra* and *Orestes,* which are still performed by major theatrical companies. Also, a play called *Thyestes,* by Roman dramatist Seneca (c. 4 BCE–65 CE), describes the butchering of Thyestes' children.

ANTHONY BULLOCH

Bibliography

Aeschylus, and A. Shapiro and P. Burian, eds. *The Oresteia.* New York: Oxford University Press, 2010.
Euripides, and P. Burian and A. Shapiro, eds. *The Complete Euripides.* New York: Oxford University Press, 2009–2010.
Harding, Anthony. *The Mycenaeans and Europe.* San Diego: Academic Press, 1984.

SEE ALSO: Agamemnon; Clytemnestra; Helen; Iphegeneia; Menelaus; Orestes; Pelops; Tantalus.

BELLEROPHON

In Greek mythology Bellerophon was a hero who tamed the winged horse Pegasus and slew a fearsome monster known as the Chimera. Bellerophon's story carried him from Greece to Lycia, in what is now Turkey, where he had most of his adventures.

Bellerophon was born in Corinth, which is a city and surrounding area in Greece that was considered sacred to Poseidon, god of the sea. Bellerophon was the son of Glaucus and Eurymede, and the grandson of Sisyphus. One mythological source claims that Poseidon was the real father of Bellerophon, although Glaucus raised him

without knowing his true origins. His travels took him to Lycia in what is now southwestern Turkey, and he is credited in legend with introducing Greek culture to that region.

The earliest version of Bellerophon's story is found in the *Iliad*, the great epic poem from the eighth-century BCE by Homer. It tells the story of the Trojan War, and in the sixth book Bellerophon's grandson, the Lycian Glaucus, narrates Bellerophon's story.

Flight to Lycia

For some unexplained reason Bellerophon had to leave Corinth and travel southward through the hills to Argos. One version has it that he fled Corinth because he had accidentally killed his brother. King Proetus (or Proitus) of Argos received him kindly, but the king's wife, Anteia (or Stheneboea), fell in love with the handsome Bellerophon as soon as she saw him. Queen Anteia wanted Bellerophon to become her secret lover. When he rejected her advances, she was furious. The spiteful Anteia lied to Proetus, announcing that Bellerophon had made advances toward her. Proetus felt betrayed and angry but could not bring himself to kill Bellerophon. Instead he sent the young Corinthian across the sea to Lycia, where Anteia's father, Iobates, was king. On arriving in Lycia, Bellerophon was to give Iobates a folded and sealed tablet containing a message for the king. Unknown to Bellerophon, the message instructed Iobates to kill the handsome Corinthian.

When Bellerophon landed in Lycia, Iobates received him with a feast that lasted nine days. On the 10th day he asked Bellerophon for the tablet and read the contents. Although stunned by Proetus' murderous request, Iobates did not want to incur the wrath of the gods by killing an important guest. Instead he sent Bellerophon on a series of dangerous tasks, not expecting him to survive.

Slaying the Chimera

First Bellerophon had to kill the Chimera. The word *chimera* is Greek for "goat," but this was a much more fearsome creature than any ordinary goat. The mythological Chimera was a fire-breathing monster with the head of a

Left: This illustration, based on a 17th-century woodcut, shows Bellerophon with the winged horse Pegasus, which he tamed.

lion, a body with a goat's head rising from it, and a snake as a tail. Bellerophon killed the monster. The king then sent him to fight the ferocious Solymi, a neighboring warrior tribe. Legends describe the battle between Bellerophon and the Solymi as the fiercest ever known, with Bellerophon emerging victorious. Bellerophon then had to fight the Amazons, a race of warrior women, but they too failed to kill him.

When Iobates heard that Bellerophon had survived the Amazons, the king sent his own soldiers to ambush him on his way back. Bellerophon killed every one of them. Then the king knew that this was a hero who was part divine, reinforcing the possibility that Poseidon was his real father. He ennobled Bellerophon and allowed him to marry his younger daughter and Anteia's sister, Philonoe. Together the couple had three children, who became the ancestors of the Lycian royal house.

The winged horse
In a parallel version of Bellerophon's adventures, the Corinthian hero was accompanied by Pegasus, the winged horse. Pegasus, according to some, was the child of Medusa and Poseidon, and in Corinth, a favorite site of

Right: This terra-cotta relief, dating from 450 BCE, shows Bellerophon slaying the three-headed Chimera. The Chimera was reputed to have the strength of three beasts and to breathe fire. An active volcano in Lycia also had the name Chimera.

Poseidon's, there was a large fountain named for the winged horse. One day Bellerophon saw Pegasus drinking water from a well. He leaped onto the winged horse but could not tame it. Then Athena, goddess of war and wisdom, gave Bellerophon a golden bridle. He slipped the bridle on Pegasus and tamed the horse immediately. The Corinthians built a temple called Athena of the Bridle in honor of the story.

Bellerophon remembered
Bellerophon's story is told in writings by Pindar, a lyric poet of the fifth century BCE, and by Pausanias, a second-century CE historian, who described the cities of Greece. Following the marriage to Iobates' daughter, the rest of Bellerophon's myth was told in two works by Euripides

Innocent Heroes and Jealous Older Women

There are many stories in which an older woman tries to seduce an innocent young man and then lies about him. One example is the Biblical character Joseph from the Book of Genesis. Joseph was sold as a slave to an Egyptian named Potiphar, whom he served well. One day when Potiphar was away, his wife tried to seduce Joseph, who ran away. Potiphar's wife then accused Joseph of raping her, and Potiphar had him cast into prison. While there he interpreted the dreams of others and by doing so earned his freedom.

A comparable Greek myth tells of the love of Phaedra for her stepson Hippolytus. When Hippolytus refused Phaedra's advances, the older woman made it seem that Hippolytus had attacked her. The young man's father then cursed him. As a result of the curse, Poseidon caused Hippolytus to be killed by his own horses.

There are also modern versions of the story, such as *The Graduate*. Originally a novel by Charles Webb, *The Graduate* was turned into a popular movie in 1967. The story is about a young college graduate, Benjamin Braddock, who is enticed into an affair by the wife of his father's friend. Benjamin, like the biblical Joseph and Bellerophon, triumphs over the jealous anger and schemes of the older woman.

Above: This fourth-century mosaic found in a building in Nabeul, Tunisia, shows Bellerophon's bride, Philonoe, the daughter of the King of Lycia.

(c. 484–406 BCE), a Greek playwright. Bellerophon, according to Euripides, never forgot Anteia's wrongs against him, and one day he mounted Pegasus and flew back to Argos. There he found Anteia crying because she still loved the hero. Pretending to take pity on her, he invited her to fly with him back to Lycia. She eagerly climbed onto Pegasus and sat behind Bellerophon, but when they were high in the sky far above the sea, he let her fall. This was Bellerophon's revenge on both her and, through Anteia's death, on Proetus. In another version Anteia committed suicide when she heard that her sister had married Bellerophon.

Flying too high

In one of Euripides' other plays, Pegasus played a key role in Bellerophon's most foolish adventure. The hero wanted to see Mount Olympus, the home of the gods. He mounted the winged horse and flew up to the mountain, but as he got closer Zeus caused him to fall off Pegasus. Bellerophon had met a similar fate to other Greek mythological characters who grew too arrogant while flying. For example, Icarus and Phaethon, both fell from the sky. Although Bellerophon did not die from the fall, he was left lame. He landed in a mysterious place called the Plain of Wandering, where, according to legend, he hobbled forever, avoiding human company and consumed with grief. Meanwhile Pegasus went on to Olympus, where the winged horse became steed of the gods.

JAMES M. REDFIELD

Bibliography

Bulfinch, Thomas. *Bulfinch's Mythology.* New York: Barnes & Noble, 2006.

Homer, and Robert Fagles, trans. *The Iliad.* New York: Penguin, 2009.

SEE ALSO: Amazons; Icarus; Phaethon; Sisyphus.

CADMUS

Cadmus was the legendary founder of Thebes and was credited with bringing the alphabet to ancient Greece. He also married Harmonia, the daughter of Ares and Aphrodite, and toward the end of their lives both were transformed into snakes.

According to legend, Cadmus (or Kadmos) was a Phoenician from the ancient city of Tyre, which still exists in modern Lebanon. The main source for the story of Cadmus is *The Library*, a collection of Greek myths attributed to Apollodorus, a writer who lived some time in the first two centuries CE. Cadmus was the grandson of Poseidon, god of the sea. His parents were Agenor, king of Phoenicia, and Telephassa, a Phoenician princess, and he had two brothers, Phoenix and Cilix, and a sister, Europa.

The search for Europa

The story of the founding of Thebes began when Zeus, ruler of the gods, disguised himself as a bull and abducted Europa. Agenor ordered his sons to search for her and not return until she was found. Each brother set off in a different direction. Phoenix looked throughout Phoenicia, Cilix went to Cilicia, and Thasus (Cilix's son who joined in the search) traveled to the island of Thasus. Eventually all gave up the search. Since each of them had failed to find Europa, they were forbidden to return home, and so they settled in the areas where they had been searching.

Cadmus had visited the islands of Rhodes, Samothrace, Thera, and Thrace before landing in Greece, where he continued to search for his sister. He arranged a meeting with the oracle at Delphi, who was supposedly able to see into the future and be all knowing, to ask where he could find Europa.

The oracle told him to abandon the search, since Zeus did not want her to be found. Instead the oracle told Cadmus to look for a cow and follow it until it lay down in weariness. On the spot where the cow lay he was to found and fortify a city. The Greek travel writer Pausanias, who lived in the second century CE, wrote that the oracle told Cadmus that the cow must have a moon-shaped mark

Right: The colorful painting inside this Italian ornamental ceramic cup depicts the transformation of Cadmus and his wife, Harmonia, into snakes.

55

Cadmus and the Greek Alphabet

Herodotus, a Greek historian who lived during the fifth century BCE, credited Cadmus with bringing the Phoenician alphabet to Greece. Although the alphabet that was used by the Greeks in Herodotus's time was indeed descended from the Phoenicians, the alphabet was not nearly as old as Thebes. Archaeologists believe that Thebes was occupied around 3000 BCE, in the Early Bronze Age. During the Late Bronze Age, around 1600 BCE, the Greeks had a writing system known as Linear B. It was adapted from the Minoan script, known as Linear A, used by the inhabitants of Crete. Linear A was actually not an alphabet but a syllabary: each symbol represented a combination of a consonant and a vowel, rather than a single sound. The system fell into disuse around 1100 BCE.

In the eighth century BCE the Greeks began to use the Phoenician alphabet (the one Cadmus is credited with introducing). In this writing system each symbol represented a single sound. The Greeks modified the Phoenician system, changing the shapes of some of the letters and adding vowels, since the original Phoenician alphabet represented only consonants. The Etruscans, who lived in Italy, borrowed the Greek alphabet and modified it again. The Romans, who conquered the Etruscans, adopted the Etruscan alphabet and made some slight variations. The Roman alphabet is used in most of the Western world today.

on each side of its body. When Cadmus left the oracle he saw just such a cow and followed it through the land of Phocis, near Delphi, and into Boeotia, in central Greece. Finally, the cow lay down to rest and Cadmus sacrificed it to Athena, goddess of war and wisdom. Centuries later Pausanias claimed to be able to identify the shrine to Athena said to have been built by Cadmus.

The rise of the *Spartoi*

After sacrificing the cow, Cadmus sent his men to a nearby spring to draw water. The guardian of the spring, a huge and ferocious serpent or dragon, killed most of Cadmus's men. The dragon was a servant of Ares, god of war. Cadmus, unaware of what had happened, went to the spring to look for his men. He found the bodies of his servants with the giant serpent looming over them. Cadmus slew the serpent. Afterward Athena told Cadmus to remove the beast's teeth and plant them in the ground (Jason did the same thing with the teeth of the dragon that guarded the Golden Fleece). From the buried teeth

immediately grew fierce, fully armed warriors, who began fighting each other. When the fighting stopped, five of the warriors survived. The warriors—Echion, Udaeus, Chthonius, Hyperenor, and Pelorus—were known as the *Spartoi*, meaning the "sown men." With the help of the *Spartoi*, Cadmus built a mighty palace and laid the foundation for Thebes, which became one of the major city-states in ancient Greece and was the setting for the story of Oedipus. Some scholars have suggested that the myth of Cadmus's founding of Thebes represents the city's actual historical association with Phoenicia (see box).

Cadmus's marriage and transformation

Another tale in the life of Cadmus involved his marriage to the goddess Harmonia, daughter of Ares and Aphrodite. The Olympian gods attended the wedding feast, and the Muses, nine daughters of Zeus who were associated with the arts, sang for the guests. Hephaestus, god of fire and metalworking, gave the couple a necklace and a robe, and some sources say that the other gods gave gifts as well. Pausanias wrote that in his time (c. 160 CE) the Thebans could identify the ruins of Cadmus's palace, Harmonia's wedding chamber, and the spot where the Muses sang.

Cadmus and Harmonia had four daughters: Agave, Ino, Autonoe, and Semele. Some sources say that they had a son, Polydorus, although Euripides, a fifth-century-BCE Athenian playwright, wrote in his play the *Bacchants*—or *Bacchae*—that Cadmus had no sons. Cadmus's daughter Semele bore the god Dionysus to Zeus, but all his other grandchildren died in tragic circumstances before marriage.

According to Ovid, a Roman poet of the first century CE, Cadmus and Harmonia went to Illyria after the tragic death of their grandchildren, where they were turned into snakes. One version explains that the couple's transformation was in revenge for Cadmus's having killed the giant serpent at the spring. Pindar, a Theban poet of the fifth century BCE, wrote that Cadmus and Harmonia joined Peleus, Achilles, and other mortals in the Elysian Fields, where they lived forever. In the *Bacchae*, Euripides seems to combine several myths, saying that the couple left Thebes, became snakes, and were finally brought to the Elysian Fields.

LAUREL BOWMAN

Bibliography

Edwards, Ruth B. *Kadmos the Phoenician: A Study in Greek Legends and the Mycenean Age.* Amsterdam: Hakkert, 1979.

Euripides, and P. Burian and A. Shapiro, eds. *The Complete Euripides.* New York: Oxford University Press, 2009–2010.

SEE ALSO: Europa; Oedipus.

CALLISTO

Callisto was one of the many sexual conquests of Zeus, king of the gods, and therefore one of many characters in Greek mythology who suffered the jealous anger of Hera, Zeus's wife and queen. Hera transformed Callisto into a bear, which according to legend is the Great Bear constellation seen in the night sky.

Above: This early diagram of the Great Bear constellation comes from an Arabic manuscript. The Greek myth of Callisto explains how the bear came to be in the sky.

Callisto was either a nymph or the daughter of Lycaon, a powerful king of Pelasgia. Both he and his sons were well known for being ruthless and untrustworthy. One day Zeus disguised himself as a humble workman and visited Lycaon to investigate his behavior.

When Zeus arrived in Pelasgia, Lycaon made a human sacrifice on Zeus's altar and then offered his guests some of the sacrifice to eat. Zeus was so disgusted by this blasphemy that he hurled thunderbolts at Lycaon and his sons, killing them instantly. Other versions of the myth have it that Zeus killed the sons but turned Lycaon into a wolf. Zeus then ordered a huge flood (Deucalion's Flood) to inundate and cleanse the earth.

After the death of her father and brothers, Callisto sought refuge with Artemis (Diana in Rome), goddess of the hunt. Artemis was renowned for her chastity and her dislike of male company. She lived in the forest, where she hunted with a select band of young women who were all sworn to virginity and loyalty to the goddess.

Zeus saw Callisto asleep in the forest. He disguised himself as Artemis and succeeded in seducing Callisto, who became pregnant. Fearful of the consequences if her pregnancy should be discovered, Callisto succeeded in hiding her condition from Artemis and her companions for nearly nine months. One hot day, however, the band of huntresses went down to the stream to bathe. As the young women disrobed, Callisto could no longer hide her secret. The goddess was furious at Callisto's breach of the rules of virginity, and in spite of the girl's pleading, Artemis exiled Callisto from the band. One of the most famous depictions of the banishment of Callisto is a painting by the Venetian artist Titian (c. 1489–1576) entitled *Diana and Callisto*. Soon after the banishment Callisto, wandering alone in the forest, gave birth to a baby boy, whom she named Arcas.

Hera's revenge

Up until this point in the story, Hera had done nothing to punish Callisto. The birth of the baby, however, was too much for the queen of the gods to endure. Hera leaped on Callisto and threw her to the ground. Callisto, pleading with Hera to spare her, could only watch with horror as her own arms and legs grew hairy and rough and her nails grew long and pointed. Soon the transformation was complete. In her jealous anger Hera had turned Callisto into a bear.

Callisto fled deep into the Pelasgian forest and lived alone in despair. Because her mind remained human, she fully understood what had happened to her. Yet her bear's mouth would not allow her to talk, only growl, so she had no way of warning hunters that she was not to be feared.

Meanwhile, Zeus had given Arcas to one of his previous lovers, Maia, to raise. Maia was the eldest of the seven sisters who form the constellation of the Pleiades. In the past Zeus had seduced her too, and she had given birth to Hermes, messenger of the Olympian gods.

When Arcas was 15 he went into the Pelasgian forest to hunt. Callisto, who was still living in the forest, recognized her son immediately. She followed Arcas because she was curious to see him and longed to be near him, but she knew she had to stay hidden. Suddenly Arcas caught sight of the bear and pursued her.

Arcas was about to kill Callisto with his bow and arrow when Zeus intervened. He snatched up Callisto and set her into the heavens, so saving Arcas from the crime of killing his mother. The god transformed Callisto into a constellation, the Great Bear and Arcas into the brilliant star Arcturus. (According to another version of the myth, Arcas became king of Pelasgia as the heir of his grandfather Lycaon, and the land of Pelasgia was renamed Arcadia in his honor.)

Hera was not happy at seeing her one-time rival's sufferings cut short, especially by the intervention of her own husband. She went to see her old nurse Tethys, the wife of the ocean, Oceanus. Tethys sympathized with Hera. She forbade the new constellation ever to plunge into the ocean to drink, which is why the Great Bear constellation never sets into the ocean, as other stars do, but always remains above the horizon.

Callisto in the heavens

In astronomy the Great Bear, which was named for Callisto, is also known as Ursa Major (meaning "Great Bear" in Latin). It is a constellation that is often seen in the northern hemisphere and includes the Big Dipper, or Plow. Another astronomical reference to Callisto is the second largest satellite (moon) orbiting Jupiter. The moon, named Callisto, is nearly as large as the planet Mercury.

PETER CONNOR

Bibliography

Apollodorus, and Robin Hard, trans. *The Library of Greek Mythology.* New York: Oxford University Press, 2008.

Bulfinch, Thomas. *Bulfinch's Mythology.* New York: Barnes & Noble, 2006.

Howatson, M. C. *The Oxford Companion to Classical Literature.* New York: Oxford University Press, 2005.

SEE ALSO: Lycaon; Pleiades.

Below: This 16th-century painting by Titian shows the moment when Artemis (Diana) banishes Callisto from her band of huntresses.

CALYPSO

Calypso was a nymph who lived on a remote island called Ogygia. She is famous for playing host to Odysseus during his journey home after the Trojan War. According to Homer's *Odyssey,* the Greek hero stayed with Calypso for seven years, during which time she tempted him with an offer of immortality. Odysseus's refusal to accept the offer reflected his love for his homeland of Ithaca and his wife, Penelope.

Different sources give various figures as the parents of Calypso. In the *Odyssey*, the epic poem by the Greek poet Homer (c. ninth–eighth century BCE), she is said to have been the daughter of Atlas, one of the Titans. Atlas was the father of a large number of daughters, many of whom, like himself, were associated with the sea and remote, otherworldly places. Other sources name other parents for Calypso, mostly associated with the sea, and the sea Titan, Oceanus, is usually said to be either a parent or grandparent. Calypso was thus a venerable and elemental figure. Calypso's name is derived from the Greek verb *kalyptein* and may mean "hider" or "concealer."

The *Odyssey* gives a full description of Calypso and the magical island of Ogygia on which she lived. Her home was a cave, warmed by a cedarwood fire. The cave was situated in a lush forest setting of alder, poplars, and cypress trees. Owls, hawks, and gulls nested there; clusters of grapes hung from a vine over the mouth of the cave; and clear water flowed from not one, but four fountains. Nearby, meadows bloomed with parsley and violets. Calypso lived on ambrosia and nectar—the food and drink of the gods. She spent her days weaving, an activity associated with femininity and domesticity.

The arrival of Odysseus

Odysseus arrived at this island paradise as a solitary castaway, bereft of everything after several years of travel and arduous adventures. The one remaining ship of his fleet had been destroyed by a storm sent by the gods and all his men had been killed. For Odysseus, Calypso was a savior, like several other women encountered by him during his travels.

At first, Odysseus was very happy to be with Calypso, but gradually he spent more and more time sitting on the rocks by the seashore, looking out to sea and yearning for his homeland of Ithaca and his wife, Penelope. When Zeus finally sent Hermes, the messenger of the gods, with instructions for Calypso to release Odysseus, she did so, helping him build a raft to continue his journey. First, though, she tried to persuade him to stay, offering him immortality and the opportunity to spend the rest of time with her on Ogygia. Odysseus's refusal, and his insistence

Above: This 17th-century tapestry depicts Odysseus arriving at the island of Calypso, one of the many islands visited by the Greek hero during his 10-year journey home from the Trojan War. In the most widely known version of the myth, Odysseus arrived at the island alone.

Above: Ulysses and Calypso *by Italian painter Luca Giordano (1641–1711). The painting shows Calypso pouring from a pitcher and attended by handmaidens, although in Homer's* Odyssey *she lived alone.*

on remaining mortal and returning to Ithaca, is a significant symbolic moment in the sequence of tests and challenges that he faces on his long journey home.

Some scholars have proposed that Calypso symbolizes one of several variant forms of marriage offered to Odysseus as alternatives to his ideal of life with Penelope on Ithaca. Calypso represents a form of utopian isolation. Other women encountered by the hero on his travels offer different forms of romantic bliss. For example, the princess Nausicaa, whom Odysseus encountered when he was shipwrecked on the island of Scheria, represented the pleasures of family life.

Calypso's children

Several sons were said to have been born to Calypso and Odysseus. Two, Nausithous and Nausinoos, have names that reflect their nautical ancestry. Another mentioned by some sources is Latinus, who became the king of the Latins in Italy. Calypso was also said by some early sources to be mother of Telegonus, although others say his mother was the enchantress Circe. Telegonus later came to Ithaca and accidentally killed his father Odysseus.

Calypso rarely featured in ancient Greek art. However, from around 1600 CE the story of Odysseus and Calypso became popular with European painters. It was around this time that Flemish artist Jan Brueghel the Elder (1568–1625) painted *Fantastic Cave Landscape with Odysseus and Calypso*, which depicted Odysseus and Calypso sitting in a romantic embrace against a lush backdrop. Around 70 years later, Dutch artist Gerard de Lairesse painted the more dramatic *Hermes Ordering Calypso to Release Odysseus*. Another 17th-century artist, the Italian Luca Giordano, also depicted the pair. His *Ulysses and Calypso* (Ulysses was the Roman name for Odysseus) shows Calypso pouring a drink for her guest.

ANTHONY BULLOCH

Bibliography

Bulfinch, Thomas. *Bulfinch's Mythology.* New York: Barnes & Noble, 2006.

Homer, and Robert Fagles, trans. *The Odyssey.* New York: Penguin, 2009.

SEE ALSO: Circe; Odysseus; Penelope.

CASSANDRA

Cassandra was the daughter of King Priam and Queen Hecuba of Troy. She was given the gift of seeing the future by the god Apollo. However, when she angered the god, he turned the blessing into a curse, decreeing that no one would ever believe her prophesies.

According to the most common version of the myth of Cassandra, Apollo first set eyes on the princess when she fell asleep in his temple. Cassandra was very beautiful, and the god immediately fell in love with her. In an attempt to seduce her, Apollo gave her the gift of prophecy. However, although Cassandra accepted the gift, she refused the god's advances. Apollo was outraged and decided to punish her. The god persuaded Cassandra to give him just a single kiss, during which he planted a curse in the young woman's mouth. Although Cassandra would be able to predict the future, nobody would ever believe her prophecies.

Most of Cassandra's prophecies concerned the Trojan War, the 10-year struggle between Troy and Greece prompted by the Trojan prince Paris's abduction of the Spartan queen Helen. Paris was Cassandra's younger brother, but when he was born she implored her father to kill the baby because she had a premonition that he would lead to the city's fall. Priam did not take his daughter's advice. Instead he ordered that Paris be taken into the wilderness and abandoned.

Paris and the war

Paris was first nurtured by a she-wolf and then raised by shepherds. As a young man he was chosen by the goddesses Aphrodite, Athena, and Hera to be the judge of a contest between them. Paris had to decide who was the most beautiful of the three goddesses. He chose Aphrodite, who had promised him the love of the world's most beautiful woman.

When Paris returned to Troy in disguise, Cassandra recognized him and he was welcomed back by his father, Priam. It was not long, though, before Paris decided to sail to Greece and visit the various kingdoms there. Cassandra warned that her brother's voyage would bring destruction on Troy, but no one believed her, and Paris set off on his travels. While in Sparta, a Greek kingdom, Paris seduced Helen, the wife of the Spartan king Menelaus, and

Right: In the late 19th century sculptor Max Klinger created this striking statue of Cassandra by using a combination of marble and alabaster. Her piercing eyes of amber suggest her visionary powers.

61

persuaded her to return with him to Troy. This abduction angered the Greeks, who raised an army to set sail for Troy. So began a war that would last 10 years.

It was at the end of this period that Cassandra made one of her most famous prophecies. In a last, desperate attempt to breach the walls of Troy, the Greeks made a hollow wooden horse and left it outside the gates of the besieged city. Believing the Greeks to have fled and the wooden horse to be an offering to Athena, the Trojans opened the gates and brought it into the city. In fact the horse was full of Greek soldiers. The only Trojans to foresee the danger were Cassandra and the priest and seer Laocoon. As the horse approached the city, Cassandra began to scream, warning her fellow Trojans of the gift's real nature. However, viewing her as a madwoman, they ignored her.

The following night the Greek soldiers climbed out of the horse and let the rest of the Greek army into Troy. They proceeded to sack the city, killing and raping its inhabitants. Cassandra fled to the temple of Athena, where she hid, clasping a wooden statue of the goddess of war and wisdom. There she was found by Ajax of Locris, who dragged her out of the temple. Accounts vary as to whether Cassandra was raped by Ajax or not. In any case she was then claimed as a prize by the Greek king Agamemnon.

Smell of death

Cassandra returned to Mycenae with Agamemnon. However, Agamemnon's wife, Clytemnestra, and her lover, Aegisthus, had been plotting to murder the Greek king. On arriving at Mycenae Agamemnon approached the palace,

Left: A French print, dating from 1730, of Cassandra warning the Trojans against accepting the gift of a wooden horse that the Greeks have left outside the walls. The print is from a series by Bernard Picart (1673–1733) illustrating scenes from ancient legends.

Right: The decoration on this ancient Greek plate shows Clytemnestra killing Cassandra with an ax.

where his wife had prepared a banquet welcoming him home. Cassandra refused to enter, claiming that she could smell blood. This was to prove to be Cassandra's last prophecy, as Clytemnestra killed both her husband and his new mistress with an ax.

Sources and variations

Cassandra appears in the *Illiad*, the Greek poet Homer's eighth-century-BCE account of the Trojan War, but in the epic poem she is described as Priam's most beautiful daughter, and there is no mention of her powers as a prophetess. Much of what is known about her is drawn from the *Aeneid*, a work by the Roman poet Virgil (70–19 BCE). Another important source is the play *Agamemnon* by the Greek playwright Aeschylus (525–456 BCE), which tells the story of Cassandra's fateful journey to Mycenae, including her murder. The figure of Cassandra also features in the work of much later writers. For example, she appears in one of William Shakespeare's plays, *Troilus and Cressida*, written in 1602.

As with other Greek myths, there are many variations on the story of Cassandra. In one, as a young child she acquires the gift of prophecy after being left, along with her twin brother Helenus, in the Temple of Apollo. In this version the two children are attacked by the sacred serpents of Apollo, after which they both acquire the gift of prophecy. However, one of the key elements of the myth is removed—the idea that Cassandra brought her misfortune upon herself by angering the gods.

ANDREW CAMPBELL

Bibliography

Homer, and Robert Fagles, trans. *The Iliad*. New York: Penguin, 2009.

Virgil, and Robert Fagles, trans. *The Aeneid*. New York: Penguin, 2009.

SEE ALSO: Agamemnon; Clytemnestra; Hecuba; Helen; Laocoon; Paris; Priam.

Ajax of Locris

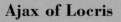

Ajax of Locris was sometimes known as Little Ajax or Ajax the Lesser to distinguish him from the huge Ajax of Salamis, who fought the Greek prince Hector, Cassandra's brother, in single combat. Little Ajax was known for his speed as a runner and for the tame serpent that he carried with him. His abduction of Cassandra brought him the enmity of his fellow Greek heroes, who believed that he had aroused the hatred of Athena by violating the sanctity of her temple. Odysseus called for Ajax to be stoned, but he was allowed to sail home to Greece.

On the way home Ajax's ship was wrecked on the Gyraean Rock. Ajax managed to swim to safety, but when he boasted of his escape he was killed by Poseidon for his vanity. In one version of the myth, however, it was the wronged goddess Athena who killed him. Because Ajax had not atoned for his crime against Athena, the inhabitants of Locris were forced to appease the goddess themselves. The Delphic oracle told the Locrians to send two girls to Troy every year for a thousand years. Each pair would serve in the temple of Athena for a year before being replaced.

CASTOR AND POLLUX

In both Greek and Roman myth the twins Castor and Pollux were seen as symbols of ideal brotherhood. Although one was mortal and the other divine, in death they were united as the constellation Gemini.

Known as the Dioscuri (literally "sons of Zeus"), Castor and Pollux (Roman)—or Polydeuces (Greek)—were thought of in classical mythology as twins, even though they had different fathers. They featured or took part in several key Greek stories, all of which occurred before the Trojan War. In addition the Roman Castor and Pollux fought alongside Roman soldiers in an early battle.

The conception of the twins occurred one night when Zeus (or Jupiter for the Romans) disguised himself as a swan and raped Leda, a mortal. That same night Tyndareos, king of Sparta and Leda's husband, made love to his wife. From Zeus's seed Leda gave birth to Pollux, while Castor was Tyndareos's offspring. According to another version that night Leda produced two eggs, one (fertilized by Zeus) containing Pollux and Helen, the other (by Tyndareos) forming Castor and Clytemnestra.

One of the Dioscuri's earliest adventures concerned their sister Helen. Before Helen was abducted by Paris, she was stolen by the Greek hero Theseus. Son of Aegeus and Aethra, Theseus was perhaps most famous for slaying the Minotaur. Several myths, including the one of the Minotaur, show Theseus treating women badly. The same was true of his abduction of Helen. She was rescued, however, by her brothers, who captured Theseus's mother, making her Helen's slave, a role she maintained until the fall of Troy.

Further adventures of the twins

The twins also sailed with the hero Jason on the *Argo,* and during the voyage Pollux killed the evil king Amycus in a boxing match. During their adventures at sea, Poseidon, according to one version, made the twins protectors of sailors and calmers of storms and waves. Greek sailors would later pray to the twins for safe voyages. It was also thought that Castor and Pollux appeared as part of the

Below: Twelfth-century statues of the Dioscuri flank the entrance to Piabba del Campidoglio, Rome, designed by Michelangelo in the 16th century.

Right: This 17th-century painting by Peter Paul Rubens, a Flemish artist, depicts Castor and Pollux abducting the daughters of Leucippus, Pheobe and Hilaeira.

natural phenomenon now known as Saint Elmo's fire, a luminous electrical discharge that is usually seen by sailors or from an aircraft during storms.

After their adventures with the Argonauts, the Dioscuri, along with other Greek heroes, took part in the legendary Calydonian boar hunt. They then returned to their native Sparta, where they abducted and raped (some versions say married) two women. Pheobe and Hilaeira were the daughters of Leucippus, and to avenge the rapes, Leucippus's nephews, Idas and Lynceus, attacked and killed Castor, the mortal twin. Another version has it that the fight between the Dioscuri and Idas and Lynceus (also known as the Messenian brothers) occurred over a disputed apportionment of stolen cattle. The Messenians had tricked the Dioscuri out of their fair share of the beef, and a fight ensued. Idas, who had earlier battled Apollo, killed Castor. Then Pollux killed Lynceus but was wounded in the head by Idas, who was in turn killed by Zeus.

Pollux was so grief-stricken at Castor's death that he pleaded with Zeus for Castor to be made immortal. As a compromise, Zeus allowed the twins to remain together on condition that they alternate days between living on Mount Olympus and in the underworld. Another version tells that Zeus transformed Castor and Pollux into the constellation Gemini.

Aiding the Romans

The Romans adopted the Dioscuri and added a significant legend. Around 500 BCE, troops of the new Roman republic fought the army of the deposed king, Tarquinius Superbus, at the Battle of Lake Regillus. The twins were seen either around the time of the battle watering their horses in the Forum, or fighting alongside the Roman soldiers on the battlefield. To honor the twins, a temple was dedicated to them in the Forum, and they appeared on Roman coinage. They also had their own secret cult.

CARL RUCK

Bibliography
Graves, Robert. *The Greek Myths.* New York: Penguin, 1993.
Howatson, M. C. *The Oxford Companion to Classical Literature.* New York: Oxford University Press, 2005.

SEE ALSO: Helen; Jason; Leda; Theseus.

CIRCE

Circe is best known from Homer's *Odyssey*, in which she plays a leading role in one of Odysseus's most important adventures. She is immortal and inhabits an island somewhere in the distant ocean, where she lives alone except for her magic servants and tame wild animals, lions and wolves that fawn on her like dogs. These are actually men she has magically transformed.

Right: Circe has captured the imagination of artists throughout the ages. This bronze figurine on a marble pedestal is the work of the Australian sculptor Edgar Bertram Mackennal (1863–1931).

When Odysseus and his men landed on Circe's island, the enchantress received them kindly, but the food she served was laced with a drug that made them drowsy. Once it had taken effect, she struck the men with a rod and turned them all into pigs, except for Odysseus. He would have suffered the same fate, too, had the god Hermes not met him previously and given him the moly plant (a species of lily), which protected him from Circe's spells.

Because Odysseus could resist Circe, she recognized him as the hero who she had been told by an earlier prophecy would one day come to her. She turned his men back into human shape, younger and more handsome than before, and became Odysseus's friend and lover.

The men stayed with Circe for a year. She told them that they must visit the land of the dead, and when they went there Odysseus was given a prophecy of his own death. They then returned to Circe for further instructions. She told them to depart, but not before warning them of the dangers of the journey ahead. In particular, she told them not to kill the cattle of the sun god, Helios, which lived on the island of Thrinacia. As it turned out, only Odysseus was resolute enough to heed her warning, and consequently he was the only member of the crew to complete the journey.

Circe also features in the story of Jason and the Argonauts. According to Apollonius of Rhodes, when the *Argo* came to Circe's island, Circe anointed Jason and Medea with pig's blood so that they could atone for their theft of the Golden Fleece. Medea and Circe were close relatives—they were both descended from Helios. The daughters and granddaughters of Helios were dangerous women; another was Pasiphae, mother of the Minotaur.

In a later version of the Circe myth, Odysseus left the enchantress pregnant. When their son, Telegonus, grew up, he went in search of his father. He came by chance to Ithaca, and, not knowing where he was, raided the island. Odysseus rushed to fight him off. Telegonus, unaware that this threatening figure was his own father, killed him. This fulfilled the prophecy made to Odysseus in the underworld that his death would come from the sea. Telegonus then

Left: This 1580 oil painting by Alessandro Allori (1535–1607) depicts Circe with the companions of Ulysses, whom she has turned into animals.

married Penelope; he and his half-brother Telemachus took Penelope with them back to Circe's island, where Telemachus married Circe. Circe then made the three of them immortal.

Comparable figures

Some scholars have seen in Circe a version of the forest witch familiar from Indo-European folktales such as the story of Hansel and Gretel. Others have suggested that Circe shares characteristics with the West Asian "Mistress of Animals," who has various names, including Ishtar, Lillith, and Anat. The name Circe means "hawk" in Greek, and the comparable West Asian goddesses are often depicted with the wings of hawks or associated with other birds of prey. In the *Epic of Gilgamesh* there are further parallels between Circe and Ishtar, the fertility goddess of the Assyrians and Babylonians: Both can control wild animals; their characters have a dangerous side connected to sexuality and magic; and they both ultimately turn from a threat into a helper. Ishtar turns her lovers into wild animals by striking them with a rod. She also sends her husband down into the underworld. These similarities can

hardly be coincidental—the myths of the two deities are interdependent, and possibly come from a common source.

Circe seems to stand mythologically for the dangers (from a male point of view) of sexual entanglement. Those who yield to her attractions may find themselves irreversibly transformed. She has links to the world of the dead, as if her attractions could be not only transformative but also lethal. She is powerful, and if her initial threat can be overcome she becomes beneficent. She is a wise woman, and the transformations she effects may be positive. The lovers who can weather the storm of her early hostility are generally enriched by their subsequent involvement with her.

JAMES M. REDFIELD

Bibliography

Bulfinch, Thomas. *Myths of Greece and Rome.* New York: Penguin, 1998.
Homer, and Robert Fagles, trans. *The Odyssey.* New York: Penguin, 2009.

SEE ALSO: Daedalus; Minos; Pasiphae; Theseus.

CLYTEMNESTRA

Clytemnestra is one of the most vilified characters in Greek mythology because of her adultery and murderous deeds. She took a lover while her husband, King Agamemnon of Mycenae, was away fighting at the Trojan War, and then she killed him on his return.

Below: Dating from around 500 BCE, this vase painting depicts Clytemnestra being restrained by one of Agamemnon's aides, Thaltybios.

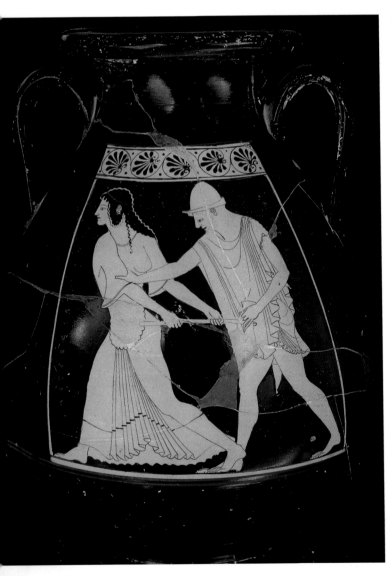

The story of Clytemnestra (or Klytaimestra) and the murders she committed was presented in several different versions. The earliest depiction of her, by the Greek poet Homer (c. ninth–eighth century BCE), presents her as a malleable character who was led astray by her lover, Aegisthus. However, later depictions of Clytemnestra by dramatists including Aeschylus, Euripides, and Sophocles generally show her as a heartless character who either led or orchestrated the killings.

Clytemnestra was the daughter of Tyndareos, king of Sparta, and Leda. Her sister was Helen (and sometimes Timandra), and her brothers were Castor and Pollux. According to some sources Helen and Pollux were the immortal children of Zeus, while Clytemnestra and the others were the mortal offspring of Tyndareos. Both Zeus and Tyndareos had slept with Leda on the same night, each making her pregnant with a boy and a girl.

According to one version of the Clytemnestra story, Agamemnon was not her first husband. She was originally married to Tantalus, the son of the Greek prince Thyestes, and they had a son. Agamemnon, who was Thyestes' nephew and ruler of Mycenae, killed both Tantalus and the boy, then married Clytemnestra. Clytemnestra and Agamemnon had three daughters and a son who each featured in dramatic stories of their own, all of which involved their mother. The daughters were Iphigeneia, Chrysothemis, and Electra; the son was Orestes. (In the *Iliad* the daughters were named Chrysothemis, Laodike, and Iphianassa.)

The murders

The story of Clytemnestra starts when her sister Helen is abducted by Paris, the incident that began the 10-year Trojan War between Greece and Troy. Helen was married to Menelaus, Agamemnon's brother, and when the war began Agamemnon became leader of the Greek forces. In an effort to ensure strong winds for his ships' speedy journey across the sea, Agamemnon sacrificed Iphigeneia. According to Aeschylus's play *Agamemnon*, Clytemnestra never forgave her husband for the death of Iphigeneia. In *Iphigeneia Among the Taurians*, a play by Euripides, at the moment the girl's throat was about to be cut, divine intervention made her vanish and a deer appear in her place on the altar.

Above: This 1817 painting by French artist Pierre-Narcisse Guérin depicts the moment before Clytemnestra and her lover stab Agamemnon.

While Agamemnon was away fighting in Troy, Clytemnestra began an affair with Aegisthus. When Agamemnon returned victorious to Mycenae, he brought with him his new mistress, Cassandra. Cassandra was the daughter of Priam, the defeated king of Troy. She was clairvoyant but cursed that no one would ever heed her warnings. Soon after their arrival, Clytemnestra stabbed (or axed) Agamemnon and Cassandra to death. When Orestes grew up, he and his sister, Electra, avenged the death of their father by killing both Aegisthus and Clytemnestra.

Dramatists and Clytemnestra

Clytemnestra held particular fascination for Athenian tragedians writing in the fifth and early fourth centuries BCE Aeschylus made Agamemnon's murder and its consequences the focus of his trilogy the *Oresteia*. In the first of the three plays, *Agamemnon*, the king, newly arrived home from the Trojan War, is murdered by his wife and her lover. In the second play, *Choephoroe* (or *The Libation Bearers*), Orestes returns to avenge his father by killing Clytemnestra and Aegisthus. He is guided by the god Apollo and encouraged by Electra, who has waited many years for Orestes' return. The title of the third play, *Eumenides*, is a reference to the Erinyes, or Furies, of Clytemnestra. The Erinyes were spirits that tormented those who wronged relatives, and in Aeschylus's play they drive Orestes insane because he killed his mother. With the help of the goddess Athena, however, Orestes is acquitted of murder at the court of the Areopagus in Athens, and the Erinyes are placated and given a new name, the Eumenides (Kindly Ones).

Although the major Greek dramatists represented Clytemnestra as a faithless wife and unloving mother, each characterized her differently. Aeschylus's Clytemnestra is at first a proud and regal figure, capable of masterful speech and manly deeds. *Choephoroe* depicts her as increasingly fearful of dreams and portents, and terrified when Orestes, whom she thought was long dead, reappears. She dies in the play while begging her son to spare her life.

The Clytemnestra of Sophocles' tragedy *Electra* is more openly hostile to her children, exulting over a false report of Orestes' death and berating Electra for moping about the death of her father. Euripides' *Electra* portrays a vain and hypocritical Clytemnestra, who is lured to her death by Electra's supposedly imminent childbirth. The relationship between the mother and daughter in the play is without love; the two women are deadly rivals.

In the early 20th century, Clytemnestra featured in two important dramatic works, *Elektra* (1909), an opera by the composer Richard Strauss (1864–1949), and *Mourning Becomes Electra* (1931), a trilogy by American playwright Eugene O'Neill (1888–1953). Strauss's opera is based on Sophocles' *Electra*, and O'Neill's trilogy is an adaptation of Aeschylus's *Oresteia*, with the drama being set in post–Civil War New England.

Deborah Lyons

Bibliography

Aeschylus, and A. Shapiro and P. Burian, eds. *The Oresteia.* New York: Oxford University Press, 2010.

Euripides, and P. Burian and A. Shapiro, eds. *The Complete Euripides,* New York: Oxford University Press, 2009–2010.

Komar, Kathleen L. *Reclaiming Klytemnestra: Revenge or Reconciliation.* Champaign, IL: University of Illinois Press, 2003.

SEE ALSO: Agamemnon; Atreus; Cassandra; Castor and Pollux; Electra; Iphigeneia; Orestes.

CYCLOPES

In Greek mythology the Cyclopes were one-eyed giants generally associated with brute force, simplemindedness, and crude, antisocial, and sometimes even psychopathic behavior. The most famous Cyclops was Polyphemus, whom the Greek hero Odysseus encountered on his journey home after the Trojan War.

In *Theogony*, the Greek poet Hesiod's (fl. c. 800 BCE) account of the origins of the universe, the Cyclopes were three immortal giants who were born to Uranus (Sky) and Gaia (Earth) at an early stage in the creation of the universe.

Gaia, one of the first four beings, created Uranus, followed by a number of elemental figures, such as the seas (Pontus) and the mountains (Ourea). Gaia then mated with Uranus to produce the first generation of gods—the 12 Titans—and the three Cyclopes. They were followed by another group of three giants, the Hundred-Handed Ones (Hecatoncheires). The Cyclopes became the workers, while the Hundred-Handed Ones had a military role and played the part of an army.

In this account of how the first beings were created, the Cyclopes were a separate and significant category of creatures. They came before Zeus, his siblings, and his children—the 12 Olympians—who took over from the Titans and whom the Cyclopes eventually served.

Forgers of thunder and lightning

The Cyclopes were called Arges, Steropes, and Brontes ("Flashing," "Lightener," and "Thunderer"). They were primitive, powerful, and unruly monsters who were twice imprisoned in Tartarus, a dark region far below the earth in Hades. Initially the Cyclopes were imprisoned by their father, Uranus. When Cronus took over power from his father, he released them, but imprisoned them again later.

When Zeus liberated the Cyclopes from Tartarus, he harnessed their power to manufacture the weaponry of his divine regime. They became the forgers of his thunderbolts and they were also said to have made instruments for Zeus's two brothers—the trident for Poseidon and the hat of invisibility for Hades. When the Olympians succeeded to power, the Cyclopes served as assistants to Hephaestus, the metalworker god, in his foundry.

According to some later accounts, the Cyclopes were killed by Apollo. Apollo's son Asclepius, the first doctor, had used his knowledge to raise people from the dead. To punish him for usurping the power of the gods, Zeus

Left: This head of Polyphemus (fourth century BCE) is a fragment from an ancient Greek sculpture. It was found in Smyrna, now Izmir, Turkey.

Polyphemus in Art

From the Renaissance onward, European artists looked back to the works of ancient Greece and Rome for inspiration. Characters drawn from Greek and Roman history and mythology became immensely popular subjects for paintings and sculpture because they enabled artists to depict larger-than-life characters and lush landscapes, bringing out the contrasts and contradictions in their stories.

The Cyclops Polyphemus is one of the characters encountered by Homer's hero Odysseus on his journey home after the Trojan War. Artists used scenes from this myth but felt free to interpret them according to their individual artistic style. Flemish painter Jacob Jordaens (below) used strong contrasts of light and shade to create a dramatic effect, whereas Alessandro Allori's palette of cool colors emphasizes his powerfully drawn figures and focuses attention on the action (see page 72). Italian artist Pellegrino Tibaldi (see page 73) was a great admirer of his fellow countryman Michelangelo's work, and his version of the myth is dominated by the powerful nude figure of Polyphemus. In complete contrast, Francois Perrier's decorative painting (see page 74) evokes no feelings of horror or drama, but depicts a pastoral scene in a romantic landscape.

Below: Ulysses in the Cave of Polyphemus.

killed him with a thunderbolt. Apollo took revenge on the makers of Zeus's weapon, the Cyclopes. As a punishment, Zeus then forced Apollo to spend a year in servitude to the mortal Admetus.

The Cyclopes were seen as brutes who provided the crude but essential "proletariat" force that drove industry. They were the ancestors of all the forge-working slaves of later European myth who labored for superior masters.

Odysseus and Polyphemus

In Homer's *Odyssey* the Cyclopes are not described as three individuals but as a whole people. However, they shared the same basic characteristics of Hesiod's Cyclopes and were an impossibly unruly group of beings. Their immediate neighbors were the Phaeacians, who were peaceful, inward-looking, and culturally advanced. Although the Cyclopes were related to the Phaeacians, the Phaeacians uprooted and moved away to escape their bullying behavior.

One Cyclops, in particular, has become particularly well-known. The *Odyssey* describes the adventures of Odysseus, (also known as Ulysses), king of Ithaca, on his 10-year journey home from Troy at the end of the Trojan War. His travels through various fantastic realms bring him to a lush region full of potential—ideal for agriculture, pasturing flocks, growing vines, and shipping. The land is inhabited by Cyclopes, giant shepherds who live in small, isolated,

Above: This dramatic fresco, The Blinding of Polyphemus, *was painted in 1580 by Alessandro Allori (1535–1607). It depicts the scene in the* Odyssey *where Odysseus and his men blind the Cyclops with a stake.*

family groups in caves high up in the mountains. They have no form of community or any social institutions, and they rely on the natural bounty of the land to provide for them without cultivation.

Odysseus and his men encounter a Cyclops named Polyphemus, a son of Poseidon, god of the sea. (Poseidon was a frequent procreator of monsters and unruly beings.) Polyphemus was as tall as a mountain peak, completely lawless, and without heed for Zeus or any other gods. Odysseus and his men become trapped inside the Cyclops' cave when Polyphemus returns home and blocks the opening with a gigantic boulder. Their visit becomes a cruel travesty of the Greek code of hospitality, as Polyphemus begins eating his guests instead of offering them food. His guest-gift to Odysseus is the promise of being eaten last.

Like the Cyclops, Odysseus inverts the hospitality code, using it as a weapon against the uncivilized giant. When Polyphemus asks Odysseus his name, the Greek hero declares that it is Nobody (Outis). He then offers Polyphemus a "counter-gift" of wine with the aim of reducing him to a drunken stupor. The Cyclops drinks the wine neat, rather than mixed with water, as was the civilized Greek custom. When he lies unconscious, in a drunken stupor, Odysseus and his remaining men put out his one eye with a wooden stake they have sharpened. The blind Cyclops calls out to his fellow Cyclopes for help, but

when they come to his cave to ask what is wrong, he says that "Nobody is killing me." The other Cyclopes leave, assuming that Polyphemus is deranged. In the morning he has to roll back the boulder to let his sheep out of the cave to graze. Odysseus and his men tie themselves to the underside of rams from the Cyclops' flock and escape.

The story finishes with a moral twist. Odysseus is unable to refrain from boasting as he escapes, and he tells the Cyclops his true name. This enables Polyphemus to appeal to his father Poseidon for revenge. The Cyclops' curse condemns Odysseus to years of wandering and troubles, pursued by the sea god: "May Odysseus either never reach home, or, if he is to return to Ithaca, may he come home late, in bad shape, after losing all his companions, in a foreign ship and to trouble at home." This curse is the primary cause of the long delay in Odysseus's return home.

Links to other mythologies

Scholars and folklorists recognized long ago that the Odysseus-Polyphemus story has parallels with the myths and legends of many other cultures around the world. In all these stories a hero encounters a terrible ogre or monster who traps him in his cave or lair. Often the ogre lives in an idyllic, pastoral setting, which contrasts with his brutishness and primitive way of life. He often possesses treasure that the hero is keen to remove from his cave (gold or silver). Before long, however, the clever hero outsmarts the stupid ogre and manages to escape. Elements of the myth of Odysseus and Polyphemus can be found in the Norse tale of the hero Beowulf and the monster Grendel, the one-eyed monster Tapagoz from Azerbaijani myth, and the northern European fairy story of Jack and the Beanstalk.

Scholars have been unable to uncover the relationship between the ancient Greek Cyclops and the ogres of other cultures or to learn whether the story passed from people to people. In fact, "influence" or "borrowing" may not be responsible for the widespread distribution and popularity of this ogre motif. Instead, it may have its origins in fears and anxieties that are common to all cultures, or to some kind of universal archetype.

Polyphemus and Galatea

Polyphemus continued to be a prominent figure in Greek myth after Homer, although increasing emphasis was placed on his simplemindedness and his pastoral setting. The Homeric Cyclops was romanticized into a country-bumpkin lover, a clumsy simpleton, who was not much of a threat to his visitors and who was pathetically unaware that his aspirations as a wooer were completely unrealistic.

From at least the fourth century BCE onward, Polyphemus was an oafish poet and singer who serenaded a sea nymph named Galatea, the daughter of the sea god Nereus. Despite being a son of another sea god, Poseidon, Polyphemus came to represent a lover who blindly pursued the impossible—a beautiful young woman who came from an element that was the opposite of his own. Polyphemus belonged on land, Galatea in the sea, so his love could never be fulfilled. Galatea, however, was often represented as enjoying teasing her amorous admirer.

The Roman poet Ovid told the story of Polyphemus and Galatea in his *Metamorphoses*. He also introduced, or maybe just gave emphasis to, a third figure in the story, creating a deadly love triangle that turned the tale of an amusingly clumsy wooer and his unrequited love into tragedy. Ovid gave Galatea a lover, a beautiful young man named Acis, who was the son of Faunus and a river nymph named Symaethis. Galatea loved Acis as strongly as she hated Polyphemus. When Polyphemus surprised Galatea in the arms of her lover, he killed Acis by dropping a massive chunk of mountainside on him while Galatea fled into the ocean. Galatea managed to turn Acis into a river, but she had lost him as her lover forever.

Above: Ulysses and the Cyclops: Escape of the Companions from the Island *(c. 1555), painted by Pellegrino Tibaldi (1527–1596). In the painting Polyphemus holds the boulder that had previously blocked the cave.*

Art, music, and literature

As the unrequited lover, Polyphemus became a common character, first of Greco-Roman pastoral (poem or play about rural life) and then of European pastoral in all its forms. Galatea and Polyphemus also became stock figures in Greco-Roman art. The one-eyed simpleton musician was always shown playing and singing to the sea nymph. The pair came to represent a suitable subject for the mosaic floors and painted walls of villas built by the wealthy, who enjoyed expressing their "sophistication" with decorative scenes from the "simple," pastoral world of ordinary, unsophisticated country men and women.

Whereas Homer's Odysseus traveled through imaginary, fantastical lands, later writers and painters often made the island of Sicily, in Italy, the setting of the pastoral world in which Polyphemus lived.

In the fifth century BCE, Athenian playwright Euripides wrote a play called *Cyclops*, which has survived, but the

Above: Acis and Galatea Hide from the Gaze of Polyphemus, *painted by Francois Perrier (c. 1594–1649). The story of the brutish Cyclops and the beautiful young sea nymph demonstrated the dangerous consequences of unrequited love.*

works of other dramatists who wrote comedies on the same topic have been lost. From the 16th century CE onward, dramatists found the foolish love of Polyphemus a good theme for comic theater, combining the absurd, but rather clever, character of Euripides' comic play with the sadly foolish Cyclops, the unrequited lover, of the Greek and Roman pastoral poets.

Composers of opera, again from the 16th century onward, also found the theme of Polyphemus's love particularly appealing. Well-known works include Lully's *Acis et Galatée*, Handel's *Acis and Galatea*, and Haydn's *Aci e Galatea*. There are also numerous works from the 19th and 20th centuries. The 18th century saw a number of ballets on the Acis and Galatea theme. In about 1888 a great French sculptor, Auguste Rodin, created a bronze statue depicting the giant burying his rival Acis under the mountain.

The term *Cyclopean* was used by Greeks to describe the great fortification walls of palaces from the Mycenaean age, such as those at Tiryns and Mycenae. The walls were constructed from enormous, mostly pentagonal to octagonal blocks of stone, which seemed too massive to have been made and moved by human effort. According to legend, such palaces were constructed by the Cyclopes in prehistoric times. Today we still use the term to describe anything massive or gigantic.

ANTHONY BULLOCH

Bibliography

Bulfinch, Thomas. *Bulfinch's Mythology.* New York: Barnes & Noble, 2006.

Hesiod, and M. L. West, trans. *Theogony* and *Works and Days.* New York: Oxford University Press, 2008.

Homer, and Robert Fagles, trans. *The Odyssey.* New York: Penguin, 2009.

Howatson, M. C. *The Oxford Companion to Classical Literature.* New York: Oxford University Press, 2005.

SEE ALSO: Galatea; Odysseus.

DAEDALUS

A native of Athens, Daedalus first found fame as a brilliant inventor. One might have expected the gods to bestow great blessings on such a worthy mortal, yet Daedalus's life was neither happy nor peaceful. He could never resist a challenge, and his downfall came when his attempts to help two desperate women, Pasiphae and Ariadne, invoked the wrath of a powerful king, Minos.

Daedalus's fatal flaw was excessive pride in his work and his personal reputation. He believed that he could find the solution to any practical problem. In many ways this self-confidence was well founded because his inventions were beneficial and admired by gods and mortals. He designed natural poses for statues, where previously their arms had been fixed stiffly to their sides. Such innovations brought him great success, but all the time he feared competition and was sometimes consumed by jealousy, most famously of his nephew Perdix.

Perdix was sent by his mother to learn mechanical arts from Daedalus, her brother. The youth showed aptitude and was a fast learner. As he walked along the seashore, Perdix picked up a fish spine and immediately imitated it by notching a piece of iron; thus he invented the saw. In another legend he devised a drawing compass by riveting together two pieces of iron.

Daedalus should have been proud of his promising student, but instead he was envious and suspicious of him. In a mad effort to rid himself of his rival, he pushed Perdix from a high tower in one of Athena's temples. Athena, who loved ingenuity, saw Perdix falling and changed him into a partridge. Partridges (Latin name *Perdix perdix*) build their nests in low hedges and do not fly high.

After killing Perdix, Daedalus fled to Crete, where he was welcomed by King Minos. Trouble soon followed, however, when Daedalus agreed to help Minos's wife, Pasiphae. Minos owned a bull that was due to be sacrificed to Poseidon, but the king did not carry out the sacrifice because he thought the bull was too beautiful to kill.

In retribution, Poseidon made Pasiphae fall in love with the animal. She appealed to Daedalus for assistance, and he could not refuse. He built a fake cow, inside which Pasiphae hid. The hollow cow was secretly left in the bull's pen. The bull mated with the fake cow and thus with Pasiphae. Nine months later Pasiphae gave birth to the fierce Minotaur, half human and half bull.

With the birth of the Minotaur, Minos grew outraged by Poseidon's act of vengeance, Pasiphae's behavior, and Daedalus's role in the conception of the Minotaur. The king demanded that Daedalus build a means to contain the horrific monster. Daedalus responded by constructing the Labyrinth. This edifice was an enormous maze with innumerable winding passages and turnings that opened into each other and seemed to have neither a beginning nor an end. According to legend, the Labyrinth was built under the Cretan royal palace at Knossos.

Death of the Minotaur

Minos exacted a yearly tribute from Athens (perhaps because Daedalus was a native of that city) of 14 Athenians (seven youths and seven maidens). These young people were sent to Crete, imprisoned in the Labyrinth, and devoured by the Minotaur. One year Theseus, prince of Athens, volunteered to be one of the sacrifices. Minos's daughter, Ariadne, fell in love with Theseus, and she begged Daedalus to help her save him from being killed by the Minotaur. Daedalus gave her a ball of thread and told her that Theseus should tie one end to the entrance of the Labyrinth and unwind the thread as he moved through the passages. Ariadne passed on the thread and the instructions to Theseus, who did as he was told. When he found the sleeping Minotaur, he killed it, either with his bare fists or with a sword given to him by Ariadne. He then found his way back to the entrance by winding up the thread.

For helping Ariadne, Minos imprisoned both Daedalus and Daedalus's son, Icarus. Some accounts say that they were locked in the Labyrinth, others that they were held in

Above: The Fall of Icarus *by Carlo Saraceni (c. 1580–1620) is one of many depictions by artists of the moment when Icarus ignored his father's warnings, flew too close to the sun, and plunged to his death.*

a tower. Escape was impossible by land or sea, so Daedalus made two pairs of wings from bird feathers held together with wax: his plan was to fly to safety. Just before Daedalus and Icarus launched themselves into the air, the father warned his son not to fly too close to the sun's heat or the sea's dampness, but to follow him closely on a middle course. However, Icarus, intoxicated with the freedom and power of flight, flew higher and higher. Daedalus cried out and warned him, but the boy paid no attention. Icarus soared too close to the sun and the wax melted; his wings disintegrated, and he plunged to his death in the sea.

Hiding in Sicily

Heartbroken, Daedalus buried Icarus's body on an island and then flew to Sicily, where he was befriended by the king. In Sicily Daedalus built a temple to Apollo and hung up his wings as an offering to the god of light.

Minos—angry, betrayed, and thirsting for revenge—did not know where Daedalus was, but he knew that he could trick the inventor into revealing his whereabouts by appealing to his vanity. He offered a great reward in a worldwide contest to anyone who could pass a thread through an intricate, spiraled seashell. Daedalus, in the name of the Sicilian king, solved the puzzle: He tied a thread to an ant and placed the creature in one end of the convoluted shell. When the ant eventually reemerged at the other end, it was clear that the thread ran through the shell's labyrinthine twists and turns. Hearing of this feat, Minos knew that there was only one man who could have thought of and implemented such a smart solution, so he went straight to Sicily to seize Daedalus. The Sicilian king refused to surrender his friend, however, and in the battle for Daedalus, Minos was killed.

After the story of the death of Minos, Daedalus does not appear in any other Greek myths. Perhaps the loss of Icarus balanced the scales for Perdix's murder, and Daedalus was of no further interest to the gods. His legacy is still with us, though. Labyrinths mirroring his invention are constructed

Modern Labyrinths

Archaeological evidence and ancient writings show that labyrinths date back many thousands of years. Their main practical use was as a defense to baffle invaders and trespassers. Today, labyrinths are designed and built for public exploration and pleasure. Modern constructions of this type are usually made of shrubbery and set in gardens, providing a place where the physical world is fashioned to evoke the spiritual world. Many people who walk labyrinths say the experience is soothing and meditative.

One modern labyrinth is found at St. Mark's Episcopal Church in Antioch, a suburb of Nashville, Tennessee. The maze is an imaginative re-creation of Daedalus's original home for the Minotaur. Nashville has long been associated with ancient Greece, and is often known as "the Athens of the South." Other famous modern labyrinths include those constructed on the grounds of Traquair House in Scotland and the maze at Hampton Court, the former royal palace on the western outskirts of London, England.

Above: Renowned throughout Britain for its intricate design, this giant maze was erected in 1980 on the grounds of Traquair House, a popular tourist attraction in Scotland.

worldwide, and the tragedy of a father's loss—the story of headstrong Icarus—and Daedalus's personality, trials, and inventions continue to provide inspiration for authors and artists of all genres. In the early 20th century, Irish writer James Joyce (1882–1941) adapted the inventor's name as Stephen Dedalus for the hero of his short novel *Portrait of the Artist as a Young Man* (1916) and again as a major character in the novel *Ulysses* (1922).

ALYS CAVINESS

Bibliography

Howatson, M. C. *The Oxford Companion to Classical Literature*. New York: Oxford University Press, 2005.

Joyce, James, and Seamus Deane, ed. *Portrait of the Artist as a Young Man*. New York: Penguin Books, 2003.

Nyenhuis, Jacob E. *Myth and the Creative Process: Michael Ayrton and the Myth of Daedalus*. Detroit, MI: Wayne State University Press, 2003.

SEE ALSO: Ariadne; Icarus; Minos; Pasiphae; Theseus.

DANAE

Danae was a Greek princess who was imprisoned by her father, Acrisius, to prevent the fulfillment of a prophecy that she would give birth to a son who would kill him. However, because of divine intervention by the god Zeus, who visited Danae in her prison, Acrisius's actions were in vain.

Left: This painting, Danae and the Brazen Tower, *is by English artist Edward Burne-Jones (1833–1898) of the Pre-Raphaelite movement.*

Danae was the daughter of Eurydice and Acrisius, king of Argos, a city of the Peloponnese peninsula in southern Greece. Acrisius tried to kill Danae and her son in order to save himself. The story began when Acrisius was told a terrible prophecy about his young daughter. The Delphic oracle foretold that Danae would give birth to a son who would one day kill his grandfather. In an effort to prevent the omen from coming to pass, Acrisius immediately imprisoned his daughter in an underground chamber made of bronze with only a small aperture for light and air. Later accounts of the legend make Danae's prison a bronze tower. The earliest work in which this version appears is *Odes* by Roman poet Horace (65–8 BCE).

Acrisius barred the doors and left poor Danae, his only child, with her nurse. No man could come in, and she could not go out. While Danae mourned the loss of her freedom, weeping in her lonely bedroom, the beautiful girl suddenly noticed a strange, sunny glow creeping through the window. She was afraid to move. Gradually the glow coalesced into a shower of gold, and then into the form of the god Zeus. He was attracted to the imprisoned girl and determined to be her lover. Danae naturally felt little loyalty to her father at this point and saw no reason why she should not have an affair with this handsome divinity. They spent many happy hours together, and at last Perseus, her son, was born.

Acrisius trembled with fear when he heard that, despite his efforts, Danae had given birth to a son. He refused to believe that Zeus was the father of his grandchild. Still determined to prevent the prophecy from coming true, he locked his daughter and grandson in a wooden chest and threw it into the sea. He hoped that this would be the end of them, but the chest was protected by Zeus. It drifted far out to sea before finally floating close to the island of Seriphos. Dictes, the brother of the local king Polydectes, was fishing in the sea that day and caught the chest in his nets. When he opened it, he was surprised to see a beautiful woman and an infant. Danae and Perseus, still alive, had found a new home.

Above: Danae, *by Italian master Titian (c. 1489–1576), shows Zeus, disguised as a shower of gold, visiting the princess.*

In later years Polydectes fell in love with Danae. Since she had a full-grown son, however, he felt embarrassed to court her. He pretended that he was in love with someone else and planned to be married. All the warriors of the kingdom were to bring him wedding gifts. Perseus, who by this time had grown into a strapping young hero, promised to bring him the head of the Gorgon Medusa, who could turn men to stone with just one look. Surely, Polydectes thought, Medusa would kill Perseus, and he would then be left to court Danae in peace without the jealous attentions of her son.

Perseus visited the Graeae, three blind, toothless witches, who told him where the Gorgon lived. He stole from them a helmet of invisibility, winged sandals, and other magical aids before proceeding on his quest. Perseus tracked down the Gorgon and slew her while she was asleep, taking care not to look at her directly, but only at her image reflected in a shield made of bronze. When he came home with Medusa's hideous, snake-covered head, he found that Polydectes had been harassing his mother, Danae, and that she had taken refuge at the altars of the gods. Furious, he confronted the king, holding up the Gorgon's head. Polydectes took one look at Medusa and turned to stone.

Perseus and Danae were finally free to leave Seriphos and return to Argos.

King Acrisius was still mindful of the oracle but was nevertheless glad to have an heir. He came to love Perseus and found it difficult to imagine him committing murder. However, one day at Larissa, a town on mainland Greece, the young man was hurling the discus at some funeral games held by the local king. Acrisius just happened to be in the way and was killed when the discus struck him in the head. The Delphic prophecy had been fulfilled.

Perseus chose not to take his grandfather's throne, but became king of Tiryns and Mycenae, two great Bronze Age cities. His children included the mighty Heracles, thus making Danae the ancestor of one of the greatest Greek legendary heroes.

Older versions of the myth

This version of the story of Danae was almost certainly not invented by the Greeks, but was based on older legends from previous civilizations. Danae was probably the same

DANAE

Right: This bronze statue by Italian sculptor Benvenuto Cellini (1500–1571) depicts Danae with her son, Perseus.

early female deity as Danu, who was worshiped in ancient Europe and gave her name to the Don River in Russia and the Danube River in Europe.

The way in which the legend of Danu has been handed down suggests that it was originally a story from a matriarchy, a culture in which women were the heads of the family and in which descent was traced through the female line. Danu was expelled from her traditional lands by invading patriarchal warrior tribes, and she and her followers fled to the edges of the continent. The story reflects the transition from the Stone Age to the Iron and Bronze Ages. Although the children of Danu did not have metal weapons, they were so skilled in magic that they later became known as the fairy folk, or Sidhe.

The Tuatha De Danann, or Children of Danu, were the mythical first inhabitants of Ireland. They were believed to have fled from warlike humans and vanished into earth mounds, from which they could enter the mystical otherworld. Danu's association with magic and the earth links her to Danae. The fact that Danae's prison was made of bronze is a reference to the emergence of metallurgy.

Danae as Diti

Farther back in time, Danae was the goddess Diti, the earth mother of the prehistoric Dravidian civilization of India. In the original story, Indra, head of the warrior pantheon, murdered Diti and her son Vrta with a lightning bolt. Mother and son were both described as serpent-demons, but after their deaths, as a cow and her calf. In both versions the animals they were identified with were the chief companions of the agricultural earth mother. The rivers flowed with Diti's blood, and from this source was born the sun god that shone on the new Brahman elite. This link with the sun reappears in the myth of Danae, who is impregnated by a shower of gold, a metal that symbolizes the sun. However, after the Aryan settlement of India in the third millennium BCE, Diti, like many Dravidian deities, was subsumed by the Vedic gods of the new, dominant culture.

BARBARA GARDNER

Bibliography

Bulfinch, Thomas. *Bulfinch's Mythology.* New York: Barnes & Noble, 2006.

Howatson, M. C. *The Oxford Companion to Classical Literature.* New York: Oxford University Press, 2005.

SEE ALSO: Gorgons; Heracles; Perseus.

cellini
danae col figlio

DAPHNE

Daphne was a nymph who was loved by Apollo. The god pursued her through a forest, but at the moment he was about to catch her, Daphne was transformed into a laurel tree. Today, a crown of laurel leaves is a symbol of success, following a tradition that began in ancient Greece, when victors in sport and music contests were awarded laurel wreaths at games dedicated to Apollo.

The nymph Daphne was the daughter of a river god, either Ladon in Arcadia or Peneius in Thessaly, and according to all accounts she was extremely beautiful. There are two stories that feature Daphne, and in both, Apollo, the god of music, poetry, and light, is madly in love with her. Although Apollo's love for Daphne was unrequited, the ancient Greeks believed that the Olympian god associated himself forever with Daphne by making the laurel tree his own.

Leucippus in disguise

The lesser known of the two myths featuring Daphne was told by the Greek writer and geographer Pausanias (143–176 CE). His version revolves around Leucippus, the son of King Oenomaus of Elis. Leucippus fell in love with Daphne the first moment he saw her in the forest near his

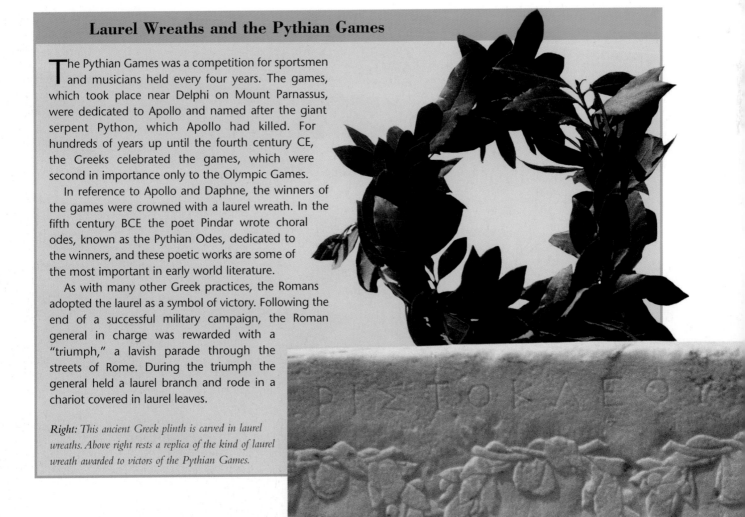

Laurel Wreaths and the Pythian Games

The Pythian Games was a competition for sportsmen and musicians held every four years. The games, which took place near Delphi on Mount Parnassus, were dedicated to Apollo and named after the giant serpent Python, which Apollo had killed. For hundreds of years up until the fourth century CE, the Greeks celebrated the games, which were second in importance only to the Olympic Games.

In reference to Apollo and Daphne, the winners of the games were crowned with a laurel wreath. In the fifth century BCE the poet Pindar wrote choral odes, known as the Pythian Odes, dedicated to the winners, and these poetic works are some of the most important in early world literature.

As with many other Greek practices, the Romans adopted the laurel as a symbol of victory. Following the end of a successful military campaign, the Roman general in charge was rewarded with a "triumph," a lavish parade through the streets of Rome. During the triumph the general held a laurel branch and rode in a chariot covered in laurel leaves.

Right: This ancient Greek plinth is carved in laurel wreaths. Above right rests a replica of the kind of laurel wreath awarded to victors of the Pythian Games.

father's kingdom, but he knew that the nymph had sworn to reject the attentions of all men and remain a virgin. Wanting to be near her even if she would not love him in return, Leucippus disguised himself as a woman and braided his long hair. He then met up with Daphne and told the nymph that he was one of Oenomaus's daughters and that he—or she—wanted to go hunting with Daphne and the other nymphs. Daphne agreed and Leucippus proved an excellent hunter, gaining her respect.

After a short while, however, Apollo, who knew that Leucippus was in disguise, grew jealous and angry. He desired Daphne for himself and did not want the beautiful nymph to fall in love with anyone else. One day, during a hunt, Apollo inspired Daphne and the other nymphs to bathe in the Ladon River. As the nymphs undressed, Leucippus refused to join in. The nymphs playfully ripped off Leucippus's clothes and discovered that he was a man. Outraged, they attacked and killed him with their spears and hunting knives.

Apollo's chase

The more famous myth featuring Daphne was told by Roman poet Ovid (43 BCE–17 CE). When Apollo boasted that he was a better archer than Eros (or Cupid, as the Roman Ovid called him), the god of love secretly shot a sharp golden arrow of love at Apollo. The arrow caused Apollo to fall in love with Daphne. Eros then hit Daphne with an arrow, but this time the arrow was blunt and tipped in lead, making the nymph reject the love of men and desire to remain a virgin.

Apollo tried to woo Daphne, but she ran from the deity of light. The Olympian god chased after her through the forest, both running as fast as the wind until Daphne reached the banks of the Peneius River. Apollo had nearly caught up to her when Daphne prayed to her divine father for help. Immediately the nymph's feet changed to roots, her chest to a tree trunk, her arms to branches, and her long flowing hair to leaves. Daphne had been transformed into a laurel tree (*daphne* in Greek).

According to Ovid, Apollo embraced the new laurel tree, kissing the trunk where Daphne's heart would have been. He spoke to her one last time: "If you cannot be my bride, you can be my tree." From that time forward, the laurel was sacred to Apollo and his worshipers.

Left: Apollo and Daphne, *painted by the Italian artist Giovanni Battista Tiepolo (1696–1770) between 1744 and 1745. The painting shows the moment when Apollo (left) catches up with Daphne and she transforms into a laurel tree. The elder figure near the bottom is Daphne's father, a river god; Eros (Cupid), the god of love, supports the nymph.*

Representations of Daphne and Apollo

Because of the myth of Daphne and Apollo, the god was often depicted wearing a crown of laurel leaves. Apollo's priestesses at Delphi and at other sanctuaries sacred to him wore similar crowns. The Delphic priestesses also burned laurel or bay leaves as part of the rituals in which they revealed the prophecies, or oracles, of Apollo.

The story of Daphne's transformation into a laurel tree has inspired both painting and sculpture from ancient times to the present. Some of the most famous paintings are by 16th- and 17th-century artists, including Nicolas Poussin, Peter Paul Rubens, Giovanni Battista Tiepolo, Jacopo Robusti (Tintoretto), and Veronese (Paolo Caliari). Perhaps the best-known statue of Apollo and Daphne is the piece by Italian sculptor Gian Lorenzo Bernini (1598–1680), which formed one of four groups of sculptures made for the gardens in Rome of Cardinal Scipione Borghese.

Daphne's sanctuary

In Greece a grove of laurel trees stood near Athens. The grove was called the Daphne sanctuary, and it was sacred to Apollo. In 480 BCE, during the Persian Wars, when the armies of King Xerxes I (c. 519–465 BCE) of Persia invaded mainland Greece, Xerxes set up his golden tent at Daphne's sanctuary. The Persian king had chosen the sanctuary partly because of its symbolic importance and partly because the spot gave him an excellent vantage point from which to watch what he expected would be the final sea battle between his large fleet and the remnants of the Greek navy, in the Bay of Salamis. As it happened, the Greek ships under the command of Themistocles (c. 524–460 BCE) encircled and destroyed the Persian fleet in one of the most famous engagements in naval history.

Today a Greek Orthodox Church stands on the site of the Daphne sanctuary. In the central dome of the church is an image of Jesus Christ. The place that was once sacred to Apollo and his love for Daphne is now a site of Christian worship.

KARELISA HARTIGAN

Bibliography

Barber, Antonia. *Apollo and Daphne: Masterpieces of Greek Mythology.* Los Angeles: Paul Getty Museum Publications, 1998.

Bulfinch, Thomas. *Bulfinch's Mythology.* New York: Barnes & Noble, 2006.

Race, William H., ed. *Pindar: Olympian Odes, Pythian Odes.* Cambridge, MA: Harvard University Press, 1997.

SEE ALSO: Pleiades.

DEUCALION

In Greek mythology, Deucalion and his wife, Pyrrha, were the ancestors of the entire human race. Like many similar figures in the myths of other cultures, they were the only survivors of a flood sent by the gods to wipe out humanity.

Deucalion was the son of Prometheus, and a grandchild of the Titan Iapetus and his niece, the Ocean nymph Clymene. Iapetus and Clymene had four sons: Atlas, Prometheus, Epimetheus, and Menoetios.

Prometheus was a frequent benefactor of human beings. For example, he is credited with introducing fire and pharmaceuticals to them. His son kept up the philanthropic tradition: Deucalion became a kind of re-founder of the human race in Greece. A survivor of an early catastrophe

that wiped out all or most of the early descendants of the first human families, Deucalion became the father from whom nearly all subsequent humans were descended. Deucalion married his cousin Pyrrha, the daughter of his uncle Epimetheus. (In some versions of the story, Pyrrha's mother was the first woman, Pandora.) Thus Deucalion and Pyrrha are functionally equivalent not only to Noah and his wife, but also to Adam and Eve in the Judeo-Christian tradition.

Zeus had become disgusted with mankind after Lycaon, the founding father of Arcadia (a region of the Peloponnese peninsula in southern Greece), sacrificed his own son and served him in a soup at a banquet for the gods. Zeus changed Lycaon into a werewolf, but he still felt vengeful, so he decided to put an end to the whole human race by sending a great flood onto Earth.

When Prometheus heard of Zeus's plans, he informed Deucalion and Pyrrha, and the two of them built an ark in which to try to ride out the flood. The entire Earth was then inundated by a torrential downpour, and all of mankind was drowned, although some cities, including Delphi, Megara, and Lesbos, claimed to have ancestors who escaped the flood by withdrawing to the mountains.

Deucalion and Pyrrha spent nine days afloat in their ark before the waters began to recede. Eventually they came to land on an exposed mountaintop. The place has been identified variously as Delphi, on the slopes of Mount Parnassus, and Dodona, in the far northwest of Greece.

Below: Deucalion and Pyrrha *(c. 1520) by Italian painter Domenico Beccafumi (c. 1486–1551). The painting depicts the pair throwing stones behind them, from which new humans are created.*

Deucalion and Pyrrha gave thanks for their deliverance by sacrificing to Zeus, the god of escape, and then set about finding how to re-create the human race. Zeus, or possibly Themis, advised them to cover their heads and throw "the bones of their mother" behind them. At first the couple wondered what that meant, but then Deucalion realized that it was a reference to the stones lying on the ground around them—the bones of Mother Earth. The stones that Deucalion threw turned into men; those that Pyrrha threw turned into women. Thus the new race of humans was a race of stone, hardy and durable. This story may be based on a pun: the Greek word for "people" is *laos*, the word for "stone" is *laas*.

Thus, ancient Greek accounts of creation place the origin of humankind before the time of Deucalion. The development of the race was then interrupted by the flood, which was sent as a punishment for errant behavior. However, although Deucalion and Pyrrha were not the very first humans, they were the survivors who started humankind over again, and most regions traced their

Below: This engraving from an 18th-century French book shows Deucalion and Pyrrha escaping Zeus's punishment of humanity.

LE DÉLUGE.
The Deluge.

Der Sündfluez.
De Sondvloedt.

Deucalion of Crete

The other Deucalion in Greek myth was a son of king Minos of Crete and his wife, Pasiphae. He had a brother, Catreus, and two sisters, Ariadne and Phaedra. Deucalion became an important ally of Theseus, king of Athens.

Deucalion had a son, Idomeneus, who led the contingent of 100 ships from Crete that took the Greek army to besiege Troy under the leadership of King Agamemnon. According to some accounts, Deucalion also had a daughter whose name, Crete, was adopted by her native island. In other versions, however, Crete was the child of Asterius and Europa, the daughter of the king of Tyre.

Deucalion also had at least one illegitimate son, named Molus, and according to Homer's *Odyssey*, another named Aethon. When Odysseus was disguised as a beggar in his palace, he introduced himself to Penelope as Aethon.

Crete was always regarded with great veneration in ancient Greece, and the Cretan character of Deucalion provides a connection between the island and some of the most important events in the mythical history of the mainland.

ancestry back to Deucalion. In Athens, Deucalion's son Amphictyon was regarded as third in the line of early kings (after the two earth-born kings, Cecrops and Cranaus). The link with Deucalion was so important that Athenians claimed he was buried in their city.

Parents of a nation

The rest of Greece also claimed descent from Deucalion and Pyrrha. One of their sons was Hellen, whose name means "Greek." It is from the root *Hell-*, from which are derived *Hellas*, their name for their country, *Hellenes*, meaning "Greeks," and *Hellenikos*, the adjective "Greek."

Among the children and grandchildren of Hellen and his wife, the nymph Orseis, were the founders of each of the primary subethnic regional groups of Greece. Two of their sons were Aeolus, the first of the Aeolians, and Dorus, the first of the Dorians. Another son, Xuthus, married Creusa and had two sons: Ion, the founder of the Ionians, and Achaeus, the founder of the Achaeans. The terms *Aeolian*, *Dorian*, *Ionian*, and *Achaean* are still used today to describe both the geographical and the dialect areas of Greece. They are surpassed in importance only by Athens and the surrounding district of Attica.

Deucalion and Pyrrha were the starting point to which all Greeks traced their origins. As their civilization developed, more and more cities and regions began to claim association with the couple, and that they were central to the story of the flood. The people of Dodona, for example, claimed that their city had been founded by Deucalion after his ark had landed there. The citizens of Kynos, the main port in Locri, maintained that Deucalion and Pyrrha had lived there, and that Pyrrha was buried there.

Meanwhile, the people of Athens responded to provincial rivalry by making new claims of their own. Deucalion was already buried among them; they later asserted that the land surrounding his grave contained a large cleft in the ground that marked the spot at which the floodwaters had first begun to recede. They commemorated this event in an annual ceremony at which they threw honey-wheat cakes into the crack.

The Parian Marble (*Marmor Parium*) is an ancient stone on the island of Paros with inscriptions that record significant events from the time of the earliest kings to the third century BCE. According to its account, Deucalion's flood took place in 1528–1527 BCE, 53 years after Cecrops became the first king of Athens, 110 years before the introduction of agriculture by Demeter, and 320 years before the Trojan War.

Other accounts of a great flood

The motif of a flood that inundates the world and destroys the human race with the exception of a select few is found in the mythology and legends of other cultures, particularly in the Mediterranean and West Asia, but also in other parts of the world. In Mesopotamia, the Sumerian Ziusudra was a pious king who was warned by one of the gods about an impending flood. He saved himself by building a boat while the rest of mankind was destroyed.

In the *Epic of Gilgamesh*, also from Mesopotamia, Utnapishtim survives the flood by building an ark. The major difference between this myth and its Greek equivalent is that the hero becomes immortal. In the Biblical book of Genesis, God decides to destroy the human race because of its wickedness, but warns Noah, who builds an ark and rescues creation by preserving a pair of each species.

Similar stories are found in northern Europe, Africa, Central Asia, China, Southeast Asia, and Australasia. In outline, they are almost always the same: A corrupt and

Below: The Parian Marble is a surviving chronicle of ancient Greece inscribed in marble. The chronicle dates the flood that wiped out all humans but Deucalion and Pyrrha to c. 1528–1527 BCE.

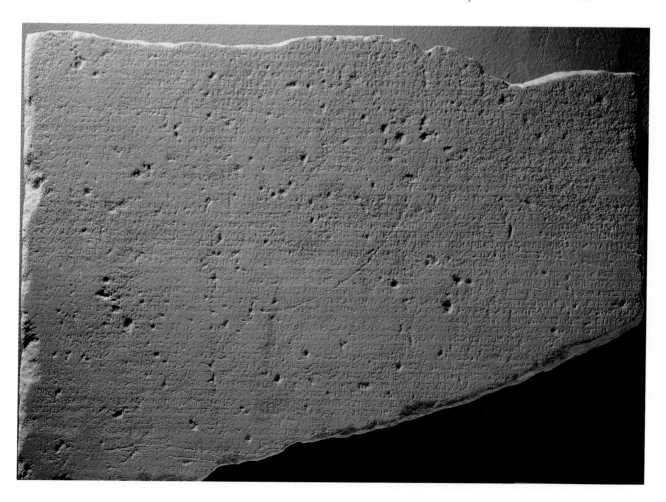

Above: The sanctuary of Athena at Delphi. Many Greeks believed that this was where Deucalion and Pyrrha's ark came to rest after the flood. It was also the site of the most famous oracle in Greece.

sinful human race is destroyed by angry gods in a great flood, but one or more persons are warned, and so he or they take refuge in a vessel to ride out the waters of the flood. The survivors then become the ancestors through whom humankind, and often other species as well, are able to continue. An occasional variant on this basic theme is that the gods send the flood because Earth was becoming overpopulated by humans.

Historical basis

Recent geological discoveries have led archaeologists and other scholars to propose that what is now the Black Sea was once an enclosed freshwater lake. In about 7000 BCE, however, it burst its banks at what is now the Bosporus and Dardanelles, and opened out into the Mediterranean Sea, causing extensive flooding in the eastern Mediterranean and beyond. If that is correct, the Greek and West Asian myths of a great flood may be a "folk memory" of this cataclysmic event.

Although the breach of the ancient topographical barrier between the Black Sea and the Mediterranean Sea is an event of immense significance, the flood myths retain a broader and perhaps even greater symbolic importance. The stories can be viewed as a metaphor for one of the most fundamental preoccupations of human experience: the fear of being engulfed and swept away in a huge, elemental catastrophe. Whether such a worldwide disaster ever actually took place is thus, to some extent, a relatively minor consideration.

Deucalion is featured very little in what remains of ancient Greek art, but the theme of the great flood became popular during the Renaissance in Europe, and various Italian painters depicted topics such as the flood involving Deucalion and Pyrrha. The leading works on these themes are by Baldassare Peruzzi (1481–1536), Lo Schiavone (1522–1563), Lelio Orsi (c. 1511–1587), and Giovanni Castiglione (c. 1616–1670). The topic was also favored for a while in minor operatic works by composers of the late 18th and early 19th centuries.

ANTHONY BULLOCH

Bibliography

Bulfinch, Thomas. *Myths of Greece and Rome.* New York: Penguin, 1998.

Howatson, M. C. *The Oxford Companion to Classical Literature.* New York: Oxford University Press, 2005.

SEE ALSO: Odysseus; Pandora.

DIOMEDES

A king of Argos and a suitor of Helen, Diomedes played a crucial role in the Greek victory in the Trojan War. His importance was partly the result of his bravery as a warrior and partly the result of his cunning, a quality that he shared with his comrade Odysseus.

Diomedes' grandfather was Oeneus, king of the city of Calydon in central Greece. His father, Tydeus, was forced to flee Calydon after killing one of his relatives, possibly his uncle or brother. In Argos he married Deipyle, daughter of King Adrastus, who bore him Diomedes. Tydeus's fate mirrored that of Polyneices, the son of the Theban king Oedipus, who also left his homeland for Argos and married a daughter of Adrastus. Tydeus supported Polyneices in his attempt to seize the throne of Thebes from his brother, Eteocles, but the expedition was a disaster and both men died.

Early exploits

Like his father, Diomedes was a valiant fighter. Ten years after Tydeus's death, he joined a force known as the Epigoni (descendants), who vowed to succeed where their fathers had failed in Thebes. The Epigoni fulfilled their vow and installed Polyneices' son on the throne. Diomedes also sought vengeance for his father's exile from Calydon. He killed the cousins who had taken the throne from King Oeneus, and crowned Oeneus's son-in-law king. Yet Diomedes' greatest achievement as a fighter was in the Trojan War, the 10-year conflict between the Greeks and the Trojans that began when the Trojan prince Paris abducted Helen, wife of the Greek king Menelaus. As one of Helen's many admirers, Diomedes had promised to defend the honor of anyone who married her, so he led a fleet of 80 ships to carry the Greek army to Troy.

The Trojan War

Diomedes was one of the greatest Greek champions in the Trojan War. In the *Iliad*, the poet Homer describes him as second only to Achilles, and makes frequent references to "Diomedes of the great war cry." In other versions, Diomedes is even braver than Achilles, whose petulant behavior when his slave girl Briseis is taken from him almost costs the Greeks victory.

Diomedes killed many Trojans in battle and, with the assistance of the goddess Athena, injured two deities. He wounded Aphrodite when she intervened to rescue her son, the Trojan hero Aeneas, from Diomedes' onslaught. In the same battle Diomedes fought Hector, Paris's brother and a favorite of Ares, the god of war. Athena helped Diomedes thrust his spear at Ares, wounding the god and causing him to flee the battle.

Diomedes' natural cunning and his partnership with Odysseus had an even more significant impact on the course of the war. Two episodes in particular illustrate the pair's capacity for deception. In one story they tricked the hermit Philoctetes out of his magic bow and arrows, which he had inherited from Heracles. The weapons allowed the Greeks to fulfill one prophecy of victory over

Left: This statue of Diomedes was carved by Polyclitus, one of the greatest Greek sculptors of the fifth century BCE.

Above: In this painting by Erasmus Quellinus (1607–1678), Odysseus and Diomedes give presents to the daughters of Lycomedes. One of the "girls" is Achilles in disguise; he gives himself away by seizing the weapons.

the Trojans. Diomedes and Odysseus fulfilled another when they stole the Palladium, a wooden statue to Athena, from inside Troy. Both the Greeks and the Trojans believed that, as long as the Palladium remained inside its walls, Troy was safe. However, disguised as beggars, the pair passed unnoticed into the city and stole the statue. These stories demonstrate the importance of sacred objects to the morale of the side that possessed them.

After the Trojan War

When Diomedes returned to Argos following the end of the Trojan War, he did not receive a hero's welcome, but discovered that his wife had been unfaithful in his absence and that his claim to the throne was disputed. Some writers suggest that this outcome was caused by the Greek prince Oeax, who believed that his brother Palamedes had been murdered by Diomedes and Odysseus. Accordingly, Oeax told Diomedes' wife that her husband was returning from Troy with a new lover. This legend may have inspired the medieval story of Troilus and Cressida, later retold by Geoffrey Chaucer (c. 1342–1400) in a long poem and by William Shakespeare (1564–1616) in a play. In the former version, Troilus, son of the Trojan king Priam, falls in love with Cressida, only to be heartbroken when the Trojan woman switches her affections to Diomedes. Other Greek sources maintain that Diomedes' ill-fortune after the war was Aphrodite's punishment for the injury he had caused her. All the sources agree that Diomedes left Greece for Italy, but there are several different accounts of what he did there. Some state that he was killed by the king of Apulia; others that he founded several Italian cities, including Brindisi and Arpi. The Greek poet Pindar (c. 522–c. 438 BCE) even suggests that Athena made Diomedes a god.

ANDREW CAMPBELL

Bibliography

Bulfinch, Thomas. *Myths of Greece and Rome.* New York: Penguin, 1998.

Homer, and Robert Fagles, trans. *The Iliad.* New York: Penguin, 2009.

SEE ALSO: Achilles; Aeneas; Helen; Heracles; Menelaus; Odysseus; Priam; Troilus.

ECHO

Echo was a nymph whose myth provided an explanation for the phenomenon of sound echoing. More important, the two main versions of her story highlight the limits of acceptable female behavior in Greek myth and culture, where lack of female sexual compliance was punished.

There are three main versions of Echo's story. In the first she incurs the anger of Hera, queen of the Olympian gods. The second myth has her falling eternally yet unrequitedly in love with the most beautiful man in Greek mythology, Narcissus. In the third she imprudently refuses the love of the god Pan, with tragic consequences. Her punishment served as a warning to young girls who rejected the attentions of male admirers in ancient Greece.

Both the Hera and Narcissus versions were recorded by Roman poet Ovid (43 BCE–c. 17 CE). As the attendant of Hera, wife of Zeus, Echo was expected to give the goddess her unswerving loyalty and devotion. Yet Echo was forced by Zeus to cover for his amorous indiscretions by distracting Hera with ceaseless chatter. When the goddess discovered this ruse, she cursed Echo, so that the nymph could not voice her own words but only repeat what others said. In classical mythology, the punishment always fit the crime: because Echo transgressed by acting on another's behalf (Zeus), her penalty was the ability to speak only through the agency of another.

In the second story, the nymph spied Narcissus hunting in the forest. Her love for him was immediate, but because of Hera's curse she could only echo Narcissus's words. When she tried to embrace the hunter, he told her to go away. Heartbroken, the nymph retreated deep into the forest, where she spent the rest of her life pining for Narcissus, until all that was left was the echoing sound of her voice.

The story of Echo and Narcissus shows us that in ancient Greece feminine expression of desire was considered inappropriate. Women were to be desired, never to be seen to desire for themselves. Narcissus's response emphasizes the impropriety of Echo's feelings. At his rejection, Echo ultimately withered away from longing. Yet this residual part of Echo really did not belong to her at all. By taking the initiative with Narcissus, she had usurped a principal male prerogative. Her punishment for failing to identify with the socially acceptable behavior of her gender was the loss of her identity.

Left: This early-20th-century illustration depicts Narcissus disappearing into the distance, leaving the heartbroken Echo to pine for him.

Above: Nicolas Poussin (1594–1665) painted this version of the rejected Echo watching over the sleeping Narcissus. Cupid, the god of love, looks on.

Rejecting divine love

The most famous version of the Pan and Echo myth was written by Longus, a Greek author of the second or third century CE. In this story, unlike Ovid's myth, it is Echo who rejects the admirer. Pan was the god of shepherds and flocks. He appeared half human and half goat and had a lustful nature. He was always chasing nymphs whom he desired. Pan encountered Echo and immediately desired her. She was not only pretty but could sing sweetly and play many musical instruments. Despite Pan's divine status, Echo rejected the god's advances. In anger, Pan incited a group of shepherds to attack Echo. They tore her body into little pieces, until all that remained was her voice echoing through the forest.

In this myth, Echo's offense falls at the other end of the spectrum from her encounter with Narcissus: instead of going too far, she fails to go far enough by not acceding to the lust of a god. The ultimate outcome of her punishment is the same in both myths, but in the second the means is much more brutal: it is arguable that Echo's violent dismemberment represents rape. This peculiar account is told as part of a larger story about the erotic maturation of a young girl named Chloe. In many myths, a girl's first sexual experience is painful, often the result of rape by some god, and tends to be transformative. In other words, becoming a woman is symbolized by her change into, for instance, a tree or a fountain. Chloe had the rare fortune in myth to love and be loved by a young man named Daphnis. Echo's myth, told to Chloe just before the climax of her own story, heightens the dramatic suspense and plays counterpoint to the happy resolution of Chloe's romance.

KATHRYN CHEW

Bibliography

Bulfinch, Thomas. *Bulfinch's Mythology.* New York: Barnes & Noble, 2006.

Ovid, and A. D. Melville, trans. *Metamorphoses.* New York: Oxford University Press, 2008.

Pomeroy, Sarah B. *Goddesses, Whores, Wives, and Slaves: Women in Classical Antiquity.* New York: Schocken Books, 1995.

SEE ALSO: Narcissus.

ELECTRA

In Greek mythology. Electra was the daughter of Agamemnon, king of Mycenae, and Clytemnestra. Years after her mother killed her father, Electra and her brother avenged their father's death.

The character Electra is not mentioned as one of Agamemnon's daughters by the earliest Greek poet, Homer (c. ninth–eighth century BCE). Instead, she makes her first dramatic appearance in the fifth century BCE in a play by Aeschylus (525–456 BCE) called *Choephoroe* (more popularly known as *Libation Bearers*), the second part of the *Oresteia* trilogy. From that time on the story of Electra was retold with several variations, but the essential plot never changed.

Electra was one of four children born to King Agamemnon of Mycenae and his wife, Clytemnestra. Their other children were a son, Orestes, and two more daughters, Iphigeneia and Chrysothemis. Electra's legend begins with the Trojan War. When Helen, wife of King Menelaus of Sparta and sister of Clytemnestra, ran away to Troy with Paris, a Trojan prince, the Greeks decided to wage war on Troy and bring back Helen. Agamemnon, Menelaus's brother, was chosen as the military leader of the Greek forces. Before the Greeks set off for Troy across the sea, a soothsayer told Agamemnon he must sacrifice his daughter Iphigeneia to the goddess Artemis in exchange for a fair wind. He did so—although in some versions Artemis spared Iphigeneia's life—and the Greek army set sail for Troy. Clytemnestra was devastated by the loss of Iphigeneia and never forgave her husband. While Agamemnon was away fighting in Troy, Clytemnestra and her husband's cousin Aegisthus became lovers, yet Electra always remained loyal to her father and longed for his return.

After 10 years of warring between the Greeks and the Trojans, Troy was finally defeated and Agamemnon came home to Mycenae, but he did not return alone. As a kind of victory trophy he had claimed Cassandra, a daughter of King Priam of Troy, as his mistress. Within hours of his arrival at the royal palace, according to some versions, Clytemnestra and Aegisthus murdered both Agamemnon and Cassandra. Clytemnestra then planned to kill Orestes, but Electra secretly arranged for her young brother to be sent to the Greek kingdom of Phocis, north of the Gulf of Corinth, where he was raised in safety.

Left: This 19th-century painting by Frederick Leighton (1830–1896) depicts Electra grieving in the tomb of her murdered father, Agamemnon.

Above: In this painting by French artist Jean Baptiste Joseph Wicar (1762–1834), a distraught Electra hugs an urn that she believes contains the ashes of her dead brother and savior, Orestes. Unknown to her, the man bearing the urn is actually Orestes in disguise.

Betrayal and revenge

For years thereafter, Electra mourned the death of her father and vowed to avenge his murder. When Orestes reached manhood, he heard about how his father had been killed, so he set off with his cousin and friend Pylades for Mycenae. When the two men reached the royal palace, they disguised themselves as travelers to gain entry. They also claimed to be carrying the ashes of the dead Orestes in an urn.

Some legends have it that, although Electra was upset at hearing the rumor of Orestes' death, she resolved to kill Clytemnestra and Aegisthus herself. Before she could act, however, Orestes and Pylades secretly revealed to her their

The Electra Complex

The phrase *Electra complex* is closely associated with famous Austrian psychoanalyst Sigmund Freud (1856–1939), although he did not use the term himself. Essentially the Electra complex is the female equivalent of what Freud called the Oedipus complex. In Greek mythology Oedipus, without realizing his true parentage, slew his father and married his mother—a metaphor, Freud believed, for a common phase of human emotional development, typically between the ages of three to five, when a child experiences a strong bond with or even sexual desire for the parent of the opposite sex and an equally strong sense of rivalry with the parent of the same sex. According to Freud, in emotionally healthy people, the phase ends once the child identifies with the parent of the same sex. The Electra complex is a way of explaining why some girls are closer to their fathers than their mothers.

true identities, and together they plotted their crime. First Orestes killed Clytemnestra by stabbing her, and, depending on the account told, Electra either encouraged him or helped him stab their mother a second time. They then showed Aegisthus Clytemnestra's body before executing him too. Another version has it that Orestes and Pylades killed Aegisthus before stabbing Clytemnestra to death.

Orestes rewarded Pylades for his help by giving him Electra to wed. Once married, Electra and Pylades moved to Phocis, where they had two sons, Medon and Strophius.

The significance of Electra's story

The ancient Greeks valued the ideals of loyalty and justice, and Electra was seen as a hero for her devotion to her father and her obsession with avenging his wrongful murder. Women were meant to be faithful and obedient to men, and

Below: This Roman statue of Orestes and Electra, made sometime between the first century BCE and the first century CE, depicts the siblings in an intimate pose, perhaps plotting the death of Clytemnestra.

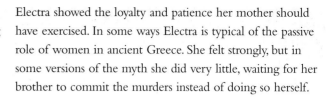

Electra showed the loyalty and patience her mother should have exercised. In some ways Electra is typical of the passive role of women in ancient Greece. She felt strongly, but in some versions of the myth she did very little, waiting for her brother to commit the murders instead of doing so herself.

Echoes of the story

In ancient Greece the earliest paintings of Electra, from the the fifth century BCE, were of her presence at the killing of Aegisthus. Later in Greek art she was featured more often with Orestes at the tomb of their father.

The most important literary depictions of Electra come in the works of three Greek dramatists, Aeschylus, Sophocles (c. 496–406 BCE), and Euripides (c. 486–406 BCE). In Aeschylus's version of her story, Electra has little to do with the murders of Clytemnestra and Aegisthus; yet in the versions by Sophocles and Euripides, both of which are titled *Electra*, she takes a more central and instrumental role. Sophocles' play puts greater emphasis on Electra's emotional torment during the years spent waiting for the return of Orestes and the agony she feels when she hears the false rumor that her brother is dead. Sophocles' Electra also encourages Orestes to stab their mother a second time. A major difference between the Sophocles and Euripides *Electras* is that in the latter play Electra grips the knife with Orestes and the two stab their mother together.

In the 20th century, Electra continued to inspire artists. Most famously, Electra is featured in a reworking of *Oresteia* by the U.S. dramatist Eugene O'Neill (1888–1953). The play, *Mourning Becomes Electra*, sets the drama among a New England family immediately following the Civil War. In 1908 the German composer Richard Strauss (1864–1949) wrote an opera based on Sophocles' *Electra*. Poet Sylvia Plath (1932–1963), whose own father died when she was young, wrote "Electra on Azalea Path" about her feelings for him.

Anna Claybourne

Bibliography

Aeschylus, and A. Shapiro and P. Burian, eds. *The Oresteia*. New York: Oxford University Press, 2010.

Euripides, and P. Burian and A. Shapiro, eds. *The Complete Euripides*. New York: Oxford University Press, 2009–2010.

O'Neill, Eugene. *Three Plays: Desire under the Elms, Strange Interlude, Mourning Becomes Electra*. New York: Vintage Books, 1995.

See also: Agamemnon; Atreus; Clytemnestra; Iphigeneia; Orestes.

ENDYMION

The mythical Greek king Endymion was the subject of two stories. In one, he introduced racing to the Olympic Games. In the other, more famous story, the moon goddess Selene fell in love with him while he was asleep. The story of the sleeping Endymion captured the imagination of several important painters, as well as English poet John Keats.

Below: French artist Nicolas Poussin (1594–1665) painted this version of the Endymion myth, but he substituted Diana for Selene.

Endymion was the son of Aethlius and Calyce, although some sources say that his father was the god Zeus. Aethlius himself was one of Zeus's sons, and Calyce was a daughter of Aeolus, the mythical ancestor of the Aeolian Greeks who lived in Thessaly, on the northeastern region of the Greek mainland. An ancient Peloponnesian legend claims that Endymion brought the Aeolians with him from Thessaly to the Peloponnese, where he became king of Elis, an area of the northwestern part of the peninsula.

Endymion the king

King Endymion fathered three sons, Paeon, Epeius, and Aetolus, and a daughter, Eurykyda. When his sons were young men, Endymion ordered a footrace to decide which of the three would inherit the throne. The only contestants were to be his sons; the winner would be ruler of Elis after

Above: *This Roman relief sculpture of Endymion sleeping, from the first century CE, is typical of depictions of the handsome youth. Endymion is asleep, and by his side is a dog either howling at the moon (Selene) or pining for the hunts he will miss because Endymion will never wake.*

Endymion's death. According to legend, this was the first footrace held at Olympia, which lies in Elis, where the original Olympic Games were held.

Epeius won the race and was proclaimed the heir. Paeon, angry at having lost, left the Peloponnese and traveled through mainland Greece, eventually settling in an area north of Macedonia that he named Paeonia. Aetolus remained in Elis and became king when Epeius died. His reign was shortlived, however, because he was exiled for having killed another king. Aetolus journeyed until, like his brother Paeon, he too founded a new kingdom on mainland Greece: Aetolia, near the Achelous River.

Eleios, the son of Eurykada, succeeded Aetolus as king of Elis, and it is said that the people of the kingdom were called Eleans in honor of him. Greek writer Pausanias (143–176 CE) noted that the Eleans kept a tomb of Endymion in Olympia at the starting place of the sprinters. The people of Herakleia, however, claimed that Endymion had left Elis and traveled to Mount Latmos, where he was buried. The people there worshiped him as a local hero.

As for the mythological fate of King Endymion, one version claims that he was invited to Mount Olympus by Zeus. There he fell in love with Hera, Zeus's wife. When he tried to make love to her, Zeus grew so angry that he banished Endymion to the underworld.

The sleeping Endymion

The other depiction of Endymion was as one of the most handsome mortals in all of Greek mythology. One night the young Endymion fell asleep under the stars when the moon goddess, Selene (known as Diana or Luna to the Romans), saw him and fell passionately in love. The goddess descended to the spot where Endymion slept and the two made love. The next morning Endymion woke with such vivid and pleasant dreams that he asked Zeus to grant him eternal sleep—and youthful beauty—so that he could repeat the pleasure forever. Zeus granted the handsome youth his wish, although some say it was Selene who asked Zeus to make the young man sleep forever. From then on Endymion slept in a cave on Mount Latmos, the place where both stories of Endymion converged.

In a similar version by Pausanias, Selene made so many nocturnal visits to Endymion that she gave birth to 50 of his daughters. Another story tells that the god of sleep, Hypnos (known as Somnus by the Romans), also loved Endymion. He made the beautifully handsome youth sleep for eternity but with his eyes open so that the god could look directly into them when he was making love to Endymion.

Endymion in art

In art from ancient Greece to the late 18th century, Endymion is depicted most often as a young man sleeping. He is sometimes portrayed as a hunter, holding a spear, or a herder, with a shepherd's crook. Occasionally, Selene stands beside him and is identified by a crescent on her forehead. In later paintings Artemis (Diana) or other mythical goddesses are substituted for Selene. Sometimes the couple are joined by a young Eros (Cupid), the god of love. Often, a dog appears in the scene, perhaps alluding to the hunt that the sleeping Endymion will only enjoy in his dreams.

In Greek vase painting, only a few representations of Endymion exist, and although Pausanias mentions an ivory statue of Endymion at Olympia, not a single Greek statue of Endymion survives. By contrast, the sleeping figure of Endymion appears often in Roman painting, sculpture, and mosaics. There are also numerous representations of Endymion and Selene in the frescoes of Pompeii, and he was a popular figure on Roman sarcophagi from the late first century BCE onward. One explanation for the popularity of Endymion in funerary art is that his death was seen as a liberation by a deity from earthly existence, followed by an eternal slumber. This is supported by Cicero (106–43 BCE), a Roman statesman and author, who wrote that the sleep of Endymion was a comforting vision of death.

Few notable sculptures of Endymion were created until the early 19th century, when Italian artist Antonio Canova (1757–1822) produced one around 1820. Of the many paintings of Endymion, the most famous are those by the late-16th-century artists Titian and Tintoretto, the 17th-century painters Van Dyck, Poussin, and Rubens, and the 18th-century painters Boucher and Fragonard.

In literature the story of the sleeping youth also inspired English poet John Keats (1795–1821). Keats wrote a long allegory titled *Endymion*, published in 1818, which was an imaginary search for ideal beauty. The poem begins with the famous line, "A thing of beauty is a joy for ever."

FEYO SCHUDDEBOOM

Bibliography

Bulfinch, Thomas. *Bulfinch's Mythology*. New York: Barnes & Noble, 2006.

Howatson, M. C. *The Oxford Companion to Classical Literature*. New York: Oxford University Press, 2005.

Sirracos, Constantine. *History of the Olympic Games*. Long Island City, NY: Seaburn Books, 2000.

Steinhoff, Stephen, ed. *Keats' "Endymion": A Critical Edition*. New York: Whitson Publishing Company, 1987.

ERICHTHONIUS

Erichthonius was a mythical king of Athens. He was usually believed to be the son of the gods Hephaestus and Athena, and was often depicted as half man, half serpent. When he became king of Athens, he promoted the worship of his mother. He is often confused with his grandson Erechtheus.

The story of Erichthonius fits into a larger body of myths whose purpose was to justify the political supremacy of Athens in Greece by contending that the early rulers of the city were autochthonous—literally, "from the earth itself." The idea was to assert that the founders of Athens did not immigrate from other places, and that thus the city did not owe its greatness to other cities, but was a self-made power. Other dynasties traced their families back through generations of humans, but Athenian kings claimed to be direct descendants of the earth, the mother of all living beings.

In most versions of the story, Erichthonius was conceived during an encounter between Athena and Hephaestus. By one account, Athena visited the blacksmith god with an order for some armor, and Hephaestus, who was lonely after having been abandoned by Aphrodite, tried to rape her. In another version, Poseidon harbored a grudge against Athena after she had beaten him in a competition for the patronage of Athens, so encouraged Hephaestus to attack her. Athena fought hard to keep her virginity, using her knee to keep the god at bay, and Hephaestus finally discharged his semen onto her thigh. Athena wiped her leg clean with a piece of wool, which she then threw onto the ground. Divine intercourse is always procreative, and Hephaestus's seed, wrapped in wool (the product of female labor), on touching the earth, which is also female, caused the conception of the baby Erichthonius. His name refers to the circumstances of his creation: *eri-* means "wool," and *chthon-* means "earth," thus giving "wool and earth man."

Poseidon later became the father of Theseus, the greatest Athenian hero, and it may be that the myth of Erichthonius was intended to strengthen the association between Athena and her city's rulers—Theseus was born to the sixth generation after Erichthonius.

Symbolism of snakes

Like many autochthonous beings, Erichthonius was associated with snakes. Snakes are symbolically complex. While their shape suggests the male sexual organ, the fact that they can shed their skin suggests the ability to regenerate themselves unaided. That, and the fact that they lived within the earth, were both regarded as female characteristics. An Athenian vase painting represents Cecrops, the first king of Athens, as human from the waist up and serpentine below. Erichthonius might have had a snakelike torso instead of legs, or perhaps snaky feet. Another version gave him human form.

After the creation of Erichthonius, Athena hid him in a covered basket, either alone or with a snake, and entrusted it to Cecrops's virgin daughters (Pandrosus, Aglaurus, and Herse), with strict orders not to look inside. The girls peeked, and saw either a baby coiled up in a snake or a biform creature. For defying the will of Athena, they were then either slain by the snake or were driven mad, hurling themselves to their deaths from the top of the Acropolis.

In Greek mythology, knowledge and sight are intimately connected. In light of the snake's sexual connotations, the sight of it could symbolize the young girls' initiation into sexuality. Alternatively, the snake could represent the secret of creation itself. This knowledge is too powerful for mortals to comprehend and results in their madness or death.

When Erichthonius grew up, he banished Cecrops and seized the crown. As king he erected the wooden statue of Athena in what became the Erechtheum, and instituted the Panathenaic festival. During this festival, virgin girls called *arrephoroi* ("bearers of unspeakable things") reenacted his myth, transporting baskets containing sacred objects from the Parthenon to an underground cave in the grove of Aphrodite. This rite, too, suggests sexual awakening.

Erichthonius was also said to have invented the enclosed chariot, perhaps to conceal his snaky feet. He later became the constellation Auriga, the charioteer. On Athena's gold-and-ivory statue in the Parthenon, Erichthonius appeared as a snake hiding behind the goddess's shield.

The best sources for the story of Erichthonius are the mythological handbook written by Hyginus in the first century CE and the ancient travel guide to Greece by Pausanias (143–176 CE).

KATHRYN CHEW

Above: The Finding of Erichthonius *(1632–1633) by Peter Paul Rubens. As her nurse watches, Aglaurus opens the lid of the basket containing the infant Erichthonius.*

Bibliography
Graves, Robert. *The Greek Myths*. New York: Penguin, 1993.
Pausanias, and Peter Levi, trans. *Guide to Greece*. New York: Viking Press, 1984.

SEE ALSO: Theseus.

EUROPA

Europa was a princess of Tyre who attracted the amorous eye of Zeus, king of the Greek gods. Disguised as a white bull, Zeus carried her off and raped her. As a result of the crime, she gave birth to three sons who would become powerful rulers of Crete.

According to legend, one day Europa and her friends were gathering flowers in a meadow near the seashore. Zeus saw the beautiful princess and desired her. He transformed himself into a magnificent bull and galloped onto the meadow. The girls were amazed at how beautiful the bull was. His coat was as white as snow and his horns shimmered like jewels. The bull was so placid that the girls slowly wandered over to pet the beast. They offered him the choicest grasses and wove garlands for his brilliant horns. Europa was so fond of the beast that she climbed on its back. Immediately the bull jumped into the sea and, with Europa unable to escape, swam off to the island of Crete.

On Crete, Zeus revealed his true identity to the girl. They mated in a cave on Mount Dicte in a bed prepared by nymphs. According to some versions of the legend, it was the cave where Zeus spent his youth hiding from his father, Cronus.

Sons of Europa

From their union, three sons were born, and each became a ruler of part of Crete. The first and most powerful was Minos, who gave his name to the culture that arose on the island, Minoan. His brothers were Rhadamanthys and Sarpedon. Minos ruled at Knossos, largest and grandest of the Minoan palaces. Rhadamanthys was king at Phaistos, near the southern coast of the island. Sarpedon's seat of power was at Mallia, east of Knossos.

Below: Europa and Zeus, disguised as a white bull, are depicted on this decorative plate made in Greece during the fourth century BCE.

Europa was widely depicted in ancient Greek art. During the 16th and 17th centuries her story was also popular with painters. The most famous depictions of her story from this period are by Italian painter Titian (c. 1489–1576), Flemish artist Peter Paul Rubens (1577–1640), and Dutchman Rembrandt (1606–1669). Europa also gave her name to the continent to which Greece belongs, Europe.

KARELISA HARTIGAN

Bibliography

Farnaux, Alexandre, and David J. Baker, trans. *Knossos: Searching for the Legendary Palace of King Minos.* New York: Harry N. Abrams, 1996.

Ovid, and A. D. Melville, trans. *Metamorphoses.* New York: Oxford University Press, 2008.

SEE ALSO: Minos; Pasiphae; Theseus.

GALATEA

Galatea was a sea nymph who became the object of the attentions of Polyphemus, the monstrous Cyclops who tried to crush her young lover Acis to death out of jealousy. Galatea saved him by turning him into a river, but was then unable to turn him back into a human. The story of the tragic affair was a popular subject for the artists of the Renaissance.

Below: This wall painting (1597) by Annibale Carracci (1560–1609) depicts Polyphemus playing the panpipes for Galatea.

Galatea was a Nereid, that is, a daughter of Nereus, the Old Man of the Sea, and Doris, the daughter of Oceanus. Since the Nereids were sea nymphs, it is likely that the name Galatea, meaning "milk white," originally referred to the milky color of the froth and crests of the waves. Homer mentions Galatea in passing when he lists the daughters of Nereus, but the story of Galatea and Polyphemus was apparently first told by the poet Philoxenus in the fourth century BCE. In Sicily, Galatea was worshiped as a protectress of the flocks.

Galatea lived on the coast of Sicily, where the Cyclops Polyphemus fell in love with her and wooed her with passionate love songs. There are two different endings to the story. According to the more popular version, as told by the poet Theocritus and others, Polyphemus's attempts to win Galatea were in vain. She would have nothing to do with the crude giant, and every time he approached her,

Redon's *Cyclops*

In his painting of Galatea and Polyphemus, French artist Odilon Redon (1840–1916) combines features of his late, colorful style with his earlier tendency to pick somewhat bizarre subject matter. The canvas depicts the one-eyed giant looking over the sleeping sea nymph. In the foreground, Galatea lies naked in a field of flowers on a hillside. The lightness of her skin contrasts sharply with the dark green and purple of the surrounding landscape. She seems quite unaware of the presence of Polyphemus, whose towering figure protrudes from behind the ridge of the hill. The Cyclops's stooping posture, and the gentle expression of the big, round eye in the middle of his face, make him look harmless and quite endearing. Instead of bombarding the nymph with love songs, it almost looks as if the Cyclops is afraid to disturb her in her delicate slumber. At any rate, this Polyphemus is quite different from the horrible monster described by Homer (ninth or eighth century BCE) or Virgil (70–19 BCE).

Left: Looking at the painting Cyclops *(1914) by Odilon Redon is like opening a window into a fantasy world.*

Galatea in art

Galatea is often depicted in art as a nude woman riding on the back of a dolphin. Usually, Polyphemus is also present in the scene, sometimes tending to his flocks, sometimes playing a lyre or flute.

The myth of Polyphemus and Galatea does not appear in ancient Greek art, which is sometimes taken to imply that the story was invented by Philoxenus. The earliest surviving representation of the sea nymph is found in a wall painting in the house of Livia, the wife of the Emperor Augustus, on Palatine Hill in Rome. It shows Polyphemus standing in water up to his chest and leaning on a rock, looking dolefully at Galatea. A young Cupid rides on his shoulders, evidently to make fun of the giant's state of mind. Meanwhile, Galatea rides a hippocampus (a mythical sea horse) in front of Polyphemus, and seems to tease him by showing him her body while staying just outside his reach.

Galatea is represented in many wall paintings, reliefs, and mosaics of the Roman Empire. In particular, there are numerous representations of Galatea in the murals of Pompeii, which was buried by a devastating volcanic eruption in 79 CE. In an interesting wall painting from the nearby town of Herculaneum, Galatea appears modestly dressed in a chiton (a loose, full-length tunic) before a seated Polyphemus.

she would escape by withdrawing into her element, the sea. In the other version of the story, however, Galatea finally gave in to Polyphemus, and married him. She had a son by him named Galas or Galates, who became the ancestor of the Gauls (the ancient people of Gallia, modern-day France, who also founded three major settlements in Galatia, a large territory in central Turkey, in the fourth century BCE). This variant of the myth is probably based on nothing more than the similarity between the words "Galatea" and "Galates."

Ovid is one of several authors who relate that Polyphemus was in love with Galatea, but that she had already given her heart to the young shepherd Acis, the son of Faunus, whom she preferred to the monstrous and clumsy Cyclops. To amuse themselves, Acis and Galatea listened to the singing of the Cyclops, until one day Polyphemus caught the couple unawares as they lay in each other's arms on the seacoast. In a jealous rage, he crushed Acis under a huge boulder, meaning to kill him. Acis, however, cried out for help to Galatea, who instantly transformed him into a river.

Above: In this wall painting (1512–1514) by Raphael, Galatea rides in a chariot drawn by a dolphin.

In later art, the motif of Galatea riding the sea alone on a dolphin or on a chariot drawn by sea creatures is quite popular. The stories of Polyphemus and Galatea, and of Acis and Galatea, also continue to be favorite themes. In the early 1500s, Raphael decorated a wall of the Villa Farnesina in Rome with a fresco of Galatea in the sea. Next to it, a work by Sebastiano del Piombo depicts Polyphemus. Annibale Carracci depicted Polyphemus wooing Galatea (1597–1600), while Nicolas Poussin painted two studies of Galatea and Acis (1630 and 1649). In the second study, Polyphemus prowls in the background. He appears as a stern, brooding figure in the painting of Gustave Moreau (about 1880) and as a lovesick colossus in Odilon Redon's painting. The story of Acis and Galatea is also the theme of several operas, notably Handel's *Acis and Galatea*.

Two other women in classical mythology also bear the name Galatea. Neither is connected to the sea nymph. One appears in the story of Pygmalion, a sculptor who became disenchanted by mortal women and so created an image of feminine perfection. When he became enthralled with his own sculpted ideal, Venus answered his prayers and brought the statue to life as Galatea.

The other Galatea is the daughter of Eurytius, who married Lampros and lived in Phaistos on the island of Crete. When she became pregnant, her husband told her that if the child was not a boy she must kill it. When Galatea gave birth to a girl, she passed her off as a boy and gave her the masculine forename Leukippos. When her deception was discovered, Galatea prayed to the goddess Leto to transform Leukippos into a boy. Leto granted her wish and the child was saved.

FEYO SCHUDDEBOOM

Bibliography

Hesiod, and M. L. West, trans. *Theogony* and *Works and Days*. New York: Oxford University Press, 2008.

Ovid, and A. D. Melville, trans. *Metamorphoses*. New York: Oxford University Press, 2008.

SEE ALSO: Cyclopes; Pygmalion.

GANYMEDE

In Greek myth, Ganymede was
the son of Tros, king of Troy. His
extraordinary beauty came to the
attention of Zeus, king of the gods.
He carried the boy off to Mount
Olympus to serve as cupbearer to the
gods. The deities were so struck by his
beauty that they did not want it to
fade with age or perish in warfare,
but to endure forever for their delight,
so they made him immortal.

*Left: This image of a naked Ganymede holding a rooster was painted in
Greece around 500 BCE.*

There are several different legends of the actual
abduction of Ganymede. In one version,
Ganymede was borne aloft by a whirlwind and
then taken to Mount Olympus by the eagle of Zeus. In
another account, Zeus first spotted Ganymede herding a
flock of sheep on Mount Ida. The god was smitten by his
good looks and offered the boy a rooster, a traditional love
gift. In this version, the story of Ganymede acquired a
homoerotic element: Zeus brought the Trojan prince to
Olympus as his young lover. The Romans were particularly
interested in the erotic element of the myth; the Latin
equivalent of Ganymede was Catamitus. According to other
accounts, Ganymede was kidnapped by Eos, goddess of
dawn, who wanted to add him to her long list of mortal
lovers. Zeus then snatched him from her. One detail,
however, is the same in all versions of the myth: when
Ganymede was installed on Olympus, he became the
cupbearer of the gods, responsible for serving them nectar.

When Tros learned of his son's disappearance, he was
devastated. His grief touched Zeus and moved the god to
offer recompense. Zeus presented Tros with a golden vine
and two swift horses that could run over water. Zeus also
reassured him by telling him that Ganymede would
become immortal. Later, Tros offered the horses to the
famous hero Heracles in payment for destroying the
sea monster sent by Poseidon to besiege the city of
Troy. Heracles kept his part of the bargain, but Tros
reneged on his, thus earning the everlasting hatred of
heroes and gods alike.

Repercussions

When Ganymede arrived on Mount Olympus, the
cupbearer of the gods was Zeus's daughter Hebe. Hebe
and Ganymede vied with each other for the honor of
serving the gods. Eventually Ganymede won the
position and became the close companion of Zeus.

Another Olympian upset by the arrival of Ganymede
was Hera, the wife of Zeus. When Zeus took Ganymede
as his lover, Hera was consumed by jealousy. In order to
protect the boy from her wrath, Zeus granted him

Above: The Abduction of Ganymede *is one of the greatest works by Flemish artist Peter Paul Rubens.*

immortality and installed him among the stars as the constellation Aquarius. There he eternally carries water for the gods, while Aquila, the eagle, stands guard nearby.

The people of Troy expected to reap some benefits from Ganymede's move to Mount Olympus, but they were sadly disappointed. In the second choral song of *Trojan Women*, a play by Euripides (c. 486–c. 406 BCE), the women of the city lament that the boy's abduction has brought them no favors from the gods, and that Ganymede himself has no concern for the fate of his native city.

Ganymede is thought to be unique among the characters of Greek mythology: he is the only mortal who did not have to win the right of abode on Mount Olympus. Pollux, Heracles, and Asclepius, each of whom had one divine parent, all had to earn their place among the gods. Tithonus, also taken aloft from Troy, was granted immunity from death, but he did not gain exemption from old age, and thus his "gift" was more of a curse than a blessing. Yet the wholly mortal Ganymede was granted

immortality without any effort on his part, or any physical transformation. His elevation to Olympus was in itself sufficient to strip away his mortality.

Ganymede in art

Ganymede has been a favorite subject for artists since classical times. In the art of ancient Greece and Rome, he is often depicted holding a rooster or receiving the rooster from Zeus as a symbol of his love. Later artists, such as Peter Paul Rubens (1577–1640), tended to focus on the dramatic moment when the eagle snatched the boy and bore him off to Mount Olympus. By the mid-16th century, the church had begun to frown on nudity and the subject became less popular.

Karelisa Hartigan

Bibliography

Euripides, and P. Burian and A. Shapiro, eds. *The Complete Euripides.* New York: Oxford University Press, 2009–2010.
Homer, and Robert Fagles, trans. *The Iliad.* New York: Penguin, 2009.

See also: Laomedon; Tithonus.

GORGONS

In Greek myth the Gorgons were three monstrous sisters. The most famous of the trio was Medusa, whose snake-covered head was so frightful in appearance that people who looked upon it were turned to stone.

The Gorgons were triplets. Their mother and father, the sea deities Phorcys and Ceto, were also the parents of the Graeae, another set of female triplets who were born old and shared a single eye and tooth. According to Hesiod, the Greek poet of the eighth century BCE, two of the Gorgons, Stheno and Euryale, were "ageless and immortal." The third, more famous, sister was Medusa: she was mortal and met a violent end. Greek artists depicted the Gorgons as grotesque creatures with snakes for hair, and usually with fixed grins or screamlike expressions, boars' tusks, brazen hands, and golden wings.

In one version of the story, Medusa was originally a beautiful priestess who was working in the temple of Athena, the goddess of war and wisdom, when she was assaulted by Poseidon, the god of the sea. Athena was outraged by this act of sacrilege, but she lacked the power to attack Poseidon directly, so she took her revenge on him by transforming Medusa into a hideous Gorgon. According to a slightly different legend, Athena turned Medusa into a monster after the priestess had boasted that she was more beautiful than the goddess she served. This theme of pride going before a fall—hubris being eventually punished—occurs quite frequently in ancient Greek mythology.

The slaying of Medusa

Polydectes, king of the island of Seriphos, fell in love with a princess called Danae, but before he could marry her he wanted Perseus, her son by Zeus, out of the way. So he ordered the young hero to bring him the head of Medusa as a wedding present. The king thought that this was effectively a death sentence: the Gorgon would surely turn Perseus to stone.

Above: The Head of Medusa *by Italian painter Caravaggio (1573–1610). Even after her head had been severed, Medusa's gaze could still turn people to stone.*

Before Perseus could find Medusa, he first had to confront the Graeae, whose main task was to bar the road leading to their sisters the Gorgons. Perseus stole the Graeae's single eye and tooth and refused to return them until they told him the location of the Gorgons, which turned out to be in the far west, the place of the setting sun and the entrance to the underworld. The gods supplied Perseus with the other equipment he needed to complete his task. That included the cap of Hades, god of the underworld, which would make him invisible (*Hades* means "unseen"); the winged sandals of Hermes, the messenger of the gods; a purse known as a *kibisis* for carrying the Gorgon's head; and a scimitar, a curved sword.

Perseus used his winged sandals to fly over the ocean to the home of the Gorgons. On the advice of Athena, he approached Medusa backward, taking care not to look at the monster directly, but observing her reflection in his polished shield. Perseus decapitated Medusa as she slept, stuffed her head into the *kibisis,* and then, without ever looking at his prize, used his winged sandals and the cap of invisibility to escape the wrath of his victim's sisters, Stheno and Euryale. In one version of this myth, it was at this point that two children of Poseidon sprang fully formed

Above: This illustration by Philip van Gunst (18th century) shows Perseus slaying Medusa. Both the hero and his winged horse, Pegasus, avert their gaze from the monster, because to look at her is fatal.

from the blood that flowed from Medusa's neck. One was Pegasus, the winged horse; the other was Chrysaor, a giant with a golden sword.

Medusa's head was a powerful weapon for Perseus. When he fell in love with Andromeda and saved her from a sea monster, he turned her betrothed and his followers to stone so that he could marry her. He freed his mother, Danae, from the evil clutches of Polydectes, king of the island of Seriphos, by turning him and his followers to stone. He then made Polydectes' brother, Dictys, king. Perseus is also said to have used Medusa's head to turn Atlas to stone, thus easing the strain felt by the Titan who had been condemned to bear the weight of the heavens for eternity. Finally, Perseus gave Medusa's head to Athena, who placed it on her aegis (shield) or her breastplate as a symbol of her protective power.

Gorgons as symbols

The image of the Gorgon appears frequently in ancient Greek temples and on coins and vases. Most scholars believe that the likeness of the monster was intended to ward off evil. However, other interpretations exist. Some commentators have seen the Gorgon as a symbol of female energy: the face of Medusa depicts the scream of birth labor, while her power to turn people to stone represents the destructive capabilities of bad women. By placing the monster's head on her armor, Athena tames and harnesses the Gorgon's wild, elemental power.

KIRK SUMMERS

Bibliography

Garber, Marjorie, and Nancy J. Vickers, eds. *The Medusa Reader.* New York: Routledge, 2003.

Wilk, Stephen R. *Medusa: Solving the Mystery of the Gorgon.* New York: Oxford University Press, 2000.

SEE ALSO: Andromeda; Danae; Harpies; Perseus.

HARPIES

In Greek myth, the Harpies (meaning "snatchers") were female monsters who caused mischief, tormented wrongdoers, and carried souls to the underworld. They were known for their hideous appearance and smell.

In the earliest accounts, the Harpies were not monstrous—they were simply spirits who represented windy or stormy weather, and they were depicted as beautiful young women with wings. Over time, however, they developed into terrifying beasts. They had long, fair hair and the faces and upper bodies of women, but the wings, tails, legs, and claws of birds of prey, with sharp talons made of metal. They were always ravenously hungry, and would steal food or even eat their victims before carrying away their souls. The Harpies were repulsive to look at, and they spread filth everywhere they went. They stank so much that whatever they touched gave off a terrible smell.

There are several different stories of how many Harpies there were and where they came from. According to the eighth-century-BCE Greek poet Hesiod, they were the daughters of Thaumas, who was a son of Gaia, the earth goddess. In Hesiod's account, the Harpies were the sisters of Iris, the personification of the rainbow and a messenger of the gods. Other sources mention that they were the daughters of Typhon, another of Gaia's sons, and Echidna, a monster who was half woman and half snake. Some stories say there were countless Harpies; in others there were between one and four of them. At least four of the Harpies had names: Celaeno, Aello, Ocypete, and Podarge.

Left: A Harpy standing between two sphinxes on a Corinthian amphora (c. 725–c. 600 BCE). Sphinxes were believed to have a woman's head and a lion's body.

The Harpies could be sent by the gods—especially Zeus, Hera, and Athena—to punish people, and they were sometimes referred to as "the hounds of Zeus," but they could also cause problems on their own by stealing, destroying property, causing storms, and kidnapping people.

The Harpies and Phineus

The most famous myth involving the Harpies is the tale of King Phineus. He was a king of Thrace, in northern Greece, who offended the gods. There are various accounts about what he did wrong, but in the best-known version he remarried after his wife died, and, in his desperation to please his new bride, allowed her to torture his children, who ended up being blinded. In another version Phineus was granted the gift of prophecy, but foretold the future so well that he infuriated the gods by revealing their plans.

As punishment, Phineus was himself blinded, and the gods also sent the Harpies to make his life a misery. The monsters constantly snatched his food from his hands or spoiled it with their foul stench, so Phineus could never get enough to eat and grew painfully thin. He was finally rescued when Jason and the Argonauts came past Thrace on their journey to fetch the Golden Fleece. Two of the Argonauts, Calais and Zetes, the brothers of Phineus's first wife, decided to help the king, and drove the Harpies away to the Strophades Islands. They were going to kill them, but the Harpies' sister, Iris, persuaded the Argonauts to spare them if they promised to keep away from Phineus. In some versions the Harpies then went to Crete; in others they stayed in the Strophades.

The Children of Podarge

Podarge, one of the Harpies, was the mother of Xanthus and Balius, the two magical horses that ran like the wind and pulled the chariot of the Greek hero Achilles during the Trojan War. The horses' father was Zephyrus, the West Wind. The gods gave Xanthus and Balius to the hero Peleus as a present on his marriage to the sea goddess Thetis—the horses then passed to the couple's son, Achilles, when he went to Troy.

Soon after the horses were born, Hera, the wife of Zeus, gave Xanthus the power of speech, and during the Trojan War he spoke to Achilles. He warned him that although he would survive a forthcoming battle, he would die soon afterward. The Furies, the spirits of vengeance, struck Xanthus dumb to punish him for what he had told Achilles. When Patroclus, Achilles' best friend, was killed at Troy, both Xanthus and Balius wept, and Zeus was sorry that he had allowed them to get involved in the fighting and violence of humans.

The Harpies and Aeneas

The Harpies also played a role in the story of Aeneas, survivor of the Trojan War and the son of Aphrodite, goddess of love. After Troy was destroyed, Aeneas wandered far and wide until, following a prophecy that he would establish a great city, he went to Italy and founded Rome.

During his journey, Aeneas sailed to the Strophades Islands, where the Harpies were living. He and his men slaughtered some wild goats and cattle for food. They made offerings to the gods before eating, but as they sat on the beach to enjoy their feast, the Harpies swooped down, snatched their food, and spread stinking filth and dirt all around. The sailors moved to another spot, but the Harpies found them and ruined their food again. Aeneas ordered his men to fight, but their blades could not harm the monsters. Celaeno, the leader of the Harpies, told the sailors that, although they would end up in Italy, they would suffer terrible hunger as a punishment for trying to kill her and her sisters, and would not be able to found a city until they were so hungry that they had eaten their tables.

In Italy, after landing at the mouth of the Tiber River, Aeneas and his men were so hungry that they ate the round bread platters on which they had been served a meal. They realized that these were the "tables" to which Celaeno had referred.

Left: The Argonauts Calais and Zetes rescue Phineus from the Harpies in this engraving by French artist Bernard Picart (1673–1733). The overturned amphora indicates the damage caused by the monsters.

Above: Aeneas and His Companions Fighting the Harpies *by French painter François Perrier (1594–1649). The mischief caused by the Harpies was a means for the Greeks to explain bad luck in their lives.*

Delivering justice; stealing souls

According to Roman poet Virgil (70–19 BCE), who recounted Aeneas's travels in the *Aeneid*, in her speech to Aeneas and his men, Celaeno refers to herself as "the eldest of the Furies." The Furies (or Erinyes) were the female spirits of justice and vengeance who punished wrongdoers, often by driving them insane. The myth of Pandareos also links the Harpies to the Furies. Pandareos was a man from Crete who upset Zeus by stealing his golden dog and giving it to Tantalus, one of Zeus's sons by the Titaness Pluto. Zeus turned Pandareos into stone as a punishment. His daughters, Clytia and Cameira, were cared for by Aphrodite, who fed them milk and honey and found husbands for them, but just as the two young women were about to be married, the Harpies took them away to be slaves to the Furies.

The Harpies' connections with the Furies, as well as their actions in other myths, suggest that people believed that they were able to carry away the souls of the dead. Female spirits or superhuman beings who had this power are found in stories from many ancient cultures. In Norse myth, the Valkyries took dead warriors into Valhalla, where they lived in a great hall alongside the chief god Odin. Like the Harpies, the Valkyries could be either beautiful or terrifying. In Egyptian myth, the goddess Taweret carried the dead into the next world, while the Celts believed that this role was performed by Morrigan, a raven-goddess who ate the flesh of dead people and carried away their souls.

The meaning of the Harpies

To the ancient Greeks, the Harpies represented the punishment that came from displeasing the gods, but they were also associated with unfairness and random bad luck. Like the winds that they originally embodied, the Harpies could come out of nowhere, ruin plans, and destroy people's lives. People blamed them for storms (see box, page 112) and for any small objects or items of food that mysteriously went missing.

In modern times, the word *harpy* is sometimes used to mean a mean, heartless woman. However, some people

Above: A terra-cotta Harpy overlooking the Aegean Sea on the Greek island of Thera. The Harpies were first known as weather spirits, and the Greeks often blamed them for causing storms.

Mythology and the Weather

The Harpies' names reflect the fact that they were originally storm spirits: *Celaeno* means "storm cloud," *Aello* means "rainstorm," *Ocypete* means "swift flier," and *Podarge* means "swift-foot." Although they developed into monstrous creatures, they continued to be associated with weather and were blamed for strong winds and storms.

Many gods, spirits, and monsters in mythologies from around the world are associated with different kinds of weather. In Greek mythology, for example, the Harpies' sister Iris was the goddess of the rainbow, and the god Aeolus controlled the winds. In Australian Aboriginal mythology, the Rainbow Serpent, one of the most powerful of all deities, controlled storms, rain, and floods. Many cultures have a god of rain, such as En-kai or Ngai, the rain god of the African Masai people. Since weather comes from the sky, it makes sense that people throughout history have interpreted rain, thunder, rainbows, and other forms of weather as signs, punishments, or rewards from the gods, who were usually thought to live above Earth.

also see the Harpies as a symbol of feminism, because they were strong female characters who represented male fears about female power.

Sources and cultural impact

A number of ancient authors gave accounts of the Harpies, including the Greeks Hesiod, Apollonius of Rhodes (third century BCE), and Apollodorus (second century BCE) and the Roman Virgil. In the *Odyssey*, Homer (ninth–eighth century BCE) describes the Harpies as wind spirits.

Many artists have depicted the Harpies. They appear in pictures on ancient Greek vases and temple carvings, and they have inspired more recent works, including paintings by French illustrator Gustav Doré (1832–1883) and British Pre-Raphaelite painter Evelyn de Morgan (c. 1850–1919).

ANNA CLAYBOURNE

Bibliography

Apollonius Rhodius, and R. Hunter, trans. *Jason and the Golden Fleece.* New York: Oxford University Press, 2009.

Rose, Carol. *Giants, Monsters, and Dragons.* New York: Norton, 2000.

Virgil, and Robert Fagles, trans. *The Aeneid.* New York: Penguin, 2009.

SEE ALSO: Achilles; Aeneas; Jason; Tantalus.

HECTOR

Hector is one of the main characters in the stories of the Trojan War. A Trojan prince and elder brother of Paris, he was viewed even by his ancient Greek enemies as being noble, honest, and fearsome in battle.

Hector was the eldest of the many children of King Priam of Troy. Although it was another of Priam's sons, Paris, who triggered the Trojan War by running away with Helen, wife of Spartan king Menelaus, the ancient Greeks viewed Hector with respect and admiration. He was their enemy, but he was also a figure of great courage and principle. The Greeks also believed that there was ill feeling between the brothers and that Hector criticized Paris for abducting Helen, even though his loyalty to his brother and his city then led him to fight for Paris's cause.

During the Trojan War, Hector was the leader of the Trojan forces in their battle against the besieging Greeks. Yet Hector's story is more than simply a tale of military might; it also emphasizes the importance the ancient Greeks placed on the institution of the family. In Homer's *Iliad*, thought to date from around 800 BCE, there is one emotional scene in particular when Hector, fresh from his feats on the battlefield, enjoys a happy moment with his wife, Andromache, and their young

Right: This is a model for the statue of Hector created by Italian sculptor Antonio Canova (1757–1822).

son, Astyanax. Later in the story Homer also tells of the deep grief felt by Andromache and the Trojans in general at the news of Hector's death.

Greece, Troy, and the Trojan War

The ancient city of Troy was part of the network of city-states around the Mediterranean with which Greece traded and interacted. According to legend, King Priam was a descendant of Zeus. A seer told him that the newborn Paris would one day bring destruction to Troy, so Priam abandoned the baby on a mountainside to die, but he was soon rescued by a shepherd. When he grew up, Paris returned to Troy. Priam then sent him to Greece, where he visited King Menelaus of Sparta. Aphrodite, goddess of love, had promised Paris that he would marry the most beautiful woman in the world, who was Menelaus's wife, Helen. Helen and Paris ran away together and settled in Troy. When the Greeks learned of this affront to the king, they assembled an army and sailed to Troy to attack the city and win back Helen. This began the Trojan War.

King Priam was very old when the war began, so his son Hector was chosen as leader of the Trojan army. Hector was the obvious choice as leader not just because he was the prince but because he was renowned for his military skill. The Greeks knew that unless they could kill him, they would probably fail to topple Troy. Hector was a formidable enemy, and he was often helped by the god Apollo (see box, page 114). This was partly why, according to legend, the Trojan War lasted for as long as 10 years.

Above: This painting by Giovanni Demin (1786–1859) depicts Hector, on the right wearing a large helmet, urging his brother Paris, in the center almost nude, to do the noble thing and join in the fight against the besieging Greeks. Helen, wearing a white dress, sits on Paris's right. The scene takes place in a temple dedicated to Aphrodite.

Even though Hector was a skilled warrior and killed many of the Greeks' best fighters, such as Epigeus and Archesilaus, he did not enjoy war but rather saw the defense of the city as his duty. On one occasion he tried to resolve the war by arranging a duel between Paris and Menelaus, but Aphrodite interfered on Paris's behalf and the duel did not have a conclusive outcome.

The death of Hector

The Greeks' best soldier in the Trojan War was Achilles. However, after a disagreement with Agamemnon, the leader of the Greek armies, Achilles refused to fight, and the Trojans gained the upper hand. At this point Achilles' best friend and companion, Patroclus, decided to go into battle in Achilles' chariot, wearing Achilles' armor. He reasoned that if the Greek soldiers thought he was Achilles, they would be encouraged to fight harder. He was right, and the Greeks began to force the Trojans back toward the city. Seeing what he thought was Achilles joining the battle,

Intervention of Apollo

The Trojan War split the loyalties of the Olympian deities, with some favoring the Greeks and some the Trojans. One of the most powerful gods to intervene in the mortal conflict was Apollo. According to Homer, Apollo's involvement in the war came late, some nine years after the fighting began, when the daughter of one of Apollo's priests was abducted by Agamemnon. The angry god sent a pestilence into the Greek camp, ailing and killing many soldiers. Several of his later involvements directly involved Hector. When Hector was badly wounded by a large bolder thrown at him by the Greek warrior Ajax, Apollo was ordered by Zeus to heal Hector's wounds. Another more famous incident occurred when Patroclus was battling Hector. Apollo first knocked off Patroclus's helmet, then his shield and breastplate, and finally the deity split Patroclus's spear, leaving the Greek hero completely defenseless against Hector. When Achilles avenged his friend's death, Apollo was unable to save Hector from Achilles' deadly spear. Yet Apollo did preserve the Trojan's body while Achilles dragged it behind his chariot. Apollo also played a part in the death of Achilles. Before Troy fell, Paris shot an arrow at Achilles and Apollo guided the arrow toward the only vulnerable part of Achilles' body, his heel.

Hector was afraid. He knew that Achilles was the only fighter who could match him. Overcoming his fear, Hector fought his enemy in single combat, and since it turned out to be Patroclus and not Achilles, Hector killed him easily. Hector took Achilles' armor from Patroclus's body and afterward wore it himself.

When he realized that Hector had killed his friend Patroclus, the grieving Achilles resolved to take his revenge and rejoined the battle. Seeing the danger from Achilles, Priam ordered the Trojan army to retreat back into the city, but Hector refused. He stayed outside to fight Achilles, but then lost his nerve and began to run away. Achilles chased him around the battlefield, until the goddess of war, Athena, who favored the Greeks, deceived Hector. She appeared to him in the form of one of his brothers, Deiphobus, and encouraged him to stand and fight. Tricked into thinking he had his brother to help him, Hector turned to face Achilles. It was then that Achilles killed Hector with a spear wound to the neck.

After Hector's death

Not content with having killed Hector, Achilles strung the Trojan's body to his chariot and dragged it around the battlefield before taking it back to his camp. Urged on by Zeus, Hector's brokenhearted father, Priam, visited Achilles and begged to be given the body. Achilles took pity on the old king and released the corpse. Priam then returned to Troy with Hector's body and prepared it for a funeral.

Not long after Hector's death, the Greeks finally tricked their way into Troy using the Trojan Horse, burned most of the city to the ground, and took Helen back to Greece. Hector's son, Astyanax, was thrown from the battlements and killed in case he tried to take revenge after he grew up, and Andromache was taken prisoner.

Hector and Troy

In the story of the Trojan War, especially in Homer's version, Hector is not only a great hero, but also acts as a symbol of Troy and its fate. Like Troy, he is strong, solid, and unyielding and stands firm against the Greek attack for a huge length of time. Troy's hopes depend on him, and while he holds out, so does the city. Yet just as Hector is

Below: This sarcophagus depicts Achilles on his chariot dragging the dead body of Hector in front of the Trojans. Achilles finally released the body to the dead hero's grieving father, King Priam, for burial.

Hector as Cult Hero

In ancient Greece from about the third to the eighth century BCE, many legendary heroes, such as Hector, Heracles, and Achilles, had cult followings that rivaled the worship of the major Olympians. Generally such heroes were considered semidivine: for example, Hector's father, Priam, was said to have been the grandson of a river god; Heracles was the son of Zeus; and Achilles the son of the sea goddess Thetis. The tradition of worshiping a particular hero is known as a hero cult, and the followers of a particular hero cult would make offerings to their hero. For instance, they would sacrifice animals, such as sheep, or pour a liquid, such as blood, wine, or oil, onto the ground at the site where the hero was believed to have been buried. They would also pray to their hero to help them, and they believed that the hero would occasionally come back to life at the spot where his body was buried.

The cult of Hector was followed mostly in and around Troy, where he was thought to have been buried. There was also a cult dedicated to Hector at the Greek city of Thebes. This was because, according to one version of the legend, Hector's body had been removed from Troy and buried there.

Left: Tears of Andromache, *by French artist Jacques-Louis David (1748–1825), depicts the widow and her son grieving beside Hector's corpse. David chose to paint Hector because his qualities made him a popular hero during the French Revolution.*

doomed, so too is Troy doomed. The way Hector is tricked just before his death, and the humiliating way Achilles treats his body, are soon echoed by the Greeks. They trick the Trojans with the hollow wooden horse, and then burn and destroy the city and humiliate its people. Troy's weakness, like Hector's, is its refusal to do anything but keep fighting. Instead of negotiating or striking a deal that might end the war, Troy relies solely on its military power—just as Hector relies on his strength—and is taken advantage of by the cunning superiority of the Greeks.

Admiration of the Greeks

Even though Hector was a Trojan, the ancient Greeks respected him and regarded him as a military leader worth emulating. They admired his calmness, courage, and sense of duty, believing that these qualities were more useful on the battlefield than the unpredictable, often childish moods of his Greek counterpart, Achilles.

Hector never lied, cheated, or resorted to underhand tricks to win his victories (although Apollo did unfairly intervene on his behalf). He was always honest and honorable, the only lapse being when he took Achilles' armor from the corpse of Patroclus and wore it himself. He could not understand how others, such as his brother Paris, could be immoral, lazy, or ungentlemanly. In addition to lauding him in epic poems and myths, the ancient Greeks also depicted Hector in their art, and some groups even worshiped him like a god (see box).

Despite all of Hector's positive qualities, he was nevertheless a tragic figure. By linking Hector so closely to his family and by showing the emotional devastation felt by his wife at the news of his death, Homer demonstrates that the victims of war are not just the soldiers but their families as well.

Various sources of Hector

Homer's *Iliad* is considered to be the first major work about the Trojan War. A significant portion of the epic poem focuses on Hector's life during the final stages of the war, and the poem ends with his funeral. The *Iliad* does not include the fall of Troy, although Homer does mention this in his other great work, the *Odyssey*. A later dramatist, Euripides (c. 486–c. 406 BCE), featured Hector's wife, Andromache, in his play *The Trojan Women*, about the fate of the women of Troy after the city's defeat. Other classical writers, such as Pindar (c. 522–c. 438 BCE), Apollodorus (third century BCE), and Ovid (43 BCE–17 CE), reworked and added to the story of the Trojan War. It is from them that most of the details about the end of the war and the fate of Hector's family have been passed down.

Although in modern terms, Hector is not as famous as some of the other Trojan War characters, such as Helen, he has featured in numerous paintings that depict scenes from the Trojan War. He also often appears in works of literature regarding the Trojan War, such as William Shakespeare's play *Troilus and Cressida* and an opera, *King Priam*, by British composer Michael Tippett (1905–1998).

ANNA CLAYBOURNE

Bibliography

Euripides, and P. Burian and A. Shapiro, eds. *The Complete Euripides.* New York: Oxford University Press, 2009–2010.

Homer, and Robert Fagles, trans. *The Iliad.* New York: Penguin, 2009.

Shakespeare, William. *The History of Troilus and Cressida.* New York: Penguin, 2000.

SEE ALSO: Achilles; Hecuba; Helen; Patroclus; Priam.

HECUBA

Hecuba was the chief wife of Priam, king of Troy, and the mother of many of his children, including sons Hector, Paris, and Troilus and daughters Cassandra, Creusa, and Polyxena.

There is no historical evidence that Hecuba ever existed, but she plays a major role in ancient Greek mythology. Ancient sources are divided on the names of Hecuba's parents. Homer, a Greek epic poet of about the eighth century BCE, described her as the daughter of Dymas, a native of Phrygia in western Asia, but according to Greek tragic playwright Euripides (c. 486– c. 406 BCE), her father was Cisseus. Other early writers give her mother's name as Evagora, Glaucippe, or Teleclia. However, Hecuba's importance in myth does not derive from her ancestry, but from her role as the wife of Priam and mother of several of his daughters and 19 of his sons, including Hector, the greatest warrior of the Trojans.

During Priam's reign, Troy was besieged for 10 years by the Greeks. According to Homer, the conflict ended when the Greek armies captured Troy, burned it to the ground, and killed or enslaved its inhabitants. All the stories about Hecuba are set against the background of the destruction of her city.

The fall of Troy

Until the war, Troy had been the wealthiest and most powerful city in Asia Minor. As Priam's chief wife and the mother of many of his children, most of them sons, Hecuba's status and happiness seemed assured. Yet the decade of the Trojan War stripped her of everything: her family, her home, her social status, and her personal freedom. During the conflict she sent her youngest son, Polydorus, to Polymestor, king of Thrace, for safety. When Troy fell to the Greeks, Hecuba was handed over to Odysseus as a slave. While accompanying Odysseus on his homeward journey to Greece, she discovered the corpse of Polydorus and avenged his murder by Polymestor by killing two of the latter's children and tearing out his eyes. Hecuba was eventually turned into a fiery-eyed dog.

Left: The Dream of Hecuba *is one of the panels in Pippi de' Gianuzzi's* Scenes from the Trojan War *fresco, painted in the late 1530s.*

Those are the bare bones of the legend of Hecuba. The story became popular with later writers, who did much to embellish her biography and character. Some of the details they appended are contradictory, however.

According to most Greek sources, the Trojan War began after the Trojan prince Paris, Hecuba's second son by Priam, eloped with the wife of Menelaus, king of Sparta. In response to this outrage, the Greeks mounted an expedition to rescue Helen from the enemy. According to Pindar (c. 522–c. 438 BCE), a poet from the city of Thebes in Boeotia (northwestern Greece), while Hecuba was pregnant with Paris she had a vivid dream that the son born to her was a firebrand that set fire to the city. The soothsayer Cassandra interpreted the dream to mean that Paris would bring destruction to the whole state. (In Homer's *Iliad*, Cassandra had been merely a daughter of Hecuba and Priam; her role as a prophetess was added by later authors.) Alarmed by this prophecy, King Priam gave orders that his child be left out to die on Mount Ida. Paris was rescued by a shepherd, however, and as a young man he was accepted back into the city, where he inevitably came to fulfill the seer's prediction.

All but one of Hecuba's children died during the Trojan War. Of the sons whose names were recorded by the author Apollodorus (fl. 140 BCE), a collector and probably an embellisher of myths, Antiphus, Deiphobus, Hector, Hipponous, Pammon, Polites, Troilus, and Paris himself were killed in combat. Polydorus, her youngest son, and her infant grandchild Astyanax (the only son of Hector) were murdered shortly after the end of the war. Her daughters Cassandra, Creusa, Laodice, and Polyxena all died during the fall of the city or shortly afterward. Hecuba's sole surviving offspring was Helenus, who spent some time after the war as a slave but later became king of Epirus.

After the war

In the *Iliad*—Homer's account of the ninth year of the Trojan war—Hecuba remains always in the background, fulfilling the role of the bereaved queen destined to survive the sack of Troy, the loss of her husband, and nearly all her children. The latter part of her life became a favorite subject of Greek tragedy. Hecuba features in two great plays by Euripides. In *The Trojan Women*, she is handed over to Odysseus at the end of the conflict and has to endure the sacrifice of her daughter Polyxena on Achilles' tomb and the murder of her grandchild, Hector's only son, Astyanax. Hecuba is powerless to intervene as her daughter Cassandra is given as a slave to Agamemnon, the leader of the Greeks, and as Andromache, her daughter-in-law, the

widow of Hector, is handed over to another Greek captain. Finally Hecuba herself is led away, lamenting the fate of her city, as the slave of the Greek Odysseus.

In *Hecuba* Euripides gives a different account of the end of the queen's life. She discovers the murder of her last remaining son, Polydorus, and the prophecy is made that she will later be transformed into a dog. Her daughter, Polyxena, accompanies Hecuba on Odysseus's ship, but the Greeks then decide to sacrifice her to Achilles. Shortly after Polyxena's death, word is brought to Hecuba that the body of her son, Polydorus, has been found washed up on shore. As in other versions of the story, Polydorus had been sent for safekeeping to Polymestor, king of Thrace, at the beginning of the war, only to be murdered by the monarch once Troy fell.

According to Euripides, Hecuba exacted a savage vengeance on Polymestor. She went to Thrace, pitched camp, and enticed him and his sons into a tent, where she and other Trojan women murdered the king's own children before his eyes, and then blinded him.

Having lost everything else, Hecuba now lost her mind, and at last even her humanity. Euripides depicts her being driven mad with grief. In the end the prophecy was fulfilled: Hecuba was transformed into a barking dog; she threw herself from Odysseus's ship and drowned in the sea.

Hecuba in art

Although many of the great characters and exciting incidents from the Trojan War are frequently represented in art, there are relatively few paintings of Hecuba. However, there are two outstanding exceptions to this general rule. Italian Renaissance artist Giuseppe Maria Crespi (1665–1747)—known as lo Spagnolo—painted *Hecuba Blinding Polymnestor*, a masterpiece which is now housed in the Musée des Beaux Arts in Brussels, Belgium. Another famous depiction of the Trojan queen appears in the series of frescoes known as *Scenes from the Trojan War*. These were painted by Pippi de' Gianuzzi (c. 1499–1546) on the walls of the Reggia di Gonzaga (the ducal apartments) in Mantua, Italy.

LAUREL BOWMAN

Bibliography
Homer, and Robert Fagles, trans. *The Iliad*. New York: Penguin, 2009.
Homer, and Robert Fagles, trans. *The Odyssey*. New York: Penguin, 2009.

SEE ALSO: Cassandra; Hector; Helen; Odysseus; Paris; Priam.

HELEN

Helen, or Helene, was a mythic heroine in ancient Greece and a local divinity in Sparta. Reputed to have been the most beautiful woman of her time, and possibly of all time, Helen was the wife of Menelaus, king of Sparta, and the lover of Paris, a prince of Troy. Her abduction by Paris caused the Trojan War, and as a result she is almost always called Helen of Troy. Helen is the subject of several plays and poems, and according to one, at the time of her death she was made immortal by Zeus.

Helen's beauty is credited with causing the Trojan War—"the face that launch'd a thousand ships" according to playwright Christopher Marlowe (1564–1593). She was the daughter of the Greek queen Leda and either Zeus or Tyndareos, a mortal. The uncertainty surrounding the true identity of Helen's father lies in the myth of Zeus and Leda. Zeus fell in love with Leda, the wife of King Tyndareos, and transformed himself into a swan in order to mate with her. The children of this union were Helen and her brother, Pollux. On the same night Tyndareos made love to Leda and she became pregnant by him with Clytemnestra and Castor, who were mortal. The brothers became known as the Dioscuri, or "sons of Zeus." In antiquity, several places in Greece claimed to display the egg from which Helen was hatched.

Another older but less common version of the story has Nemesis, goddess of retribution, as Helen's mother, making Helen the daughter of two divine parents. In this version, in which Zeus was also said to have used the swan disguise, Helen was given to Leda to raise as her daughter. Nemesis was a divine personification of the punishment that awaits those who step out of bounds and commit the crime of *hybris* (exaggerated pride). The role of Nemesis as mother of Helen connects with a tradition that makes the Trojan War a form of divine retribution against mortals.

According to Stesichorus (fl. 600–550 BCE), a poet of ancient Greece, Helen's mortal father, Tyndareos, forgot to perform a sacrifice of thanks to the goddess Aphrodite during his wedding. Angry at the mortal's mistake, the goddess punished him by making his daughters faithless to their husbands: Helen was unfaithful to Menelaus and Clytemnestra murdered her husband, Agamemnon. Even as a young girl Helen's beauty made her vulnerable. In one myth she was carried off by Theseus, the Greek hero and slayer of the Minotaur, but was reclaimed by her brothers before any harm could come to her. Another similar version has it that as a result of her relationship with Theseus, Helen was the mother of Iphigeneia and entrusted the young girl to her sister, Clytemnestra, who was married and who raised the girl as her own. Most other accounts of Iphigeneia have Clytemnestra and Agamemnon as her real parents.

When Helen was a young woman, the news of her beauty spread throughout Greece, and as a result she had many suitors, especially from powerful, aristocratic families. Not wanting the young men's competition for Helen to cause strife, Tyndareos made her many suitors swear to support the claim of whomever Helen chose to marry and to avenge any attempts to take her from her legitimate spouse. In the end Helen married Menelaus, a son of Atreus of Argos, and they had a daughter, Hermione.

The abduction of Helen

Paris's seduction of Helen was the result of an incident known as the Judgment of Paris. Eris, the goddess of strife and discord, was angry at not having been invited to the wedding of Peleus and Thetis, so she disrupted the party by casting in the midst of the divine guests a golden apple, inscribed "To the Fairest." A dispute arose among the goddesses Hera, Athena, and Aphrodite over who deserved the honor, and Paris, prince of Troy, was chosen as the judge.

Right: This depiction of Helen, by German artist Franz von Stuck (1863–1928), was painted in the early 20th century. It shows Helen in classical pose surrounded by furniture and images of antiquity.

TADELT·NICHT·DIE·TROER·VND·HELLVMSCHIENTEN·ACHÆER·
DIE·VM·EIN·SOLCHES·WEIB·SO·LANG·AVSHARREN·IM·ELEND!
EINER·VNSTERBLICHEN·GŒTTIN·FVERWAHR·GLEICHT·JENE·VON·ANSEHN!

HOMER·ILIAS.

Right: The fourth-century-BCE sketchings on this bronze mirror depict Menelaus and Helen. The scene, one of the most popular in ancient Greek art, shows the moment when, after Troy has fallen, Helen reveals herself naked to her husband to stop him from killing her.

The three contestants were brought to the wilds of Mount Ida in Anatolia, where Paris, who lived as a shepherd, was tending his flocks. Each goddess offered a reward should he choose her. Hera offered rule over men; Athena, victory in battle; and Aphrodite, the most beautiful woman on earth. Paris gave the apple to Aphrodite, but soon discovered that his prize, Helen, was already married.

Intending to seduce Helen, Paris went as a guest to the house of Menelaus, where he succeeded in winning her over. Paris took Helen away, together with precious objects from the palace. This violation of hospitality angered the gods, particularly Zeus, protector of the relationship between host and guest, and Hera and Athena, who had a grudge against Paris because he chose Aphrodite over them.

The Trojan War

Menelaus and his brother, Agamemnon, called on all the suitors who had sworn the oath to Helen's father. They gathered a great fleet and sailed to Troy to reclaim her. Thus began the Trojan War, which, according to the poet Homer (c. ninth–eighth century BCE), lasted for more than 10 years.

Homer's *Iliad* is the most famous narrative of the war, and in it he portrays the relationship between Helen and Paris as less than harmonious. During the war she berates him for physical cowardice on the battlefield and resists his amorous approaches. She recalls the virtues of her previous husband and curses her own faithlessness, but after Aphrodite threatens her, Helen finally goes to Paris's bed.

Homer depicts Helen as a woman full of shame and at the mercy of desire. Although Helen was reviled by Priam's other sons, in Book Three of the *Iliad*, the old men of Troy see her and declared that there was no shame for the Greeks and Trojans in fighting over her beauty. Paris repeatedly refuses to give her up, and an attempt to settle the matter by a duel between him and Menelaus is deliberately sabotaged by Aphrodite.

After the war

The *Iliad* ends before the fall of Troy, so much of Helen's story comes to us from other sources. Late in the war, after Paris had been killed, Helen married another Trojan prince, Deiphobus. According to the poet Hesiod, who lived around 800 BCE, Helen and Deiphobus were the parents of a son, Nicostratus.

After the taking of Troy, Menelaus went in search of his wife with the intention of killing her for her faithlessness. In a scene frequently depicted on Greek vases, when he found Helen, she removed her robe and stood naked in front of him. He took one look at her beauty and the sword dropped from his hand.

The *Odyssey*, another epic poem attributed to Homer, gives a glimpse of the couple's home life back in Sparta in the years after the Trojan War. Helen is once again an obedient wife, but underlying tensions in her relationship with Menelaus are hinted at in a pair of stories that the couple tell separately to Telemachus, a guest who has come seeking news of his father Odysseus.

In Helen's story, she was loyal to the Greeks. For example, she says that she had recognized Odysseus when he disguised himself as a beggar to spy on Troy. When she realized it was the Greek king, she treated him well. Menelaus, on the other hand, answered with a story in which Helen teased the men inside the Trojan horse by

Below: The Love of Paris and Helen *by French artist Jacques-Louis David (1748–1825). As testament to the enduring popularity of the myth, this painting was made in 1788, over 2,500 years after Homer created his version of the story.*

Helen in Egypt

Egypt appears in several ways in Helen's story, not least in a version of the myth in which Helen never actually went to Troy. At the beginning of his *Histories*, Greek writer Herodotus (c. 484–425 BCE) traces the origins of hostility between Greece and Anatolia (Troy) to the stealing of Helen, and later tells of her stay in Egypt. In the *Odyssey* Homer says that, while attempting to return to Sparta, Menelaus and Helen are blown off course to Egypt, where they become guests of the king and are given many rich gifts.

In *Helen*, a play by Euripides (c. 486–c. 406 BCE), a phantom Helen goes to Troy while the woman herself stays in Egypt, where she is the guest of the king. The play begins as Menelaus arrives, conveniently at just the moment when Helen can no longer resist the king's demands to marry her. She meets Menelaus, who has been traveling with the phantom Helen, and confusion ensues. Once matters are cleared up, she tricks the king into letting her go back to Greece with Menelaus.

This alternate version of Helen's story dates back to a poem on the Trojan War by poet Stesichorus (fl. 600–550 BCE). In Stesichorus's poem Helen went willingly with Paris to Troy. According to legend, the poet was stricken with blindness as punishment for this slander against Helen. Stesichorus then wrote a palinode (recantation) in which he corrects himself and says that Helen actually never went to Troy. His revision worked and the poet recovered his sight.

Helen as goddess

According to legend, both Helen and Menelaus were given divine honors after their deaths. Menelaus, although not a particularly highly regarded figure among Greek heroes, had an exalted position in the afterlife, apparently because he was the son-in-law of Zeus. He was said to have gone to the Isles of the Blessed, which were reserved for those of uncommon privilege. There was a shrine dedicated to him at Therapne near Sparta, known as the Menelaion. The couple was supposedly buried there, which suggests it was a hero shrine rather than the temple of a god. However, according to the fourth-century-BCE orator Isocrates, they were worshiped there not as heroes but as gods. One of the earliest inscriptions found in the region, a dedication inscribed on a sacrificial fork "to Helen," was found at this sanctuary.

The immortality of Helen is also suggested by Homer, who calls her "daughter of Zeus," a formula that he otherwise reserves for goddesses such as Athena. Some writers tell of Helen's posthumous marriage to Achilles on the island of Leuke, or White Island, in the Black Sea. Other suggestions of divine status for Helen come from the island of Rhodes, where she was supposed to have been hanged in revenge for the deaths of men in the Trojan War, and where there was a shrine to Helen of the Tree. Herodotus, a fifth-century-BCE Greek historian, tells the tale of an ugly baby girl in Sparta whose nurse brought her every day to pray in front of Helen's image at the Menelaion. One day a woman appeared, stroked the young girl's cheek, and predicted that she would grow up to be the most beautiful woman in Sparta. Indeed, so beautiful did she become that, like her patroness, she was also stolen from her first husband.

Helen as icon

Many other ancient Greek writers were fascinated with the figure of Helen. Sappho (fl. c. 610–c. 580 BCE), a female poet, wrote that the most beautiful thing is whatever one loves. She then used Helen as an example, not only of a desirable but also of a desiring woman, who followed "the thing she loves," leaving behind her husband and baby.

Just as Euripides' treatment of the phantom Helen (see box) was influenced by contemporary philosophical thought about the nature of reality, orations by Isocrates in praise of Helen focused on the power of both eros (erotic love) and rhetorical persuasion. In this way, Helen, the most beautiful woman in the world, came to stand for any number of

using a divine talent she possessed to imitate the voices of their wives. She nearly induced them to betray themselves, but Odysseus prevented them by clamping a hand over their mouths. While each of these stories glorifies Odysseus in some way, they also reveal Helen's uncanny powers of recognition and imitation, as well as the difficulty of determining to whom she was loyal. In the same episode Helen eased the painful memories of all present by adding a drug to the wine. This drug, a gift from an Egyptian queen, called to mind a detour that Helen and Menelaus took on the way back from Troy (see box).

Throughout the *Odyssey*, as Odysseus struggles to return home and his wife, Penelope, resists the attentions of her many suitors, Helen and her sister, Clytemnestra, stand as cautionary figures for them both. In the underworld, Odysseus was warned by Agamemnon that he must return stealthily to his home on the island of Ithaca in case his wife turned out to be treacherous like Clytemnestra. Meanwhile Penelope strove to be a faithful wife in the face of great odds, and not a faithless one like Helen.

Right: Helen on the Steps of Troy *(c. 1870) by French artist Gustave Moreau (1826–1898). Moreau painted several versions of Helen, all of which depict her as the femme fatale who caused the destruction of Troy.*

Homer and Helen

Although Homer reproaches Helen in his epic poem, he also associates her closely with epic poetry, which indicates his respect for her. When Helen appears for the first time in the *Iliad,* she is weaving a cloth showing the battles of the Greeks and Trojans—a type of textile counterpart to the poem itself, especially since ancient Greek poets are sometimes said to "weave" their poetry. In another scene, Helen stands on the wall of the city and identifies the Greek heroes for King Priam, providing the sort of heroic catalog that is typical of epic poetry. Only Achilles, of all the characters in the *Iliad,* is similarly associated with epic: when he has withdrawn from the battlefield, he sits alone and sings "the deeds of men." Helen, unique among Homer's characters, seems to understand the function of epic poetry and the meaning of mortal suffering. She tells her brother-in-law, Hector, that their sufferings are given by Zeus so that they will be the subject of song for generations to come. This is a succinct description of the function of Greek epic poetry, which is to provide lasting fame for heroic deeds.

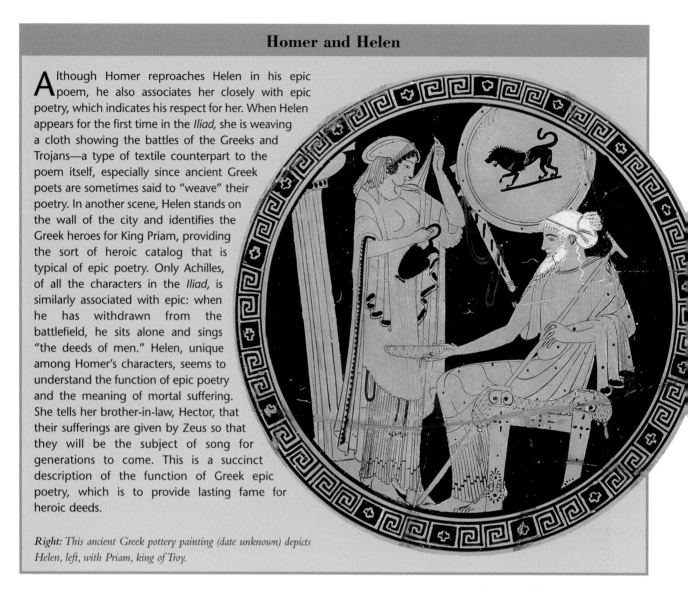

Right: This ancient Greek pottery painting (date unknown) depicts Helen, left, with Priam, king of Troy.

philosophical issues with which ancient Greek thinkers grappled. Helen is also an important figure in Euripides' dramas *The Trojan Women* and *Orestes.* In the former, she is reviled by all the captive women of Troy, while in the latter, Orestes and Pylades plot to kill her. Another classical writer who used Helen was the Roman poet Ovid (43 BCE–17 CE). He included a fictional letter from Helen to Paris in his work *Heroides.*

Helen has continued to play an important role in later Western literature. Medieval romances about Troy helped to keep Helen alive in the imagination. Edmund Spenser's *Faerie Queene* (1590) features a reworked version of Helen called "Hellenore." In the myth of Faust, as told first by the Elizabethan dramatist Christopher Marlowe and later by the German poet and playwright J. W. Goethe (1749–1832), the sight of Helen is one of the enticements with which Mephistopheles persuades Faust to sell his soul to the devil. Twentieth-century American poet H. D. (Hilda

Doolittle, 1886–1961), frustrated with the male perspective on Helen, wrote from the point of view of the ancient Spartan beauty herself in her long poem "Helen in Egypt."

The fate of the Trojan Women and the story of Faust feature in operas including, among others, *Les Troyens* (The Trojans) and *The Damnation of Faust,* both by French composer Hector Berlioz (1803–1869), and *The Egyptian Helen,* by German composer Richard Strauss (1864–1949).

DEBORAH LYONS

Bibliography

Homer, and Robert Fagles, trans. *The Iliad* and *The Odyssey.* New York: Penguin, 2009.

McLaren, Clemence. *Inside the Walls of Troy.* New York: Simon Pulse, 2004.

SEE ALSO: Agamemnon; Castor and Pollux; Clytemnestra; Hecuba; Iphigeneia; Menelaus; Odysseus; Paris; Theseus.

HERACLES

A national hero of ancient Greece, Heracles performed a series of arduous labors, and his name became a byword for physical strength and bravery. He was worshiped as a god in Greece from at least the sixth century BCE, and his cult was probably the earliest nonindigenous form of worship accepted in Rome.

Heracles was one of the greatest of all ancient mythological heroes. His amazing exploits and accomplishments took place over an enormous geographical area that stretched beyond his native land into the farthest corners of the known world. Unlike the deeds of lesser figures, his actions benefited all of Greece rather than just one particular region or city, and Heracles is therefore sometimes described as "panhellenic." He destroyed or subdued a host of monsters. Even the gods marveled at his enormous strength. Numerous kings, emperors, and generals appropriated Heracles' two most distinctive symbols—the lion skin and the club—in order to associate themselves with the hero in the hope that they might bask in some of his reflected glory.

The main source for the story of the labors of Heracles is the second-century BCE mythographer Apollodorus, but he is also mentioned by much earlier authors, including Homer (c. eighth–ninth century BCE). In the *Odyssey,* Homer describes how Odysseus meets Heracles' spirit in the underworld. For the Greeks he personified superhuman courage and strength. His life was one of toil and hardship on behalf of humankind; his reward was to become immortal after his death.

Heracles became the object of cult worship in Greece, where his rituals involved feasting and sacrifice. Animals

Right: This sculpture of Heracles is an ancient Roman copy of a Greek original dating from the fourth century BCE.

were lifted onto the sacrificial altar in an echo of Heracles' great feats of strength. At Thebes in Boeotia the temple of Heracles was attached to a gymnasium, in commemoration of the hero's athletic prowess.

Circumstances of his birth

Heracles was the son of Zeus and Alcmene, a descendant of Perseus and the wife of Amphitryon. While Amphitryon was away at war, Zeus came to Alcmene disguised as her husband. To satisfy his lust, the god caused the night to stretch out to three times its normal length. On the same night, however, Alcmene's husband returned and also had intercourse with her. As a result she became pregnant with two male children, one the semidivine Heracles, the other the mortal Iphicles. Most ancient writers say that Heracles was born at Thebes, because that is where Amphitryon lived, but in some accounts he is linked with Argos, which was Alcmene's family's home. Some mythographers suggest that Heracles—"glory of Hera"—was so named to appease the wrath of Zeus's wife, who was jealous of the children that Zeus had through other females.

It was Hera who caused most of Heracles' subsequent troubles. Zeus had foolishly boasted that the next child born in the line of Perseus would rule over Argos; Hera responded by making her daughter, Eileithyia, goddess of childbirth, delay the birth of Heracles so that his cousin, Eurystheus, could be born first (and prematurely). Alcmene eventually carried her twins for a painful 10 months. Even so, after Heracles was born some of the other goddesses tricked Hera into briefly suckling the baby with her own milk in order to ensure his immortality. When he clamped down too hard on her nipple, however, Hera yanked him away, and the spurting milk formed the Milky Way.

After the baby was returned to his mother, Hera sent serpents into his nursery to try to kill him. Since she was unsure which of the two newborn children belonged to Zeus, she sent two snakes to kill both twins. The mortal baby began to cry when he saw the danger, but Heracles grabbed both snakes and strangled them. The parents were shocked when they rushed into the room. They knew then that they had a supernatural child who possessed fantastic strength, and they decided that he deserved a special education. The best teachers were appointed, one of whom was Linus. While Heracles excelled in the more physically demanding arts, such as archery and wrestling, he failed miserably at music, Linus's specialty. One day, when Linus was ridiculing Heracles for being clumsy and incompetent, the boy picked up the instrument that he was playing and struck Linus over the head with it, killing him.

The 12 Labors of Heracles

1. Skinning the Nemean Lion.
2. Killing the Hydra of Lerna.
3. Capturing the Arcadian stag.
4. Capturing the Erymanthion boar.
5. Cleaning the Augean stables.
6. Shooting the birds of the Stymphalian marshes.
7. Capturing the Cretan bull.
8. Capturing the human-eating horses of Diomedes.
9. Obtaining the belt of the Amazon queen Hippolyte.
10. Driving the cattle of Geryon from the far west to Greece.
11. Fetching the golden apples of the Hesperides.
12. Capturing Cerberus, the three-headed watchdog of the underworld.

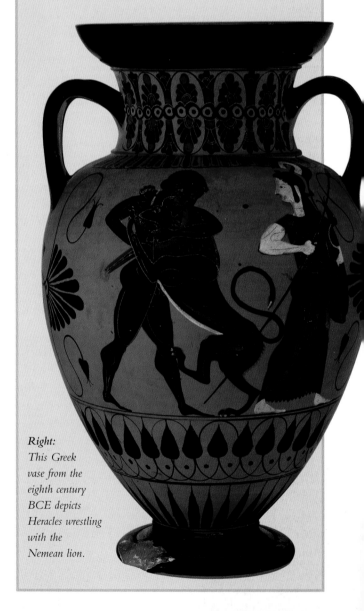

Right:
This Greek vase from the eighth century BCE depicts Heracles wrestling with the Nemean lion.

Early feats

Heracles' parents feared his temper and his strength, so they sent him off into the country to tend the flocks on Mount Cithaeron, between Thebes and Thespiae (ruled by Thespius). The boy grew tall and continued to show signs of exceptional athleticism. He killed a ferocious lion with his bare hands. This so impressed King Thespius that he invited Heracles to stay in his palace and dine with him. Thespius and the Thespians, meanwhile, were suffering at the hands of Erginus, king of nearby Orchomenus, who was demanding from them a heavy tribute. Thespius was secretly hoping to strengthen his kingdom by having the powerful Heracles produce children with his daughters. At the dinner party, Thespius got Heracles drunk on wine, then sent him in to his daughters—all 50 of them. Heracles had intercourse with every one, producing a child through each union. Soon afterward, when envoys from King Erginus came to Thespiae to exact the tribute, Heracles cut off their ears and noses, hung them around their necks, and sent the envoys packing back to Orchomenus. This sparked the outbreak of a war between the two states, but with Heracles fighting on the side of the Thespians and rearming them with weapons stored in a temple, the Thespians prevailed and began to exact their own tribute from the Minyans of Orchomenus.

Soon Heracles married Megara of Thebes, and they had several children together, all of whom he loved very much. Hera, however, was not content to let the hero lead a happy life. She sent a fit of madness on him, and he began to slay everyone in his family, either by throwing them into a fire or by shooting them with arrows. The only way that Heracles could atone for these murders was by submitting to his cousin Eurystheus, who set him 10 tasks. Because Heracles cheated on two of the original tasks, the number was later increased to 12.

The first 10 labors of Heracles

The first labor Eurystheus ordered Heracles to perform was to kill the Nemean lion, which was not a normal lion but a creature born from monstrous parents and brother to the famous Sphinx of Thebes. For years it had ravaged the land around Nemea in the Peloponnese, where it lived in a cave with two exits. Because its hide was invulnerable, Heracles could not harm it with his arrows. So he fashioned a club for himself, and used it to drive the lion into its cave, where he had blocked up one of the exits. He then strangled the beast with his bare hands. He used the dead lion's own claws to flay its skin, which from then on he wore as a distinctive coat and helmet.

Eurystheus never liked Heracles, and the hero's slaying of the Nemean lion only made him fear and loathe him more. The second labor that he imposed on Heracles was to kill the Hydra, a giant, multiheaded, snakelike creature that spewed venom from its mouth. Even the breath that

Below: This statue by French sculptor François-Joseph Bosio (1768–1845) depicts Heracles slaying the monstrous Hydra, the second of his 12 labors.

Heracles and Antaeus

Heracles encountered Antaeus on the way back to Greece from his 11th labor in the garden of the Hesperides, which was situated in the far west of the known world. Antaeus, a son of the earth goddess Gaia, was a giant who challenged every traveler he met to a wrestling contest. He had never lost a fight, and he had killed all his previous adversaries.

When Heracles and Antaeus came to grips, the hero soon discovered that, no matter how many times he threw Antaeus off and tossed him to the ground, he derived no advantage from his opponent's falls. On the contrary, the giant appeared to draw even greater strength from every throw. Heracles eventually deduced that the giant derived his power from contact with the earth, which was his mother, so he held Antaeus aloft until all his power had drained away, and then strangled him.

After Heracles had disposed of Antaeus, he proceeded safely back to his taskmaster and cousin, King Eurystheus of Argos, to receive instructions for his final labor.

Right: This painting by Antonio Pollaiuolo (c.1431–1498) depicts Heracles grappling with the giant Antaeus. Heracles defeated his opponent by lifting him from the ground and strangling him.

issued from it while it slept was poisonous enough to kill anyone nearby. The Hydra lived in Lerna, a swampy area of the Peloponnese. When he confronted the monster, Heracles discovered that every time he cut off one of the Hydra's heads, two would grow back in its place. He ordered his nephew, Iolaus, to sear the neck-stumps whenever he cut off a head, so that new ones would not be able to grow back. After successfully beheading the monster of its many heads, Heracles discovered that the middle head was immortal. He took a huge rock and buried the head beneath it, after which he dipped his arrows into the Hydra's venomous blood. Because Heracles used the services of his nephew Iolaus, this labor did not count toward the 10 that he needed to complete.

Heracles' third labor involved capturing the golden-horned stag of Ceryneia. This creature was extremely swift, though it was larger than a bull. The collar that it wore around its neck bore a legend saying that it was dedicated to Artemis, meaning that it would be an act of great impiety to hunt it. As in the case of the boar, deer often symbolize the rite of passage from childhood to adulthood. Heracles chased the stag for a full year until finally he was able to get close enough to wound it, then catch it. As Heracles returned to Argos, Artemis and her brother Apollo stopped him and tried to wrestle the animal away from

him. They relented only after Heracles explained to them that he was merely following the orders of Eurystheus and that he would not harm the deer.

Next, as a fourth labor, Eurystheus ordered Heracles to bring back alive the monstrous Erymanthion boar. The creature haunted the slopes of Mount Erymanthus and was causing considerable havoc in the countryside. (Boars in myth often symbolize the passage of young boys into manhood.) Heracles managed to drive the Erymanthian boar into deep snow, throw a net over it, and carry it back to Eurystheus. The king, terrified by the sight of the boar, hid in a huge pot in the ground.

As a fifth labor, Eurystheus ordered Heracles to clean the stables of Augeas, the king of Elis in the western Peloponnese. Augeas's father had given him great herds of cattle, but Augeas had failed to clean up their dung. As a result, the countryside was being deprived of fertilizer and therefore becoming infertile. Heracles went to Augeas and arranged a deal by which he would be paid for cleaning out all the dung. He then diverted a nearby river to run through the stable and thereby cleaned it thoroughly. When Heracles went back to Augeas for his money, Augeas refused to pay him on the grounds that the river had done the work, not Heracles. Eurystheus was unwilling to count this as one of the original 10 labors, since Heracles had asked for money. Later, Heracles returned to punish Augeas, whom he eventually killed. During that adventure, near Elis at Olympia, Heracles founded the Olympian Games.

The sixth labor that Eurystheus imposed on Heracles was to rid Lake Stymphalus of a huge flock of birds that were devouring everything in sight and making excessive noise. Some ancient authors say that their droppings were acidic and that they would shoot their metal-tipped feathers at

passersby. Heracles used castanets to drive the birds from hiding and then downed them with his arrows, the tips of which were steeped in Hydra venom.

For his seventh labor, Heracles was ordered to bring back alive the bull of Crete. This was the white bull that Poseidon had sent to King Minos but which Minos had failed to sacrifice to him in return. Heracles captured the bull and swam with it from Crete to mainland Greece. After showing it to Eurystheus, he tried to dedicate it to Hera, but the goddess, still angry, refused the gift.

Eurystheus then told Heracles that, for his eighth labor, he must capture the mares of Diomedes, king of the savage Thracians, and bring them back alive to him. The four horses were unique in that they lived on human flesh. Heracles was able to tame the animals by feeding Diomedes himself to them. After they had eaten their fill, it was no problem to lead them back to Argos. By overcoming Minos and Diomedes, Heracles had subdued the closest and most fearsome leaders of the Greeks' rivals.

It was during the eighth labor that Heracles visited the town of Pherae in Thessaly. There he met Admetus on the very day that his wife, Alcestis, had died. When Heracles discovered that the couple had entered a compact by which the wife would die in her husband's place, the hero wrestled Thanatos (Death) and stole Alcestis back, returning her to the selfish and now embarrassed Admetus.

The ninth labor of Heracles involved stealing the girdle or belt of Hippolyte, the queen of the Amazons. The Amazons were a tribe of women warriors who lived on the southern shore of the Black Sea. Although Hippolyte willingly agreed to give Heracles the girdle, the vengeful Hera caused a misunderstanding between them, and Heracles slew Hippolyte. The Amazons attacked, but during the battle, Heracles took so many hostages that the Amazons were forced to trade the belt for them.

For his 10th labor, Heracles was sent to retrieve the cattle of Geryon, a three-bodied giant, from a distant island either in the far reaches of the Mediterranean Sea or in the Atlantic Ocean. In order to traverse the vast ocean, Heracles borrowed from Helios, the

Left: This Etruscan bronze sculpture of the fifth century BCE shows Heracles subduing the carnivorous horses of Diomedes.

sun god, the cup in which he returned to the east after sunset every evening. When Heracles reached the island, he struck down Orthus, Geryon's two-headed guard dog, with a single blow of his club, then slew the giant with his arrows. After returning to Europe in Helios's cup, Heracles then drove the cattle all the way through Spain, Gaul (modern France), Italy, and on to Greece.

The final two labors

Heracles then went back to Argos to receive instructions from Eurystheus about his two additional tasks. For his 11th labor he had to travel to the western extremity of the world and bring back some golden apples. The tree on which they grew was tended by the Hesperides, daughters of Atlas. They had been set to look after the tree by Hera, who had been given it by Gaia as a wedding present. The golden apples of the Hesperides were guarded by Ladon, an immortal dragon with a hundred heads. Heracles traveled across northern Africa on his way to Mount Atlas. At some point during this journey, he met up with Prometheus and freed him from his captivity, during which he had been constantly gnawed by Zeus's eagle. In Libya Heracles encountered the giant Antaeus (see box, page 130), who wrestled and killed everyone he met. Antaeus was invincible so long as he was attached to the earth. Heracles lifted him on his shoulders and choked him to death.

Some ancient writers recount that on his way to the garden Heracles visited Atlas and agreed to hold up the sky while the Titan went to retrieve the apples. When Atlas

Right: This sculpture of Heracles with the Erymanthion boar is by the Flemish-Italian artist Giovanni Bologna (1529–1608), commonly known as Giambologna. The 12 labors of Heracles have been a popular subject for artists for many centuries.

Heracles in Art

The oldest surviving artistic depictions of Heracles date from the ninth century BCE. Hundreds of vases and bowls of the period depict the hero's everyday life as well as his 12 labors.

In many of the scenes showing Heracles fighting the Nemean lion, Athena is in the background to reassure the viewer of the hero's ultimate victory. Although the beast was supposedly invulnerable to weapons, Heracles is often shown attacking it with a club.

Another commonly depicted labor is the theft of the girdle of Hippolyte. There are nearly 400 examples, in some of which Heracles is killing the Amazon queen. The 11th labor is usually represented, not by the theft of the golden apples, but by Heracles seated before Atlas asking for his help.

Most of the images relating to the fourth labor show Heracles presenting the Erymanthion boar to Eurystheus, who is hiding in a vase.

returned, he decided that he wanted to take the apples to Eurystheus himself, and so refused to take the sky back on his shoulders. Heracles pretended to agree to this plan, and asked only that Atlas hold up the sky while he shifted his shoulders into a more comfortable position. When Atlas held the sky once more, Heracles grabbed the apples and promptly departed. Other accounts say that Heracles found the garden, slew the dragon, and retrieved the apples by himself. After Heracles showed the apples to Eurystheus, Athena returned them to the garden of Hera.

For the 12th labor Heracles had to descend into the underworld and bring out Cerberus, the three-headed guard dog of the underworld. In the underworld Heracles came across the imprisoned Theseus and Peirithous, two heroes who had tried to kidnap Persephone, the queen of the underworld. The goddess permitted Heracles to free Theseus, who was stuck in the chair of forgetfulness, but not Peirithous. Then Heracles grabbed Cerberus and dragged him up to Eurystheus. When Eurystheus saw the dog, he again took fright and jumped into his clay pot for safety. The dog was then returned to its master, Hades.

Life after labors

After the last of his labors, Heracles had finally atoned for the murder of his family. It was by no means the end of his adventures, however. He mounted many expeditions against various enemies, including the Trojans (Heracles lived one generation before the Trojan War), Augeas, and the people of Pylos (in the Peloponnese) and Sparta. He came into contact with Priam and Nestor, who were in the twilight of their lives when the Trojan War began.

While in the underworld, Heracles had promised the Greek prince Meleager that, when he went back to the world above, Heracles would marry his sister, Deianeira of Calydon. When Heracles returned, he headed for Calydon, where he found Deianeira being wooed by the river god Achelous, who was able to turn himself into any creature. When Deianeira expressed the desire to marry Heracles instead of Achelous, the two suitors became locked in mortal combat. In the end Heracles defeated Achelous while the latter was in the form of a bull. Heracles ripped off one of his horns, at which point Achelous admitted defeat and conceded the hand of Deianeira to Heracles.

Later, Heracles won a girl named Iole in an archery contest. Because her father refused to hand her over to Heracles, the hero had to take her by force. According to some versions, he killed her father. Most versions agree that in a fit of madness he killed her brother, who may have been one of his supporters, and so had to pay for his sins again. The oracle at Delphi was so appalled by his repeated crime that she refused to tell him what to do. Heracles became enraged, took the tripod of the Pythian priestess, and threatened to set up his own oracle. Apollo arrived, and he and Heracles came to blows until Zeus unleashed a thunderbolt to separate them. The oracle then told Heracles that to purify himself he must become a slave of Omphale, queen of Lydia, for three years. This was a humiliation for Heracles, because Omphale dressed him in women's clothes and took his lion skin and club for herself. Heracles even learned weaving from the queen.

Deianeira, meanwhile, had become jealous that Heracles might love Iole more than her. One day, while Heracles and his wife were crossing a dangerous river, a centaur named Nessus appeared and offered Deianeira a lift on his back to the further bank. Once on land, Nessus assaulted Deianeira. Heracles, on seeing what was happening, shot one of his poisonous arrows into Nessus. Before Nessus died he told Deianeira to take some of his blood because it had special qualities: "If ever Heracles begins to lose affection for you," he told her, "this blood can be used to restore his love." It was a trick, since the blood had been tainted by the venomous arrows. When Deianeira finally decided to act, she rubbed some of the supposed love-potion on a shirt and sent it to Heracles to wear. When he put it on, the fiery acid burned his skin. When he could bear the agony no longer, Heracles built a funeral pyre for himself and climbed on top. He begged servants and passersby to set fire to the wood, but no one would until a certain Philoctetes wandered by and lit it. As a reward, Heracles gave him his unerring bow and arrows. In some mysterious way, the fire only purged Heracles of his mortal parts, so that with a clap of thunder and the descent of a cloud, Heracles was lifted up to heaven to live with the gods there. In some versions of the myth, the mortal side of Heracles dwelled with the other shades in the underworld. The now divine Heracles was reconciled once and for all with Hera, and married Hebe, the goddess of youthfulness.

KIRK SUMMERS

Bibliography
Apollodorus, and Robin Hard, trans. *The Library of Greek Mythology.* New York: Oxford University Press, 2008.
Bulfinch, Thomas. *Bulfinch's Mythology.* New York: Barnes & Noble, 2006.
Graves, Robert. *The Greek Myths.* New York: Penguin, 1993.

SEE ALSO: Amazons; Hesperides; Hippolyte.

HERO

The tale of Hero and Leander is one of Greek mythology's most tragic love stories. Although a relatively minor myth, it remains enduringly popular and has caught the imagination of writers and artists through the ages.

Geography plays an important part in the myth of Hero. An exceptionally beautiful young woman, Hero, lived in the city of Sestos in Thrace (modern Turkey). Sestos stood on the shore at the narrowest point of a strait called the Hellespont, now known as the Dardanelles. On the opposite shore stood another city, Abydos, in the western Asian region of Dardania. The Hellespont, which divides Europe from Asia, took its name from a young girl named Helle. She had fallen into the strait and drowned while flying over it on the back of a magical ram, whose golden fleece featured in the story of Jason and the Argonauts.

Hero was a priestess of the goddess Aphrodite. Her name comes from the ancient Greek word *heros*, meaning "hero," which was used to describe men or women who were honored after their death. Hero dedicated her life to serving the goddess Aphrodite, making sacrifices to her and worshiping her in a temple. Since Aphrodite was the deity of love, Hero might have been expected to celebrate the goddess by being in love herself. Instead, according to the wishes of her parents, she lived alone in a high stone tower, with only an old maidservant to look after her. She kept away from boys, and also from other girls her own age, fearing that they would be jealous of her beauty.

Hero's love for Leander

According to the myth, every year the people of Sestos held a festival to celebrate the beautiful youth Adonis and his lover, Aphrodite. The festival may well have been the Adonia, in which worshipers planted seeds in shallow soil that sprang up and quickly died. The seeds symbolized the brief nature of Adonis's life, which ended when he was killed by a wild boar. Although she normally avoided parties, Hero had to take part in the festival since she was a priestess of Aphrodite. Many people came to the festival, some traveling great distances. All the young men were amazed at Hero's beauty and talked about how they would love to marry her. One youth, Leander, approached Hero in silence, showing his feelings for her only in his face and his gestures, and in this way they fell in love.

When he did finally speak, Leander told Hero that he came from Abydos, the city on the opposite shore from Sestos. He said that if she lit a lamp in her tower late at night, he would swim across the Hellespont to visit her in secret, using the light to guide him. Leander assured her that Aphrodite would approve of their relationship, to which Hero agreed. Every evening Hero lit a lamp in the tower, and Leander, seeing it from Abydos, swam across the water to spend the night with her. He always swam back before dawn so as not to be discovered by Hero's parents.

A tragic end

For several months Leander visited Hero every night, relying on Aphrodite to protect him as he battled the strong currents of the Hellespont. Then winter came, and the sea grew rougher and more dangerous, but the young couple were so in love that they could not bear to be apart for long, so Leander continued to make his perilous journey. One stormy night, when the sky was pitch black with clouds, a gust of wind blew out Hero's lamp. Before she could light it again, Leander, with nothing to guide him, lost his way and drowned. The next morning his battered body washed ashore on the rocks at the foot of Hero's tower. Seeing him lying there, Hero was so overcome with grief that she threw herself from the top of the tower and fell to her death at his side. No one had ever known of their love except Hero's maidservant.

Star-crossed lovers

Mythology and folklore are littered with tales of young lovers thwarted by circumstance—usually because their parents or society condemns the relationship—but who refuse to be separated by death. Hero came from Thrace, which was part of the Greek empire, while Leander came from Dardania, part of the Persian empire. Between 492 and 449 BCE the Greeks were involved in a series of wars

Above: A second-century-CE Roman mosaic, in Dougga, Tunisia, depicts Leander swimming, surrounded by Nereids (sea nymphs) and the heads of the four winds.

against the Persian Empire to keep their independence. This historical background suggests that neither the inhabitants of Sestos nor of Abydos—both of which stand as ruins today—would support a love affair between citizens from either city, and that Hero and Leander's love was in opposition to their societies' wishes.

Other stories with the theme of thwarted love include the Greek myth of Pyramus and Thisbe and the Indian tale of Khamba and Thoibi. Pyramus and Thisbe grew up as neighbors and fell in love, but both sets of parents forbade them from being together. Instead, they agreed to meet in

secret, but Pyramus, finding Thisbe's bloody veil on the ground, believed she had been eaten by a lion and so killed himself. Thisbe, on finding Pyramus's body, decided to kill herself, too. In contrast, Khamba and Thoibi's love for each other promised to unite their clans, the Khumals and the Moirangs, but the Moirangs' chief rejected their marriage out of jealousy or spite. The lovers killed themselves and war broke out. The doomed lovers and warring families have parallels with the tale of Romeo and Juliet, which was used in a play by William Shakespeare (1564–1616).

The lovers in these stories are star-crossed, meaning that fate obstructs their love. Some writers have interpreted such myths as reminders that happiness is temporary and that death comes to everyone. Other people have observed that, by dying together when young, the lovers preserve their love for all eternity instead of letting it grow stale. They argue that the appeal of the stories lies in the universal recognition of the passion and power of young love.

Below: This painting, Hero Holding the Beacon for Leander, *is by English artist Evelyn De Morgan (c. 1850–1919).*

Lord Byron and Leander

English romantic poet Lord Byron (1788–1824) was alive at a time when many artists and poets were especially interested in tales from Greek mythology. An adventurer who traveled a great deal, Byron decided to try to swim the Hellespont himself while on a tour of Europe in 1810. He undertook the challenge along with his friend Lieutenant William Ekenhead, who was a member of the British Navy and a good swimmer. It took the pair two attempts, but on May 3, 1810, they succeeded. Although at its narrowest point the Hellespont is less than a mile wide, because of strong currents the two men swam a total of 4 miles (6.5 km). Their swim took them just over one hour.

Byron was hugely proud of his achievement and recorded it in the poem "Written After Swimming From Sestos to Abydos." He also mentioned the feat in his long comic poem, *Don Juan,* in which he wrote:

A better swimmer you could scarce see ever,
He could, perhaps, have pass'd the Hellespont,
As once (a feat on which ourselves we prided)
Leander, Mr. Ekenhead, and I did.

Hero and Leander in literature and art

The story of Hero and Leander is mentioned in the work of Roman writers Ovid (43 BCE–c. 17 CE) and Virgil (70–19 BCE), while the fifth- or sixth-century-CE Greek poet Musaeus wrote a lengthy poem about the lovers. Scholars believe that all three writers copied the story from an earlier version that is now lost.

Hero and Leander have appeared in the work of many writers and artists since classical times. In the 16th century, English poet and playwright Christopher Marlowe wrote a long poem retelling the story, and the tale became especially popular in the 18th and 19th centuries, when it was retold by German poet Johann Schiller and English poets John Keats and Lord Byron (see box). Meanwhile, many artists, including Peter Paul Rubens (1577–1640) and J.M.W. Turner (1775–1851), have depicted scenes from the story.

ANNA CLAYBOURNE

Bibliography
Ovid, and A. D. Melville, trans. *Metamorphoses.* New York: Oxford University Press, 2008.
Virgil, and Robert Fagles, trans. *The Aeneid.* New York: Penguin, 2009.

SEE ALSO: Adonis; Jason.

HESPERIDES

The Hesperides were nymphs who, according to Greek myth, lived in a beautiful garden and guarded a tree that bore golden apples. The nymphs played a minor role in a number of stories, but their apples were of great significance in accounts of the Trojan War, among other tales.

The ancient Greeks compared the sun, when it set over the sea, to a golden apple. They believed such golden apples were produced by a tree that stood on an island at the end of the earth. The third-century-BCE Greek poet Apollonius wrote that the island was near Mount Atlas, in northwest Africa, while the second-century-BCE Greek scholar Apollodorus suggested it was in the far north. The Greeks believed that the Hesperides were two (or seven) beautiful sisters who wandered through the garden, singing to the tree. They were its protectors, together with a serpentlike dragon called Ladon.

The name Hesperides can be translated as "daughters of evening" and derives from the Greek word *hesper,* which not only means "evening," but also refers to the evening star, which the Romans renamed Venus. In some sources, the Hesperides were the offspring of the Titaness Hesperis, who married her uncle, the Titan Atlas. In other accounts, notably that of the eighth-century-BCE poet Hesiod, the Hesperides were the daughters of Nyx (Night) and her brother Erebus (Darkness, or the underworld). Hesiod's description of their parentage would make the Hesperides sisters to the Fates, the Keres (Destinies), Pain, Blame, Sleep, and Dreams, among others. In yet another version, however, the sea god Phorcys and the sea monster Ceto are the father and mother of the Hesperides—meaning that they would be sisters to Ladon, as well as to the three strange old women, the Graeae, and the three monsters, the Gorgons, who also lived near Mount Atlas. The number of Hesperides varies between accounts from two to seven. In some cases at least three were named: Aegle ("brightness"), Erytheis ("scarlet"), and Hesperethusa ("sunset glow").

Below: A scene depicting the Hesperides in their garden, on a fourth-century-BCE Greek vase. To the left of the image is the tree bearing golden apples, around which coils the dragon Ladon.

Male and female power

The tree that the Hesperides kept watch over was originally a gift from the earth goddess Gaia to her granddaughter, Hera, on Hera's marriage to Zeus, the ruler of the Olympians. Hera set her own dragon, the serpent Ladon, to guard it, before giving the magic tree to Zeus. Some scholars believe the story of the tree—originally possessed by Mother Earth, then by the Queen of Heaven, before finally passing to the chief Olympian god—reflects a transition in the Greek pantheon from female, mother-centered power to male-dominated, patriarchal rule.

In two famous myths involving the golden apples, bribery or trickery enables a man to win a wife. In the first myth, Eris, the goddess of discord, rolled one of the apples across the floor at the wedding of the mortal Peleus and the sea goddess Thetis. The apple was inscribed "To the Fairest," and three goddesses claimed the apple and the title: Hera, Athena, and Aphrodite. Zeus appointed Paris, the son of King Priam of Troy, as judge, and each goddess tried her best to bribe him. Paris chose Aphrodite, who promised him the most beautiful woman in the world for his wife—Helen, who was married to King Menelaus of Sparta. Paris abducted Helen to Troy, which led directly to the Trojan War.

In the second myth, the virgin princess Atalanta, a renowned runner, refused to marry anyone she could defeat in a footrace. However, her most determined suitor, Melanion (or Hippomenes), obtained three golden apples from the sympathetic Aphrodite before his race. As they ran, he tossed one of the apples ahead of Atalanta. The princess was unable to ignore the beautiful apple and stooped to pick it up, allowing Melanion to gain on her. He repeated the trick with the second and third apples, thus winning the race and her hand in marriage.

Heracles and the theft of the apples

The Hesperides and their apples played a significant role in the story of Heracles, in which the theme of trickery is also evident. One of the Greek hero's final labors for King Eurystheus was to steal three of the golden apples. Heracles

Left: This painting depicts Hercules [Heracles] Killing the Dragon of the Hesperides, and is by Italian artist Lorenzo dello Sciorina (c. 1540–1598).

had no idea where to find the fruit, but brutally forced the secret out of the ancient sea god Nereus. The sea god told Heracles that the Hesperides' garden lay near the mountains where Atlas supported the sky on his shoulders. In one version of the story, Heracles himself held up the sky while Atlas took the apples. On his return, Atlas was unwilling to resume his burden, but was tricked by Heracles. The hero asked the Titan to briefly hold the sky while he assumed a more comfortable position. Atlas agreed, and Heracles walked away.

In another version, Heracles stole the apples himself after killing Ladon. Hera honored her dragon by setting his form in the heavens as the constellation Draco, but she never forgave Heracles for the murder. The Hesperides also grieved, and in one account turned into elm, poplar, and willow trees in their sorrow over Ladon's death and the theft of the apples.

Explaining natural forces

The story of the Hesperides represents an attempt by the ancient Greeks to explain what they saw when the sun set. They pictured dramatic and beautiful evening skies as a protected mountain garden, which was usually hidden from mortal eyes but for brief moments was visible at sunset. The Hesperides were some of many spirits and deities that the Greeks believed controlled natural phenomena—a belief that linked them to other peoples and other mythologies throughout the world.

KATHLEEN JENKS

Bibliography

Bulfinch, Thomas. *Bulfinch's Mythology.* New York: Barnes & Noble, 2006.

Hesiod, and M. L. West, trans. *Theogony* and *Works and Days.* New York: Oxford University Press, 2008.

SEE ALSO: Atalanta; Helen; Heracles; Paris.

HIPPOLYTE

Hippolyte, whose name means "horse releaser" or "one born of the stamping horses," was a queen of the Amazons, a mythical race of female warriors. She played a major part in the myths of the Greek heroes Heracles and Theseus.

Above: A Greek amphora (c. 480 BCE) depicting Theseus abducting Hippolyte. In some versions of the story, Theseus kidnapped Antiope, who may have been the sister of the Amazon queen.

According to Greek myth, Hippolyte was the daughter of the war god Ares and a mortal woman called Otrera. She grew up to become ruler of the Amazons, a tribe of warrior women who lived on the Thermodon River on the shore of the Black Sea. Most scholars believe that Hippolyte and the Amazons were entirely mythical, although some commentators think that the notion of a warlike group of females may have been based on the "masculine" practices adopted by women in some cultures in western Asia, including those of the Scythians and Sarmatians. However, the historical figure Alexander the Great (356–323 BCE), a Macedonian king and conqueror, allegedly encountered the Amazons and their queen during his travels.

Hippolyte and Heracles

The ninth of the Greek hero Heracles' 12 labors, which he performed for King Eurystheus as a penance for killing his own family, was to obtain Hippolyte's belt or girdle— a gift from her father, Ares, and a potent symbol of her power. According to Greek writer Apollodorus (second century BCE) and Roman poet Ovid (43 BCE–17 CE), Eurystheus's daughter Admete coveted the girdle because of its magical powers. In one version of the story, Hippolyte willingly surrendered the girdle, but Hera— perpetually jealous of Heracles because her husband, Zeus, had fathered him by another woman—planted suspicions in the minds of the Amazons that their queen had been abducted. The Amazons attacked Heracles and, in response, he killed Hippolyte. In another version, Heracles gained the girdle by capturing Hippolyte's sister, Melanippe, and demanding the belt in exchange.

Hippolyte and Theseus

In some accounts, the Athenian hero Theseus accompanied Heracles on his journey to the Amazon capital. In return, Heracles gave him Hippolyte as a gift. In other accounts, Theseus kidnapped Hippolyte and took her back to Athens. The abduction led the Amazons to march to the Greek city to reclaim their queen—they were defeated in the battle known as the Amazonomachy. Still other accounts say that the Amazons approached Athens only after Hippolyte gave birth to Theseus's son Hippolytus.

There are several different tales of how Hippolyte died. Greek poet Simonides (c. 556–c. 468 BCE) suggested that Hippolyte was fiercely jealous of Theseus's subsequent marriage to another woman, Phaedra. Hippolyte led a charge into Theseus's palace on his wedding day and was killed in the fray. Apollodorus also questions whether Theseus himself or his men killed her intentionally, or if

Above: This 1470 illustration from Giovanni Boccaccio's poem Teseida *(c.1341) depicts the battle between the Greeks under Theseus and the Amazons under Hippolyte.*

Penthesilea, a future Amazon queen, killed Hippolyte accidentally. One reason for the number of stories surrounding her death could be the confusion between Hippolyte and Antiope, another Amazon queen who may or may not have been Hippolyte's sister. Some writers suggest that it was Antiope whom Theseus took back to Athens; others, such as Greek dramatist Euripides (c. 486–c. 406 BCE), maintain that it was Hippolyte. The confusion demonstrates how, over time, storytellers could lose track of names in their desire to tell a good tale.

Hippolyte in ancient and modern cultures

The story of Hippolyte and the Amazons in general is significant because it involves the reversal of traditional gender roles. Whereas ancient Greeks and Romans saw women as silent, unobtrusive wives and mothers, Hippolyte and her followers placed little importance on masculinity—they only required male genes to further the Amazon race. Some present-day feminists have identified with the Amazons because the Amazons asserted themselves against the male-dominant world. Others point out

that Hippolyte's story actually reaffirms the power of men—a belligerent queen, who would never surrender to a man, ultimately did so and had a child with her former abductor.

Hippolyte's likeness has been discovered on temples, pottery, and sculpture fragments dating from the sixth century BCE, but she has also figured in a variety of other artistic genres. In English playwright William Shakespeare's comedy *A Midsummer Night's Dream* (c. 1595), Hippolyte is the fiancée of Theseus. In the 20th century the Amazon queen began to appear in popular culture. In 1941 she was described as the mother of D.C. Comics' newest creation, Wonder Woman. Around the same time, Julian Thompson's play *The Warrior's Husband* starred American actress Katharine Hepburn as Hippolyte. At the start of the 20th century the character of Hippolyte featured in television programs, books, and even video games.

DEBORAH THOMAS

Bibliography

Apollodorus, and Robin Hard, trans. *The Library of Greek Mythology.* New York: Oxford University Press, 2008.
Bulfinch, Thomas. *Bulfinch's Mythology.* New York: Barnes & Noble, 2006.

SEE ALSO: Amazons; Heracles; Hippolytus; Theseus.

HIPPOLYTUS

Hippolytus was the son of Theseus, king of Athens, by his second wife, the Amazon queen Hippolyte. The meaning of Hippolytus's name foretells his fate: "one who is destroyed by horses." His story demonstrates the importance for the Greeks of maintaining a balance between opposing practices in life—in this case, between abstinence and sex.

The Greeks believed that over the course of a person's life there were appropriate times for chaste behavior and for sexuality. The former stage was overseen by the virgin goddess of hunting, Artemis; the latter stage by the love goddess Aphrodite. Before puberty, youths would devote themselves to nonsexual pursuits, such as hunting, but when they reached maturity they would embrace the world of sexuality and, eventually, marriage. In the most famous version of the Hippolytus myth, in the play *Hippolytus* by Greek dramatist Euripides (c. 486–c. 406 BCE), Hippolytus refused to make the transition from a chaste youth to a mature man. Like Peter Pan, he effectively refused to grow up.

In Euripides' play, Theseus sent Hippolytus to nearby Troezen in preparation for his son's rule of that city—a sign that Theseus considered Hippolytus to be entering adulthood with all its responsibilities. However, in an act of adolescent rebellion, Hippolytus refused to acknowledge his maturity. He clung to his solitary hunts and his favor with Artemis, and he failed to worship Aphrodite. The love goddess was therefore enraged. She caused Hippolytus's stepmother, Theseus's third wife, Phaedra, to fall in love with him when she and Theseus visited the city.

Phaedra revealed her desire to Hippolytus through her nurse. When Hippolytus angrily rejected her invitation, Phaedra became so upset that she resolved to commit suicide. Yet, because she lacked the courage to admit to her perverse desire, and because she resented Hippolytus for rejecting her, Phaedra left a suicide note, charging that Hippolytus had raped her and driven her to kill herself.

When Theseus discovered the note he cursed his son and prayed that his father, the sea god Poseidon, would destroy the young man. Poseidon sent a bull from the sea, which frightened Hippolytus's horses as they pulled his chariot along the shore. Hippolytus was caught in the reins and dragged behind his steeds. Theseus went to his son's side and, before Hippolytus died, learned about Phaedra's lie from Artemis.

A different account

In other tellings of the story, however, Phaedra is portrayed as a shameless woman who fell in love with Hippolytus but failed to seduce him. She told Theseus that Hippolytus had raped her; after Hippolytus died, Phaedra hanged herself. The mythical character Phaedra came from a family beset by sexual problems. Her father was Minos, king of Crete, who had difficulties ejaculating, and her mother was Pasiphae, who fell in love with a bull.

Below: A relief showing Phaedra professing her love to Hippolytus, on a third-century-CE Roman sarcophagus. The myth emphasizes the importance of moving from one stage in life to another.

141

Back from the dead

According to some sources, Hippolytus was brought back to life by Asclepius, the god of healing. He then journeyed to Aricia in Italy, where he became king and established a festival in honor of Diana, the Roman name for Artemis. Eventually he was honored in Aricia as the god Virbius, who was regarded as a companion to Diana. At Troezen, in Greece, young girls came to dedicate their hair to Hippolytus before marriage, a ritual that symbolized an end to their chaste lives and their progress into adulthood. There was a shrine to Hippolytus in Sparta, and, because of the manner of his death, he became associated with the constellation Auriga (the Charioteer).

Meaning and parallels in other myths

Hippolytus's tale encouraged reluctant youths in Greece to accept adulthood and its responsibilities, of which marriage was one of the most important. The Greeks regarded it as vital to the survival of their society, since it guaranteed the reproduction of its citizens and the growth of its cities. Hippolytus's resistance to accepted customs was prefigured by that of his mother, Hippolyte, who belonged to a race of women—the Amazons—that defied the conventions of the Greeks' patriarchal society and civilization.

Above: The Death of Hippolytus *by Flemish painter Peter Paul Rubens (1577–1640). In one version of the myth, Hippolytus came back from the dead and went to Italy, where he was honored as a god.*

Many other Greek myths have parallels with the story of Hippolytus. The mortal Myrrha, for example, scorned Aphrodite—as a result, the goddess made her fall in love with her own father. In another tale, Artemis enjoyed the company of the hunter Orion so much that she planned to marry him. However, the sun god Apollo became alarmed by Orion's relationship with his sister and tricked Artemis into killing him with an arrow. The first of these myths implies that no one should ignore the worship of deities, while the second suggests that there are some situations in which only chaste behavior is acceptable.

KATHRYN CHEW

Bibliography

Bulfinch, Thomas. *Bulfinch's Mythology.* New York: Barnes & Noble, 2006.

Euripides, and P. Burian and A. Shapiro, eds. *The Complete Euripides.* New York: Oxford University Press, 2009–2010.

SEE ALSO: Amazons; Hippolyte; Myrrha; Orion; Theseus.

ICARUS

Icarus was the son of the mythical inventor and craftsman Daedalus and Naukrate, a slave of King Minos of Crete. He is famous for flying too close to the sun, wearing a pair of wings built by his father. Some writers have seen Icarus's fate as a warning for people to be aware of their limitations.

Below: Daedalus and Icarus, *by Italian sculptor Antonio Canova (1757–1822), shows Daedalus securing wings onto his son.*

Daedalus was Minos's chief artisan. He constructed many fabulous inventions for his employer, including a hollow wooden cow in which Minos's wife, Pasiphae, hid in order to seduce a bull. Pasiphae's union with the animal resulted in the birth of the Minotaur—a monster who was half man, half bull—and led to another of Daedalus's creations, the labyrinth in which Minos concealed the creature, but the king became angry with Daedalus, either because of his role in the queen's adultery with the bull or because he helped the hero Theseus kill the Minotaur. Consequently, Minos put his inventor in prison, along with Icarus, now a young man.

Walls could not hold Daedalus, however. He constructed wings of feathers and wax for himself and Icarus, and the two flew out of the prison and away from Crete. Before their departure, Daedalus warned his son not to fly too low, in case the sea spray should soak his wings, or too high, in case the rays of the sun should melt the wax, but once he was in the air, Icarus soared higher and higher, ignoring his father's calls. Their route led north from Crete across the Aegean Sea, where, off the island of Samos, Icarus flew so close to the sun that his wings melted and came apart, and the youth plunged to his death. His body washed ashore on a nearby island, where it was found by the Greek hero Heracles, who buried the body and named the island Icaria and the sea around it Icarian in honor of Icarus. Other accounts, however, relate that Daedalus himself buried his son.

Origins of the story

The pairing of a legendary craftsman with a protégé, or apprentice, is a common theme in a number of ancient eastern Mediterranean myths. Examples include Kothar and Khasis, whom inhabitants of the city of Ugarit (in present-day Syria) believed to be artisans to the gods, and Bezalel and Oholiab, who, according to the Bible, built the tabernacle, or sanctuary, for the Ark of the Covenant.

143

Since some of these cultures predate the arrival of the Greeks in the region, the story of Daedalus and Icarus was probably adapted from an earlier tale. Its connection with Crete supports the idea of adaptation, since the island was home to the Minoan civilization—named by scholars for the mythical King Minos—which enjoyed extensive contacts with other cultures and was eventually absorbed into mainland Greek civilization. The technological achievements of the Minoans—including their buildings, writing systems, and works of art—may have seemed almost miraculous to the early Greeks. The myth of Daedalus and Icarus might well have been a means for them to conceptualize both their wonder at, and fear of, this technology.

Below: Daedalus and Icarus *by French painter Charles-Paul Landon (1760–1826). Some people interpret Icarus's fall as a symbol of human folly; others believe it shows humanity's desire for progress.*

Sources for the Icarus myth

The earliest known reference to Icarus comes from a pottery fragment, dating from mid-sixth-century-BCE Athens, on which is inscribed the character's name and a pair of winged feet. No surviving poem or play is devoted to Icarus; instead, information about him comes from Greek sources such as *The Library*, a handbook of mythology attributed to the second-century-BCE Athenian Apollodoros; the *Bibliotheca historica* (Universal History), by first-century-BCE Greek Diodoros Siculus; and a second-century-BCE traveler's guide to Greece by Pausanias. Roman writers also told Icarus's story: one of the best-known accounts of his death is by Ovid (43 BCE–17 CE) in his epic *Metamorphoses.*

Different authors emphasize different aspects of the myth. Ovid portrays Icarus as a young man who ignored his father's advice to pursue a moderate course and ended up destroying himself. On the other hand, Roman poet Horace (65–8 BCE), comparing writing poetry to taking flight, presents Icarus positively, as one whose fame he wishes to surpass. Historical writers and scholars have tended to rationalize the myth. According to many of them, Daedalus and Icarus did not "fly" from Crete, but left on a ship for which Daedalus invented sails. In these writers' accounts Icarus fell from a ship, and not from the sky.

Icarus in art and music

Icarus has inspired many artists. Flemish painter Pieter Brueghel the Elder (c. 1525–1569) inverted Ovid's description of laborers who marveled at Icarus's flight—instead, Brueghel depicts the youth's fall into the sea as a tiny splash in the corner of his painting, while laborers proceed with their tasks, unconcerned. The view of Icarus as a symbol of the human desire to "fly higher," which Horace emphasized, has been the dominant perspective on him in the modern era of technological advance. For French artist Henri Matisse (1869–1954), Icarus symbolized the dream of flight, while the American composer Ralph Towner (b. 1940) entitled his theme music for the first lunar flight in 1969 "Icarus." A number of aircraft, aircraft carriers, and aircraft systems have been called *Icarus.*

JIM MARKS

Bibliography

Apollodorus, and Robin Hard, trans. *The Library of Greek Mythology.* New York: Oxford University Press, 2008.
Ovid, and A. D. Melville, trans. *Metamorphoses.* New York: Oxford University Press, 2008.

SEE ALSO: Daedalus; Heracles; Minos; Theseus.

IDOMENEUS

Idomeneus was a king of Crete, the son of Deucalion and the grandson of King Minos. His story revolves around the events of the Trojan War, where he led the Cretan contingent, which fought on the side of the Greeks.

Above: This engraving by Luigi Schiavonetti (1765–1810) depicts a kneeling Mentor, a valued friend of Odysseus, giving advice to Idomeneus.

The story of Idomeneus falls into two parts, one of which took place before and during the Trojan War, the other after it. Before the start of the war, Idomeneus competed with Odysseus, Ajax, and Menelaus for the hand of Helen, the daughter of Zeus and the most beautiful woman in Greece. Helen married Menelaus, but was then abducted to Troy by Paris. Idomeneus and the other defeated suitors had pledged to Agamemnon, king of Mycenae and brother of Menelaus, that they would try to recapture Helen. Greek poet Homer (c. ninth–eighth century BCE) wrote in the *Iliad* that Idomeneus and his nephew Meriones led 80 Cretan ships to Troy. Idomeneus was one of the principal warriors in the ensuing war, and one of the few Greeks to return home after the long conflict.

The Trojan War

Idomeneus fought with distinction throughout the hostilities in Troy. According to the *Iliad*, he slew Phaestus, the son of Borus the Maeonian, before volunteering—one of only nine men to do so—to fight the Trojan champion Hector in single combat. This task, however, fell to Ajax. Later in Homer's account, Idomeneus instructs the aged Nestor to save the wounded healer Machaon from battle. Idomeneus's most fearsome fighting is described in Book 13 of the *Iliad*: urged on by the sea god Poseidon and accompanied by Meriones, he stands firm against an onslaught from the Trojan ranks led by Deiphobus and Aeneas. Later still, Idomeneus fought for the body of Patroclus, the beloved companion of the Greek champion Achilles. Idomeneus accompanied Odysseus, Nestor, and Phoenix when they went to comfort Achilles. Finally,

Pausanias and Idomeneus

Idomeneus was descended from Helios, the sun god, through the god's daughter Pasiphae. This was made clear by Greek travel writer Pausanias (143–176 CE), who described his visit to the temple of Zeus at Olympia. There Pausanias saw eight of a set of nine statues representing the warriors who rose to fight Hector at Troy—the ninth had apparently been taken to Rome by the emperor Nero. Although the only statue with an inscribed name was that of Agamemnon, Pausanias decided that another of the monuments must represent Idomeneus, because the shield of the statue in question bore the image of a rooster. The rooster was the sacred bird of the sun god Helios.

Above: The Greek fleet sails toward Troy, from an illustration in a 15th-century French book. According to Homer, Idomeneus took part in all the Trojan War's main battles and related events.

during the funeral games to honor Patroclus, Idomeneus quarreled with Ajax while watching the chariot race. In classical art, most of the surviving representations of Idomeneus show him during the Trojan War: for example, leading a sacrifice with Agamemnon, or during Patroclus's funeral games. However, much of his fame derives not from the Trojan War itself, but from his journey back to Crete.

The journey home

Like many other Greeks, Idomeneus ran into difficulties on his way home from Troy. During a fearsome storm, he promised Poseidon that, if he were delivered from the tempest, he would sacrifice the first being he saw on his return to Crete. Poseidon accepted the offer and calmed the storm, but the first person to greet Idomeneus when he reached dry land was his own son, Idamantes. There are several different versions of the subsequent events. In the *Aeneid*, by Roman poet Virgil (70–19 BCE), Idomeneus sacrificed his son, thus angering the gods, who drove him from Crete to Calabria in southern Italy. In another account, the sacrifice sparked a plague, which enraged the Cretan people, who, in turn, forced Idomeneus off the island. In the second century BCE, Greek scholar Apollodorus related a third version of events. While Idomeneus was in Troy, his wife Meda took a lover, Leucus, who killed both Meda and her daughter before usurping the throne and forming alliances with 10 other cities. When Idomeneus returned home and attempted to sacrifice his son, a plague broke out. This event gave Leucus a perfect excuse to banish Idomeneus.

In all three versions, the story of Idomeneus is a sad one. His hasty oath to Poseidon and the subsequent sacrifice of his son cast a shadow over the reputation he had made for himself at Troy. However, a happy ending did come in the form of an opera by composer Mozart (1756-1791), *Idomeneo, rè di Creta* (1781), in which Neptune (the Roman Poseidon) released Idomeneus from his vow.

BRIAN SEILSTAD

Bibliography

Homer, and Robert Fagles, trans. *The Iliad*. New York: Penguin, 2009.

Virgil, and Robert Fagles, trans. *The Aeneid*. New York: Penguin, 2009.

SEE ALSO: Agamemnon; Ajax; Hector; Helen; Menelaus; Minos; Pasiphae; Patroclus.

IPHIGENEIA

In Greek mythology, Iphigeneia was taken by her father, Agamemnon, to be sacrificed to the goddess Artemis. In most versions of the story, Artemis saves her life at the last moment and makes her into a priestess. In one account, however, Iphigeneia has her throat cut on the altar.

Iphigeneia was the daughter of Agamemnon and Clytemnestra, and the sister of Orestes, Electra, and, in some accounts, Chrysothemis and Laodice (although that is possibly another name for Electra). Agamemnon was the king of Mycenae or Argos; his brother was Menelaus; they were both sons of Atreus. The royal house of Atreus was doomed to a series of tragic misfortunes by a curse placed on it as a result of the deeds of Atreus's father, Pelops, and his grandfather, Tantalus.

In one of the most famous of all Greek legends, Iphigeneia was offered up for sacrifice by her own father Agamemnon. After the Trojan prince Paris abducted Helen of Sparta, a Greek fleet assembled at Aulis ready to attack Troy. Agamemnon, brother of Helen's husband Menelaus, was commander of the Greeks. For a long time, however, the warships were unable to set sail because Artemis was making the winds blow either in the wrong direction or not at all. The goddess did this because she had a grudge against Agamemnon. There are various accounts of why she was so angry. One is that Agamemnon had shot a stag, possibly in Artemis's sacred grove, and then boasted that he was a better hunter than the goddess. This is an example of hubris (pride), which in Greek mythology always invites nemesis (an act of vengeance against the proud person). According to other accounts, Agamemnon had traditionally sacrificed to Artemis the most beautiful creature born each year, but in the year of Iphigeneia's birth, this was the princess herself, and Agamemnon dishonestly withheld his daughter. Another version is that Agamemnon's father,

Atreus, had promised Artemis the finest animals in his flocks, and then withheld a golden lamb.

Whatever the reason, the soothsayer Calchas told Agamemnon that the only way he could appease Artemis was to sacrifice his virgin daughter. So Agamemnon sent word to his queen, Clytemnestra, that she should bring Iphigeneia to Aulis so that she could be betrothed to Achilles. When mother and daughter arrived, however, he offered the princess up for sacrifice. The winds blew, the fleet sailed, and the Trojan War began.

In most versions of the story, Artemis substituted a deer for Iphigeneia on the altar, snatching the girl away at the very last moment as the knife went to her throat. Iphigeneia then became a priestess in the land of the Taurians (today part of the Crimea on the Black Sea).

Iphigeneia in art and literature

Agamemnon's daughter has inspired artists and writers throughout history. She is the subject of two great plays by Euripides (c. 486–c. 406 BCE). *Iphigeneia at Aulis* has political overtones, because the heroine is portrayed as an idealistic young woman willing to die for a unified Greece. When the play was first performed (408-406 BCE), Athens and Sparta had been locked in the Peloponnesian War for more than 20 years, and the concept of Greece as a single, unified nation was still wishful thinking, not a practical possibility.

The Prototype Heroine

Most Greek myths survive in several versions, and the details sometimes contradict each other. For example, Penelope was originally a model of chastity, but later accounts make her the lover of all her suitors and the mother of the god Pan. Similarly, according to some legends, Iphigeneia was not Clytemnestra's daughter at all: she had been adopted to conceal the fact that her real mother was Helen of Troy, who had been raped as a child by Theseus. As a daughter of Zeus, Helen was a deity, so Iphigeneia had one mortal and one immortal parent—in this, she was like the heroes, men of mixed parentage. Iphigeneia is thus sometimes regarded as the first heroine.

Above: The Sacrifice of Iphigeneia, *by Giovanni Battista Tiepolo (1696–1770), shows the goddess Artemis substituting a deer for Iphigeneia.*

An earlier (and less political) play by Euripides, *Iphigeneia among the Taurians*, tells the rest of the story. Iphigeneia has arrived on the Black Sea coast of the Crimea and become a priestess of Artemis. The cult there was unusually bloodthirsty, requiring the sacrifice of all foreigners who were shipwrecked in the vicinity. The action begins when Iphigeneia encounters a castaway Greek who turns out to be her own brother, Orestes. Having discovered his true identity in the nick of time, Iphigeneia hatches a plot to allow them both to escape with the image of Artemis and return to Greece. The play ends with the appearance of the goddess Athena, who decrees that Iphigeneia will serve as priestess to Artemis at the shrine of Brauron in Attica, where young girls served the goddess. Artemis will no longer receive human sacrifices, and must henceforth be satisfied by a symbolic spilling of a tiny amount of blood at her sanctuary in Aulis, where Orestes is commanded to found a temple.

In *Catalogue of Heroines*, a fragmentary work usually attributed to the Greek poet Hesiod (fl. 800 BCE), Agamemnon's daughter, here called Iphimede, is rescued by Artemis and becomes the goddess Einodia. This version was later recalled by Pausanias (143–176 CE), according to whom the princess became Hecate, a better-known goddess who, like Einodia, is sometimes treated as an aspect of Artemis and at other times as a distinct divinity.

In *Agamemnon*, the first play of the *Oresteia* (458 BCE)—a dramatic trilogy by Aeschylus (525–456 BCE) that also comprises *Choephoroe* (*Libation Bearers*) and *Eumenides*—the eponymous king returns in triumph from Troy to Argos with a captive, the Trojan prophetess Cassandra. The pair are then murdered by Agamemnon's wife Clytemnestra and her lover Aegisthus. The queen is inspired to commit this crime, not by Agamemnon's adultery—she has also been unfaithful—but by his earlier sacrifice of their daughter Iphigeneia. In this version there is no reference to a last-minute substitution at the altar: the princess dies painfully.

The tragic figure of the young Iphigeneia, sacrificed for her father's ambitions, continued to inspire later writers.

Roman poet Ennius (239–169 BCE) wrote an *Iphigeneia* that survives only in fragments. For Lucretius (c. 100–c. 53 BCE) in *De rerum natura* (*On the Nature of Things*), the story of Iphigeneia's sacrifice was an indication of the evils that religion could cause.

Iphigeneia's story has remained a popular subject throughout history. French playwright Jean Racine (1639–1699) wrote *Iphigénie* (1674). German composer Christoph Gluck (1714–1787) wrote two operas— *Iphigeneia in Aulis* (1772) and *Iphigeneia in Tauris* (1779)— the first of which was inspired by Racine's play. In the 19th century Austrian composer Franz Schubert (1797–1828) set to music the poem "Iphigeneia" by Johann Mayrhofer. German Nobel laureate Gerhart Hauptmann (1862–1946) wrote *Iphigenie in Delphi* (1941) and *Iphigenie in Aulis* (1944), the first two plays in his *Die Atridentetralogie*, a series of four works that gave an account of the ancient myth in the context of World War II (1939–1945).

The story continues to inspire reinterpretation. In 1977, Greek director Michalis Kakoyannis filmed a highly influential *Iphigeneia in Aulis*. In the 1990s American composer and satirist Peter Schickele wrote the cantata *Iphigeneia in Brooklyn* under the pseudonym P. D. Q. Bach, a mythical son of J. S. Bach. *The Songs of the Kings* (2002), a novel by Barry Unsworth, is another modern reworking of the myth of Iphigeneia.

In the footsteps of the princess

To commemorate Iphigeneia's role as a priestess, some young Greek women were chosen to spend time in seclusion at the temples of Artemis. The girls were known as *arktoi* (bears), and their time there was known as the *arkteia*. Small vases found at these sanctuaries show girls taking part in races and other games, and there are statues of girls holding animals, presumably symbolic offerings to Artemis, who protected the young of all species.

In *Lysistrata*, a comedy by Greek playwright Aristophanes (c. 450–c. 388 BCE), this ritual is said to have been carried out by all Athenian girls before marriage. Yet the weight of evidence suggests rather that only a small number of girls from elite families were selected to perform this service on behalf of all girls. Unlike the widely practiced custom of dedicating toys to Artemis before marriage, the *arkteia* seems to have been carried out only by very young girls, and thus its connection to marriage remains unclear.

DEBORAH LYONS

Above: An ancient Roman fresco depicting Iphigeneia in Tauris. The exact date of composition is unknown, but is no later than 79 CE. According to Greek historian Herodotus (c. 484–425 BCE), the Taurians made human sacrifices to a deity whom they identified with Iphigeneia.

Bibliography

Bulfinch, Thomas. *Bulfinch's Mythology.* New York: Barnes & Noble, 2006.

Euripides, and P. Burian and A. Shapiro, eds. *The Complete Euripides.* New York: Oxford University Press, 2009–2010.

SEE ALSO: Agamemnon; Atreus; Electra; Helen; Orestes; Paris; Pelops; Tantalus.

JASON

The Greek hero Jason was the son of Aeson, king of Iolcus in Thessaly, and was brought up in secret after his father was deposed. As an adult Jason attempted to win back his father's kingdom. He was set the task of bringing back the Golden Fleece, which was guarded by a sleepless dragon.

Below: This 15th-century bronze statue is a copy of a second-century Roman original depicting Jason with a winged genius, or guardian spirit.

After the death of King Cretheus of Iolcus, who was Jason's grandfather, the throne should have gone to his eldest son, Aeson, born of his wife Tyro. However, Tyro had another son, Pelias, from an earlier relationship with the god Poseidon. Pelias seized the throne from the rightful heir, Aeson, whom he then kept a prisoner in his palace. Aeson's wife, whom the Athenian grammarian Apollodorus (fl. 140 BCE) names Polymede, gave birth to Jason in captivity. Fearing for the child's safety, she pretended that the baby had been stillborn. The child was smuggled out of the palace and placed into the care of the centaur Cheiron, who reared the boy in his cave on Mount Pelion. When Jason grew up, he went down the mountain to reclaim the throne.

By this time Pelias had managed to incur the anger of the goddess Hera, to whom he had neglected to sacrifice. He had also been warned by an oracle that he would be killed by a man wearing one sandal. While making his way toward Iolcus, Jason had to cross the Anaurus River. There he was approached by an old woman (really Hera in disguise) who begged him to carry her across. While doing so, he lost one of his sandals in the river. When he reached Pelias, who was celebrating a festival in honor of Poseidon, Jason appeared wearing one sandal. Pelias recognized his future murderer and slyly asked him what he would do if he learned that somebody was destined to kill him. Prompted by Hera, Jason replied that he would send him to fetch the fabled Golden Fleece (see box, page 151). Pelias replied that when that was done, he would gladly give up his throne to Aeson's son.

Summoning the Argonauts

Pelias confidently expected Jason to fail in this quest, because the fleece was guarded by a sleepless dragon, but Jason intended to prove himself and commissioned a 50-oared ship, called the *Argo*. To man the ship he summoned the best youths in Greece. Known as the Argonauts, they included Heracles, Theseus, Meleager, Orpheus the musician, the twins

Castor and Pollux, Zetes and Calais (winged sons of Boreas, the north wind), Telamon (Ajax's father), Peleus (Achilles's father), and Augeas (whose filthy stables Heracles cleaned for his fifth labor). Some accounts say the group also included the athlete Atalanta, but others say that Jason rejected her, fearing that a woman would cause trouble.

The Argonauts sailed at dawn one morning and were to have many adventures before reaching Colchis. Landing first on Lemnos, they found an island with no male inhabitants. Sometime earlier the men of Lemnos had rejected their wives because of their unbearable smell, a curse put upon them for insulting Aphrodite. The men had taken Thracian girlfriends and the Lemnian women had murdered them in revenge. However, the women now realized that their population was in danger of dying out. They welcomed the Argonauts with open arms, and many children were conceived before the *Argo* set sail again.

After sailing through the Hellespont, the strait that separates the Aegean Sea from the Sea of Marmara, the

Below: The Argonauts, *by Italian artist Cesare Dell 'Acqua (1821–1904), depicts the adventurers leaving their homeland.*

The Legend of the Golden Fleece

The Golden Fleece had once graced the back of a miraculous flying and talking ram. The story of the fleece began in Thebes, where the firstborn children of King Athamas, a boy Phrixus and a girl Helle, incurred the hatred of their stepmother, Ino, who wanted her own son to succeed to the throne. When the crops failed, Ino announced that an oracle had decreed that Phrixus must be sacrificed to avert famine. As Athamas prepared to slaughter his son, Hermes, messenger of the gods sent a golden-fleeced ram to Phrixus and Helle. They jumped on the creature's back and were whisked away.

During the flight Helle lost her grip on the ram and fell to her death in the sea named for her, the Hellespont. Phrixus held on until the ram reached Colchis. He settled there, sacrificed the ram to Zeus, and hung the fleece in a grove dedicated to the god Ares. However, when Phrixus died (some sources say he was murdered), he was not given a proper burial, and an oracle proclaimed that the land of Iolcus would fail to prosper until the Golden Fleece was brought back to Greece and the ghost of Phrixus liberated.

Argonauts landed at Arcton, where they were welcomed and feasted by the Doliones people. The Argonauts set sail for the Bosporus, the channel leading to the Black Sea, but were blown back to Arcton by a headwind. In the darkness the Doliones mistook their former guests for pirates and attacked them. Many died on both sides, including the Doliones' king, and the Argonauts hastened away again.

Some time later, during a rowing contest between Jason and Heracles to see who could row the longest, Heracles broke his oar. The Argonauts landed so that he could cut another. Heracles's lover, a beautiful youth called Hylas, also disembarked and went in search of water. At the pool he was seen by a water nymph, who fell in love with him and abducted him. Heracles searched for the boy in vain. At dawn, when neither Hylas nor Heracles had reappeared, the *Argo* sailed, leaving both behind.

A boxing match and Clashing Rocks

On the island of Bebrycos in the Bosporus, the Argonauts were challenged to a boxing match by Amycus, king of the Bebrycians. After a long fight, Pollux killed Amycus with a blow to his skull. When they saw their king was dead, the Bebrycians attacked the Argonauts. Easily overcoming their foes, the Argonauts sacked their palace and sailed on again.

After stopping at Salmydessus to save its king, Phineus, from the Harpies (see box, page 153), the Argonauts then

Above: This Roman sculpture depicts King Aeetes watching Jason as he grapples with one of two fire-breathing bulls before harnessing them to plow a field and sow dragon's teeth, as commanded by the king.

approached the Symplegades, the "Clashing Rocks" that guarded the far end of the Bosporus and smashed anything moving between them. On Phineus's advice, the Argonauts sent a dove through first, and then quickly tried to follow it. However, they would have been crushed had the goddess Athena not restrained the rocks. When the Argonauts were safely through, the Symplegades froze in place forever, as the gods had decreed would happen should any man survive the crossing.

The Argonauts arrive at Colchis

After sailing for many days and surviving many more adventures, the Argonauts finally landed at Colchis, on the eastern shore of the Black Sea. Jason sought out King Aeetes and demanded the return of the fleece. Aeetes agreed, on condition that Jason carry out a seemingly impossible task: he was to yoke two fire-breathing bulls, plow a field, and sow dragon's teeth from which would spring fearsome warriors whom he would have to kill.

At this point the goddesses Hera and Athena stepped in to help their favorite, Jason. They invoked the help of Aphrodite, goddess of love, to make Aeetes' daughter,

King Phineus and the Harpies

King Phineus lived in Salmydessus in eastern Thrace. He was a seer who had offended the gods by his all-too-accurate predictions. He had been punished with blindness and the constant torment of two Harpies, winged fiends who snatched away his meals and fouled the leftovers with an unappetizing stench. When the Argonauts arrived, Phineus ordered a banquet to be spread before them. However, the Harpies immediately swooped down and fouled the food. Zetes and Calais, the winged sons of Boreas, jumped up and, sword in hand, flew off in pursuit of the Harpies. They caught up with them on the Floating Islands, where, according to different accounts, either the monsters dropped dead from exhaustion, the gods called them off, or the Harpies themselves promised not to bother Phineus again. Because of this, the isles were renamed the Turning Islands.

In gratitude for being delivered from the Harpies, Phineus gave Jason valuable advice on how to navigate the Bosporus and warned him of some of the dangers the Argonauts would face on their voyage.

Medea, fall in love with Jason. Medea was a powerful sorceress. She gave Jason a magic potion to smear over his body, which protected him from fire. When the armed warriors sprang from the seeds he planted, Jason threw a stone among them so that they attacked each other. While they did so, he killed them one by one.

When Jason completed this task, Aeetes decided to kill the Argonauts. He unwisely confided his plans to Medea, who warned the Argonauts and took them by night to the sacred grove where the fleece hung. She drugged the dragon so that Jason was able to take the fleece. Medea fled with the Argonauts, taking her young half-brother Apsyrtus with her. When Aeetes sailed in pursuit, Medea and Jason distracted him by murdering Apsyrtus, dismembering his body, and tossing his limbs upon the waves. While Aeetes gathered his son's remains, the Argonauts escaped.

Return to Thessaly

There are several accounts of how the Agonauts returned to Greece. Some say that Jason and Medea traveled all the way to Italy's western coast to seek purification from Circe, Medea's aunt, for the murder of Apsyrtus. At some point during their return, Jason married Medea so that she could not be returned to her father.

Back in Iolcus, Jason discovered that Pelias had killed Jason's parents and newborn baby brother. In order to depose Pelias, Medea told Jason to remain hidden while she ingratiated herself with Pelias's daughters. She demonstrated to them how she could transform an old ram into a young lamb by mincing and boiling it with some special herbs. She then suggested that the daughters could restore Pelias to youth by using the same method. The daughters killed their father, chopped him up, and boiled the pieces—but Medea had been lying. However, Jason and Medea were unable to profit from this because Pelias's son Acastus took the throne and expelled them. The couple fled to Corinth, where they found refuge with King Creon.

For 10 years Jason and Medea enjoyed happiness in Corinth and had three children, but eventually Jason's ambition destroyed them. King Creon offered Jason his daughter Glauce (or Creusa) as his wife. When Medea discovered Jason's plan to divorce her and marry Glauce, she devised a fearful revenge.

Feigning joy at the prospective marriage, Medea sent the bride a beautiful garment that she had steeped in a lethal poison. The bride died in agony. Creon clasped his daughter in his arms, and he too died from the poison. Medea then slaughtered two of her children by Jason before fleeing to Athens. The story of Medea's revenge was dramatized by the playwright Euripedes in his tragedy *Medea* (431 BCE). Without Medea, Jason achieved very little. He never ruled Iolcus, and he died when a rotting piece of the *Argo* fell upon him as he sat beneath it.

Jason in literature and art

The main sources for Jason's myth are in Apollonius of Rhodes' epic the *Argonautica* (third century BCE) and Pindar's *Fourth Pythian Ode*. The mythological handbooks of Apollodorus, Ovid, and Hyginus also contain accounts of his story.

The myth of Jason and the Golden Fleece was widely represented in ancient art. Notable modern paintings include Alfred Waterhouse's *Hylas and the Nymphs* (1896) and *Jason and Medea* (1907), Maxfield Parrish's *Chiron and Jason* (1908), Evelyn De Morgan's *Medea* (1889), and Salvator Rosa's *Jason Charming the Dragon* (1665).

KATHRYN CHEW

Bibliography
Apollonius, and Peter Green, trans. *The Argonautica*. Berkeley, CA: University of California Press, 1997.
Pindar, and Anthony Verity, trans. *The Complete Odes*. New York: Oxford University Press, 2008.

SEE ALSO: Castor and Pollux; Harpies; Heracles; Medea; Orpheus; Theseus.

LAOCOON

Laocoon, a priest to either Apollo or Poseidon, figured prominently in the fall of Troy as the voice of caution whose efforts were frustrated by both Greek cunning and the intervention of two serpents. Laocoon's origins are unclear—he was either the son of the Trojan king Priam or the son of Antenor, one of Priam's confidantes who betrayed the Trojans during the war.

Laocoon met his horrific fate during the last days of the Trojan War. Roman poet Virgil (70–19 BCE) retold the priest's story in his epic poem *Aeneid*. After nearly 10 years of fighting, the Greeks built an enormous wooden horse and placed inside its hollow belly their fiercest warriors. They then rolled the horse up to the gates of Troy, and the armies retreated to their ships, appearing to sail away, presumably to Greece. However, they only sailed out of view of the Trojans, behind an island called Tenedos. Upon seeing the horse, Laocoon immediately warned the gathering crowd by saying that he feared the Greeks, even when they were bearing gifts. According to Greek writer Apollodorus (fl. 140 BCE), Laocoon suggested that there could be armed men within, waiting to lay waste to the city. For a few moments the Trojans were convinced by the priest's words, and they debated how to dispose of the horse. Laocoon even hurled his spear into the horse's belly, and the hollow boom from within would have heightened the Trojans' suspicions had a Greek named Sinon not appeared before them.

Lies and sea serpents

Sinon had been left behind as part of a Greek plan hatched by the hero Odysseus. A convincing storyteller, Sinon would persuade the Trojans to take the horse inside the city gates. He told the assembled crowd that the goddess Athena was angry with the Greeks because they had stolen the Palladium, a statue made in her honor, from inside the city. The only way for the Greeks to ensure a safe passage back

Left: The Laocoon Group, Vatican City, Rome. The statue (created c. second century BCE–first century CE) depicts a sea serpent strangling Laocoon and his sons.

Ancient Superstitions

Superstition played a significant role in the fall of Troy. The Trojans feared Athena's wrath if they did not take the wooden horse into the city, and they took Laocoon's death as a definite sign that he had displeased the gods. After interpreting these apparent messages from the gods, the Trojans took the horse inside the city gates and had a huge celebration, complete with the singing of hymns and decoration of the city's temples. Little did they know that death, destruction, and the fall of their city awaited them.

Ancient people were extremely superstitious and considered many occurrences to be divine messages. The Romans, for instance, believed that anyone who stumbled on the threshold when leaving their house in the morning should go back inside. They also believed that bad dreams would come true, that a black cat should never enter a house, and that it was an ominous sign if a rooster crowed during a party. Superstitions were often grounded in polytheistic beliefs—the worship of many different gods and goddesses—which provided numerous opportunities for offending deities and invoking unhappy consequences. The Greeks and Romans, in particular, were careful to make appropriate sacrifices, follow procedures in every ceremony, and give due credit to their deities.

Right: An engraving of Laocoon from the Italian book Historia deorum fatidicorum *by Pierre Mussard (1675). The words above the image relate that Laocoon was the son of Priam and Hecuba.*

home was to make a sacrifice to appease Athena. The lying Greek told the Trojans that he was the intended sacrificial victim, but that he had escaped after his fellow soldiers sailed away. He added that the Greeks also hoped to regain the goddess's favor by building a wooden horse to replace the Palladium. According to Sinon, the Greeks made the horse extremely large in the hope that it would not fit through the city gates since, if it were to get inside, it would grant Troy Athena's protection.

Both Sinon and his story were very convincing, but the Trojans' fate was sealed by what happened next. As Sinon was finishing his story, Laocoon was tending to the sacrifice of a bull. Suddenly, from the direction of Tenedos where the Greeks were hiding with their ships, two serpents glided over the waves, with enormous coiled bodies, bloodred eyes, and flickering tongues. Once ashore, they made their way toward Laocoon's young sons. Accounts vary about what happened next. According to Virgil and Greek poet Euphorion (c. third century BCE), the serpents

strangled and devoured Laocoon's sons before attacking Laocoon himself. Arctinus (c. eighth century BCE), another Greek poet, says that Laocoon and only one of his sons were killed. A third account, corroborated by Apollodorus, the Greek poets Bacchylides (c. fifth century BCE) and Quintus Smyrnaeus (c. fourth century CE), and the Athenian playwright Sophocles (c. 496–406 BCE), is that only Laocoon's sons were killed. All sources agree, however, that as the Trojans scattered in horror, the serpents left the remnants of the bodies on the shore and disappeared within Athena's temple inside the city.

The Trojans' fatal error

Ancient writers differ in their accounts of why Laocoon was attacked. Euphorion wrote that the sun god Apollo sent the serpents because Laocoon and his wife had offended the deity by making love in sight of his statue. Other writers maintained that the sea god Poseidon, who was on the side of the Greeks, sent the serpents to destroy

Above: Laocoon *by Spanish artist El Greco (1541–1614). The painting depicts the serpents' attack on the priest and is one of the most famous visual representations of the episode.*

Laocoon because the god feared that the Trojans would destroy the horse if the priest were not silenced. Regardless of who sent the serpents, their gruesome actions had the desired effect. The Trojans opened their arms to Sinon and took him and the wooden horse inside the city gates. That night, Sinon let the soldiers out of the horse and lit a beacon on the shore to signal to the other Greeks, waiting in their ships. The Greeks massacred the city's sleeping inhabitants and captured Troy.

Laocoon in art

The story of Laocoon survives on two frescoes in Pompeii, a Roman city buried after the eruption of Mount Vesuvius in 79 CE; in addition, El Greco, a Spanish artist born in Crete, paid tribute to the Trojan priest and his sons in his painting *Laocoon* (1610). In the 19th century, French composer Hector Berlioz (1803–1869) wrote the opera *Les Troyens*, in which Laocoon has a key role in the first act. Perhaps the most compelling reminder of Laocoon's demise is a nearly eight-foot- (2.4-meter-) tall statue that now stands in the Vatican in Rome. Sometime between the second century BCE and the first century CE, three sculptors from Rhodes immortalized the anguish of Laocoon and his sons in marble. When fragments of it were discovered in the 16th century, renowned Italian sculptor Michelangelo (1475–1564) was asked to restore the statue, which has been widely lauded for its realism and emotional impact.

DEBORAH THOMAS

Bibliography

Apollodorus, and Robin Hard, trans. *The Library of Greek Mythology.* New York: Oxford University Press, 2008.
Virgil, and Robert Fagles, trans. *The Aeneid.* New York: Penguin, 2009.

SEE ALSO: Odysseus.

LAOMEDON

In Greek mythology, Laomedon was a king of Troy. His name became a byword for anyone who reneges on a deal. He behaved unscrupulously toward gods and mortals alike, and his conduct brought him to a violent end.

Laomedon's father was Ilus, a mythical king of Troy—it was in reference to him that the city was known alternatively as Ilion, hence the *Iliad* of Homer. Laomedon's mother was Eurydice, the daughter of Adrastos, king of the Greek city-state of Argos. Laomedon had one sister, Themiste, whose grandson, Aeneas, became the legendary founder of the Roman race.

Laomedon either had several wives, or else a different wife in several stories. Among them were Strymo, whose father was Scamander, a god associated with a river at Troy; Placia, the daughter of Otreus, a king of nearby Phrygia; Calybe, a local nymph; and Leucippe, about whom nothing is known other than her name.

Numerous offspring

Laomedon's marriage or marriages produced many children, although it is not always clear which child was born to which wife. His most famous sons were Priam and Tithonus. The former's mother may have been either Strymo or Leucippe; Tithonus is usually described as the child of Strymo. Calybe was the mother of another boy, Boucolion, who became the father of two sons killed by the Greeks in the Trojan War. According to some sources, Ganymede was also a son of Laomedon, although in most accounts his father was Tros (Laomedon's paternal grandfather). The other sons of Laomedon were Lampos, Clytios, and Hicetaon.

Laomedon had several daughters, too, including Hesione, Cilla, Astyoche, Aithylla, Medicaste, and Proclia. Some of them married Greeks, and as a result Laomedon's grandchildren fought on both sides during the Trojan War. Hesione, for example, became the concubine of the Greek hero Telamon; their son Teucer took his father's side during

Above: A medieval tapestry depicting the incident, recounted in some myth collections, in which Jason and the Argonauts tried to enter Troy but were refused access by Laomedon. According to some accounts, this action enraged Heracles, one of the Argonauts, who returned to kill Laomedon.

the 10-year conflict. Some or all of Laomedon's other daughters escaped the destruction of Troy and accompanied Aeneas to Italy, where they burned their boats in order to force their husbands to settle there. Laomedon was thus an ancestor of Trojans, Greeks, and Romans.

Invoking the wrath of the gods

The downfall of Laomedon came about as an indirect result of a rebellion on Mount Olympus by Apollo and Poseidon. After Zeus had suppressed their uprising, he forced them to offer their services to Laomedon for a

157

whole year during the construction of walls around Troy—working under the supervision of a mortal was one of the greatest possible humiliations for any god. Zeus was also aware of Laomedon's reputation for dishonesty, and he saw this as an opportunity to test the Trojan's good faith.

The *Iliad* gives two different accounts of which god did what: in Book 7, both gods worked on the walls; in Book 21, Poseidon is said to have worked on the walls while Apollo looked after Laomedon's cattle on Mount Ida. In several other versions of the story, Apollo and Poseidon were helped by a mortal, Aeacus, the first king of Aegina. That was because, if they had carried out the work unaided, Troy would have been impregnable, and it was preordained that the city would fall to the Greeks. In one

Below: This 19th-century engraving shows Heracles rescuing Hesione from the rock on which she had been offered for sacrifice to a sea monster.

account, when the walls were completed, three snakes tried to surmount the ramparts: two fell dead, but the third succeeded in gaining entrance to the city through the part of the wall that Aeacus had built. This was taken as an omen that Troy would be taken by Aeacus's descendants.

The wages of sin

When Apollo and Poseidon had finished their work, Laomedon refused to pay them the agreed sum. This was an affront to divine honor, so Apollo infested Troy with a plague, and Poseidon sent a sea monster that snatched people from the shore. In an effort to find a remedy for these afflictions, Laomedon consulted various oracles. They foretold that relief would come only if he gave Hesione to be devoured by the sea monster, so he chained his daughter to the rocks near the sea. Just then, however, the hero Heracles arrived and offered to kill the monster on the condition that he would be rewarded with the divine horses that Zeus had given to Laomedon's grandfather, Tros, in exchange for Ganymede. Laomedon accepted the terms, but after Heracles had killed the monster and reunited father and daughter, he went back on the agreement. Heracles left Troy empty-handed, but vowed to return and take his revenge.

Heracles was as good as his word. He came back with an army, which besieged and then captured Troy. He killed Laomedon and all his sons except Tithonus, who had previously been carried off by Eos, and Priam, who was spared because he alone had counseled Laomedon to honor his agreement. Finally, Heracles gave Hesione as a concubine to his companion Telamon, the son of Aeacus.

Laomedon was buried at the Scaean Gate, one of the main entrances to Troy, and it was said that the city would remain unconquered for as long as his body remained undisturbed. His tomb was eventually destroyed during the Greek siege of Troy; the city fell soon afterward.

In the modern remains of the temple of Aphaea on the Greek island of Aegina, carvings on one of the pediments depict Heracles' sack of Troy. The bearded warrior shown collapsing in the corner is thought to be Laomedon.

JIM MARKS

Bibliography

Gardner, Jane F. *Roman Myths*. Austin, TX: University of Texas Press, 1993.

Homer, and Robert Fagles, trans. *The Iliad*. New York: Penguin, 2009.

SEE ALSO: Aeneas; Ganymede; Heracles; Jason; Priam; Tithonus.

LEDA

In one of the most famous stories of Greek mythology, the beautiful Leda became an object of the amorous attentions of Zeus, who took the form of a swan in order to pursue her.

Leda was the daughter of King Thestius of Aetolia and sister of Althaea, the mother of Meleager. She married Tyndareos, the king of Sparta. Her beauty was so great that she attracted the attention of Zeus, the king of the gods. When he went off on his various amorous adventures, Zeus took on a wide range of physical forms in order to escape the watchful eye of his jealous wife, Hera. He came to Leda disguised as a great white swan that flew into her arms for protection from a pursuing eagle.

According to the most popular version of the myth, after her union with Zeus, Leda laid two eggs. From one egg hatched two sons. Although they were known together as the Dioscuri, from the Greek *dios kouroi*, "sons of Zeus," only one of them, Pollux (or Polydeuces), was the son of the god. The other son, Castor, was sired by Tyndareos. From the second egg two daughters were born: Clytemnestra, who was fathered by Leda's mortal husband, and Helen, who claimed Zeus as her father.

A less familiar version of the story suggests that Leda laid only a single egg, from which the Dioscuri hatched. Clytemnestra, the daughter of Tyndareos and Leda, was born in the normal way. Helen, meanwhile, was a child of Zeus and Nemesis, who mated while transformed into birds. Their egg was tended by Leda. When Helen hatched,

Below: Leda and the Swan *was painted in 1601 by Flemish artist Peter Paul Rubens (1577–1640).*

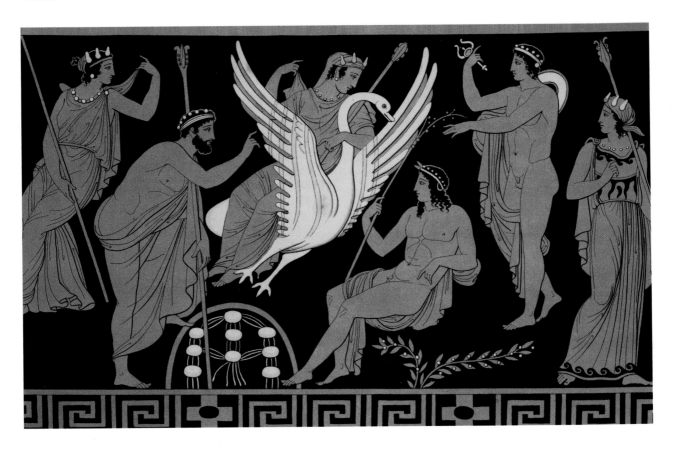

Above: This ancient Greek painting of unknown date depicts Zeus, in the form of a swan, abducting Leda.

Leda raised the child as her own daughter. Helen grew up to believe that the sufferings of her life sprang from the bizarre circumstances of her birth. To commemorate the form Zeus had taken during his union with Leda, the god placed the constellation Cygnus (Latin for "swan") in the Milky Way.

Leda also had three other daughters by Tyndareos: Timandra, who married Echemus, king of Arcadia, but then ran off with Phyleus, king of Doulichium; Philonoe, who was made immortal by Artemis; and Phoebe, who is mentioned only once in ancient literature, in the play *Iphigeneia at Aulis* by Greek dramatist Euripides (c. 486–c. 406 BCE), but who appears on several Attic vases depicting Leda's family.

Leda in art

Whatever the story, the egg is central to it. It features in numerous vase paintings from about 450 BCE, and Greek travel writer Pausanias (143–176 CE) claimed to have seen the shell itself suspended on ribbons from the rafters of a temple in Sparta. Leda's story has remained popular throughout history. Among the artists who have painted Leda and the swan are Leonardo da Vinci (1452–1519),

Michelangelo (1475–1564), Correggio (Antonio Allegri, 1494–1534), Tintoretto (c. 1518–1594), Caliari (1528–1588), Peter Paul Rubens (1577–1640), François Boucher (1703–1770), and Eugène Delacroix (1798–1863). In English verse, perhaps the greatest treatment of the subject is found in "Leda and the Swan" by Irish poet W. B. Yeats (1865–1939).

There seems to have been no cult or ritual associated directly with Leda. Her fame rests entirely on her unusual union with Zeus and the offspring she bore to him and her mortal husband.

The fate of Leda's sons

When they grew up, the Dioscuri excelled almost equally in male pursuits, even though Castor was mortal and Pollux the son of Zeus. Castor was a skilled horseman; his brother a great boxer. The heavenly twins took part in two great mythical exploits. The first was the Calydonian boar hunt, in which a group of heroes was hired to kill a boar that had been sent by Artemis to ravage the kingdom of Calydon. The second was Jason's expedition with the Argonauts in search of the Golden Fleece.

In time Castor and Pollux came into a fatal conflict with their cousins, Idas and Lynceus, the sons of Aphareus, king of Messenia. The cause of their disagreement was either the ownership of some cattle or the Dioscuri's desire for the women betrothed to Idas and his brother. In the latter version of the story, the Dioscuri abducted their cousins' brides on their wedding day and took them off as their own wives.

Whatever the cause of the dispute, the four eventually went into battle against each other. Idas stabbed Castor, Pollux killed Lynceus, and then Zeus intervened by blasting Idas with a thunderbolt. When Pollux found that his brother had been mortally wounded, he begged Zeus to be allowed to die in his place. The chief god denied this request but offered a compromise: Pollux could share his immortality with Castor. Henceforth the brothers spent alternate days in the realm of the dead and on the heights of Mount Olympus. Finally they were turned into stars, the Gemini, and from their place in the night sky became the guiding gods for sailors. To this day Castor and Pollux are associated with Saint Elmo's fire, dual balls of light that play around the masts of ships during thunderstorms. This meteorological phenomenon was taken as an omen that the Dioscuri would protect ships in bad weather.

Helen and Clytemnestra

Leda's two daughters, Helen and Clytemnestra, both figured prominently in Greek mythology. Clytemnestra murdered her husband Agamemnon and was killed in turn by her son Orestes. Her story was popular with classical authors

and was the subject of the Oresteia trilogy of plays by Aeschylus (525–456 BCE). Helen's abduction by Paris was the cause of the Trojan war. Her importance was so great that she was worshiped as a goddess. She is honored in archaic poetry as a divinity, and, according to Euripides, she was transformed into a star at the end of her mortal life. Other accounts relate that she was buried with her husband, Menelaus, in a grave at Therapne, near Sparta.

In Sparta itself Helen became the focus of a cult of tree worship. Young girls would dance around a special tree in honor of the most beautiful woman in history. They would place a wreath on the tree and pour olive oil drawn from a silver flask onto its roots. The first celebration of the rite concluded when the girls cut an inscription into the bark: "I am Helen's tree."

KARELISA HARTIGAN

Bibliography

Euripides, and P. Burian and A. Shapiro, eds. *The Complete Euripides.* New York: Oxford University Press, 2009–2010.
Pausanias, and Peter Levi, trans. *Guide to Greece.* New York: Viking Press, 1984.

SEE ALSO: Atalanta; Castor and Pollux; Clytemnestra; Helen; Menelaus.

Right: The story of Leda and the swan has remained popular with artists through the ages. This sculpture is by Bartolommeo Ammannati (1511–1592).

LYCAON

In the mythology of ancient Greece, Lycaon was the legendary first king of Arcadia. He offended the god Zeus by serving him human flesh and was turned into a wolf as a punishment.

Lycaon's father was Pelasgus, the mythical ancestor of the Pelasgians, the earliest inhabitants of Greece. His mother is given various names, but she is always associated with springs or the ocean. Lycaon was thus a child of earth and water. He founded Lycosoura, the "first city the sun shone on." The games celebrated on Mount Lycaon were sometimes said to be the oldest festivals of their kind held in Greece. Lycaon's birthplace, Arcadia, the landlocked mountainous area in the center of the Peloponnese, was also the native land of the chief god Zeus himself. The Arcadians and their predecessors the Pelasgians were believed to have existed before the moon and to have lived off acorns before the development of agriculture. In the archaic and classical period they remained, from the Greek point of view, somewhat primitive—herdsmen more often than agriculturalists, living in scattered settlements that were not as dignified as a *poleis*, the Greek name for a civilized city–state. Instead of proper shields, the Arcadian warriors carried the skins of bears and wolves.

Flesh-eating

Scholars believe that Lycaon's name is derived from *lykos*, the Greek for "wolf." Wolves in Greek stories are typically hungry for human flesh, and Lycaon's story includes themes of cannibalism and lycanthropy—the transformation of humans into wolves. Zeus was entertained by Lycaon at a feast during which someone—either Lycaon himself or one of his 50 sons—served Zeus the flesh of a young boy. Zeus kicked over the table (the regular response in myth to a cannibalistic meal) and struck the household with lightning, killing all the sons. Lycaon himself was turned into a wolf. In some versions of the story, Lycaon's crime provoked Zeus to destroy the entire human race with a great flood, of which the only survivors were Deucalion and Pyrrha.

The child butchered at Lycaon's feast is variously identified. In some stories he is an anonymous waif, in others he is Lycaon's son Nyctimus; in at least one version he is Lycaon's grandson Arcas, whom Zeus later restored to life so that he could become the collective ancestor of the Arcadian people, who bear his name. Arcas's name seems related to *arktos* or *arkos*, the Greek for "bear"; Arcas's mother, Callisto, Lycaon's daughter, was turned into a bear. The Arcadians thus appear to originate from a wolf and a bear—further confirmation of their closeness to animals.

These themes reappear in the rituals that were said to have been held by the Arcadians on Mount Lycaon in honor of Zeus. In one, for example, a sacrificial meal was prepared of animal entrails stewed in a pot. A single piece of human flesh was included, and the worshiper who ate it was turned into a wolf for eight or nine years, at the end of which, if he had abstained from further cannibalism throughout the intervening period, he would be restored to human form. This story was related by Greek philosopher Plato (c. 428–c. 348 BCE), who clearly believed that the transformation was imaginary. He was probably right to think that the cannibalism was imaginary as well—modern archaeologists who have studied the sacrificial residue on Mount Lycaon have found no trace of human remains. While it is certain that some sort of ritual was conducted in this sanctuary, it seems that the widely circulated account of what took place there was substantially different from what really went on. It is more likely that the ceremonies symbolized cannibalism but did not actually involve it. One possibility is that rituals were performed in which the participants dressed as wolves and pretended to eat human flesh.

Whatever the truth of these stories of cannibalism and lycanthropy, they tell us something about the meaning of the ritual. It is probably significant that, in several tellings of the story, those who served Zeus human flesh did so in order to test whether he was really a god. A god, it seems, could tell the difference between humans and animals, but

Right: This engraving by French painter Bernard Picart (1673–1733) depicts the transformation of Lycaon into a wolf.

B. Picart sculp. dir.

LYCAON TRANSFORMÉ EN LOUP.

Lycaon metamorphosed into a Wolf.

Lycaon in einen Wolf verändert

Lycaon in een Wolf verandert.

Above: The modern remains of the walls of Messene. This ancient city of the southwestern Peloponnese was originally part of Arcadia.

humans could not. Humans avoid eating each other not naturally but through obedience to an externally imposed cultural rule—abstinence is learned behavior. The Lycaon story and the ritual that commemorated it help to account for the separation of gods from humans. The moral seems to be that, if humans are to survive, they must be careful to restrain their animal nature.

Lycaon had one daughter, Callisto, who became a nymph of Artemis but was raped by Zeus. In some versions of the legend, Lycaon served Zeus human flesh as an act of revenge for the violation of his daughter. This rape resulted in Callisto's transformation into a bear. The child of the union was a boy named Arcas. When he grew up, he came upon his mother while hunting and (without recognizing who she was) pursued her. She fled into a sacred sanctuary of Zeus and was about to be killed when Zeus took pity on her and placed her among the stars as the Great Bear constellation, Ursa Major. Zeus also carried Arcas to the stars, making him the star Arcturus or "bear guardian" so that he followed his mother across the night sky. In this story, the transformation into an animal is linked with the violation of a sacred space (like cannibalism, something taboo), and with immortality.

Magical sanctuary

Mount Lycaon was always a place of deep magic and transformations. Historians believe that the mountain was the location of an *abaton*. People who entered it were known as "deer" and were doomed to die within a year. Once again, transformation was linked to annihilation. Animals who took refuge there were not pursued. People and animals within this precinct were believed to cast no shadow, perhaps because they were already classified with the dead: ghosts are immaterial and cannot be grasped, so the light goes right through them. Any place struck by lightning was, for the Greeks, sacred to Zeus. Probably the precinct on Mount Lycaon was thought to be the place where the sons of Lycaon had been struck by lightning.

According to another story about Mount Lycaon, every year one young man was chosen by lot to go to an oak tree on the edge of a lake. There he would hang his clothes, and he'd swim across the water. On the further bank he would be turned into a wolf, in which form he would remain for eight years. Only if he abstained from eating human flesh for the whole time would he again become human. Greek travel writer Pausanias (143–176 CE) claimed to have seen at Olympia a statue of an early Olympic victor who had survived this very ordeal.

JAMES M. REDFIELD

Bibliography

Pausanias, and Peter Levi, trans. *Guide to Greece*. New York: Viking Press, 1984.

Plato, and Robin Waterfield, trans. *Republic*. New York: Oxford University Press, 2008.

SEE ALSO: Callisto; Deucalion.

MAENADS

In ancient Greece, maenads were female worshipers of Dionysus, god of wine, whose behavior was often regarded as unacceptable by conventional society. Maenads also played a role in myth, notably the murder of King Pentheus.

Above: Dating from between 900 and 200 BCE, this carved head of a maenad adorned the walls of a temple of Juno (the Greek Hera) in Tuscany (part of modern Italy).

Maenads were the votaries of Dionysus. They were known by numerous other names, including Bacchantes (Dionysus later became the Roman god Bacchus), potniades ("mistresses"), and thyiades ("mad women"). While they were believed to have magical powers, maenads were ordinary women who took time out from their domestic lives to answer the call of the god.

Wild ceremonies

Dionysus was a god of nature and fertility, and those who worshiped him were encouraged to cast aside their everyday inhibitions. The consumption of wine was central to their ceremonies, because alcohol was thought to be the blood of Dionysus, his very essence. Celebrations included dancing, which was performed either in silence or to the accompaniment of bells, castanets, and clashing cymbals. The movements were deliberately asymmetrical—a reaction against the structured forms associated with Terpsichore, the Greek Muse of dancing—and usually based on walking or running, although they were sometimes performed on the tip of the toes. The maenads' torsos were twisted loosely backward and forward, in imitation, it is thought, of sexual ecstasy, and their hands held above the head to make a shape like a letter *W.*

Maenads also performed in specially composed dramatic scenes and playlets—Dionysus was the god of the theater—and engaged with actors dressed as satyrs in banter of sexual nature. In myth, satyrs were grotesque creatures, of human form for the most part but with the tail of a horse or with the horns, ears, and often the legs of a goat.

Far from the crowd

Dionysian ceremonies were performed well away from centers of population, typically in the mountains, where the maenads could cavort unobserved. Many Greeks believed that the maenads, inspired by Dionysus or more particularly by wine, performed preternatural feats of strength, such as uprooting trees. They were also reputed to have captured wild animals, shredded them alive with their bare hands (a ritual known as *sparagmos*), and then eaten them raw (a ceremony known as *omophagia*).

Additional stories about the maenads related that they possessed magic powers. They could charm snakes, which they placed in their hair or around their bodies. They could not be harmed by fire, which they carried in their hands or

Left: Dance of the Maenads (1526–1535). This fresco by Pippi de' Gianuzzi (c.1499–1546) decorates the walls of the Palazzo del Te in Mantua, Italy.

on their heads. The leading maenads would brandish a *thyrsos*, a rod made of ivy or fennel branches and tipped with a pinecone. When they tapped the ground with their staffs, it would flow with honey, milk, or wine.

The worship of Dionysus was not condoned by conventional Greeks, who perceived it as a flagrant disregard for social norms and a threat to civilization. Hence the word *maenad* derives from the verb "to be insane," for maenads were thought to have been driven mad by Dionysus. For all their wildness, however, the activities of the maenads represented a useful outlet for repressed feelings. The cult of Dionysus was popular because it served a need for catharsis (emotional release), particularly in women, that was not satisfactorily provided by mainstream festivals. Although events such as the Adonia (a celebration of Adonis) or the Thesmophoria (a three-day annual festival held in Athens in honor of Demeter) were useful safety valves for pent-up emotions, they did not offer the uninhibited release that came from being a maenad.

A form of liberation

While it was highly unusual for the principal followers of a male god to be female, the worship of Dionysus may be explicable in sociological terms. In ancient Greek society, women were treated as inferior to men because they were physically less strong and were thought to lack self-control and rationality. The prevalence of women among Dionysus's followers may thus have been a consequence of their desire to live with such stereotyping without fear of criticism.

Within the cult of Dionysus, these supposed characteristics ceased to be faults and became assets that helped the maenads to abandon social conformities and participate fully in the god's wild rites.

Maenads in art and literature

While maenads are depicted on many ancient vase paintings and in sculptures, the most abundant classical source of information about them is *The Bacchae*. First performed in Athens in 405 BCE, this play by Euripides (c. 486–c. 406 BCE) concerns the events that unfolded after Dionysus visited his cousin, Pentheus, king of Thebes. The puritanical young monarch denied that Dionysus was a god and tried to ban the celebration of his ecstatic rites. Greatly offended, the god caused the Theban women—led by Agave, Pentheus's mother—to mistake the king for a wild animal. As they set upon it with their bare hands, the king identified himself and pleaded for mercy. However, the maenads, under the spell of Dionysus, were not capable of charitable or maternal feelings and tore the king limb from limb.

KATHRYN CHEW

Bibliography
Euripides, and P. Burian and A. Shapiro, eds. *The Complete Euripides.* New York: Oxford University Press, 2009–2010.
Graves, Robert. *The Greek Myths.* New York: Penguin, 1993.

SEE ALSO: Adonis; Satyrs.

MEDEA

In Greek myth, Medea was the daughter of King Aeetes of Colchis and the nymph Eidyia; her two grandfathers were the sun god Helios and the sea god Oceanus. Medea was a sorceress, renowned for crimes that seemed especially horrible to the Greeks since they were committed against the men of her own family.

The story of Medea is closely wound with that of Jason, the Greek hero and captain of the Argonauts, who came to Colchis in his quest for the Golden Fleece. According to Apollodorus of Athens, a second-century-BCE collector and recorder of myths, King Aeetes agreed to give Jason the fleece if he would first single-handedly yoke two huge fire-breathing bulls, plow a field with them, and sow the field with dragon's teeth. Jason would surely have been killed by the bulls had Aphrodite, the goddess of love, not caused Medea to fall hopelessly in love with him. The king's daughter secretly offered Jason her assistance, giving him an ointment to spread on his skin and armor that would make him invulnerable to wounds or flames for one day. In exchange, Medea asked him to take her away with him on his ship the *Argo* and marry her. Jason accepted the sorceress's offer, and the next day he used the ointment to successfully complete the task. After he had sowed the dragon's teeth, ferocious armed warriors sprang up. On Medea's advice, Jason threw a rock into the middle of the group to make them fight among themselves, giving him the opportunity to kill them all.

Medea's murders

Aeetes, however, went back on his word and refused to give up the Golden Fleece. Instead, he planned to burn the *Argo* and kill its crew. Medea saved Jason again, leading him by night to the sacred grove where the fleece hung on a tree, protected by a giant dragon or serpent. She lulled the monster to sleep with her charms and drugs, allowing Jason to take the fleece. She then boarded the *Argo* with him, accompanied by her young brother Apsyrtus. According to Apollodorus, when Aeetes pursued the ship, Medea committed her first murder, chopping her brother into pieces and throwing them into the sea. Aeetes was forced to delay his pursuit while he collected the pieces of his son's body in order to give him a proper burial. As a result, Medea escaped on the *Argo* with Jason and the Golden Fleece.

Left: Medea, by English painter Frederick Sandys (1829–1904), depicts the sorceress concocting a magic potion, with the Argonauts' ship and the grove where the Golden Fleece hung in the background.

The king of the gods, Zeus, sent a storm in punishment for the killing of Apsyrtus, and the *Argo* took shelter at the island of the sorceress Circe, Medea's aunt, who cleansed her niece and Jason, absolving them of blame for the murder. They continued to the island of Scheria, where Queen Arete married them, and then to Crete, where they were prevented from landing by a bronze giant, Talos, who protected the island by ceaselessly running around it. A nail in one of Talos's ankles kept all the ichor, or divine blood, in his body, without which he would die. Medea killed the giant by means of her magic, which caused the nail to come free.

When Jason returned home to Iolcus in Greece, he delivered the fleece to his uncle Pelias, who had usurped the throne of Jason's father, Aeson, and, according to Apollodorus, driven Aeson himself to suicide. When Pelias refused to give up the throne, Medea tried to help Jason by persuading Pelias's daughters that she was capable of turning their father back into a vigorous young man. To demonstrate, she killed and chopped up an aged ram and threw it into a boiling cauldron of water with magical herbs. A young lamb leaped out of the pot. The daughters then killed their father and threw his body into the cauldron. For Pelias, however, there was no magical

Below: Jason Swearing Eternal Affection to Medea *by French painter Jean-François de Troy (1679–1752). Jason agreed to marry Medea in return for her assistance in his quest for the Golden Fleece.*

reprieve. The people of Iolcus blamed Jason and Medea for Pelias's death. Pelias's son Acastus took the throne and forced Jason and Medea to flee to Corinth.

A sorceress's revenge

Jason and Medea lived in Corinth for 10 years, where Medea bore her husband two sons, Mermerus and Pheres. However, when King Creon of Corinth offered his daughter Glauce to Jason, Jason was quick to accept, and divorced Medea. In vengeance, Medea sent a poisoned dress to Glauce. It clung to her skin and burned her to death, and it also killed her father, who tried to rescue her. Most sources agree that Medea then murdered her own two small sons in order to complete her revenge on Jason. However, according to another version of the story, Medea fled Corinth, leaving her sons in the sanctuary of the goddess Hera. The citizens of Corinth stoned them to death. The ghosts of Medea's sons terrorized the city, taking the lives of its citizens' children until yearly sacrifices were established in their honor.

Above: This illustration of Medea charming the serpent that guarded the Golden Fleece is by British artist Maxwell Armfield (1881–1972). After Medea lulled the serpent with her charms, allowing Jason to obtain the Golden Fleece, she fled with him aboard the Argo *and murdered her own brother to delay her father's pursuit.*

> ## Medea the Monster
>
> For the Greeks, Medea represented one of the most frightening monsters of all: a powerful woman. She was intelligent, dangerous, and determined and refused to conform to the ideal of loyalty expected of women toward their male family members. She chose her own husband instead of allowing her father to arrange her marriage; she also betrayed her father, murdered her brother and her husband's uncle, and tried to kill her stepson. When her husband discarded her, she destroyed his life by killing his new wife and father-in-law, and, in the most common version of the story, she murdered her own sons, too. The play *Medea*, by Greek dramatist Euripides (c. 486–c. 406 BCE), portrays Medea sympathetically, outcast and powerless in Corinth following her divorce. However, Euripides never lets us forget that Medea is a monster.

In this version of the myth, Medea took refuge in Athens after her escape. There she married King Aegeus and bore him a son, Medus. When Theseus, Aegeus's son by another union, arrived incognito in Athens, Medea persuaded Aegeus to allow her to poison him. At the last second, Aegeus recognized Theseus by the carved sword-hilt he carried, a family heirloom, and struck the poisoned cup out of his hand. Medea fled again. She returned to Colchis and discovered that her father had been deposed by his brother Perses, whom she killed, restoring Aeetes to his throne. This was her last recorded act. No one tells the story of her death, but Apollodorus and Apollonius say that she married the Greek hero Achilles and lived with him in a paradise known as the Isles of the Blessed.

Medea's story has inspired artists and composers through the ages. The myth has been reproduced in operas by Luigi Cherubini in the 18th century and Giovanni Mayr in the 19th century and by Rolf Libermann in the 20th, as well as in the score *Medea*, written for ballet by American composer Samuel Barber (1910–1981). French painter Eugène Delacroix and English painter John William Waterhouse (1849–1917) painted scenes from her life, and her story influenced Toni Morrison's novel *Beloved* (1987).

LAUREL BOWMAN

Bibliography

Apollodorus, and Robin Hard, trans. *The Library of Greek Mythology.* New York: Oxford University Press, 2008.
Graves, Robert. *The Greek Myths.* New York: Penguin, 1993.

SEE ALSO: Achilles; Circe; Jason; Theseus.

MEMNON

Memnon, king of Ethiopia, was the son of Eos, goddess of the dawn, and of a mortal named Tithonus. Toward the end of the Trojan War, Memnon joined the Trojans in their fight against the Greeks, but he was killed by Achilles during combat. Zeus, who favored Memnon, granted him immortality.

Below: This Greek vase from around 500 BCE depicts Achilles (left) and Memnon fighting. Their mothers stand behind them.

Memnon's mother, the goddess Eos, took several lovers, some of whom were mortals. The best-known of these was Tithonus, the son of King Laomedon of Troy, and brother of Priam, who ruled Troy during the Trojan War. Eos seized Tithonus, who was said to be the most handsome man alive, and carried him off to Ethiopia, the edge of the known world and the place where the sun rose and the dawn originated. There she gave birth to Memnon and his brother, Emathion. Both Memnon and Emathion grew up to become kings in the east, taking the thrones of Ethiopia and Arabia respectively.

Eos was so in love with Tithonus that she begged Zeus, king of the gods, to make Tithonus immortal so that he would be her companion for eternity. Zeus granted her request but not in the way Eos expected. He made Tithonus immortal yet prone to the ravages of time. Tithonus aged and withered until, increasingly frustrated with her unattractive lover, Eos either locked him up in their bedchamber or, according to other accounts, transformed him into a grasshopper, which renews itself periodically by shedding its skin.

Memnon at Troy

In the last year of the Trojan War, after the Trojan hero Hector had been slain by Achilles, King Priam sent for help from his brother Tithonus. Memnon set off with a force of 2,000 men and 200 chariots to aid the hard-pressed and demoralized Trojans. Marching north toward Troy, Memnon subdued all the nations he encountered on the way.

Memnon was an impressive commander and an imposing warrior who, like Achilles, wore armor forged by Hephaestus, the god of fire and metalworking. When he arrived at Troy he engaged the Greeks in a tremendous battle, killing several Greek heroes, including Antilochus, son of Nestor, who was trying to protect his father from Memnon's forces. The same day, emboldened by the successes of their Ethiopian reinforcements on the field, the Trojans attempted to burn the Greek ships, but darkness fell before they could accomplish this task.

Achilles was absent from the Greek camp during this engagement. The following day, told by his mother, a sea goddess, of the death of his friend Antilochus, Achilles hurried back to the scene of the action. There he found Memnon engaged in single combat with the Greek hero Ajax. Brushing Ajax aside, Achilles attacked Memnon with ferocity. While the two were locked in battle, their mothers, Eos and Thetis, each pleaded with Zeus to save her own son. As Zeus ceremoniously weighed the fates of the warriors in his scales, Memnon's pan sank below the other and he received a death blow from Achilles. Grief-stricken by Memnon's death, Eos tearfully begged and received honors for her son from Zeus (see box).

Shortly after this, Achilles also died. Paris, the Trojan prince who had abducted Helen from Sparta, mortally wounded Achilles with an arrow that was guided to Achilles' heel by the god Apollo. Ajax, Achilles' close friend, carried his body from the field while Odysseus kept the Trojans at bay. Yet once the body was safe, Ajax and Odysseus argued as to which of them should inherit Achilles' armor.

Memnon and Egypt

In the Egyptian city of Thebes, a famous pair of statues guard the mortuary temple of the pharaoh Amenhotep III (called Amenophis III by the Greeks), who reigned from 1417 BCE to 1379 BCE. Amenhotep III was confused, for

Memnon's Honors

There are several accounts of the honors Zeus awarded Memnon in the afterlife. According to one told by Greek philosopher Proclus (c. 410–485), Zeus granted Memnon immortality. In another, by Ovid (43 BCE–17 CE), Zeus changed the smoke and ashes from Memnon's funeral pyre into birds, called Memnonides or "descendants of Memnon." These birds circled his pyre, crying for him, and then reenacted Memnon's martial prowess by dividing into two groups and fighting each other to the death, falling into the flames and returning to ashes themselves. Zeus decreed that this self-sacrifice should take place each year in memory of Memnon.

According to Pausanias (143–176), who wrote a book about his travels in Greece, these birds swept Memnon's tomb clear every year. They then wet their wings with water from the nearby Aesepus River and sprinkled his tomb with the water, as a sort of funerary rite. It was also thought that the tears Eos constantly shed for her son were transformed into the dew that comes with every dawn.

Below: This illustration depicts the funeral of Memnon. The smoke and ashes from the pyre are transformed into birds by Zeus because of the pleas of Memnon's mother, Eos, seen at top left.

Above: Although these statues were built in honor of Egyptian pharaoh Amenhotep III during the 14th century BCE, they have been commonly referred to as the Colossi of Memnon.

some unknown reason, with Memnon, and the two statues became referred to as the Colossi of Memnon. In 27 BCE an earthquake caused part of one colossus to collapse, and it was damaged in such a way that it made ringing noises early in the morning. Scientists suggest that air trapped in a pocket within the statue caused the mysterious noise as it expanded when heated by the morning sun. The supernatural view, however, was that because the ringing only happened at dawn, it was Memnon singing to his mother, Eos.

The statues became famous, so much so that Roman emperor Hadrian (76–138 CE) came to view these 65-foot (20-m) high colossi on a sightseeing tour. In the early second century CE, Roman emperor Septimius Severus (c. 145–211 CE) had the damaged statue repaired, which ended the morning ringing. Even so, the name of Memnon remained attached to the statues.

Memnon in art

The most famous work of art from the Greek world featuring Memnon was a painting by Polygnotus, a fifth-century-BCE Greek artist. In a building in Delphi called the Club Room, so named for its use as a meeting place for serious discussion, the Cnidians, who came from Lacedaemon, had commissioned Polygnotus to depict scenes from the Trojan War. In the painting, which has not survived,

Memnon was depicted grieving with Sarpedon, a Trojan ally from Lycia; another Trojan hero, Paris, and the Amazon queen Penthesileia stood nearby. Memnon had his hand on Sarpedon's shoulder in a gesture of comfort, and birds embroidered on his cloak alluded to his honors. Other artworks from ancient Greece having depictions of Memnon include vase paintings showing Eos holding Memnon's dead body, Memnon and Achilles fighting, or Zeus weighing on scales the warriors' fates.

The story of Memnon was also told in "Aethiopis," a poem from the *Epic Cycle*, which is now lost. The *Epic Cycle* was a collection of ancient poems covering events around the Trojan War. "Aethiopis" (also spelled "Ethiopis") was the sequel to the *Iliad*, and was supposedly written by Arctinus of Miletus (dates unknown). Scholars think that the poem's title is a reference to Memnon as the king of Ethiopia. The best sources for Memnon's myth are now found in the summary of the *Epic Cycle* by Proclus (c. 410-485 CE) and in the writings of Pausanias (143–176 CE) and Ovid (43 BCE–17 CE).

Kathryn Chew

Bibliography

Homer, and Robert Fagles, trans. *The Iliad*. New York: Penguin, 2009.

Pausanias, and Peter Levi, trans. *Guide to Greece*. New York: Viking Press, 1984.

See also: Achilles; Ajax; Nestor; Priam; Tithonus.

MENELAUS

Menelaus, king of Sparta and brother of Agamemnon, was one of the central figures of the Trojan War. Although not one of the main warrior heroes of the epic tale, Menelaus, as the betrayed husband of Helen, forced the leaders of the other Greek city-states to lay siege to Troy. Some say that long after the war, he was made immortal by Zeus.

Below: This bust of Menelaus is housed in the Vatican in Rome. It is a Roman carving based on a Greek original.

The deeds of Menelaus are recorded in the poems attributed to Homer, who lived around the ninth or eighth century BCE, and in works by later Greek authors, such as Pausanias (143–176 CE). There is no evidence that Menelaus ever existed outside the realm of myth, but the ancient Greeks believed that he, like all the other characters in Homer's poems, was a historical figure. For example, Pausanias, a Greek travel writer, claimed that he could identify the house in Sparta where Menelaus had lived 1,400 years before.

The curse of the House of Atreus

According to Apollodorus, a second-century-BCE collector and recorder of myths, Menelaus's mother was Aerope, the daughter of Catreus, king of Crete. Atreus, king of Mycenae, was either Menelaus's father or in some accounts his grandfather. This meant that Menelaus was a member of the cursed House of Atreus, also known as the House of Pelops.

In the tragedy *Agamemnon* by the fifth-century-BCE Athenian dramatist Aeschylus, the prophetess Cassandra says that the family from which Menelaus sprang had been cursed for generations. Certainly a reading of the deeds committed by the family supports this view. Every generation saw some monstrous crime, including cannibalism, incest, and murder, usually committed by one member of the family against another.

Tantalus, the clan's founder, killed his own son, Pelops, and served him to the gods in a stew. Pelops, when resurrected by the gods, murdered his prospective father-in-law as well as his own best friend in order to win Hippodameia in marriage. Atreus and Thyestes, the sons of Pelops, quarreled over the rulership of Mycenae and over Atreus's wife, Aerope, whom Thyestes seduced. In vengeance Atreus boiled Thyestes' children and served them to him in a stew. Thyestes also committed incest with his surviving daughter (who later murdered him) in order to conceive a son who would avenge him by killing Atreus.

In the next generation, Agamemnon, one of Atreus's sons, sacrificed one of his own daughters, Iphigeneia, in order to gain a fair wind from the gods and sail the Greek army to Troy. While Agamemnon was away fighting the Trojans, Thyestes' son Aegisthus seduced Agamemnon's wife, Clytemnestra, and on Agamemnon's return Aegisthus and Clytemnestra murdered him. Years later Orestes, Agamemnon's son, avenged his father's death by murdering Aegisthus and Clytemnestra.

The early life of Menelaus

As far as Menelaus's early life is concerned, few tales exist. However, Apollodorus says that during a civil war between Agamemnon's father, Atreus, and his uncle Thyestes, Atreus was murdered by Aegisthus, after which Menelaus and Agamemnon fled into exile. On their return, Menelaus married Helen, whose mother, Leda, was the wife of Tyndareos, king of Sparta, and whose father was Zeus (see box, page 175). Menelaus became king of Sparta when Tyndareos died.

All sources agree that Menelaus and Helen had a daughter named Hermione. Apollodorus wrote that after the war Helen also bore Menelaus a son, Nicostratus. Besides his child—or children—by Helen, Menelaus had another son, Megapenthes, by a slave, as well as a son called Xenodamus, whose mother was a nymph.

When Hermione was nine years old, Paris, a prince of Troy, visited Sparta and eloped with Helen. Menelaus turned to his brother, Agamemnon, for assistance in retrieving his wife. Agamemnon, who by this time was king of Mycenae, called together an alliance of the Greek city-states and launched a campaign against Troy.

The Greeks were initially prevented from setting sail for Troy by an ill wind that held them in the harbor at Aulis. The seer Calchas revealed that

the wind could only be made favorable if Agamemnon sacrificed his eldest daughter to the goddess Artemis. In the play *Iphigeneia at Aulis* by Euripides, a Greek dramatist of the fifth century BCE, Agamemnon hesitated to pay such a terrible price. Nevertheless, Menelaus, who was afraid of losing the respect of the army if they did not sail, pressed Agamemnon to sacrifice the girl and in the end he did so.

During the war, Menelaus figured rarely except for one significant episode. Agamemnon sanctioned a duel to be

Right: This is an ancient Greek stone relief carved around the sixth century BCE depicting King Menelaus and Queen Helen. It is located in Sparta, the city that the couple are said to have ruled.

Above: Found among the ruins of Pompeii, this fresco depicts the Trojan king Priam (center), Menelaus (left of Priam), and Helen (far right). Menelaus is about to kill Helen's most recent lover, Deiphobus, after the fall of Troy. The Romans were fascinated with the Trojan War and believed that they themselves were descended from Aeneas, a Trojan prince.

fought between Menelaus and Paris. The outcome of the duel was to determine the fate of Helen and the result of the war. If Paris won, then Agamemnon agreed to have the Greeks leave, and Helen would remain in Troy. If Menelaus won, then Helen would be returned to her husband and the Greeks would depart only after the Trojans paid them compensation for the cost of waging the campaign. The duel took place as arranged, but when Menelaus was on the verge of victory, Aphrodite shrouded Paris in a heavy fog and spirited him away from the battlefield.

Returning to Sparta

Paris, however, was killed in the final stages of the war when Greek warrior Philoctetes shot him with the great bow of Heracles. Helen was then given to Paris's brother Deiphobus. Their union did not last long, however. Soon afterward the Trojans fell victim to a cunning Greek plan. They unwittingly let into the walled city a few Greek soldiers who were hiding inside a giant wooden horse.

The Suitors' Oath

Helen was the most beautiful woman on earth, and when the time came for her to marry, she had so many suitors, all from royal families of Greece, that her stepfather Tyndareos was afraid that all the disappointed suitors would quarrel with whomever he chose as her husband. Apollodorus wrote that Odysseus, the wise king of Ithaca, suggested to Tyndareos that he make all the suitors swear an oath to defend Helen's husband, whoever was chosen, against anyone who damaged their marriage. All the suitors agreed to the oath, and Tyndareos then safely chose Menelaus. When Paris, who was not among Helen's suitors, later eloped with her to Troy, Agamemnon used the oath the former suitors had taken to coerce them to form an alliance against Troy.

Several classical authors mention the suitors' oath. In addition to Apollodorus, it is referred to by Pausanias, as well as by the fifth-century-BCE Athenian historian Thucydides, among others. Homer, however, who tells the story of the Trojan War in the greatest detail, never mentions the oath. It is possible that the oath was invented by a poet after Homer's time, but it is equally possible that Homer chose to omit the story of the oath from his poems. This left him free to depict the Greeks as allying voluntarily against Troy.

Left: This illustration depicts Menelaus (left) after the fall of Troy sparing the life of Helen because of the intervention of Odysseus (right). A more popular version has it that Helen stood naked in front of Menelaus to stop him from killing her.

During the night the Greeks emerged from the wooden horse and opened the city's gates, enabling the rest of the Greek army to invade the fortress.

Reunited with Helen

When Menelaus reached Helen's chambers, he killed Deiphobus and, according to Pausanias, intended to kill his wife, too. One popular version has it that he entered her room, sword at the ready, but Helen dropped her cloak, beneath which she was naked. At the sight of her, Menelaus lost his resolve and instead brought her back to Sparta. This scene was reproduced many times in Greek art and is by far the most common depiction of Menelaus.

In the play *Trojan Women*, Euripides tells the story that Menelaus took Helen back to Sparta over the strong objections of Hecuba, queen of Troy. Hecuba, who blamed Helen for the war, begged Menelaus to kill Helen before he left Troy, since she rightly distrusted his ability to kill Helen after he had spent any great length of time with her. In the end, however, Menelaus ignored Hecuba's plea and spared Helen's life.

However, Menelaus did not go directly home to Sparta after the war. All sources agree that he quarreled with Agamemnon and set off before his brother's fleet, then was blown off course in a storm. Menelaus and Helen traveled for eight years before they found their way back to Sparta. On their journey, the couple were near Egypt when, according to Homer, Menelaus sought the guidance of Proteus, the Old Man of the Sea. Proteus predicted a safe return to Sparta for Menelaus and Helen, and afterward a long life together for the couple. He also promised Menelaus that in the end he and Helen, who was Zeus's daughter, would be made immortal and live forever in the Isles of the Blessed. According to Apollodorus, all this came to pass.

When Menelaus finally disembarked in Greece, he found that his brother had been killed and the funerals for his brother's wife, Clytemnestra, and Aegisthus, the usurper, were in progress. He lived thereafter a peaceful life at Sparta, before being made immortal along with Helen. Another version by Pausanias says that the couple died as mortals and mentions the tomb of Menelaus and Helen in Therapne, in Sparta. Menelaus was succeeded as king of Sparta by his son Megapenthes. His daughter Hermione married Orestes and had a son, Tisamenus, who later became king of Mycenae.

Menelaus is depicted by Homer as a powerful warrior at Troy—certainly stronger than Helen's lover, Paris—but not one of the greatest fighters in the war. He was not as powerful as his brother, Agamemnon, the leader of the Greeks, nor as successful in combat as the great Greek warriors Diomedes and Achilles. Neither was he the most intelligent of the Greeks, a position held by Odysseus. He is depicted as a worthy fighter and leader, but one consistently overshadowed by the heroes who surrounded him.

LAUREL BOWMAN

Bibliography

Homer, and Robert Fagles, trans. *The Iliad*. New York: Penguin, 2009.

Homer, and Robert Fagles, trans. *The Odyssey*. New York: Penguin, 2009.

McLaren, Clemence. *Inside the Walls of Troy*. New York: Simon Pulse, 2004.

SEE ALSO: Agamemnon; Atreus; Cassandra; Clytemnestra; Hector; Hecuba; Helen; Iphigeneia; Odysseus; Orestes; Paris; Pelops; Tantalus.

MIDAS

In Greek mythology Midas was a king of Phrygia, part of what is now Turkey. He famously wished that everything he touched would turn to gold. When his wish was granted, Midas realized he had made a terrible mistake.

Above: This illustration by Arthur Rackham (1867–1939) captures the moment when Midas sees that he has turned his daughter into gold.

Although the stories about Midas are mostly myth and folklore, he was a real person. Also known as Mita, he ruled Phrygia in modern Turkey in the eighth century BCE, and archaeologists have found what they believe to be his tomb (see box, page 179).

In real life, as in legend, Midas was famed for his wealth as well as for his beautiful rose gardens. His kingdom, Phrygia, also known as Lydia or Mygdonia, was very prosperous. Midas is said to have founded the ancient city of Ancyra, which is now Ankara, the capital of Turkey.

The golden touch

The most famous story about Midas is the tale of his golden touch. According to this legend, Dionysus, the Greek god of wine, was passing through Phrygia when his old adviser, Silenus, a satyr, lost his way and ended up in Midas's gardens. Midas held a feast for Silenus, then helped him to find Dionysus again. To reward Midas for his help, Dionysus offered to grant him a wish.

Midas was very greedy, so he asked for everything he touched to be turned to gold. As promised, Dionysus granted his wish. At first, Midas was delighted with his golden touch. Then he realized that any food or drink he touched turned to gold too, and he could no longer eat or drink. He began to worry, and in despair he hugged his daughter, but she, too, turned to gold.

Midas soon asked Dionysus to undo his wish. Dionysus agreed and told Midas to go and bathe in the Pactolus River. Midas did so, taking his daughter with him. She was brought back to life and Midas was restored to normal. According to legend, ever since Midas touched its waters, the river has contained flecks of gold. Gold does naturally occur in the Pactolus River, and the story of Midas bathing in the river probably came about as a way of explaining the gold deposits there.

How Midas was given donkey's ears

Another story tells of how Midas was called upon to judge a music competition between Apollo (who was, among other things, the god of music) and Marsyas, a satyr. Apollo played his lyre, a harplike instrument, while Marsyas played a flute belonging to the goddess Athena. The other judges chose Apollo as the winner, but Midas disagreed and said

Above: This painting by Peter Paul Rubens (1577–1640) depicts Midas judging the music competition between Apollo and Pan.

Marsyas should win. In another version of the story it was Pan, the fertility god, who competed with Apollo, playing on his panpipes.

In both versions of the tale, Apollo was furious with Midas for choosing his opponent and punished him for his poor judgment by giving him the ears of an ass. Midas was terribly ashamed of his huge ears and kept them covered with a turban. One person found out about them, however—the servant who cut the king's hair.

The servant was forbidden to gossip about the ears, but, desperate to tell the king's secret, he whispered it into a hole in the ground, which he then filled with earth. Reeds grew on the spot where the secret had been whispered, and every time the wind blew, the reeds repeated what the servant had said: "Midas has ass's ears." Midas became a laughingstock.

The death of Anchurus

Despite the unfortunate things that happened to him, the mythical Midas never seemed to learn his lesson or acquire better judgment. According to one story, a huge hole opened up in the ground at a city named Celaenae. An oracle told Midas that he could only close the abyss by throwing his most precious possession into it. Midas still valued money above all else, and he threw vast amounts of gold and silver into the hole, but to no avail. His son, Anchurus, however, realizing that human life was more precious than anything, rode into the gaping hole on his horse. As the boy really was Midas's most precious possession, the hole closed up, and Midas lost his son forever.

The Tomb of Midas

What might be the 2,700-year-old tomb of the real King Midas was discovered in the 1950s near the small village of Yassihoyuk in central Turkey. The tomb was located under a conical hill, which is today known as the Midas Mound. Inside, archaeologists found the body of the old king, who probably died when he was about 60, lying on a thick layer of cloth inside a wooden coffin. With him in the tomb were items of wooden furniture as well as bronze goblets, bowls, pots, and pans—but nothing at all made of gold.

One of the most interesting things about Midas's tomb, however, was that it contained evidence of a huge funeral feast that would have been held to mark the king's death. Midas was buried with the dirty plates, cups, and utensils still in the tomb with him. By studying the leftovers, archaeologists have concluded that the feast probably included a spicy lamb stew, hummus (a paste made from chickpeas), broad-bean paste, halva (a dessert made from sesame seeds, honey, and nuts), and an alcoholic drink made from honey, grapes, and barley. In 2000, scientists re-created the original funeral menu for a Midas feast, which was held at the University of Pennsylvania Museum.

Below: This royal burial mound in Gordion, Turkey (formerly Phrygia), is similar to the one thought to house the body of Midas.

Midas himself is also said to have committed suicide by drinking bull's blood. According to different versions of the story, this was either because his kingdom was being invaded or because of his shame about his ass's ears.

Handing down the story

Several ancient writers mention Midas. They include Greek historian Herodotus (c. 484–425 BCE), Greek geographer Strabo (c. 64 BCE–23 CE), and Greek travel writer Pausanias (143–176 CE). The latter is thought to have come from the same region as Midas and wrote about him in his *Description of Greece*. Midas also appears in the work of Roman poet Ovid (43 BCE–17 CE) and that of Gaius Julius Hyginus, a Latin poet of the late first century BCE.

The tale of Midas's golden touch has been retold many times as a children's story, and he is often mentioned in literature as an example of someone who loves wealth. Attributing the "Midas touch" to someone can also refer to that person's ability to create wealth.

Midas has been depicted many times in art, especially in paintings showing the ill-fated music competition that he judged.

ANNA CLAYBOURNE

Bibliography

Pausanias, and Peter Levi, trans. *Guide to Greece*. New York: Viking Press, 1984.
Pinsent, John. *Greek Mythology*. London: Hamlyn, 1982.

SEE ALSO: Satyrs; Silenus.

MINOS

In Greek mythology Minos was the semidivine ruler of an empire based on the island of Crete. Although he is most famous for forcing the Athenians to send a small group of youths to Crete, where they were fed to a monster known as the Minotaur, Minos was viewed by some as a wise and just king.

Below: This photograph shows a throne at the palace of Knossos on Crete, the legendary home of King Minos.

Minos was the son of Zeus, ruler of the gods, and Europa, a beautiful Phoenician princess. Zeus lusted after Europa and transformed himself into a bull to carry the princess away to Crete. There, according to most versions of the story, she bore him three sons—Minos, Rhadamanthys, and Sarpedon—although Greek poet Homer (c. ninth–eighth century BCE) does not cite Sarpedon as Minos's brother. After Zeus left the island, Europa married the Cretan king Asterius, who raised the three boys as his own. When they were young men, all three of the brothers fell in love with Miletus, a semidivine son of Apollo. They quarreled over Miletus and, in some accounts, Minos expelled his brothers from the island forever.

With his brothers banished, Minos ascended the Cretan throne unchallenged on the death of Asterius. Still, he felt the need to demonstrate to his Cretan subjects that the gods wanted him to be king, so he prayed for a divine sign that would publicly acknowledge his right. Poseidon, god of the sea, answered Minos's prayer and sent a beautiful bull from out of the waves. Poseidon made Minos promise that once all the Cretans had recognized the significance of the bull, Minos was to sacrifice the animal to the sea god. However, when the bull appeared and Minos was universally proclaimed king, he ignored Poseidon's instructions. Some versions claim that he could not bring himself to kill the bull because the creature looked so majestic. Others say that the bull reminded him of the form Zeus took when he wooed Europa, and that he could not kill something that resembled his own father. Whatever the reason, instead of sacrificing Poseidon's bull, Minos killed

Below: This sculpture of a pair of bull horns is located at the palace of Knossos on Crete. Bulls featured prominently in Cretan religion.

Minoan Worship

Cretan, or Minoan, influence may be seen in many Greek myths. For example, ancient Greeks believed that in order to protect the infant Zeus from being devoured by his father, Cronus, his mother, Rhea, hid the divine baby in a cave on Mount Dicte in Crete, where he was raised by nymphs. Caves were of great significance to Minoans: within them they seem to have practiced a religious cult celebrating fertility gods. Numerous votive offerings have been found in such locations—these were usually in the form of domesticated animals such as sheep, goats, and bulls, but in one particular cave a large cache of turtles was excavated.

Minoans also worshiped their gods in sanctuaries and at altars on the tops of mountains. The altars, built in the form of stylized bull horns, marked the location of cave sanctuaries; the bull horns topped the peak sanctuary building as well. However, modern archaeologists have not yet been able to ascertain the exact forms of worship that took place in these isolated sacred sites.

Right: This Roman floor mosaic from the fourth century CE depicts Greek hero Theseus fighting the Minotaur in the Labyrinth.

the best bull from his own herd. This did not satisfy Poseidon. On the contrary, the sea god viewed Minos's failure as blasphemy, and he swore revenge.

Pasiphae and the Minotaur

Minos had married Pasiphae, a daughter of the sun god Helios, and made her his queen. Together they had four sons—Catreus, Deucalion, Glaucus, and Androgeos—and five daughters—Ariadne, Phaedra, Acacallis, Xenodice, and Euryale. Minos also had many illegitimate children. After years of enduring her husband's infidelities, Pasiphae concocted a potion that made Minos imagine that snakes and scorpions were coming out of his body whenever he made love to another woman.

Poseidon finally took his revenge on Minos by causing Pasiphae to fall helplessly in love with the bull from the sea. However, the animal did not reciprocate her affections. While Minos was abroad expanding his empire, Pasiphae summoned Daedalus, the court inventor, to devise a contraption that would enable her to make love with the bull. He built a hollow statue of a cow inside which Pasiphae could lie. When the bull saw the effigy in his pasture, he mistook it for a real cow and mounted it, thus impregnating the queen of Crete. The product of this union was a baby boy with a bull's head. Our primary source for the story of Pasiphae and the bull is *The Cretans*, a play credited to Greek dramatist Euripides (c. 486–c. 406 BCE). Now lost, the work is reputed to have had Pasiphae arguing that it must have been the gods who made her fall in love with the bull in order to punish Minos, and denying that it was as a result of anything she had done.

When Minos returned from his travels, he was so disgusted at the sight of the bull-headed infant that he commissioned Daedalus to create a home for it hidden deep beneath the royal palace. Daedalus built a massive, complex maze from which the monster was unable to escape because it could never find the exit. Named the Minotaur, the bull-headed creature lived on human flesh.

Events outside of Crete provided a gruesome supply of food for the beast. Minos's son Androgeos was a great athlete. He won the Panathenaic Games, which were held in Athens in honor of the goddess Athena, but was murdered shortly after his victory. In vengeance, Minos laid siege to Athens. Although he had a mighty army, he was unable to conquer the city. Minos prayed to his father for help. In response, Zeus sent a plague and famine to Athens.

The Athenians, desperate to find ways of ending their suffering, sought the advice of an oracle who told them that they should submit to whatever terms Minos demanded. In return for ending the siege, Minos required that a tribute of seven youths and seven girls be sent to Crete (either annually or every nine years) as food for the Minotaur. The tribute ended only when the Athenian hero Theseus killed the Minotaur and escaped from the Labyrinth with the help of Minos's daughter Ariadne.

Pursuit of Daedalus

Theseus was able to find his way out of the Labyrinth with the help of a plan devised by Daedalus. When Minos discovered the inventor's role in the death of the Minotaur, he threw Daedalus and his son, Icarus, into the Labyrinth.

Drawing Parallels

The story of Ariadne and Theseus is thought by some to parallel the rise of Athens and the fall of Crete. As Attica (a peninsula of mainland Greece) became the commercial and artistic center of the Mediterranean world, the old mother goddess–worshiping civilization of Crete became an increasing menace. When Theseus made his way to the heart of the Labyrinth and slew the Minotaur, metaphorically he murdered the ancient civilization that had ruled over the incipient democracy and its patriarchal culture. In the story of the escape of Theseus and Ariadne from Crete, he abandons the daughter of Minos on the island of Naxos. Some argue that Theseus's cruelty to Ariadne is a metaphor for the passing of the old tradition and the beginning of the new order of the sky god. Heedless of Ariadne's grief-stricken cries, Theseus left her weeping and sailed home alone. His punishment was that his return to Athens would cause his own father to commit suicide.

Ever the inventor, Daedalus fashioned two pairs of wings out of wax and feathers, one pair for himself and the other for Icarus. After escaping from the Labyrinth, the two flew high into the sky away from Crete. Yet only Daedalus reached safety. Icarus, ignoring his father's warnings, flew too close to the sun. The heat melted the wax in his wings, and the boy fell to his death. Daedalus eventually found refuge in Sicily at the court of King Cocalos.

Minos tries to capture Daedalus

Minos became obsessed with capturing Daedalus. He devised a cunning plan to flush the inventor out of hiding by appealing to his vanity. The king traveled the world offering a prize to anyone who could pass a thread through a spiral-shaped seashell, knowing that only Daedalus had the skill to accomplish such a feat. For years Minos traveled to all the major courts offering his challenge, but no one proved clever enough to solve it. Finally he reached Sicily and the court of Cocalos. Daedalus, in disguise, examined the seashell carefully and took it away with him. After only a few moments he returned, having threaded the shell. He had solved the puzzle by boring a hole in the closed end of the shell and tying a thread to an ant. He then made the ant walk through the shell, pulling the thread behind it.

Minos recognized Daedalus and demanded that Cocalos hand over the inventor. Reluctantly the Sicilian king agreed, but he would not do so until after a night's rest. Believing that his years of search were at an end, Minos decided to relax in a bath poured for him by the daughters of Cocalos. Unknown to Minos, the girls adored Daedalus and were not willing to let him be taken away. According to some versions of the story, the girls poured either boiling water or pitch over Minos, scalding him to death. In other accounts the girls conspired with Daedalus to run a pipe through the roof of the room in which Minos was bathing. The girls filled the pipe with boiling water and, while Minos was relaxing in his bath, they poured it on him.

In the afterlife Minos became one of three judges of souls in the underworld. Rhadamanthys, Minos's brother, was the judge of Europeans; Aeacus—another of Zeus's semidivine sons—presided over Asians; while Minos determined the fate of those whose lives had been most complicated or difficult to judge. The ancient Greeks believed that both good and bad deeds were repaid a hundredfold in the afterlife, so the judgment of Minos

Left: This Roman bas-relief carving shows King Minos (right) making an offering to the god Neptune (the Roman equivalent of Poseidon).

Above: The entrance to Knossos. This ancient palace on Crete was first excavated by English archaeologist Arthur Evans around 1900.

was a terrifying prospect to people who feared retribution for the wicked deeds they had performed during their time on earth.

Uncovering the real Crete

According to legend, King Minos made Crete a center of commerce in the eastern Mediterranean and received tribute from cities such as Athens as a sign of his hegemony. Although it is known that from around 3500 BCE to 1100 BCE Crete was indeed wealthy and powerful, no archaeological evidence has been found to prove the existence of a historical Cretan ruler named Minos. Nevertheless, when British archaeologist Arthur Evans (1851–1941) first excavated the palace of Knossos, he named the ancient Cretan civilization thus uncovered "Minoan" in honor of the mythical king.

Minoan Art

Minoan art of the Bronze Age (which started around 3000 BCE) reveals a culture that was rich in the pleasures of the senses. The severe, abstract art of Neolithic Crete gave way about 2400–2300 BCE to curves, spirals, and meanders. These designs are reminiscent of the labyrinth at Knossos. Some Cretan artistic conventions were clearly borrowed from the culture of Egypt. Cretan figures, however, suggest the idea of a subject, such as the cat, while Egyptian figures capture the details. The paintings of bulls and bull dancers are the most evocative works of Minoan art. They reflect a fascination with the bull as a figure of fertility and power, combining both feminine and masculine divine powers. In the legends of Minos, the labyrinth and the bull are recurrent themes. Minos thus becomes the representative and champion of an ancient culture that was threatened by the rise of the Greeks and their maritime empire.

Above: This illustration by French artist Gustave Doré (1832–1883) shows Minos (foreground) judging souls in the underworld.

On the walls of the palace of Knossos there are frescoes depicting festivals, domestic parties, and nature scenes. It appears that the Minoans, like the ancient Etruscans of Italy, lived in a hedonistic society in which pleasure and freedom were of great importance. Although little is known of the Minoan social structure, it is thought that men and women had similar rights, and that wives were not mere subjects of their husbands. By 1500 BCE, Greek-speaking Mycenaeans began to settle the island, and Minoan culture was adapted and later replaced.

Cataclysmic event

One explanation historians cite for the downfall of the Minoan culture is a series of earthquakes followed by the largest recorded volcanic eruption on the island of Thera, to the north of Crete. It is known that Thera was once a thriving stopover port on the busy shipping route between Crete and Athens. The fact that archaeologists have found no evidence of human remains there has led them to conclude that the earthquakes must have forced the island's inhabitants to leave in a great hurry just before the catastrophe. The eruption is thought to have sent a tidal wave to the north coast of Crete, and to have caused a cloud of ash to reach as far as the easternmost parts of the Mediterranean. The tidal wave and ash cloud would have had a devastating impact on Minoan culture. The nature of Thera's fate is often associated with the myth surrounding the lost city of Atlantis. Some time later the island was repopulated by non-Minoan peoples.

BARBARA GARDNER

Bibliography

Farnaux, Alexandre, and David J. Baker, trans. *Knossos: Searching for the Legendary Palace of King Minos.* New York: Harry N. Abrams, 1996.

Macgillivray, Joseph Alexander. *Minotaur: Sir Arthur Evans and the Archaeology of the Minoan Myth.* New York: Hill and Wang, 2000.

SEE ALSO: Ariadne; Daedalus; Deucalion; Europa; Icarus; Pasiphae; Theseus.

MYRMIDONS

In Greek legend, the Myrmidons were a race of people famous for their devotion to duty. Although originally from an island in the Saronic Gulf about 17 miles (27 km) southwest of Athens, the race eventually settled at Phthia in Thessaly, a mainland region of east-central Greece on the Aegean Sea. They were best known as the people whom the great Greek warrior Achilles led in the siege of Troy.

Below: This 16th-century engraving depicts Aeacus discovering that the ants of his island have been transformed into people. Zeus watches from above.

Etymologically, the name *Myrmidon* is related to the Greek word *myrmex* ("ant"), and there are various accounts of how the link was formed. According to some, the Myrmidon tribe took its name from that of a legendary ancestor, Myrmidon, a son of Zeus, who was said to have been conceived when the chief god came to Myrmidon's mother, Eurymedusa, in the form of an ant. According to other versions, Zeus took the form of an eagle and pursued the nymph Aegina, daughter of the river god Asopus. When he caught her he took her to an island called Oinone. There she bore him a son, Aeacus, who became the first permanent inhabitant of the island, which was henceforth named Aegina for his mother. Zeus then turned the ants of the island into people so that Aeacus would have a proper kingdom over which to rule. Aeacus was renowned for his piety and discernment, and after his death he became a judge in the underworld.

Other accounts say that Aeacus originally had a people to rule on Aegina, but that Hera, angry at the infidelity of her husband, Zeus, sent a plague of snakes,

Aeacus married twice. By his first wife, a princess from Megara, a powerful city not too far away on mainland Greece, Aeacus had two children, Telamon and Peleus. His second marriage, to a sea nymph, produced one son, Phocus. Telamon and Peleus inevitably became jealous of their half brother and feared that he rather than they would inherit their father's kingdom. This sibling rivalry ended when Phocus was killed. In some versions his death was murder—Telamon stabbed Phocus with a spear while they were out hunting, and Peleus then finished him off with an ax. In others Phocus was killed accidentally when he was hit by a discus thrown by Telamon. In both versions, Telamon and Peleus concealed the body.

From island to mainland

When Aeacus found out what his surviving sons had done, he furiously exiled them both. Telamon and his followers went to the neighboring island of Salamis, where he became ruler and had a son, the famous hero Ajax. Peleus and his acolytes moved to Phthia in Thessaly, where they were warmly received by Eurytion, king of the region. Eurytion ritually purified Peleus of his guilt for the death of Phocus, then offered him the hand in marriage of his daughter, Antigone (not to be confused with the daughter of Oedipus of the same name), along with part of his kingdom. Thus Peleus became the first king of the Myrmidons after they had settled on the Greek mainland. Later, after the death of Antigone, Peleus married the sea nymph Thetis. They had a son, Achilles, who became the leader of the Myrmidons after the Phthians decided to join Agamemnon's expedition against Troy. After Achilles died at Troy and the city was sacked, the Myrmidon contingent returned home safely, and Achilles' son Neoptolemus ascended to the throne of Phthia.

Myrmidons are best remembered as fierce and devoted followers of Achilles. Even today, subordinates or henchmen who carry out their orders assiduously and devotedly are still sometimes called myrmidons—their name is a byword for loyalty, even when that loyalty is misplaced.

ANTHONY BULLOCH

Bibliography

Homer, and Robert Fagles, trans. *The Iliad*. New York: Penguin, 2009.

Ovid, and A. D. Melville, trans. *Metamorphoses*. New York: Oxford University Press, 2008.

SEE ALSO: Achilles; Ajax.

Above: This is a detail from The Death of Achilles *by Peter Paul Rubens (1577–1640). The man trying to hold up the mortally wounded hero is one of his faithful Myrmidons.*

which killed almost all of the island's animals and people. She also sent a devastating drought, which made it impossible for crops to grow. Aeacus noticed a column of ants gathering grain on an oak tree and prayed that he might have as many people as there were ants. His wish was granted by Zeus. That night Aeacus had a dream in which the ants turned into people. When he woke up, he found one of his sons, Telamon, running to tell him that the island was populated again with large numbers of inhabitants. Aeacus named them Myrmidons with an intentional reference to the word for "ant." The people of the island were indeed thrifty, hardworking, and resolute in achieving their goals and in holding on to what they had achieved. Appropriately for an island people, the Myrmidons were reputedly the first to build seagoing ships and to equip them with sails.

MYRRHA

Myrrha was the mother of the Greek hero Adonis. The story of how she came to be pregnant with her son is a sad one. It was the result of a divine punishment and involved an incestuous relationship with her father.

Above: This illustration by Bernard Picart (1673–1733) from an edition of Ovid's Metamorphoses *shows Myrrha changing into a tree and the birth of Adonis.*

Several versions of the story of Myrrha exist, although the variations in detail are minor. All agree that Myrrha lived somewhere in a land in western Asia known for its sweet-smelling incense and perfumes. That the story originated in this region is suggested by its reference to the myrrh tree. Arabic was widely spoken in western Asia, and the word *myrrh* comes from the Arabic word for "bitter." The tree grows naturally in western Asia, as well as in parts of northern Africa.

According to one account, the Greek goddess Aphrodite punished Myrrha because Myrrha's mother boasted that her daughter was more beautiful than Aphrodite. In revenge, Aphrodite made the girl have a sexual desire for her father, who was King Theias of Assyria (which covered present-day northern Iraq and southeastern Turkey).

With the help of her nurse, Myrrha managed to deceive her father. Instead of visiting his mistress, as was his custom, Theias visited his daughter. On 12 successive nights the two were lovers. On the last night Theias discovered the trick and was so filled with revulsion that he chased his daughter with a sword, intending to kill her.

The gods took pity on Myrrha, however, and transformed her into a myrrh tree. Nine months later the bark of the tree split open and the infant Adonis emerged. He later became the object of the affections of both Persephone, the underworld goddess, and Aphrodite.

Myrrha in the *Metamorphoses*

In the *Metamorphoses*, Roman poet Ovid (43 BCE–17 CE) set the story of Myrrha on the island of Panchaia in the Arabian Sea and identified the girl's father as Cinyras, a king of Cyprus. Ovid attributed Myrrha's desire for her father not to Aphrodite but to one of the Furies, female spirits whose responsibility it was to secure love between children and their parents. According to Ovid, Myrrha's devotion went too far. She refused to choose among the many suitors who came to woo her and instead doted on her own father.

The pain of Myrrha's unfulfilled desires proved to be too much, and she began to make preparations to hang herself. Her nurse, upon discovering Myrrha's plans, pleaded with her to share the cause of her unhappiness. The nurse then understood that, to live, Myrrha had to satisfy her passion. During a festival in which the girl's mother was otherwise occupied, the nurse told Cinyras that a young girl was interested in him, without revealing who the girl was. The story ends as the previous version does, with the father pursuing his daughter angrily and the girl throwing herself on the mercy of the gods.

Even after her transformation, Myrrha's tears continued to fall in a dewy resin that people collect from the tree and call by her name. Myrrh is an aromatic gum that was highly valued in ancient times as an ingredient in incenses, cosmetics, perfumes, and medicine. In the New Testament of the Bible it was one of the gifts that the three magi gave to the infant Jesus, along with gold and frankincense.

KIRK SUMMERS

Bibliography

Ovid, and A. D. Melville, trans. *Metamorphoses*. New York: Oxford University Press, 2008.

SEE ALSO: Adonis.

NARCISSUS

The Greek myth of Narcissus, whose pride caused him to fall in love with his own reflection, has inspired artists and writers since the classical period. Some people have seen the story as a warning against the dangers of vanity; others have viewed the tragedy of Narcissus as the result of his grieving over the death of his sister.

Narcissus was the son of the river god Cephissus and the nymph Liriope; he was born when Cephissus enveloped Liriope in his waters. According to Roman poet Ovid (43 BCE–17 CE), who wrote about Narcissus in *Metamorphoses*, Narcissus's mother was curious to know what sort of life awaited her son. She sought out Tiresias, the blind Greek prophet, and asked him how long Narcissus would live. Tiresias replied vaguely that Narcissus would enjoy a long life if he did not come to know himself. His mother wondered at the meaning of the prophecy, but was encouraged by the prospect of her son thriving to a ripe old age. It was not until Narcissus was 16 years old that his story began to unfold, and his life began to end.

Rejecting suitors

According to Ovid, the adolescent Narcissus was so beautiful that he was constantly fending off the advances of young men and women alike. One maiden in particular was so infatuated with Narcissus that she followed him when he was hunting in a forest. This maiden was the mountain nymph Echo, whom Hera, queen of the Olympians, had punished for distracting her attention with relentless conversation while her husband Zeus conducted one of his love affairs. Hera's punishment was for Echo always to have the last word, but never the first—all the nymph could do was repeat the words of others.

As she followed Narcissus on his hunt, Echo's passion grew stronger and stronger, as did her desire to reveal herself

to the youth. When Narcissus became separated from his fellow hunters, Echo began to move among the shadows of the forest. Aware he was being watched, Narcissus called out, "Is there anyone there?" Echo, however, could only repeat his last words, and this exchange continued until he beckoned her out of the woods. When she tried to run into his arms, he resisted her advances, saying that he would rather die than let her possess him. Humiliated and hurt, Echo retreated into the hollows of the mountains and never showed her face again. Only her voice remained, which, for Greeks and Romans, served as an explanation of the echoes they heard in hills and valleys.

Condemned to self-love

While some suggest that it was Narcissus's rejection of Echo that brought about his fate, others claim that his treatment of Echo was part of a pattern the arrogant youth had established with previous suitors. He had scorned so many potential lovers that one of them, in a moment of vindictiveness, prayed that Narcissus might fall in love and not be able to possess the object of his desires. According to Ovid, this prayer was answered by Nemesis, the goddess of retribution. In other versions, the deity was the virgin goddess Artemis. Either way, the prayer was answered: while Narcissus rested by a pool to quench his thirst, he caught sight of his own reflection and was so captivated by it that he tried to embrace it. After trying repeatedly to grasp the image in his arms, he began to weep, but his tears only created ripples in the pool, thus hampering his efforts to see his own reflection. He ripped open his shirt and began to beat his chest in frustration and anguish. Narcissus was doomed, since he could not tear himself away from the image he saw in the pool. As he wasted away with longing he repeatedly cried, "Alas!" Echo, who was nearby, echoed his anguish with her own voice. At last Narcissus died, but even as his spirit made its way to the underworld it was fixated on its own reflection in the waters of the Styx River.

Not everyone agreed with Ovid's version of the myth. For example, Greek travel writer Pausanias (143–176 CE) maintained in his *Description of Greece* that the idea of Narcissus falling in love with himself was absurd. Instead, Pausanias suggested that the reflection that Narcissus

Above: This painting of Narcissus gazing at his own reflection is by Italian artist Caravaggio (1573–1610).

saw in the pool reminded him of his dead twin sister, whom he adored.

When Narcissus died, his sisters—water nymphs known as Naiads—began preparing for his funeral, but they found in place of his body the yellow-and-white flower of a plant in the amaryllis family that became known as the narcissus in his memory. The flower, one of the earliest to bloom in spring, has a head that points slightly downward, as if Narcissus himself were still pining away, gazing at himself in the pool (see box, page 191).

Flora and Fauna in Greek Myth

Just as the ancient Greeks and Romans developed stories to explain natural phenomena such as thunder—they believed that Zeus's weapon was the thunderbolt—so their myths explained the origins of different plants and animals. Ovid's *Metamorphoses*, which can be translated as "transformations," is a comprehensive collection of such explanatory myths. While many of Ovid's tales highlight the transformations of mythological characters such as Narcissus, who displeased the gods, the poet also treated his audiences to more compassionate myths. For example, when the youth Hyacinthus was accidentally killed, the god Apollo, who loved him, transformed him into the hyacinth flower. Another deity who fell in love with a mortal was the goddess Aphrodite, who pined for the beautiful boy Adonis. When Adonis died, Aphrodite caused the anemone flower to spring up from the drops of his blood. Ovid also included stories of couples whose love was commemorated in nature, such as the minstrel Orpheus, whose love for Eurydice survived in the song of the nightingales at the foot of Mount Olympus, and the elderly couple Baucis and Philemon, who were spared death by being transformed into intertwining oak and linden trees.

Right: Like other members of the plant genus Narcissus, *the daffodil appears to look downward, as if contemplating its reflection.*

Interpretations and inspiration

As well as explaining the origins of the narcissus flower, the story of Narcissus perhaps served as a warning to Greek and Roman people that vanity and self-absorption were not characteristics that befitted members of their societies. Another, related suggestion is that the story owed much to the ancient Greek superstition that it was unlucky to look at one's own reflection. In the modern era, Narcissus has provided a name for a psychological condition. A person who has an excessive degree of self-esteem or self-absorption, and is thus unable to identify with the feelings of others, is often diagnosed with narcissistic personality disorder, or narcissism. The condition was first named by Sigmund Freud (1856–1939), Austrian neurologist and the founder of psychoanalysis, who believed that many classical myths provided insights into human psychology.

The story of Narcissus's demise has also served as inspiration for English poets Geoffrey Chaucer (c. 1342–1400), Edmund Spenser (1552–1599), John Milton (1608–1674), Percy Bysshe Shelley (1792–1822), and John Keats (1795–1821). Among the numerous paintings that depict Narcissus are nearly 50 murals found on the walls of houses excavated in the Roman city of Pompeii—which was buried in ash after a volcanic eruption in 79 CE—and works by Nicolas Poussin (1594–1665), Elihu Vedder (1836–1923), John William Waterhouse (1849–1917), and Salvador Dali (1904–1989). As a trait in people, narcissism was satirized in the 18th century in a comic play entitled *Narcissism, or The Self Admirer* by Swiss philosopher Jean-Jacques Rousseau (1712–1778). The story of Echo and Narcissus also inspired a poem by French writer Jean Cocteau (1889–1963), which in turn formed the basis for the ballet *Le Jeune Homme et la Mort* (The Young Man and Death) by French choreographer Roland Petit (b. 1924).

DEBORAH THOMAS

Bibliography

Ovid, and A. D. Melville, trans. *Metamorphoses.* New York: Oxford University Press, 2008.

Pausanias, and Peter Levi, trans. *Guide to Greece.* New York: Viking Press, 1984.

SEE ALSO: Adonis; Echo; Orpheus.

NESTOR

Nestor was one of the Greek rulers drawn into the Trojan War. He was known for the beauty of his voice, and his persuasive oratory was described in the epic poem the *Iliad* as "sweeter than honey," even though his tales were often long and rambling.

Nestor was the youngest of the 12 sons of Neleus, king of Pylos in Greece, and Chloris. While Nestor was away from Pylos, the legendary Greek hero Heracles slaughtered Neleus and all of Nestor's brothers. Heracles had been angry at Neleus for not cleansing him of the sin of having killed Iphitus, the son of Neleus's close friend. When Nestor returned to Pylos, he ascended his father's throne.

The Trojan War

It is in the *Iliad*, the epic poem of the Trojan War by Greek poet Homer (c. ninth–eighth century BCE), that Nestor appears most often. Although Nestor was very old when the war began, he still had much to offer—his ability to fight courageously was undiminished and, with his sons Antilochus and Thrasymedes, he brought 90 ships to the Greeks' cause.

The attribute Nestor was most admired for, however, was his wisdom, which came to the Greeks' assistance at several crucial moments during the war. After the Greek hero Achilles and the Greek commander Agamemnon quarreled—the result of Agamemnon taking Achilles' concubine to be his own—Nestor attempted to mediate between the two men. He suggested that an embassy go to Achilles' tent and inform him of Agamemnon's remorse at his action and his offer of riches if Achilles rejoined the fighting. This advice was in vain, but at other times Nestor had more success, such as when he calmed the Greeks after Achilles' death. Furthermore, Nestor had the foresight to sail away from Troy sooner than most other Greeks. His sense of an impending catastrophe was well founded. In revenge for the Lesser Ajax's rape of Trojan princess

Above: This image of Nestor was painted on a Greek vase in the fifth century BCE.

Cassandra in her sanctuary, the war goddess Athena sent a storm that destroyed much of the Greek fleet. Nestor, in contrast, returned to Pylos safely.

Legends

According to Homer, Nestor enjoyed telling long, rambling stories. He would recount how, as a young man, he fought against the centaurs, performed heroically in the Epeian War, won boxing matches and spear-throwing contests at the funeral games of Amarynceus, and nearly defeated the Moliones, twin sons of Poseidon.

As for Nestor himself, there are no tales of his death and no records of a King Nestor of Pylos ever having existed. In 1939, however, archaeologists discovered the site of a large, ancient palace near Pylos. It is referred to as the palace of Nestor.

BARBARA GARDNER

Bibliography

Homer, and Robert Fagles, trans. *The Iliad*. New York: Penguin, 2009.

SEE ALSO: Achilles; Agamemnon; Ajax; Heracles; Odysseus.

NIOBE

The Greek queen Niobe boasted that she was more fortunate than the goddess Leto because she had more children than her. She was punished severely for this act. Niobe is a prime example of a familiar type from myth—one who destroys her own happiness by foolishly boasting of it.

Niobe was the daughter of Tantalus and the wife of Amphion, king of Thebes. Her mother was usually said to be Euryanassa, but in some accounts of her story other names are given. According to Greek poet Sappho (fl. c. 610–c. 580 BCE), Niobe was originally a companion of the goddess Leto. However, one day she made the mistake of boasting that she had more children than the goddess. This act enraged Leto to such an extent that she called on her children Artemis and Apollo to punish Niobe for her hubris.

Using the bow and arrow that were their traditional attributes, the god and goddess shot and killed all of the children of Niobe, the Niobids. As Greek writer Homer (c. ninth–eighth century BCE) says in his epic poem the *Iliad*: "Though they were only two, yet they destroyed them all." Artemis took aim at the girls while Apollo killed the boys. This is in keeping with the tradition that Artemis's arrows were a cause of death for women. Niobe's husband Amphion died immediately thereafter, either by suicide or at the hands of Apollo.

According to Homer, the gods turned all the local inhabitants to stone. So, for nine days, the children remained unburied. Finally, on the 10th day, the gods

Below: This illustration from a Greek vase depicts Niobe and was created around 460 BCE. The artist is now known as the Niobid Painter.

Above: The Massacre of Niobe's Children *by Charles Dauphin (1620–1677) depicts Apollo and Artemis slaughtering the Niobids.*

took pity and buried the children themselves. Niobe's grief was unrelenting, and she herself was eventually turned to stone. Her name became a byword for sorrow in antiquity.

Niobe in the *Iliad*

Homer's version of the story of Niobe appears toward the end of the *Iliad*. It occurs when the Greek hero Achilles is urging King Priam to break a fast caused by his grief over the death of his son Hector. Achilles invokes the story of Niobe, observing that even she stopped weeping long enough to eat. From this it is clear that from a very early date Niobe's grief was proverbial. At the same time, she was also a cautionary figure, warning people of the dangers of committing hubris by boasting of their good fortune and offending the gods.

The exact number of Niobe's children varies from source to source, but there is almost always an equal number of sons and daughters. In Homer's account, Niobe had six sons and six daughters. In a poetic version of her story by Hesiod (fl. 800 BCE), she had five of each. Elsewhere she had seven or even as many as ten of each. Various lists of names are given. For example, in *The Library*, a summary of Greek mythology attributed to the writer Apollodorus (fl. 140 BCE), the following names are

given for the male children: Sipylus, Damasichthon, Eupinytus, Ismenus, Agenor, Phaedimus, and Tantalus. The female children are listed as Ethodaia, Cleodoxa, Astyoche, Phthia, Pelopeia, Astycrateia, and Ogygia. Ovid (43 BCE–17 CE) uses most but not all of the same names for the boys, but does not name the girls. In general, such lists of names are not to be taken very seriously. The fact that many of them are also used for numerous other mythic figures suggests that they may have been made up by the writers.

In some versions of the story, two children of Niobe were said to survive. Meleboea was saved because she prayed to Leto. She was henceforth known as Chloris ("grass-green" or "pale") because she turned pale with fear and never regained her normal complexion. Together with her brother Amyklas, she built a temple to Leto. Chloris married Neleus, a son of the sea god Poseidon, and gave birth to 12 sons including Nestor, who later fought in the Trojan War. The ancient travel writer Pausanias (143–176 CE) claimed to have visited the temple that Chloris built. Pausanias also wrote that he had seen the tombs of the other children of Niobe in Thebes, and the spot on Mount Sipylon near his hometown in Asia Minor where the rock that had once been Niobe stood.

Several features of Niobe's story are echoed in other ancient Greek myths. One common theme is that of a small band of children, equally divided between boys and girls, who face some terrible danger. Some of these myths can be connected with apparently initiatory rituals in which children were secluded in temples to serve a god. For example, one legend tells of how a regular tribute of seven Athenian girls and seven boys had to be sent to the Cretan labyrinth to feed the Minotaur as compensation to King Minos for the murder of his son Androgeos. This myth was commemorated in an annual festival, the Oschophoria, in which boys paraded to the sea dressed as girls. Their mothers ran behind them offering them snacks for the long trip ahead. In Corinth, a ritual was performed in which seven girls and seven boys lived at the temple of Hera Akrai. During this period, they served the goddess as expiation for the Corinthians' murder of Medea's children in that very temple.

The myth of Niobe, with its preoccupation with the bearing of children and their subsequent death or survival and the detail of the equal number of boys and girls, suggests that she may have been connected to a similar ritual, although no evidence for one has come down to us. In any case, the myth is concerned with

Right: This marble statue, known as the Niobid of the Sallustian Gardens, was sculpted in the fifth century BCE. It shows the death of one of Niobe's daughters, killed by an arrow from Artemis.

similar issues of the survival of children and the grief of parents when they do not survive. The myth of the Niobids does not, however, contain the feature of retribution for the death of children that we find in these other examples.

Niobe in art and literature

Aeschylus (525–456 BCE) and Sophocles (c. 496–406 BCE), two of the most famous Athenian dramatists, wrote tragedies based on the myth of Niobe. However, only a few fragments of these plays survive. One of the most famous retellings of Niobe's story is found in Ovid's *Metamorphoses*. Ovid's Niobe is not merely proud of her many children, but openly contemptuous of the goddess Leto. She actively dissuades other women from worshiping at her festival. Not only is Niobe turned to stone because of her incessant mourning, but the stone weeps. Finally she is whisked away to her native country of Lycia, where the poet tells us that the mountain continues to weep still. The scene of the death of the Niobids is depicted on a famous vase by the Niobid Painter, who takes his name from this piece, while a famous sculpture of Niobe and her children existed in ancient Greece. A Roman imitation of this work is now housed in the Uffizi Gallery in Florence, Italy.

While the myth of Niobe is well known, it has produced more allusions than full-scale responses by literary artists. Shakespeare's Hamlet describes his mother at his father's funeral as "Like Niobe, all tears." Phillis Wheatley, an 18th-century African-American poet, wrote a poem inspired by both Ovid's account and a painting by Richard Wilson. Musical compositions drawing on the myth include Giovanni Pacini's opera *Niobe* (1826), and Benjamin Britten's six-part piece for oboe, "Metamorphoses after Ovid" (1951), one part of which is called "Niobe." A recent piece by American composer Stephen Scott, "The Tears of Niobe" (1990), is composed for a grand piano plucked and bowed by 10 musicians. American poet Kate Daniels's 1988 volume *The Niobe Poems* draws on the myth to deal with the theme of a contemporary mother's loss of a child.

DEBORAH LYONS

Bibliography

Homer, and Robert Fagles, trans. *The Iliad*. New York: Penguin, 2009.

Ovid, and A. D. Melville, trans. *Metamorphoses*. New York: Oxford University Press, 2008.

SEE ALSO: Achilles; Minos; Priam.

ODYSSEUS

Odysseus is most famous for his ten-year journey home from the Trojan War. The Greek hero was renowned for his intelligence and cunning, and his love for his family. He could also be arrogant, impulsive, and even cruel. In Roman mythology, Odysseus was called Ulysses.

Below: Romans called Odysseus by the name Ulysses. In his adventures, Ulysses often used a disguise to deceive an enemy. This first-century-BCE Roman coin depicts Ulysses disguised as a beggar.

In Greek myth, Odysseus was the son of Laertes, king of Ithaca, an island kingdom in northeastern Greece. Odysseus's mother was Anticleia, the granddaughter of Hermes, son of Zeus and the messenger of the gods. Odysseus married Penelope, and before he went to Troy, they had a son named Telemachus. According to some myths, after Odysseus returned from Troy they had two more sons, Poliporthes and Acusilaus. Odysseus also had several other children with women he met on his travels.

Did Odysseus really exist?

The main sources for the myth of Odysseus are the *Iliad* and the *Odyssey*, the two great surviving works of ancient Greek poet Homer (c. ninth–eighth century BCE). Many other ancient writers also wrote about Odysseus, including the great playwrights Sophocles (c. 496–406 BCE) and Euripides (c. 486–c. 406 BCE).

As in the case of many mythical heroes, the character of Odysseus could have been based on that of a real person. If this is true, the real Odysseus would have lived in the 13th century BCE, more than 3,000 years ago. Archaeologists believe that this was when the ancient city of Troy (in modern Turkey) was besieged. This battle is thought to have been behind the legend of the Trojan War. There is also an ancient tomb near Ithaca, which some archaeologists think could be Odysseus's tomb.

Odysseus's childhood

When Odysseus was born, his grandfather Autolycus came to visit and was asked to name the baby. He called the baby Odysseus, which can be translated as "victim of anger" or "the one people hate," suitable names for him in some ways.

As an older boy, Odysseus visited his grandfather and went hunting wild boar in a forest. When he was about to kill a fierce boar with his spear, it tore his leg open with one of its tusks. Odysseus had a long, thin scar on his left leg, above his knee, for the rest of his life.

Marriage and war

When he grew up, Odysseus became one of many princes and kings who went to Sparta and attempted to woo Helen, the most beautiful woman in the world. Helen's stepfather Tyndareos was afraid the suitors might fight, especially when Helen chose her husband. With typical cunning, Odysseus told Tyndareos that he had a plan to ensure that the suitors did not fight. He promised to tell Tyndareos the plan if he could marry his niece, Penelope. Tyndareos agreed. Odysseus told the king to make all the suitors swear an oath promising to respect Helen's choice, and to fight anyone who tried to part her from her husband. Helen chose Menelaus, and thanks to his plan, Odysseus also came home with a wife, Penelope.

When Trojan prince Paris fell in love with Helen and took her away to Troy, the suitors who had taken the oath were forced to go to Troy to win Helen back. Odysseus had taken the oath too, but he did not want to go; he loved his life in Ithaca with Penelope and their baby, Telemachus. Odysseus had also heard a prophecy that if he went to war, he would be away for many years.

When Odysseus did not come forward, Palamedes, a Greek prince renowned for his ingenuity, was sent to Ithaca to fetch him. Odysseus tried to avoid going to war by pretending to be insane, but Palamedes proved he was not. Palamedes took the baby Telemachus and threatened him with his sword (in some versions of the myth, Palamedes laid the baby in front of a plow Odysseus was driving). Odysseus immediately ran to save his son, thus demonstrating that his insanity was an act. Lacking any further excuses, Odysseus had no choice but to set off for Troy.

Right: This sculpture of Odysseus's head was carved by Greek sculptor Polydorus (first century BCE).

Odysseus at Troy

Odysseus was one of the greatest assets to the Greek army at Troy. He was a brave fighter and a brilliant strategist. He carried out a number of successful spying missions with his friend Diomedes. On one occasion, they captured a Trojan named Dolon and forced him to reveal where they could find King Rhesus of Thrace, who was helping the Trojans. They killed Dolon, then went and killed Rhesus and his men as they slept. Odysseus was so cunning that he was even able to sneak inside the walled city of Troy. Disguised as a beggar, he stole a statue of Athena called the Palladium.

The Trojan Horse

The Greeks finally won the Trojan War by playing a trick on the Trojans. They built a huge wooden horse and left it outside Troy, then sailed away and hid at a nearby island. One Greek man, Sinon, was left to explain to the Trojans that the Greeks had retreated and gone home, leaving the horse as an offering to the goddess Athena. The Trojans took the horse into Troy. They did not realize that a band of Greek soldiers, including Odysseus, was hiding inside it. The hideaway Greeks climbed out of the horse and opened the gates of Troy to let in the rest of the Greek armies, who had sailed back to Troy, and the city was destroyed.

When she saw the horse being brought into Troy, Helen suspected something. She walked around it, calling out the names of Greek soldiers she knew, and imitated their wives' voices in the hope of making them call out if they were inside. A soldier named Anticlus nearly called out. To stop him, Odysseus held his hand over Anticlus's mouth for so long that he suffocated the man to death. This is one example of Odysseus's uncompromising nature.

Below: This 16th-century fresco by Italian painter Giulio Romano (c.1499–1546) depicts the construction of the Trojan horse.

At Troy, Odysseus also took his revenge on Palamedes. He had a Trojan captive write a fake letter, making it appear that Palamedes was spying for the Trojans. Then Odysseus buried some gold in Palamedes' tent. When the letter and the gold were discovered, Palamedes was accused of treachery and was stoned to death. According to some versions of the myth, Odysseus came up with the idea for the wooden horse, an invention that was decisive in the Greek victory at Troy.

The Odyssey

The Odyssey was the name given to Odysseus's travels after the Trojan War, as he made his way home from Troy with his men and ships and encountered a range of problems, including hostile peoples, monsters, and divine wrath.

First, Odysseus came to the land of the Ciconians. They had sided with Troy during the war. Odysseus and his men attacked them, killed many citizens, and stole food and

wine. Eventually the Ciconians called on neighboring peoples for help, and after a battle in which 70 of his men died, Odysseus fled.

Next Odysseus and his men came to the land of the Lotus-eaters, where some of Odysseus's men ate the fruit of the lotus plant. The lotus fruit made them forget their homes and families, and they wanted nothing more than to stay there and eat from the plants forever. Odysseus had to drag them back to the ships and chain them up. Finally, his fleet sailed on.

The Cyclops Polyphemus

Odysseus's most famous enemy was the Cyclops Polyphemus, a giant with one eye in the middle of his forehead. Odysseus and his crew arrived at Polyphemus's cave while he was out. Instead of taking some food and escaping, Odysseus wanted to wait and meet the monster. When Polyphemus returned with his flock of sheep, he

shut the men inside his cave and ate several of them for his supper, planning to eat the rest later.

Odysseus came up with a plan. First, he told Polyphemus his name was Nobody. Then he persuaded the monster to drink lots of wine. When the Cyclops was asleep, Odysseus and his men blinded the giant by driving a sharpened stake into his eye. Polyphemus called to his friends for help, but when he cried "Nobody has hurt me!" they ignored him. The next day, Odysseus and his men tied themselves under the Cyclops's sheep, and in this way escaped from the cave.

However, as he set sail, Odysseus could not resist taunting Polyphemus. He boasted about how he had escaped and revealed his real name. Polyphemus threw a rock at Odysseus in anger and missed. Finally, the Cyclops called on his father, the sea god Poseidon, to curse Odysseus and to cause him trouble on his journey home.

So near, and so far

Next, Odysseus visited Aeolus, the keeper of the winds. Aeolus welcomed the travelers. He gave Odysseus a bag containing all the winds so that he could sail wherever he wanted. Odysseus could return directly to Ithaca. As they approached the shore, Odysseus fell asleep. Hoping to find treasure, some of his men looked inside the bag Aeolus had

Above: This Roman mosaic depicts Odysseus and one of his men trapped in Polyphemus's cave. As part of his plan to escape the cave, Odysseus offers wine to the Cyclops in the hope of intoxicating him.

Who Was Homer?

Homer was a poet who lived around the 8th century BCE. He composed two great epic poems, the *Iliad* and the *Odyssey*. These poems were about the Trojan War, which, if it happened, took place in the 12th or 13th centuries BCE. In Homer's time, poets composed their work in their heads and recited it aloud. Homer's poems were eventually written down and passed on to later generations. The ancient Greeks who lived after Homer regarded him with great respect. Homer's poems were treasured and were central to Greek culture. According to legend, Homer was born in a Greek settlement on the coast of Asia Minor (modern Turkey), and was blind.

However, many modern experts think that poems attributed to Homer were actually written by more than one person and were probably changed and added to over time. Some people have even suggested that there was really no such person as Homer. We know so little about his period of history that the truth may never be discovered.

Right: In this fresco, Italian painter Alessandro Allori (1535–1607) depicts the meeting in Hades between Odysseus and the aged seer Tiresias.

given Odysseus. The winds escaped and blew up a storm, the ships were blown away from Ithaca, and Odysseus was lost again. He returned to Aeolus to ask for more help, but Aeolus was angry that his gift had been misused, and he sent him away.

Odysseus next stopped at the land of the Laestrygonians, a fierce cannibal tribe. While Odysseus moored his own ship outside the bay, the captains of his other ships decided to sail into the harbor. The Laestrygonians attacked the ships, pelting them with rocks. Trapped in the harbor, they could not escape. Only Odysseus's ship and crew survived.

Circe

Odysseus's ship then came to the island of Aeaea, home of the enchantress Circe. Circe used her magic to turn some of Odysseus's men into pigs, but the god Hermes came to their rescue. He gave Odysseus a magic herb, moly, that would help him resist Circe's magic. When Circe met

Odysseus and realized she could not control him, she fell in love with him. She returned his men to their human forms and invited them all to stay.

Odysseus and his men stayed with Circe for a year. Before they left, Circe gave them directions to Hades, the land of the dead, where they could find the soul of Tiresias, a seer who would tell Odysseus his future. Odysseus reached Hades by sailing down the River of Ocean (Oceanus). Tiresias told him not to harm the cattle on Helios's island of Thrinacia, which he would soon visit. He also warned Odysseus that in Ithaca, his wife Penelope was being harassed by suitors who believed Odysseus was dead and wanted to marry her and take over the throne. Finally, Tiresias told Odysseus he would live to be old, and that death would come to him out of the sea. In Hades, Odysseus also met his mother, Anticleia, who had died while he was away, and Greek leader Agamemnon, who had been murdered by his wife on his return from Troy.

The Tomb of Odysseus

Some people believe that an ancient Greek tomb at Poros, on the island of Cephalonia, could be the grave of Odysseus. The tomb is a *tholos*, a dome-shaped underground chamber containing many graves. It dates from the Mycenaean period (1400–1100 BCE), when the events leading up to the Trojan War are thought to have occurred.

Cephalonia is the closest island to Ithaca, and since Homer does not mention it as a separate kingdom, some experts think Cephalonia might originally have

been part of the kingdom of Ithaca. If this is true, it would make sense that Odysseus is buried there. *Tholos* tombs were often used to bury royalty, and the graves in the Poros tomb contained gold and jewelry, suggesting that the person who was buried there was very wealthy.

However, with such an old tomb, it is very hard to prove who was buried there. Even if it was Odysseus, his life was probably very different than that of the famous mythical hero.

Further trials

Next, Odysseus encountered the Sirens, beautiful but deadly bird-women. The Sirens sang a haunting melody that lured men toward the treacherous rocks where they lived. In this way, countless sailors had lost their lives. Wishing to hear the song, Odysseus followed Circe's advice and plugged his men's ears with wax, then told them to tie

him to the mast. When Odysseus's ship came near the Sirens and he heard their singing, he begged to be set free, but his men refused, and they passed the Sirens safely.

Odysseus then had to sail between Charybdis, a deadly whirlpool, and Scylla, a six-headed monster. Scylla and Charybdis were on opposite sides of the Straits of Messina, which separate Sicily and mainland Italy. Circe had told him the only way to survive would be to sail close to Scylla, who would snatch six of his men. Keeping this secret from his crew, Odysseus did as Circe had said and escaped. Six of his men paid with their lives.

Below: In this vase painting, Odysseus is tied tightly to the mast of his ship. Safely bound, he cannot succumb to the winged Sirens' enchanting songs as they circle him and his men.

Left: This illustration by the British artist H. J. Ford (1860–1941) depicts the encounter between Odysseus and Nausicaa. Although Nausicaa is surprised by the naked man, she rescues Odysseus and delivers him to her father, King Alcinous.

but with the help of other gods, Odysseus was washed ashore at Phaeacia, a land near Ithaca.

Odysseus was rescued by Nausicaa, the princess of Phaeacia, who took him to her father, King Alcinous. Alcinous threw a banquet for him, and at the table Odysseus revealed who he was and told everyone about his amazing adventures. The next day, a Phaeacian ship took him to Ithaca and left him on the shore. However, the goddess Athena, who had been protecting Odysseus, now told him he must disguise himself before going home. She warned him that Penelope's suitors—Ithacan nobles who had invaded Odysseus's home and, believing him to be dead, sought to marry his wife—would kill him unless he took them by surprise. After reuniting him with his son Telemachus, who was told about the plan, Athena made Odysseus look like an old beggar, and in this disguise he went home to his palace.

Almost 100 suitors had taken over the palace. They were eating Odysseus's food and drinking his wine while bullying Penelope and Telemachus. Penelope had run out of hope and decided to marry the suitor who was strong enough to string and fire Odysseus's old bow. The suitors failed, but Odysseus, still disguised, took the bow and fired it with ease. Then, with the help of an old swineherd, Eumaeus, a young cowherd, Philoetius, and the goddess Athena disguised as an old friend of Odysseus named Mentor, Odysseus and Telemachus killed all the suitors in a gruesome bloodbath. At first Penelope could not believe her husband had returned, but his old nursemaid, Eurycleia, knew him by his scar. When he was able to describe their marriage bed exactly, Penelope finally knew it was Odysseus.

Old age and death

Odysseus's travels were not yet over. The families of the slain suitors complained to King Neoptolemus of Epirus, and he ruled that Odysseus must be exiled. Odysseus eventually returned to Ithaca and lived to be an old man. Tiresias's prophecy about the death of Odysseus was fulfilled. Telegonus, the son of Odysseus and Circe, came to Ithaca to find his father. He came in peace, but when Odysseus confronted him, Telegonus did not recognize Odysseus and wounded him with his spear. The spear was tipped with a poisonous stingray spine, and Odysseus died.

Finally, Odysseus reached the island of Thrinacia, where the cattle and sheep of the sun god Helios were grazing. Because of Tiresias's warning, Odysseus was reluctant to land there, but his men were tired, so he said they could rest there for one night as long as they left the cattle alone. While Odysseus and his men were at Thrinacia, a storm blew up and they could not leave. They ran out of food, and one day, while Odysseus was busy praying for help, his men slaughtered some of the sacred cattle to eat. Helios begged Zeus to punish them, so when they set sail again, Zeus sent a thunderbolt to destroy the ship. The crew drowned, and only Odysseus survived. He drifted for many days until he came to the island of Ogygia, home of the nymph Calypso.

Calypso was lonely, and she was delighted to see Odysseus. She cared for him in every way she could. She also held him prisoner, keeping him on her island for seven years, though he longed to go home. Finally the gods agreed he must be set free. They sent Hermes to tell Calypso to let him go. Odysseus made a boat and set off. Poseidon still tried to stop him by sending another storm,

James Joyce's *Ulysses*

Irish writer James Joyce (1882–1941) is famous for his novel *Ulysses*, published in 1922. Joyce wanted to create a modern version of Homer's poem the *Odyssey*. Instead of a ten-year journey, Joyce made the action take place over the course of a single day, June 16, 1904, in Dublin. The hero, Leopold Bloom, represents Ulysses (or Odysseus) as he wanders around his city. Bloom's wife Molly stands for Penelope, and his friend's son, Stephen Dedalus, is Telemachus.

Each chapter in Joyce's *Ulysses* corresponds to an episode of Homer's poem. For example, Chapter 12, known as the Cyclops chapter, has several parallels with Homer's Cyclops myth. It is set in a dark Dublin bar, representing the Cyclops's cave, and Bloom, the hero, uses a fake name, as Odysseus does. At the end of the chapter, someone throws a biscuit at Bloom and misses, just as the Cyclops throws the errant rock at Odysseus.

Left: This photograph of Irish writer James Joyce was taken in 1938. The author of Ulysses *was visiting Zurich, Switzerland.*

A popular hero

Despite his shortcomings, Odysseus has always been regarded as a hero. The ancient Greeks admired his cunning and wit and saw him as a fine leader. Although he was merciless toward his enemies and could often be unnecessarily cruel, he always acted with courage. Odysseus's decisiveness during the Trojan War and on his travels averted many potential disasters.

Odysseus's adventures also contain many moral lessons. Whenever Odysseus is arrogant, boastful, or complacent, fate and the gods punish him. His adventures suggest that there is often a bad consequence for someone who carries out a bad deed. As well as being clever and brave, Odysseus sometimes makes mistakes or loses control, and he always suffers for it. Perhaps this is why Odysseus is such a well-loved character, even though his personality is often disagreeable. He is a kind of everyman: someone that is easy to identify with since he does his best in life's journey; he goes through ups and downs, and he has to struggle against his own weaknesses to survive.

The Odyssey as inspiration

Odysseus is most famous for his epic journey, which has now become part of modern speech. The word *odyssey* is used to describe any long journey, especially one that teaches someone a lot about themselves, whether it is a physical journey or an inner journey of self-discovery.

The *Odyssey*'s simple structure of disaster and recovery, the exciting monsters, and the universal theme of longing for home make the poem enduringly popular. The *Odyssey* has been translated and retold countless times in books, films, and literature. A famous example is Irish writer James Joyce's novel *Ulysses,* which is based on the *Odyssey.* The poem has also inspired more recent works such as *2001: A Space Odyssey* and the TV series *Star Trek: Voyager*, in which the crew of a spaceship encounters many monsters and strange peoples on their long journey home. Odysseus and his adventures have been depicted in many carvings, paintings and sculptures, from ancient Greek times to the present day.

ANNA CLAYBOURNE

Bibliography

Apollodorus, and Robin Hard, trans. *The Library of Greek Mythology.* New York: Oxford University Press, 2008.

Graves, Robert. *The Greek Myths*. New York: Penguin, 1993.

Homer, and Robert Fagles, trans. *The Iliad*. New York: Penguin, 2009.

Homer, and Robert Fagles, trans. *The Odyssey.* New York: Penguin, 2009.

SEE ALSO: Achilles; Agamemnon; Calypso; Circe; Cyclopes; Helen; Penelope; Tiresias.

OEDIPUS

In Greek mythology Oedipus was the son of Laius, King of Thebes, and Jocasta, who is also known as Epicasta. He is renowned as a man who endured a life that was full of misfortune, during which he unwittingly killed his father and married his mother.

The oldest version of the Oedipus myth appears in Homer's (c. ninth–eighth century BCE) epic poems the *Iliad* and the *Odyssey*. Homer's version of the myth is different from later versions found in fifth-century-BCE Greek tragedies. The most famous of these tragedies were written by Sophocles (c. 496–406 BCE)—*Oedipus the King* and *Oedipus at Colonus*—and by Aeschylus (525–456 BCE)—*The Seven Against Thebes*. Some scholars speculate that tragedians changed the myth to make it more politically and socially relevant to contemporary Greek society. The plague mentioned in the opening of *Oedipus the King*, for example, is thought to refer to a great plague that affected Athens in 430 BCE. Scholars also suggest that in *Oedipus at Colonus*, King Theseus's sympathy for Oedipus, who had been exiled from Thebes, offers an insight into how democratic Athens was during this period.

Homer's Oedipus

According to Homer, Oedipus was a prince of the house of Cadmus in Thebes. Before his birth, his father, King Laius, had been warned by a prophet that he would be killed by his son, so he ordered a herdsman to abandon the baby Oedipus in the woods. (In many ancient cultures, "exposure" was used as a form of birth control. Unwanted newborn babies were abandoned to die or to be picked up by a passerby. If the baby was adopted, he or she might be raised in a family or become a slave.) Oedipus was adopted by King Polybus and Queen Periboea of Corinth and lived peacefully until he unwittingly killed his real father during a chance encounter on the road to Thebes. Oedipus then married the widow of Laius, who was his own mother.

In the *Odyssey*, Homer names the queen Epicasta. When the incestuous marriage comes to light, Epicasta kills herself and Oedipus is cursed by being pursued by the Erinyes (Furies). Unlike in later versions of the myth, Oedipus did not gouge out his eyes and was not exiled from Thebes. Instead, he continued to rule Thebes and married again. Finally, he died a hero in battle, and at his funeral, games were held in his honor.

Other versions of the myth

Later versions of the Oedipus myth give more details in the story. They recount that Laius, king of Thebes, married Jocasta, daughter of Menoeceus, uniting two branches of the royal house of Thebes. Laius became anxious about the couple's difficulty in producing a child and consulted the oracle at Delphi. The oracle warned Laius not to have a son because that son was fated to kill his father. To prevent the prophecy from being fulfilled, Laius avoided making love to women, including his wife. (In one version of the myth, Laius kidnapped Chrysippus, the son of King Pelops of Pisa, to be his companion. Since the Thebans did not reprimand Laius for this action, the gods sent the Sphinx, a winged creature with a woman's head and a lion's body, to punish them.) However, Laius did not tell his wife why he was avoiding her, which made Jocasta unhappy, so she plotted to seduce her husband. One night, when he was drunk, Jocasta succeeded and became pregnant. Jocasta knew nothing of the prophecy. She was therefore horrified when the fearful Laius took away their healthy baby and abandoned the boy. In an effort to ensure that the baby was not adopted, Laius pierced his ankles with brooches or spikes. Then the king instructed a herdsman to leave the baby on Mount Cithaeron, between Boeotia and Attica. There, the baby was either found by servants of King Polybus of Corinth or given to them by the herdsman. The servants took the baby to Corinth, where Polybus's wife, Queen Periboea, healed the baby's ankles and adopted him. She named him Oedipus, which means "swollen feet" in ancient Greek. In a variation of the myth, Oedipus was born to Laius and his first wife; Jocasta was Laius's second wife. As a baby Oedipus was put into a chest and tossed

into the sea. The chest floated to Sicyon and was discovered by Polybus, who was king of Sicyon. In this version, Oedipus also eventually married Jocasta, his stepmother.

Oedipus grew up as prince and heir to the throne of Corinth, but his companions taunted him. They insisted that Oedipus could not be Polybus's son because the king was so mild and Oedipus was so aggressive. Oedipus approached the queen about the rumor, but she told him nothing of his adoption. The young man went to Delphi to consult the oracle about his parentage. The oracle advised Oedipus not to return to his native land. If he did, the oracle warned him, he would murder his father and sleep with his mother. Believing that the oracle was referring to Polybus and Periboea, Oedipus did not return to Corinth.

Patricide

Oedipus traveled in another direction, toward Daulis. On his way, on a narrow road, Oedipus encountered a chariot driven by two men, one of whom, unknown to Oedipus,

Above: This painting by an anonymous 17th-century artist depicts the discovery of Oedipus by servants of King Polybus after the baby had been abandoned on Mount Cithaeron.

was his natural father, Laius. Laius was going to consult the oracle at Delphi about how to rid Thebes of the Sphinx that was terrorizing the city. In another version of the myth, Laius was visiting the oracle because he had witnessed omens that foretold his death, and he wanted to discover if they were true. When father and son met on the narrow road, the king's herald Polyphontes ordered Oedipus to give way. According to some versions, Oedipus hesitated, so the herald killed one of his horses; in another the king urged his horses forward and a wheel bruised one of Oedipus's feet. In both stories Oedipus killed the herald with his spear, then dragged Laius from the chariot and killed him.

King Damasistratus of the nearby city of Plataea presided over Laius's funeral. Jocasta's brother and Oedipus's uncle, Creon, became regent in Thebes. During his rule the

Sphinx continued to terrorize Boeotia. It destroyed the fields around Thebes and killed anyone who failed to give the correct answer to a riddle, which it had learned from the Muses. The riddle is well known today: "What creature walks on all fours in the morning, two legs at noon, and three legs in the evening?" Some tragedians claimed that the Sphinx also had a second riddle: "There are two sisters. One gives birth to the other, then that one gives birth to the first. Who are they?" The answer to the second riddle is Night and Day, which are both feminine nouns.

In ancient Greece there were two versions of how the Sphinx forced the Thebans to guess its riddles. In one the monster came to the city each day to ask its riddle. Each time it was answered incorrectly, it devoured one of the citizens. In other versions of the story it perches on top of the citadel, or by the side of the road, and prevents travelers from passing if they provide an incorrect answer. The Thebans were desperate to escape the curse. There are stories that they gathered in the Agora (a marketplace found in most ancient Greek cities) to debate possible answers to the riddle, but without success. According to one version of the myth, Creon's own son Haemon was eaten by the Sphinx. However, Haemon also appears in the play *Antigone,* which is set after the death of the Sphinx.

Whether Creon was grief-stricken at the loss of his son or was simply a frustrated ruler, he promised the kingdom

Below: This third-century-BCE marble relief depicts Oedipus dragging Laius from his chariot to kill him.

of Thebes and the hand of his sister, Jocasta, to the person who could rid Thebes of the Sphinx. Many men came to try, but they all failed and were killed by the monster. News of the proclamation eventually reached Oedipus, and he headed for Thebes, where he met the Sphinx. Oedipus solved the riddle. The answer was a man. As an infant, humans are four-footed, crawling on their arms and legs; as adults they go on two feet; when they are elderly they walk using a cane like a third leg. On hearing the right answer, the Sphinx threw itself to its death.

Oedipus was welcomed into Thebes as a hero. He was crowned king and offered the hand of the widowed queen. Oedipus thus unwittingly married his mother. According to Sophocles' play *Oedipus the King,* when Oedipus became king he decreed that the murderer of Laius was to be found and brought to justice, and that he or she would be killed or banished from the kingdom.

Incest

According to some accounts Oedipus and Jocasta had four children: Eteocles, Polyneices, Antigone, and Ismene. Other accounts attribute other wives to the hero, possibly to overcome audiences' distaste at the idea of incest between a mother and son. In these accounts Euryganeia, the second wife of Oedipus, was sometimes credited as the mother of Eteocles, Polyneices, Antigone, and Ismene. Jocasta was childless, or their children were two obscure mythological characters called Phrastor and Laonytus. In some versions of the myth Oedipus married again after Euryganeia, to a

The Greek Sphinx

According to different myths, the Greek Sphinx was the female offspring of the monster Typhon and the snake-woman monster Echidna, or of the two-headed hound Orthus and the fire-breathing she-goat monster Chimaera. Her sister was the Nemean Lion, a murderous beast that Heracles had to kill for his first labor. Hera, the goddess of marriage, sent the Sphinx to terrorize Thebes because she held the Thebans accountable for Oedipus's marriage to his mother. Although Homer and tragedians agree that Oedipus solved the Sphinx's riddle, there are various accounts of how the Sphinx met her death. The most common version states that the Sphinx threw herself from a great height onto rocks, but another version claims that Oedipus pushed the Sphinx to her death. While both accounts are equally dramatic, the second undermines the exercise of solving the riddle and is not traditional.

Right: Oedipus confronts the Sphinx in this painting by French artist Gustave Moreau (1826–1898). The Sphinx was a monster with a woman's head, eagle's wings, and lion's body.

princess named Astymedusa. Some scholars speculate that the extra marriages were intended to avoid any implication that the Theban royal family was incestuous.

When Oedipus and Jocasta's children were reaching adulthood, a plague came upon the city. Eventually the plague became so bad that the Thebans consulted the blind seer Tiresias. Tiresias declared that the pestilence would cease if a descendent of the founders of Thebes died voluntarily to save the city. Menoeceus, father of Jocasta, threw himself to his death from the walls of the city. The plague ceased but Tiresias now said that although the gods were content with the death of Menoeceus, they had originally referred to another man. Tiresias told Jocasta that this man was Oedipus, and when she told her husband, he arrogantly refused to believe her. Around this time, however, Oedipus received a letter from his adoptive mother, Queen Periboea of Corinth. The letter, written following the death of King Polybus, revealed Oedipus's true identity. He was Jocasta's son and Laius's murderer. Menoetes, the herdsman who had exposed Oedipus when he was a baby, also identified him by the scars on his feet and ankles as the son of Laius. On hearing the news, Jocasta either hanged herself or killed herself with a sword, while Oedipus blinded himself with brooches that he tore from

Jocasta's robes. Following the sentence he himself had decreed for the murderer of Laius, Oedipus went into exile, accompanied by his daughter Antigone. Before leaving, Oedipus handed the kingdom of Thebes to his sons Polyneices and Eteocles. Some versions of the myth claim that his sons imprisoned him before he could leave Thebes, hoping that his disgrace might be forgotten. Oedipus cursed his sons so that they would never agree between them who should become the next king of Thebes.

The Oedipus Complex

Sigmund Freud (1856–1939) was a psychologist who is regarded as the father of psychoanalysis by psychologists today. He used Oedipus's name as shorthand for instances when his patients experienced a sexual attraction to their parents; his interpretation of the myth is renowned. Freud's theory of the Oedipus complex centers around the idea that between the ages of 3 and 5 a child experiences feelings of attraction toward the parent of the opposite sex. At the same time, the child experiences a feeling of rivalry with the parent of the same sex. Freud argued that these issues were part of normal human development. Modern psychologists argue that Freud's theory is not correct and interpret the Oedipus myth differently; they explain the relationship between Oedipus and his parents in terms of resentment of parental authority, not sexual rivalry.

Below: This illustration from de Claris Mulieribus, *by Italian author Giovanni Boccaccio (1313–1375), depicts different stages of the Oedipus myth. The woman stabbing herself is Oedipus's mother Jocasta, who can not bear the fact that she has married her son.*

Polyneices and Eteocles tried to avoid the curse by agreeing that they should rule Thebes alternately for a year at a time. This agreement did not last long, however: Eteocles seized power and refused to share the throne with his brother.

Meanwhile, Oedipus had taken refuge at Colonus in Attica, where he was welcomed by King Theseus of Athens. While he was in Colonus, the disagreement between his sons worsened and war approached. Before conflict broke out, an oracle stated that the victor would be allied with Oedipus. Creon came to Oedipus on behalf of Eteocles and attempted to persuade him to return to Thebes. When Oedipus refused, Creon endeavored to take him there by force. Theseus intervened in time to save Oedipus, who remained in Colonus.

Aided by King Adrastus of Argos, Polyneices raised an army to march against his younger brother, who had banished Polyneices from Thebes and now controlled the city. Polyneices went to his exiled father at Colonus and asked for his support. Oedipus responded to the request by issuing another curse, in which he doomed his sons to kill each other.

The Thebans prepared for war by taking their treasures out of the city. Soon after, allies of Polyneices known as

Above: This painting by French artist Ernest Hillemacher (1818–1887) shows Antigone guiding her blind father, Oedipus. In some versions of the myth, Oedipus blinds himself after discovering that he has killed his father and married his mother.

the Seven Against Thebes attacked the city. Polyneices' forces were defeated, Oedipus's sons killed each other in battle, and Creon came to power again. Oedipus's daughter Ismene also perished during the war. She was killed in bed by Tydeus, king of Argos, while she lay with her lover Theoclymenus.

After the war King Creon decreed that the body of Polyneices be left on the battlefield to rot. In ancient Greece, this was an undignified end for fallen soldiers. When Creon's niece Antigone learned of her brother's death and Creon's edict, she insisted that Polyneices be buried. When Creon discovered her disobedience, he imprisoned her for failing to follow his decree. Antigone killed herself in captivity. Ten years later, sons of the seven allies of Polyneices, known as the Epigoni, captured Thebes to avenge the death of their fathers.

Shortly after meeting with Polyneices, Oedipus died. Some versions of the myth say that he died at Colonus, others say that it was Thebes. Again, accounts differ as to whether he died of natural causes or killed himself. Although Oedipus was an exile and an outcast in most versions of the myth, his grave was regarded with reverence by ancient Greeks because of a prophecy which said that any land containing his tomb would be blessed by the gods.

LYN GREEN

Bibliography

Bulfinch, Thomas. *Bulfinch's Mythology.* New York: Barnes & Noble, 2006.

Homer, and Robert Fagles, trans. *The Iliad.* New York: Penguin, 2009.

Homer, and Robert Fagles, trans. *The Odyssey.* New York: Penguin, 2009.

Howatson, M. C. *The Oxford Companion to Classical Literature.* New York: Oxford University Press, 2005.

SEE ALSO: Antigone; Cadmus; Heracles; Theseus; Tiresias.

ORESTES

In Greek mythology Orestes is usually described as the son of Agamemnon and Clytemnestra, mythical king and queen of the ancient city of Mycenae, although in some accounts they are said to have come from nearby Argos, in Laconia. Orestes' life was blighted by the curse that his great-grandfather Pelops had brought on himself and all succeeding generations of his family.

The roots of the tragedy of Orestes can be traced back two generations before he was born. Pelops, founder of the Pelopid dynasty of Mycenae, wanted to marry Hippodameia. Hippodameia's father, Oenomaus, king of Pisa in Elis, would allow the union only if Pelops could beat him in a chariot race. Pelops won the contest by driving winged horses given to him by the sea god Poseidon and by offering a bribe to Myrtilus, Oenomaus's charioteer, to remove pins from his master's chariot. Oenomaus was killed, but Pelops drowned Myrtilus to avoid paying the bribe. As he was dying, Myrtilus cursed Pelops and his descendants. The numerous misfortunes that subsequently befell the house of Atreus, Pelops's son, are all attributed to this curse. Agamemnon was Atreus's son, and Orestes the son of Agamemnon.

The sins of the fathers

When Orestes was a baby, his father Agamemnon left home to lead the Greek armies in the Trojan War, leaving his wife, Clytemnestra, in charge of Mycenae. The campaign took a long time to prepare, and the war itself lasted 10 years, so Orestes was in his early teens by the time his father returned.

The Trojan War had not even begun when Agamemnon provoked the anger of the gods. While the Greeks were still gathering their fleet at the port of Aulis in readiness to transport their army to Troy, Agamemnon boasted that he was a better hunter than the goddess Artemis. To punish Agamemnon's hubris (pride), Artemis angrily stilled the winds so that the Greek ships could not set sail. A soothsayer told Agamemnon that the winds would return only if he sacrificed his daughter Iphigeneia to the offended goddess. With great sadness and reluctance, Agamemnon did his penance and had Iphigeneia killed on Artemis's altar. Clytemnestra never forgave her husband for allowing their daughter to be sacrificed and sought ways to avenge her death. Before long she joined forces with her cousin, Aegisthus, who hated Agamemnon as a consequence of an earlier conflict between their fathers, Thyestes and Atreus, respectively.

Left: Orestes consulting the oracle at Delphi. This marble bas-relief from the first century BCE was excavated from Herculaneum, one of the towns destroyed by an eruption of Mount Vesuvius in 79 CE.

Clytemnestra was at first reluctant to conspire with Aegisthus, but they later became lovers and she yielded to her desire for revenge and power. With Agamemnon away at Troy, the pair began to rule Mycenae as king and queen and made plans to kill Agamemnon when he returned. They forced Clytemnestra's surviving daughters to accept the new regime, but one of them, Electra, sent Orestes for safety to Agamemnon's ally Strophius, king of Phocis. That saved Orestes, for Aegisthus would not have allowed the heir to the throne to live.

When Agamemnon returned home to Mycenae with a mistress, the Trojan princess Cassandra, Clytemnestra and Aegisthus murdered the pair of them. They then ruled Mycenae for seven years. Orestes remained with Strophius, whose son Pylades became his close friend. When they reached manhood, they resolved to reclaim Orestes' birthright and avenge Agamemnon's death. They consulted the oracle of Apollo at Delphi, and Orestes was told to slay the killers of his father. The friends then proceeded to Mycenae and entered the city in secret. They made contact with Electra, who in one version had been compelled to marry a farmer so that her children would be ineligible to inherit the kingdom. Electra idolized her dead father and hated her mother and stepfather. She was therefore willing to help her brother. Together, the three young people managed to kill Aegisthus and Clytemnestra.

Although Orestes had acted with Apollo's approval, he was still guilty of matricide (killing one's mother), so he was vulnerable to attack by the Erinyes (Furies), goddesses of vengeance who tormented all criminals. These hideous demons pursued Orestes across Greece until he at last came to Athens. There a group of citizens assembled to hear his case, which Apollo defended since he originally supported Orestes' cause. The prosecution was presented according to some accounts by the Erinyes, in others by Clytemnestra's father, Tyndareos, or by Erigone, daughter of Aegisthus and Clytemnestra. The jury was divided, so Athena, the city's patron goddess, cast the deciding vote. Since Athena herself was born directly from Zeus and had no mother, she sympathized with Agamemnon as a father

figure. She ruled that Orestes' revenge was justifiable homicide. After she delivered her verdict the Erinyes agreed to become patrons of Athens, and were renamed the Eumenides ("Kindly Ones").

In search of a cure for madness

Despite his acquittal, Orestes' mind was still disturbed by all that had happened, so he and Pylades went in search of a cure for his madness. On the instructions of an oracle, they went to retrieve a sacred wooden image of Artemis from the Taurians, a savage northern people who were known to kill strangers on sight. Orestes and Pylades secretly entered the temple where the image

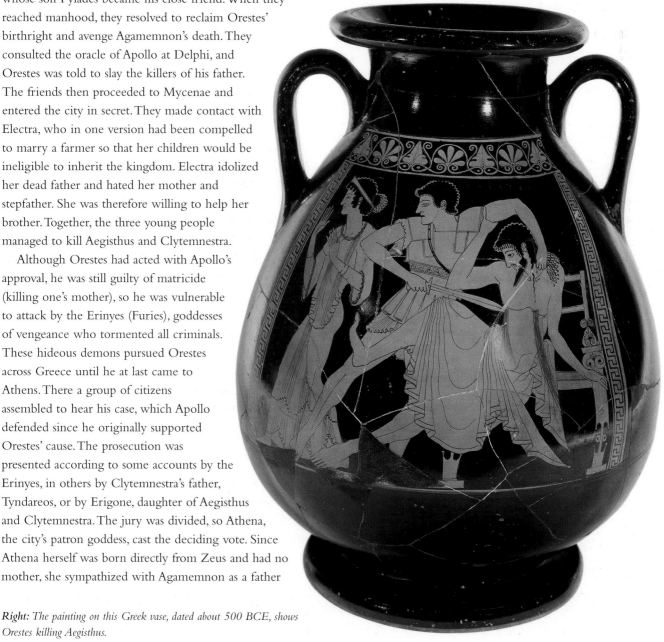

Right: The painting on this Greek vase, dated about 500 BCE, shows Orestes killing Aegisthus.

The Many Oresteias

The story of Orestes, otherwise known as the Oresteia, is represented in virtually every period of ancient Greek literature and art. An early and influential account of the Oresteia is elaborated in the *Odyssey*, an epic poem attributed to Homer (c. ninth–eighth century BCE). The poem refers to the seduction of Clytemnestra by Aegisthus, implicates both in the death of Agamemnon, and praises Orestes for killing Aegisthus. The Erinyes, Electra, and Pylades do not appear in Homer, and neither do the killing of Clytemnestra nor Orestes' trial. *Catalogues of Women*, a fragmentary epic attributed to Hesiod (fl. c. 800 BCE), mentions the sacrifice of Iphigeneia, the affair between Aegisthus and Clytemnestra, and her murder by Orestes.

A number of lyric poets who were familiar with the work of Homer and Hesiod also refer to the Oresteia. Stesichorus (fl. 600–550 BCE) wrote a long poem on the subject that includes a recognition scene between Electra and Orestes, and his pursuit by the Erinyes. Supporting characters emerge in an ode by Pindar (c. 522–c. 438 BCE) in which Orestes is saved from Aegisthus by a nurse named Arsinoe and taken in by King Strophius. These poems emphasize Clytemnestra's role in Agamemnon's death, and Orestes' role in hers, while the Homeric account plays down these events. Stesichorus and Pindar both locate Agamemnon's kingdom in Amyclae, a town near Sparta, not Mycenae.

The Oresteia is best known, however, from plays by the major tragedians of fifth-century-BCE Athens—Aeschylus (525–456 BCE), Sophocles (c. 496–406 BCE), and Euripides (c. 486–c. 406 BCE). Each develops the storyline in his own way, often by focusing on the female characters. All three set the action in Argos.

The *Oresteia* of Aeschylus is a trilogy consisting of *Agamemnon*, *Choephoroe* (*Libation Bearers*), and *Eumenides*. The three plays focus on the duty of children to their fathers and justify the role of the state in settling family feuds. Aeschylus's Clytemnestra manipulates her weak husband and justifies killing him with powerful rhetoric; Aegisthus is comparatively feeble, appearing only after the killing. As in the *Odyssey*, Orestes' deeds are praiseworthy, but Aeschylus confronts conflicting loyalties that the epic ignores. Electra plays a small role in Aeschylus's trilogy, and Pylades appears only to steel his friend's resolve to carry through the matricide. Aeschylus develops both the role of the Furies and the trial of Orestes more than any of his predecessors.

Sophocles may have been present at the first performance of Aeschylus's *Oresteia* in 458 BCE. In his own surviving play on this theme, *Electra*, the heroine is a passionate young woman and the driving force behind the plot to avenge her father, Agamemnon. Orestes is fairly passive, relying on Electra and a servant to direct his actions; Pylades is a silent character. Sophocles' Clytemnestra and Aegisthus are wicked and tyrannical; Orestes does not hesitate to kill his mother, and no Furies appear.

At about the same time as Sophocles was writing, Euripides was creating a unique vision of the Oresteia in four plays of his own: *Electra*, *Iphigeneia in Tauris*, *Orestes*, and *Iphigeneia at Aulis*. Euripides depicts Orestes and Pylades as homicidal thugs, while Clytemnestra is sympathetic and Aegisthus a popular leader. It was Euripides who first made Electra a farmer's wife, and he who developed the reunion of Orestes and Iphigeneia. Electra and Orestes regret the killings; the Erinyes are his guilty conscience.

Below: The story of Orestes appears on the side of the Sarcophagus of the Poet, a tomb from the third century BCE.

Above: After their murder of Aegisthus and Clytemnestra, Orestes, Electra, and Pylades are pursued by the Furies (Erinyes). This engraving originally appeared in an 18th-century dictionary of mythology.

was kept, but they were discovered and sent by the Taurian king Thoas to be sacrificed by the priestess of Artemis. The priestess, however, turned out to be Iphigeneia. She had not after all died at Aulis, but had been spirited away to serve Artemis in Tauris. Iphigeneia helped her brother, and she, Orestes, and Pylades escaped together. They fled with the sacred image—in some versions of the story, they took it to Athens, in others to the island of Rhodes.

Pylades then married Electra, and they seem to have lived happily ever after. Orestes, however, was less fortunate. In one version of events, he was due to wed his cousin Hermione, daughter of Agamemnon's brother Menelaus, but during one of his fits of madness she was carried off by Pyrrhus (also known as Neoptolemus), a distinguished Trojan war veteran. Orestes pursued them and killed Pyrrhus in Apollo's temple at Delphi.

Torment to the end

Most accounts agree, however, that Orestes finally did marry Hermione, and had a son, Tisamenus, who later ruled Achaea. However, Orestes did not remain with his family for long. As an additional reparation for killing his mother, or perhaps as a penance for killing Pyrrhus on ground that was sacred to Apollo, he had to endure a year's exile in Arcadia, a region of the Peloponnese peninsula in southern Greece. There he was bitten by a snake and died. He was buried near the city of Tegea.

The curse upon the house of Atreus was so strong that, even in death, Orestes did not find a permanent resting place. A Spartan, acting on instructions from an oracle, later dug up his bones and brought them to Sparta. The Spartans believed that once they were in possession of these relics, they would vanquish their neighbors and perpetual enemies the Tegeans. This seems to have been no more than wishful thinking, for in reality the Tegeans continued to be formidable opponents in battle, and it was diplomacy, rather than war, that finally brought them into the great Hellenic military alliance known as the League of Sparta.

JIM MARKS

Bibliography

Aeschylus, and A. Shapiro and P. Burian, eds. *The Oresteia*. New York: Oxford University Press, 2010.
Homer, and Robert Fagles, trans. *The Odyssey*. New York: Penguin, 2009.

SEE ALSO: Agamemnon; Atreus; Clytemnestra; Iphigeneia; Pelops.

ORION

In ancient Greek mythology, Orion was a giant hunter. He features in numerous legends, many of which give contradictory accounts of his life and exploits. Every version agrees, however, that after his death he became a constellation in the night sky—the outline of the group of stars named for him appears to show the hunter wearing a lion's skin, carrying a club, and accompanied by two hunting dogs.

Below: One of the brightest star clusters in the night sky, the constellation named for Orion has inspired artists for thousands of years.

In most accounts, Orion was either the son of Hyreius, king of Boeotia, or of the deities Dionysus and Demeter. A few myths state that his mother was Gaia, the earth goddess; elsewhere his parents are said to have been either Poseidon and Euryale or Hyrieus and the nymph Clonia. One myth attributed Orion's origin to a bull hide: childless Hyrieus asked for an heir by sacrificing a bull to Zeus, Hermes, and Poseidon; they urinated on the hide, and Orion was born from it.

Love stories

As a young man Orion courted Merope, one of the Pleiades, seven nymphs who were companions of the Greek goddess Artemis (the others were Alcyone, Celaeno, Electra, Maia, Sterope, and Taygete). Merope rejected his advances. In one story, she married a mortal, Sisyphus, king of Corinth. According to another version, Merope became betrothed to Orion, but her father—Oenopion, king of Chios, an island in the Aegean Sea—kept postponing the

date of the wedding. Eventually Orion lost patience and raped Merope; Oenopion blinded him in revenge. Orion then wandered helplessly until the god Hephaestus took pity on him and sent his own attendant, Kedalion, to help the blinded man. Sitting on top of Orion's shoulders, Kedalion guided him to the abode of Helios, the sun god, and Eos, goddess of the dawn. When Eos saw Orion she was moved to tears—they became the glistening morning dew—and immediately restored his sight. On seeing his savior, Orion fell in love with her, but this angered the gods, who ordered Artemis, goddess of hunting, to slay the man with her arrows. Before he died, however, Orion repaid his debt to Hephaestus by building a subterranean temple in his honor in Sicily. He also built walls around the island's coast to protect it from the sea.

Another legend states that Orion and Artemis fell in love and planned to marry. Their relationship was sabotaged by Artemis's brother, Apollo, who disapproved of the union between a goddess and a human. Apollo pointed to a small bobbing object far out to sea and challenged Artemis to hit it. The goddess would never turn down a chance to show off her marksmanship, so she shot an arrow from her bow and hit the center of the distant speck. The target disappeared beneath the waves. Not long afterward the body of the victim was washed up on shore—it was

Above: This 19th-century engraving shows Orion, on a hunting expedition, being fatally bitten by a scorpion.

Orion, as Apollo well knew. Artemis, grief-stricken, asked Zeus to place her dead lover among the stars.

Several mythological accounts of the life of Orion end with his being stung fatally by a scorpion. According to some sources, the venomous creature was set upon him by Artemis after he had raped one of her followers. In other accounts, Orion boasted that he could slay any animal, so the scorpion was his comeuppance. In a variation on this theme, the earth goddess Gaia sent the scorpion. It stung Orion, but he survived thanks to an antidote promptly administered by Asclepius, god of medicine.

A modern place among the stars

Every legend of Orion agrees that after the hunter's death, Zeus granted the wish of Artemis and placed him in the heavens. The constellation still known as Orion, the Hunter, is the most spectacular and one of the most easily recognized in the sky. The stars represent the hunter holding a shield in his left hand and a club in his right. Betelgeuse, one of the largest stars known, marks his right shoulder. Bellatrix marks his left shoulder, and Saiph and Rigel mark his two legs. Other notable parts of the

The Australian Pleiades

The Aboriginal peoples of Australia have their own myth of the creation of the Pleiades and Orion, which are visible in the southern hemisphere during Australia's winter months. The Pleiades were seven beautiful sisters who roamed the land during the day and returned to their sky home at night. A man named Wurrunnah captured two of them but discovered that their beautiful hair was like icicles. He tried to melt the sisters' cold crystals over his campfire; the water put out his fire and dimmed the sisters' brightness (thus accounting for the two dimmest stars of the Pleiades). During their captivity, many men admired the sisters, but Berai Berai (two brothers) honored them most. They hunted for food for the sisters but knew that they longed for their home in the sky. Each night, their five sisters twinkled, beckoning them. One day Wurrunnah told the sisters to gather pine bark from a tree. As they began, the pine tree extended itself to the sky, and the sisters escaped home. Berai Berai laid aside their weapons and mourned until death's shadow overtook them. The fairies then placed Berai Berai in the sky, where they could always hear the sisters singing; the brothers became Orion's sword and belt.

Other Myths about Orion's Belt

Above: The constellation of Orion appears in the Book of Fixed Stars, *an Arabic astronomical treatise of the 11th century CE.*

Many peoples saw significance in the three bright stars of Orion's belt—which today we call Mintaka, Alnilam, and Alnitak—that form an almost straight line. Peruvians believed the middle star was a criminal; the moon goddess sent Pata, the two outside stars, to capture him. In South African myth, Orion associated with Isilimela (the Pleiades), daughters of a sky god. Their husband (the star Aldebaran) unsuccessfully shot an arrow (Orion's sword) at three zebras (Orion's belt), and remained in the cold sky: he dared not return without game, and he dared not retrieve his arrow; a fierce lion (Betelgeuse) watched the zebras. In other South African myths, Orion's belt stars were lions that had been transformed by a magical girl child, and three pigs chased by three dogs. Siberians and Mongolians saw stags, while California Native Americans saw mountain sheep, antelope, and deer. Hindu myth said the belt stars were an arrow fired at creator-god Prajapati, who lusted after his daughter (Aldebaran). Northern Australian Aboriginals saw three fishers in a canoe, as did the Wasco of Oregon. Ancient Jews saw Nimrod, bound to the heavens for disobeying God. Early French agriculturalists called Orion's belt *le râteau* (the rake).

constellation include Orion's belt, consisting of three bright stars and including the dark Horsehead nebula; and Orion's sword, where the bright Orion nebula is visible to the naked eye. The constellation is located near the celestial equator and dominates the night sky of the northern hemisphere in winter. The nearby constellations of Canis Major and Canis Minor represent Orion's two hunting dogs. Also in the same part of the sky is Taurus, the Bull, which was often seen as Orion's prey. Among the stars of this constellation are the Pleiades—this is particularly an allusion to Orion's pursuit of Merope, but also to a version of the story in which Orion pursues the seven sisters and their mother, Pleione, until the gods turn them into doves.

Another astronomical reference to the story of Orion is the constellation of Scorpius, the Scorpion, which is never visible at the same time as Orion—according to legend, that is because Zeus ordered the killer and its victim to be kept apart.

Similar legends in other cultures

The legends of Orion and his link with the stars have notable parallels in other ancient cultures. Sumerians saw the constellation as Sibzianna, a shepherd god; the neighboring stars were his flock. Mesopotamians called it

Uru-anna (Light of Heaven), who, as Gilgamesh, battled Gut-anna (Bull of Heaven), which is represented by the Taurus constellation. What modern Westerners know as Orion was known to Hittites as Aqhat, a hunter. The battle goddess Anat loved Aqhat, but Aqhat rejected her and refused to lend her his bow. Anat sent a man to steal it, but the man killed Aqhat. Aqhat fell into the sea, an explanation for the constellation's disappearance below the horizon in spring. The ancient Egyptians were among the many other civilizations that attached mythic significance to the constellation. They regarded it as a manifestation of Osiris in his sky barge.

ALYS CAVINESS

Bibliography

Bulfinch, Thomas. *Bulfinch's Mythology.* New York: Barnes & Noble, 2006.

Gayley, Charles Mills. *The Classic Myths in English Literature and Art.* Boston: Ginn and Company, 1893.

Hamilton, Edith. *Mythology: Timeless Tales of Gods and Heroes.* New York: Grand Central, 2011.

Ovid, and A. D. Melville, trans. *Metamorphoses.* New York: Oxford University Press, 2008.

SEE ALSO: Pleiades.

ORPHEUS

In Greek mythology, Orpheus was a musician from Thrace, a region occupying parts of what are now eastern Greece and western Turkey. There are many legends about his magical skill on the lyre, which enabled him to charm trees, rivers, and stones, as well as wild beasts.

Below: This marble statue of Orpheus with his lyre was carved by French artist Pierre de Francheville (1554–1618).

Orpheus was the son of Calliope, the Muse of epic poetry; in most versions of his story, his father was Oeagrus, a Thracian river god, one of the children of Ares. As a child Orpheus learned music from Apollo, the greatest master of the art. In some versions, Apollo is said to have been Orpheus's real father. Orpheus was a gifted pupil, and before long he was able to calm the people of his native Thrace, who were notorious for their barbarism, by playing to them on his lyre, a stringed instrument, which he had had fashioned out of a hollow tortoise shell. According to one legend, Orpheus invented the cithara, a stringed musical instrument that was widely used in ancient Greece. Similar in shape to the lyre, it had from 5 to 11 strings that were plucked with a plectrum or with the fingers. The guitar and the zither derive their names from the cithara.

Adventures with the Argonauts

Orpheus had many adventures. For example, he accompanied Jason and the Argonauts on their voyage to retrieve the Golden Fleece. While they were at sea, he calmed the waves during storms, distracted the Sirens who were trying to ensnare the crew with their songs, and quietened the sailors when they became unruly. According to some accounts, it was Orpheus who lulled the dragon to sleep so that Jason could grab the Golden Fleece.

On his return to Thrace, Orpheus lived in a cave and spent his time charming the countryside with his music. He fell passionately in love with the Dryad Eurydice and wanted to marry her. On their wedding day, however, many dreadful things happened. Hymen, god of marriage, came to the ceremony. This was normally an auspicious sign of a good life ahead for the happy couple, but on this occasion Hymen was unable to keep his sacred wedding torch alight. No matter how much he shook it or blew on it, it just produced smoke that irritated the eyes of the guests and made them cry. That was a bad omen. The same day, Eurydice was chased through the meadows by Aristaeus, the son of Apollo and Cyrene and the husband of Autonoe. He was herdsman and beekeeper to the gods. As Eurydice fled from him, his bees pursued her; she accidentally stepped on a snake, which bit her. She died as a result.

Orpheus in the underworld

Orpheus was overwhelmed with grief by the death of Eurydice. He ceased to sing and play and instead moped around in silence. Finally he resolved to search for the entrance to the underworld so that he could at least see— and, if possible, retrieve—his lost love. When he found the entrance in southern Italy, he made his way into the passage. Once inside, he began to play his lyre again. The

Below: A mosaic from the third century CE from Tarsus, Turkey, shows Orpheus playing his lyre and enchanting animals and charming birds from the trees.

Enduring Myth

The story of Orpheus is one of the oldest Greek myths. Its enduring popularity has given rise to many variations on the basic legend, as each new teller has added his or her own embellishments. In particular, the imagery of the story of this musical hero, master of the lyre and inventor of the cithara, was adopted by the esoteric religious movement known as Orphism to reinforce and legitimize its doctrine. It has also been invoked by many poets for inspiration. As an allegory, the pagan story even found its way into early Christian iconography. In the catacombs of Jerusalem, for example, Jesus was depicted in the guise of Orpheus with the lyre. In some later Christian tombs Orpheus is shown delivering the Sermon on the Mount or acting as "the Good Shepherd."

One of the myth's most potent and enduring images is of the power of music to achieve effects that are unattainable by other means. Orpheus used his celestial harmonies in an attempt to raise Eurydice from the dead and influence the shades of the underworld. If he had not made the mistake of looking back, he would probably have succeeded—the technique was faultless, only the practitioner was flawed by his humanity. Such ideas are more than artistic fantasy. A modern form of psychological treatment known as music therapy uses harmonious sounds to calm anguished people and improve their state of mind.

Above: This oil painting by the German artist Friedrich Brentel (1580–1651) depicts the ascent of Orpheus from the underworld. Eurydice is dragged back into Hades when Orpheus turns to look at her.

music that he played charmed Charon, the boatman of the Styx River, and Cerberus, the three-headed dog that guarded the entrance to Hades, into letting him pass. All the inhabitants of the underworld were likewise captivated by Orpheus's music: even Tartarus stopped torturing the souls of his victims. In *Metamorphoses*, Roman poet Ovid (43 BCE–17 CE) described the scene this way: "Tantalus stopped reaching for the receding waters, the wheel of Ixion stopped in wonder, the vultures ceased tearing at the liver of Tityus, the Danaid sisters left their urns empty, and Sisyphus sat on his throne to listen." In the *Georgics*, Virgil (70–19 BCE) described how thousands of flitting shades and spectral images of the departed flocked to see Orpheus, moved by his music. The Furies abandoned their vengeful ways to listen to his song. Death itself seemed suspended.

Even the gods Hades and Persephone were softened and were temporarily rendered speechless by the sound of Orpheus's lyre. The grieving hero took this opportunity to explain to them how his bride Eurydice had died before her time. He implored them to let her return with him to earth, pointing out that they would inevitably have her back in their kingdom one day, so a temporary reprieve

would make no difference. Desperately, Orpheus then announced that he would not, and could not, return without her. Moved by his appeals and the intensity of his devotion, the gods decided to let Orpheus take Eurydice, but on one condition: he must lead the way out of the underworld and not look back at her until they reached the upper air. Orpheus agreed. So he departed, his beloved behind him, his eyes fixed ahead.

While he was leading her up the steep path through the black vapors, however, just as the end of the passage was in sight and light was visible ahead, he could not refrain from turning and gazing at his wife's face—he wanted to make sure that she was still with him. At that very moment, Eurydice turned into a mist. Orpheus tried to grab her but could not prevent her from being sucked back into the underworld. Hermes, the escort of souls, led her down the path into the dark abode. Orpheus tried to follow, but this time even his music failed to overcome the guards. Charon would not allow him back on the boat.

Above: Orpheus leads Eurydice out of the underworld. This painting is one of the greatest works by the French painter Jean-Baptiste-Camille Corot (1796–1875).

Orpheus reluctantly returned to the world above and became like a lost soul on earth, wandering here and there, living as a recluse, avoiding the company, above all, of women. He still sang, but only songs of mourning and lament. He remained attractive to women, however, and many of them tried to cajole him out of his devotion to his dead lover. Yet Orpheus remained adamant that he would have nothing to do with any other female.

Death of a hero

One day on his aimless wanderings Orpheus happened upon a group of Thracian women who were taking part in an orgiastic ritual in honor of Dionysus, god of wine and intoxication. When they saw Orpheus, they went into a frenzy and rushed after him. Their weapons, however, fell to the ground around him, charmed by his music. The women grew more hostile and bold, abandoning all restraint. As they began to play their raucous Dionysian music, the curved pipes, pounding drums, and whooping and shrieking all combined in a great cacophony that eventually drowned out the sound of the hero's lyre.

The women were able to capture Orpheus. They ripped him to shreds with their bare hands. Their crime is usually said to have been motivated by their anger at having had their amatory advances rejected—as English playwright William Congreve (1670–1729) put it, "Hell hath no fury like a woman scorned." Some accounts, however, claim that their actions were inspired by Dionysus himself, who resented Orpheus's advocacy of the worship of Apollo.

As the women tore him apart, Orpheus's head rolled down a hill into the Hebrus River and was washed down to the sea, rolling this way and that and constantly crying, "Eurydice! Eurydice!" Eventually it came ashore on the island of Lesbos. The local inhabitants placed the talking head in a cave, where it functioned as an oracle for those who came with questions. Orpheus was said to have inspired the work of Sappho (fl. c. 610–580 BCE), a great female poet who lived on Lesbos. In another legend, Orpheus was torn apart by Maenads—the Muses gathered the pieces of his dismembered corpse and buried them in a single place near their home on Mount Olympus. A nightingale sang over the tomb of Orpheus, and his musical instrument was placed in the heavens as a constellation. This is the modern Lyra, the brightest star of which is Vega.

The cult of Orphism

The cave on Lesbos containing the head of Orpheus functioned for many years as an oracle until one day the head ceased to speak. Much of what it had said had been recorded, however, and this information formed the basis of a new religion that emerged around 600 BCE. Orphism, as it was known, claimed to have at its core the revelations given by the head of Orpheus after it had been detached from his body. The records—known as the Orphica—contain hymns, poetry, and commentaries.

Orphism developed an elaborate cosmogony (a theory explaining the creation of the universe) that focused on the killing and eating of Dionysus by the Titans and Zeus's subsequent destruction of the Titans, from whose ashes

arose the human race, part Dionysiac (divine and good) and part Titan (earthly and evil). Through initiation into the Orphic mysteries, and by living an ascetic life of abstention from meat, wine, and sexual activity, individuals sought to suppress their earthly nature. Full liberation of the divine soul could be achieved only through a cycle of incarnations. Orphism was never a widespread cult, although its ideas were influential.

Thus, in Greek mythology, Orpheus evolved from a gifted musician into a theologian of unassailable authority. The explanation of this development is to be found in the myth itself. Orpheus had achieved something that few mortals had ever done: he had entered Hades as a living being and reemerged from it unscathed. In essence, he had conquered death and thereby weakened its fearful grip on humankind. In addition, Orpheus's round-trip to the underworld cast reassuring new light on the mystery of death by opening up the possibility of rebirth. Orphian scholars concluded that their hero had been forbidden to turn around and look at Eurydice while they were emerging from the underworld because by doing so he would have been able to see something the gods did not

Below: The story of Orpheus has remained perennially popular in art. In this French oil painting of the late 19th century, he is shown on the seashore lamenting the death of Eurydice on their wedding day.

Orphic Religion

Central to Orphic religious practices was the belief in the transmigration of souls, which, if properly understood and dealt with, could lead to ultimate bliss on the Isles of the Blessed or in the realm of the starry ether. The goal of every Orphic disciple was to learn how the human soul had become stained with evil and the means by which it could be purified. Orpheus had taught the proper rituals and incantations necessary for purification, and he recommended a lifestyle of asceticism that included vegetarianism, a general respect for the value of all life, expiation of sins, and sanctity of conduct. Orphics dressed in white to indicate their aspirations to purity, and they did everything in their power to avoid any form of impropriety. The strict rules of Orphism, together with the prominence it gave to music, caused the cult to be identified with other mystery religions, such as the Bacchanalia and the Eleusinian Mysteries of Demeter. The revelations witnessed by these cults tended to result in joy and the hope for an afterlife of bliss.

Left: This painting by Gustave Moreau (1826–1898) shows Orpheus's detached head in the arms of a suitor after he had forsworn all contact with women.

want him to see; namely, the process of regeneration. Thus the very act that stole Eurydice from Orpheus forever is the same act that revealed to him the secret that all humans would like to share.

Orphism in art

Since the decline of Orphism as a religious cult, the term has come to denote the style of painting created and practiced by French painter Robert Delaunay (1885–1941). First called "orphic cubism" by French poet Guillaume Apollinaire (1880–1918), the style is characterized by an approach in which color (identified with light) is the primary pictorial element. The theory on which orphic cubism is based comes from the recognition that the constant movements and changes of light produce color

shapes that are independent of objects, and that create patterns resembling those of abstraction. By an extension of this theory, certain combinations of colors can be juxtaposed in such a way as to produce harmonic contrasts with each other and thus represent the movement of light. Delaunay's series *The Windows*, painted between 1910 and 1913, exemplifies the kaleidoscopic possibilities of orphism, as does his *Window on the City No. 4* (1911). Orphism was built on the achievements of earlier movements such as impressionism, cubism, and futurism, and especially on the 19th-century color theories studied and explored by, among others, Georges Seurat (1859–1891), the French artist who founded pointillism. In modern English usage, the term *Orphian* or *Orphean* means anything that is outstandingly melodious or tuneful.

KIRK SUMMERS

Bibliography

Bulfinch, Thomas. *Myths of Greece and Rome.* New York: Penguin, 1979.

Ovid, and A. D. Melville, trans. *Metamorphoses.* New York: Oxford University Press, 2008.

SEE ALSO: Jason; Maenads.

PANDORA

In Greek mythology, Pandora is the first woman, a beautiful but problematic creature designed by the gods as a punishment for mortal men. Traditionally, curiosity compels Pandora to open a jar containing all kinds of ills and suffering, freeing the afflictions on humankind.

The principal accounts of the myth of Pandora are found in two works by Greek poet Hesiod (fl. 800 BCE), *Theogony* and *Works and Days*. While both versions have much in common, there are also many significant differences. *Theogony* gives her no name, but in *Works and Days* the name Pandora and its etymology play a central role. Pandora is sometimes compared to Eve from the Book of Genesis in the Bible, another first woman whose curiosity leads to trouble for humans. The problems that arose from Pandora's curiosity have become proverbial, giving rise to the common expression *to open a Pandora's box*.

In *Theogony*, which recounts the births of the gods, the creation or invention of humans requires no explanation. Although female divinities exist from the beginning of time, the first mortals are assumed to be male. Scholars of Greek mythology suggest that, because men were fashioned to appear like the gods and because asexual reproduction occurs among the gods, female partners for men were unnecessary. Unlike the account given in the Book of

Below: In Eva Prima Pandora, *French painter Jean Cousin the Elder (1490–1560) compares the biblical figure of Eve to Pandora, the first woman in Greek mythology. Her left hand rests on a jar that she will eventually open, releasing suffering into the world.*

Genesis, where woman is created as man's companion, here woman is created as a source of woe for man. In each case the creation of woman is the beginning of human marriage, but in *Theogony* this too is presented as an evil. Hesiod held a pessimistic view of human existence that led him to conclude that children are more a burden than a cause for rejoicing. He likewise undervalued other female contributions to the family. Rather than offering physical and emotional companionship, contributing to the household resources, and bearing children, Hesiod declared that woman is a drain on resources, whose curiosity causes disaster.

In Hesiod the first woman is created by Hephaestus, god of fire and metalworking, who molds her out of clay. In this way she is like Adam in the Book of Genesis, who is also made from the earth, but unlike Eve, who is fashioned from Adam's body. The Greek woman is made at the command of Zeus, chief of the gods, not to complete human existence, but as a punishment for mortals because

Below: Spanish artist Diego Rodriguez (1599–1660) depicts the god Apollo visiting the forge of Roman god Vulcan (Hephaestus in Greek mythology). In this smithy, Pandora is fashioned from clay.

they were enjoying the benefits of the gift of fire given to them by the Titan Prometheus. Womankind is only one of a series of deceitful gifts given to mortal men in the lengthy conflict involving Prometheus and Zeus.

Hesiod's version of the myth

The story of the gods' feud is most fully recounted in *Theogony,* in which Prometheus, although divine, is a protector of mortals. The conflict begins when he sets out a sacrifice to Zeus and divides the portions unequally into meat and bones wrapped in fat. Since Zeus knows all things, it is doubtful he was truly deceived, but he takes the bones and leaves the meat for mortals, thus setting the sacrificial protocol for all time. Angered by Prometheus's trick, Zeus denies mortals the use of fire, but Prometheus endeavors to steal it and return it to them. To achieve this end, Prometheus travels to Mount Olympus and takes a glowing charcoal from a torch. Securing it in a large stalk of fennel, he smuggles it back to the mortal world. In exchange for this insult, Zeus decides to create an inescapable evil for men and commands the gods to make woman. Hephaestus fashions her from the earth using clay, while Athena, goddess of war and handicrafts, dresses and

adorns her. Hesiod notes that the "race of women" is descended from the gods' creation and that she brings trouble to men, but he adds that any man who avoids marriage will also suffer from the lack of children to care for him in his old age and to inherit his property. This is known among scholars of Greek mythology as the "misogynist's dilemma" and is considered to be a major factor in the Pandora myth, which makes the evils brought by women truly "inescapable."

A longer account of the myth in *Works and Days* lists the gifts given to the woman by each god: she is dressed and adorned by Athena, the Graces, Persuasion, and the Hours; while Hermes, messenger of the gods, gives her a deceitful nature and teaches her to lie. In some versions of the myth the final gift, given by Zeus, is a jar that she is instructed not to open; in other versions the jar belongs to Epimetheus or Prometheus. Zeus then names the first woman Pandora, "All gifts," because each of the gods gave her a gift. Epimetheus ("Afterthought"), the dim-witted brother of Prometheus ("Forethought"), accepts the gift of woman despite his brother's warnings and marries Pandora. Until then men had lived lives of ease. However, once Pandora released diseases and toil from the jar,

The Role of Hope

The most puzzling aspect of the Pandora myth is the role of hope, alone left in the jar after all the evils have flown. Various interpretations of the myth have tried to determine if hope brightens the otherwise grim picture of human life, if it remains inaccessible because it is trapped in the jar, or if it is an evil that prevents mortals from seeing things clearly.

A later version of the myth, told by second-century-BCE Greek writer Babrius in his collection of fables, offers a different interpretation. In this version Zeus gathers all good elements and, placing them in a jar with a lid, leaves them among humans. They are unable to contain their curiosity and open the jar, at which point all the good things fly away, leaving only hope. Here the culprit is not a woman but a generic human being (*anthropos*). While there is still a moral message in this version, it emphasizes human folly but is less pessimistic than Hesiod's account.

Below: In this painting by German artist Johann Heiss (1660–1704), the Roman god Vulcan (Hephaestus) presents the naked first woman Pandora to the Roman god Jupiter (Zeus).

Left: This illustration by English artist Arthur Rackham (1867–1939) depicts Pandora as an innocent girl opening a box, which sets free all kinds of evil into the world.

Pandora's name

There are various interpretations of the meaning of Pandora's name. Hesiod explains that it means "she who is given all gifts." In other accounts Pandora is an epithet of the goddess Gaia, the earth, who is the source of all life for mortals, "she who gives all gifts." This interpretation is reinforced by an image on an Attic vase depicting the creation of woman, which labels the central figure *Anesidora,* which unambiguously means "she who sends up gifts [from the earth]."

The ambiguity of Pandora's name can be interpreted in either of two ways. One possibility is that the divine epithet indicates that Pandora was originally a goddess. This type of explanation was popular when scholars of Greek religion believed that all mythic figures were based on deities whose power had faded. Another interpretation considers what the myth suggests about the valuation of women. Some scholars have argued that Hesiod's rejection of women's contributions to human existence points to a desire to obscure the degree to which men actually depended on them. The ambiguous nature of the name has continued to shape the reception of Pandora throughout the centuries. She can stand for good or evil, depending on whether the myth or the meaning of the name is given prominence.

Pandora is not mentioned by name in either of the epic poems of Homer (c. ninth–eighth century BCE), the *Iliad* or the *Odyssey,* but she serves as Homer's model for the mythological figure Helen, wife of Menelaus, king of Sparta. Scholars argue that when Paris carries Helen from Sparta at the urging of the goddess Aphrodite, and when the old men of Troy say that there is no shame in risking everything for so beautiful a woman, they collectively assume the role of a latter-day Epimetheus deceived into accepting a treacherous and ruinous gift. Pandora does not play a large role in later Greek literature, although there are traces in other myths of the misogynistic attitude found in Hesiod's record of her myth.

Changing representations of Pandora

Since classical times representations of Pandora have adorned various vases and appeared on different buildings. The importance of the myth for classical Athens is demonstrated by Greek travel writer Pausanias (143–176 CE), who reports that the creation of Pandora was depicted

men's lives became miserable, and the world became a place that was hard to tolerate. However, one element remained in the jar after the other miseries had escaped: hope. Although there are many interpretations of the myth that attempt to explain why hope remained, there is no conclusive reason.

Pandora's jar also hints at the part of women's role that Hesiod criticizes. The word *pithos,* used for the jar, indicates a large jar used for long-term storage of grains and other necessities, but *pithos* can have another meaning. The belly of the jar can also represent a womb, and thus the evils that Pandora brings forth are her offspring. This pessimistic reading is in keeping with Hesiod's largely negative attitude toward childbearing.

on the base of the famous statue of Athena Parthenos in the Parthenon on the Acropolis. The myth of a first woman made of clay was of special interest to the Athenians, who claimed to be autochthonous (born from the earth of Attica). Few if any images from antiquity show Pandora with a jar; the often repeated image of Pandora lifting the lid of a box rather than a jar to let out the evil contents dates only from the Renaissance (c. 1375–c. 1575).

Roman authors had little to say about Pandora. It was the fathers of the Christian church in the late Roman Empire (30 BCE–476 CE) who first equated Pandora with Eve, a comparison that was to have a lasting impact on Western culture. Tertullian (c. 155 or 160–after 220 CE) uses Pandora as both a positive and a negative figure, while for Greek prelate Gregory of Nazianzus (c. 330–c. 389 CE) she exemplifies vanity, unhealthy curiosity, and other negative traits. Greek Christian writer and teacher Origen (c.185–254 CE) explicitly compares the *pithos* or jar with the forbidden fruit in the garden of Eden. He was familiar with Hesiod's version of the Pandora myth, which he ridicules while quoting it at length. English poet John Milton (1608–1674) also compared Eve to Pandora in his poem *Paradise Lost* and in other writings.

The myth of Pandora has given English and many other languages the phrase *Pandora's box*. In the book *Pandora's Box* (1961), American art historians Erwin (1892–1968) and Dora (d. 1965) Panofsky detail how the figure of Pandora became associated with a box that does not appear in ancient art or in ancient literature. They trace this change to the great Dutch humanist Erasmus of Rotterdam (c. 1466–1536), who used the myth to illustrate the perils of "becoming a wise man too late." Erasmus turned the *pithos* into a *pyxis*, a small box or casket, a change that has had a great influence on the iconography of the Pandora myth. In his account, Erasmus drew upon a version of the myth attributed to Greek poet Philodemus (c. 110–c. 35 BCE), which stated that Epimetheus rather than Pandora opened the box.

By the 16th century Pandora was described as a mixture of good and evil, which allowed French poets Pierre Ronsard (1524–1585) and Joachim du Bellay

(c. 1522–1560) to use her in their poetry. Ronsard compares Pandora to a beloved lady, while du Bellay compares her to the ambiguous city of Rome, a city that is not always kind to its inhabitants. The city of Paris was represented as a "New Pandora," which only gave out good things, in contrast to the ambiguous city of Rome, the "Old Pandora." As the century progressed, however, even the "Old" Pandora was redeemed and the meaning of her name came to stand for all good things. *Pandora* was even used as an honorific title for Queen Elizabeth I of England, along with the more familiar *Gloriana*.

The myth of Pandora was also popular with dramatists of the 17th and 18th centuries, from Spanish playwright Calderón (1799–1867) to French writer Voltaire (1694–1778) and German poet Goethe (1749–1832), all of whom took great liberties with the myth while using it

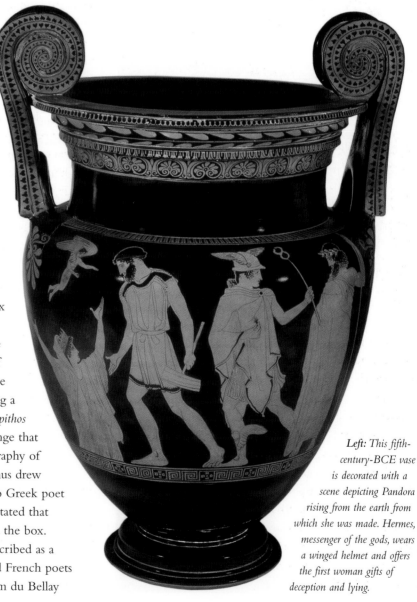

Left: This fifth-century-BCE vase is decorated with a scene depicting Pandora rising from the earth from which she was made. Hermes, messenger of the gods, wears a winged helmet and offers the first woman gifts of deception and lying.

to explore a variety of philosophical issues. In plays by these writers, Pandora is respectively a creation of Prometheus representing science and art, a frail woman enthralled by love, and a divine bringer of peace and beauty to human beings.

In the early 19th century, English artist John Flaxman (1755–1826) painted a series of images illustrating a translation of Hesiod that adhered closely to the myth, although it omitted some of the harsher details in order to turn Pandora into a more admirable figure. English pre-Raphaelite artist Dante Gabriel Rossetti (1828–1882) painted a number of versions of Pandora, depicting her as an intense-looking young woman holding down the lid of a casket with great concentration.

Below: While early versions of the Pandora myth recount that she opens a jar full of evil, later the vessel was often described as a box. English artist Dante Gabriel Rossetti's impression of Pandora depicts her clutching a box, from which issues a plume of evil smoke.

Other Pandoras, Other Creation Myths

The name *Pandora*, as well as being an epithet of Gaia, the earth, is also given to several other minor figures in Greek mythology. One is a daughter of the legendary Athenian king Erechtheus, who together with her sister sacrifices herself for the benefit of the city. Another Pandora has an intriguing connection to the theme of human origins. She is the mother of Graecus, whom the Greeks were named for, and either the daughter or the wife of Deucalion, son of Prometheus. Deucalion is usually said to be married to Pyrrha, the daughter of his brother Epimetheus. After Zeus floods the earth to punish human misdeeds, Deucalion and Pyrrha, the sole survivors, are told to repopulate the earth by "casting the bones of their mother over their shoulders," according to Roman poet Ovid (43 BCE–17 CE) in his *Metamorphoses*.

In another myth, Prometheus creates human beings out of clay. This version may explain his close relationship with mortals and his willingness to defy Zeus on their behalf. It also explains why Zeus chooses to punish mortals for Prometheus's transgressions. In all these versions, the name Pandora is somehow connected to the family of Prometheus and to the creation of man. As the first woman, Hesiod's Pandora is a creator of the female half of humankind.

Swiss painter Paul Klee (1879–1940) represented Pandora's box in a 1920 drawing, turning it into a threatening-looking urn suggestive of the female body. German filmmaker G. W. Pabst's (1885–1967) *Pandora's Box* (1929) examined the myth in the context of contemporary society, and featured American actress Louise Brooks (1906–1985) as a tragic femme fatale. German painter Max Beckman (1884–1950) revised an earlier painting after World War II (1939–1945) to equate the contents of Pandora's box with the evils of the atomic bomb. People continue to use the phrase *Pandora's box* today to refer to the unwelcome and unintended consequences of ill-conceived human actions.

DEBORAH LYONS

Bibliography

Hesiod, and M. L. West, trans. *Theogony* and *Works and Days*. New York: Oxford University Press, 2008.

Homer, and Robert Fagles, trans. *The Iliad*. New York: Penguin, 2009.

Pausanias, and Peter Levi, trans. *Guide to Greece*. New York: Viking Press, 1984.

SEE ALSO: Deucalion; Helen; Paris.

228

PARIS

In Greek mythology Paris was a handsome Trojan prince who eloped with Helen, wife of Menelaus, king of Sparta, and later married her. He is often blamed for causing the Trojan War and instigating the fall of the great Phrygian city of Troy.

Above: In this illustration by British illustrator H. J. Ford (1860–1941), Paris begs forgiveness from his former wife, Oenone. The Trojan prince left the nymph, who had magical healing powers, for Helen, wife of the king of Sparta. He returned to seek treatment for a fatal wound he received during the Trojan War.

While Paris was still in the womb, his mother, Hecuba, queen of Troy and wife of Priam, dreamed that she gave birth to a firebrand. Paris's sister, the seer Cassandra, told her parents that the child about to be born would bring ruin upon the city and that he would be a firebrand of destruction for Troy. Although Cassandra had been cursed by Apollo so that no one ever believed her predictions, Priam decided to avoid any danger his son might pose to the Trojans. He gave the baby to a servant to take him far away from Troy. The servant left the child on Mount Ida. Abandoning unwanted children to die in the wilderness or be found for adoption, known as exposure, was an accepted Greek practice, and not uncommon.

Like Oedipus in ancient Greek mythology and Moses in the Old Testament, Paris did not die in the wilderness. He was found by a shepherd who raised him and taught him to be a shepherd himself. On Mount Ida Paris grew up to become an attractive young man and eventually married the nymph Oenone. The couple lived a peaceful rural existence until several of Priam's servants seized one of Paris's favorite bulls. The bull would serve as a prize in funeral games that were being held at Troy (some versions of the myth state that these games were being held in honor of Priam and Hecuba's lost son, Paris). Paris went to Troy to reclaim his bull. According to different versions of the myth, when Paris won all the contests at these games, he was recognized by either Cassandra or Hecuba. The king and queen welcomed back their son, putting aside the firebrand dream and Cassandra's prophecy.

The Judgment of Paris

Before Paris went to Troy to retrieve his bull, the goddesses Hera, Athena, and Aphrodite had visited him while he was watching his flocks on Mount Ida. They came to settle the challenge Eris had issued at the wedding of Peleus, son of Aeacus, king of Aegina, and the Nereid Thetis. Eris, goddess of discord, had not been invited to the event, so she appeared at the wedding to create disharmony among the guests. Into the midst of the wedding guests she rolled a golden apple inscribed with a single line: "To the Fairest." Three of the guests—Hera, Athena, and Aphrodite—all claimed the apple but could not agree to whom it should belong. Neither Zeus nor any other immortal wanted to judge which of these three powerful deities was the fairest. Eventually Zeus instructed Hermes, messenger of the gods, to descend to the earth and appoint a mortal judge. Hermes selected Paris to make this difficult decision.

Each of the goddesses appeared before Paris and offered him a gift to win his favor. Hera offered him rule over all men, Athena offered wisdom and victory in battle, and

Aphrodite offered him the most beautiful woman in the world as his wife. One version of the myth recounts that Aphrodite also offered Paris the quality of powerful sexual attraction. Paris chose Aphrodite, either for her beauty or for the gift she had to offer.

Helen of Troy

The most beautiful woman in ancient Greece was reputed to be Helen, daughter of Zeus and Leda, and wife of Menelaus, king of Sparta. Despite warnings from Cassandra and other seers of Troy—and the objections of his wife, Oenone—Paris set sail for Sparta to claim the prize Aphrodite had promised him. Menelaus and Helen welcomed Paris as a guest in their home and entertained him for nine days. During Paris's stay Menelaus was called to Crete to bury his grandfather, leaving his wife with their guest. This was the opportunity Paris had been waiting for. Before Menelaus returned home, Paris abducted Helen from Sparta.

The couple became lovers on the island of Kranai, off the coast of Greece, then returned to Troy. One version of the myth claims that their journey lasted many weeks while they visited other cities; another reports that they reached Troy in three days. Upon their arrival, the city

Below: The Judgment of Paris *by Italian artist Sandro Botticelli (1445–1510). Despite the offers of gifts made to him by the goddesses Hera and Athena, the Trojan prince hands the golden apple of Eris to Aphrodite, goddess of love. Hera and Athena look on.*

Helen in Egypt

Scholars speculate that Helen might not have gone to Troy at any point. One sixth-century-BCE version of the myth suggests that it was only a cloud image that Paris took to Troy. The real Helen was wafted by the gods to Egypt, where she stayed, safe and pure, hoping that someday she would be able to return to Sparta and her beloved husband. Euripides' *Helen* gives the most complete account of this version. The playwright develops the character of the world's most beautiful woman; meanwhile the play allowed Euripides to speak out against the war that Athens was waging against Sparta at the time.

celebrated their marriage. The Trojans welcomed the prince and his new wife into the city, even though some members of Paris's family had reservations. Cassandra maintained that the marriage was fated to bring ruin to the city of Troy. However, because of Apollo's curse, her protestations were ignored.

Accounts of Helen's departure from Sparta differ: some say she was abducted against her will, others say that she was spellbound by Paris and followed him. Whether Helen went willingly or not, Paris was guilty of violating one of the most fundamental laws of Greek society: the law of *xenia* (hospitality). Ancient Greeks believed that the bond between host and guest was sacred and was governed by Zeus himself. Anyone who failed to abide by *xenia* was sure to suffer terrible consequences.

Above: In this 18th-century painting, Italian artist Giovanni Scaiaro depicts Paris forcefully loading Helen, wife of Menelaus, the king of Sparta, onto a boat destined for Troy. In some versions of the myth Helen is abducted by Paris; in others she accompanies Paris willingly.

Meanwhile Menelaus returned to Sparta and flew into a rage at discovering what had happened to his wife. He and his brother Agamemnon, king of Mycenae, determined to bring Helen back to Sparta and gathered an army of Greek soldiers for this purpose. Some of these soldiers had been Helen's suitors before she married Menelaus and were bound by an oath they had taken swearing to attack any person who endangered Menelaus's marriage to Helen. The bond had been engineered by the hero Odysseus many years earlier.

Following Helen's departure from Sparta, the Greek fleet set sail from Aulis to Troy. The army had been delayed at Aulis until King Agamemnon appeased the anger of Artemis, goddess of the hunt. She demanded that he sacrifice his firstborn daughter, Iphigeneia, before she would send a wind to carry the fleet to Troy. Iphigeneia's death instilled in Agamemnon a desire to bring a special vengeance upon the Trojans and their prince.

The Trojan War

During the course of the Trojan War, which lasted 10 years, Paris's courage was tested by Hector, his brother. Before the conflict Hector, leader of the Trojan forces, accused Paris of being deceitful, obsessed with women, and a coward. He taunted Paris and urged him to stand against Menelaus. He argued that this would be a contest in which the good looks of the wife-stealer would be of little use. Eventually Paris confronted Menelaus to prove how unfair Hector's accusations had been. However, the contest was not a straightforward duel: when Menelaus was about to capture Paris, Aphrodite intervened and spirited him from the battlefield. Paris did not stay away from the conflict for long, however. In his epic the *Iliad,* Homer (c. ninth–eighth century BCE) describes how Paris returned to the fray later. He draws comparisons between Paris running to the battlefield and a horse galloping free across a plain. Hector witnessed this enthusiasm for war and praised his brother.

Although it was clear to some Trojans that Paris was responsible for inciting the war, he did not feel responsible. On occasion he justified his role in events leading up to the conflict. He asserted to Hector that a man is obliged to accept any gifts the gods give; Paris was adamant that he had no choice but to pursue Helen and that she could not resist following him (in *The Trojan Women* by Euripides [c. 486–c. 406 BCE], Helen justified to Hecuba her departure from Sparta with the same explanation). Late in the war Helen rued her captivity in Troy and related to her husband her anguish at being surrounded by devastation, but throughout the conflict her attraction to Paris did not falter.

Although Paris was derided by Hector at times, he played a major role in the long war by avenging the death of his brother and killing Achilles, champion of the Achaeans. Before Hector died he warned Achilles that he would die at Paris's hands. One version of the Achilles myth reports that the Greek hero had a vulnerable heel, the one place not protected by the magical powers of the Styx River into which his mother Thetis had dipped him as a child. Assisted by the god Apollo, Paris managed to fire an arrow that struck mighty Achilles at this vulnerable point, killing him.

Below: In the foreground of this painting by German artist Matthias Gerung (c. 1500–1568/1570), Paris judges which of the three goddesses, Athena, Hera, or Aphrodite, is the most attractive. The Trojan War rages behind them.

Although Aphrodite protected Paris throughout the war, the Trojan prince did not survive the fall of Troy. Once the Trojan horse had been brought into the city and the Greeks rushed through the streets, Paris was hunted down to his father's palace. One of Helen's previous suitors, Philoctetes, who fought with the bow of Heracles, shot an arrow that mortally wounded Paris.

As Paris lay on his deathbed, he remembered his first wife, Oenone, who had the power to heal any wound from which he might suffer. He asked to be taken to her on Mount Ida. Oenone was still angry about being replaced by Helen, however. She refused to help Paris and sent him back to Troy. Later she felt remorseful and rushed to Troy to save him, but she was too late: Paris had died from the wound inflicted by Philoctetes. He did not live to witness the slaughter of his fellow Trojans or to see the walls of Troy catch fire and the great Phrygian city collapse.

Paris in art

Of all the ancient Greek legends, the Judgment of Paris was one of the most popular in postclassical art. Artists favored the scene because of its aesthetic appeal. Many artists have used this part of the myth to reflect contemporary culture. German painter Lucas Cranach

Above: In this painting by Italian artist Giovanni Domenico Tiepolo (1727–1804), Trojans heave the wooden horse through the streets of Troy. The horse concealed enemy soldiers.

(1472–1553), for example, depicted Paris as a knight in armor and Hermes as a faithful attendant at his side, wearing a winged hat and holding his caduceus (a wing-topped staff entwined with two serpents). The three goddesses are naked except for necklaces that match their German-style coiffures. It is not clear which deity is Athena or Hera, but Aphrodite can be identified as the figure pointing to the sky where Eros, the god of sexual love, aims his bow at her.

Flemish painter Peter Paul Rubens (1577–1640) often represented the female figure nude. In his *Judgment of Paris*, the hero is depicted as a shepherd and Hermes stands behind him. While the figures of the goddesses are similar to each other in appearance, a peacock, the sacred bird of Hera, struts near her and a shield rests behind Athena. In his version, Rubens suggests the final destructive outcome of Paris's judgment by placing a Fury (a deity of retribution) in the sky above the scene.

American artist Bob Thompson (1937–1966) represented the scene more recently. In his version the goddesses are painted in vibrant colors, and the characters appear in an exotic setting, far removed from the carefully constructed landscapes painted by Rubens and Cranach. The myth also appealed to the Spanish surrealist painter Salvador Dalí (1904–1989), whose 1965 lithograph depicts the naked Hera, Athena, and Aphrodite towering above a small and confused Paris. In stark contrast to the ancient vase paintings in which the Judgment of Paris was first recorded is American painter Charles Bell's (1935–1995) rendition of the event. In 1986 Bell arranged a number of Barbie dolls to reflect Cranach's *Judgment of Paris* and painted the scene. Female dolls represented Hera, Athena, and Aphrodite, while male dolls represented Hermes and Paris. Although the myth of Paris has its roots in ancient Greece, the Judgment of Paris remains a source of inspiration for artists today.

KARELISA HARTIGAN

Bibliography

Bulfinch, Thomas. *Bulfinch's Mythology.* New York: Barnes & Noble, 2006.

Euripides, and P. Burian and A. Shapiro, eds. *The Complete Euripides.* New York: Oxford University Press, 2009–2010.

Graves, Robert. *The Greek Myths.* New York: Penguin, 1993.

Homer, and Robert Fagles, trans. *The Iliad.* New York: Penguin, 2009.

SEE ALSO: Achilles; Agamemnon; Cassandra; Hector; Hecuba; Helen; Heracles; Menelaus; Odysseus; Philoctetes; Priam.

PASIPHAE

Pasiphae was a daughter of Helios, the Greek sun god. Her mother, Perse, was the daughter of the Titans Oceanus and Tethys, who were parents of numerous marine divinities. In addition to Pasiphae, the children of Perse and Helios included Circe, Aeetes, and Perses.

Like her sister Circe and her niece Medea, Pasiphae possessed powers of sorcery. She was married to Minos, the king of the island of Crete, and is famous for giving birth to the monstrous Minotaur, the product of an unnatural love affair with a white bull. It was her husband's offense against Poseidon that brought tragedy upon unsuspecting Pasiphae, and her myth illustrated that innocence was no protection from harm.

After defeating his brothers to claim the throne of Crete, Minos still had many challengers and sought to cement his authority. He declared that the gods would validate his right to rule by granting him whatever he prayed for. Minos asked his uncle Poseidon, god of the sea, to send him a bull, which he would then sacrifice to the god. A beautiful snow white bull emerged from the sea, guaranteeing Minos's succession to the throne.

Minos, however, considered the creature too beautiful to sacrifice, so he put it to pasture and killed another in its place. This breach of a promise incurred Poseidon's wrath. The god made Pasiphae, not Minos, the direct victim of his revenge, however, and caused her to fall in love with the bull. This act ensured that Minos, to his eternal shame, would be forever remembered less as a king than as a husband whose wife had cheated on him with a bull. Unlike other cultures that embraced animal gods, in Greek mythology, animals ranked far below gods and humans. Sexual relations with animals brought shame and dishonor.

According to another, very different version, however, Pasiphae herself neglected to offer due sacrifices to Aphrodite. The goddess was so angry that she punished Pasiphae by making her fall in love with the bull.

Driven mad by her unspeakable passion for the bull, Pasiphae finally sought the assistance of Daedalus, the master architect and inventor in the palace. At the queen's request he built a hollow wooden cow and covered it with cowhide. He made the sham cow so craftily that it could be mistaken for the real thing. Pasiphae hid inside the cow, and when it was wheeled to the bull's pasture, the bull copulated with it and at last satisfied Pasiphae's desire.

Later, to her horror, Pasiphae gave birth to a creature with a bull's head and tail and a man's body. It was named Asterius but was usually called the Minotaur ("bull of Minos"), for it was an enduring reminder of Minos's folly.

Like all hybrid creatures in Greek mythology, the Minotaur's monstrous appearance was matched by its violent nature. The horrified Minos asked Daedalus to build an asylum for the man-beast. So Daedalus designed the Labyrinth, a vast underground maze of a palace that kept the Minotaur confined. The Labyrinth was so cleverly constructed that anyone going in would never find his way out again.

Right: In Greek mythology gods often changed shape to seduce mortals. In this Greek mosaic, Phoenician princess Europa is abducted by the god Zeus, who has changed shape to become a bull.

Below: This 16th-century painting by an anonymous artist often referred to as Master of the Cassoni Campana (fl. c. 1510) depicts Pasiphae setting off to visit the white bull with whom she is having an affair.

Gods, Women, and Animals

Women having amorous relationships with animals is a recurring feature of Greek mythology. In most instances the animal in question was actually a god using a disguise to seduce the woman. If gods took on animal forms, they could always regain their divine shapes. For instance, Poseidon appeared as a bird to Medusa, as a bull to Canace, as a dolphin to Melantho, as a horse to Demeter, and as a ram to Theophane. Zeus's bestial forms included appearing as a swan to Leda and as a bull to Europa, who bore him Minos.

Seduced women were also transformed by gods into animals: Zeus made Io into a cow and Callisto into a bear, and Poseidon made Theophane into a ewe. Women's transformations into animals or other forms, such as trees or streams, were usually permanent. There are no examples of goddesses in animal form seducing men. Scholars speculate that various principles held by ancient Greeks could explain why in mythology women were seduced by animals. In the patriarchal ancient Greek society virginity and chastity in women were highly valued qualities. One theory claims that animal disguises adopted by the gods symbolically overcame any resistance that a woman made to protect her sexual purity. Scholars also attribute the permanence of most transformations of women to this high regard for the preservation of sexual purity.

Ocean Monsters

It is no coincidence that Pasiphae and her sorcering relatives are all related to ocean divinities. The ocean was a mysterious place in Greek myth. It had unseen depths and could change unpredictably. Not only did most monsters have their origins in the deep, but many of them were female. Some scholars have argued that these female characters reflected attitudes toward women held by male storytellers—who may have regarded women as mysterious and unknowable, like the sea.

These ocean-bred female monstrosities include Scylla, Charybdis, the Gorgons, the Harpies, Chimaera, the Sphinx, Ceto, the Graeae, and Echidna. Scylla, Charybdis, and Echidna preyed upon sailors. The Gorgons petrified men with their gaze. The Harpies, the hounds of Zeus, plagued Phineas (a blind seer-king) and harassed the hero Aeneas and his men. The Sphinx terrorized young Theban men, and Chimaera ravaged the Lycian countryside (a region in western Asia). All these monsters were given to sudden attack and could be overcome only by cunning.

Pasiphae and her relatives were not monsters, but they possessed extraordinary powers that disrupted the natural world. Pasiphae put an end to Minos's sex life by making him ejaculate snakes and scorpions. Her sister, Circe, unmanned her male visitors by transforming them into sentient animals. Medea, Aeetes' daughter and Pasiphae's niece, helped Jason, the hero who went on a quest for the Golden Fleece. She put to sleep a sleepless dragon, rejuvenated a ram, and slew her own brother, her children, and the family of Jason's intended Greek bride. Despite their charms, these ocean offspring could never have successful relationships with mortal men.

Left: Flemish artist Bartholomaeus Spranger (1546–1611) depicts an encounter between Glaucus and the water nymph Scylla. Scylla was later turned into a fearsome sea monster.

Pasiphae and Minos's children

Pasiphae bore Minos many children: Androgeos, Catreus, Deucalion, Glaucus, Acacallis, Xenodice, Ariadne, and Phaedra. Most of them lived unfortunate lives and suffered violent and premature deaths. Androgeos grew up in Athens and met an early death, either fighting the Marathonian Bull—the same bull that Pasiphae had desired—or by ambush. Blaming King Aegeus of Athens for his son's demise, Minos demanded that every nine years Athens send a tribute of seven young men and seven young women to be sacrificial victims for the Minotaur.

This practice continued until Athenian hero Theseus killed the Minotaur. Theseus succeeded where others had failed because he seduced Ariadne, who secured him Daedalus's assistance in entering and leaving the Labyrinth. Their love did not last. After eloping with her, Theseus abandoned her on the island of Naxos. Ariadne either took her own life or married the god Dionysus.

Phaedra, who did marry Theseus, also died by her own hand out of shame. According to one version, Aphrodite made her fall in love with her stepson, Hippolytus, and the boy rejected her advances.

The curse of Pasiphae

Like his philandering father Zeus, king of the gods, Minos repeatedly cheated on his wife. According to Greek scholar and historian Apollodorus (fl. 140 BCE), Pasiphae was furious with Minos for his affairs, and she showed herself much more adept than Zeus's wife, Hera, at punishing both her husband and his mistresses. She shrewdly resorted to her powers of sorcery and put a curse on Minos so that whenever he had sex with another woman, he ejaculated scorpions and snakes. This put a damper on his sexual escapades, for all his lovers perished.

However, in spite of his affliction, Minos was able to have an affair with Procris, who sought refuge on Crete after her husband, Cephalus, had discovered her infidelity with a man named Pteleon. According to Apollodorus, Minos wanted to make Procris his mistress, but she declined because she perceived that he had been enchanted. Once Procris found out about Minos's sexual

Left: This bust is an anonymous sculptor's impression of the Minotaur. In Greek mythology this fearsome monster has a human body and a bull's head and tail.

problems, however, she gave him a healing potion that enabled her to sleep with him without coming to any harm. In the racier account by Greek mythographer Antoninus Liberalis (second century CE), Procris made a condom of sorts out of a goat bladder. Minos would have sex and ejaculate the dangerous creatures into the condom.

In gratitude, Minos awarded Procris with a javelin that never missed its target and his hound Laelaps, who always caught whatever it chased. Procris then returned home, where she was reunited with her husband. The pair went hunting—making use of the gifts acquired from Minos—only for Procris to die when Cephalus threw the infallible javelin at her by mistake.

Pasiphae's curse, meanwhile, had ultimately backfired, since it was overcome by the very thing she had meant to deny her husband—another adulterous affair.

Depictions of Pasiphae

According to Greek travel writer Pausanias (143–176 CE), there were bronze statues of Pasiphae and Helios in the sanctuary of Ino at Thalamae in Laconia (a region in Greece). There, Pasiphae, which means "all-shining," was a title of the moon goddess Selene. Ino, escaping her husband Athamas's murderous rage by jumping into the ocean, had been transformed into the sea deity Leucothea. This "white goddess" helped sailors at sea, hence her association with other divinities who provided means of navigation, such as the sun (Helios) and the moon (Pasiphae).

A first-century-CE wall painting in the House of the Vettii in Pompeii, Italy, depicts Daedalus, Pasiphae, and the wooden cow. French painter Henri Matisse (1869–1954) made two graphic prints: *Pasiphae* and *Pasiphae Hugging an Olive Tree*. American artist Jackson Pollock (1912–1956) also represented Pasiphae in a painting called *Pasiphae*.

KATHRYN CHEW

Bibliography

Apollodorus, and Robin Hard, trans. *The Library of Greek Mythology*. New York: Oxford University Press, 2008.
Howatson, M. C. *The Oxford Companion to Classical Literature*. New York: Oxford University Press, 2005.
Pausanias, and Peter Levi, trans. *Guide to Greece*. New York: Viking Press, 1984.

SEE ALSO: Ariadne; Daedalus; Minos; Theseus.

PATROCLUS

Patroclus is famous for his loyal friendship to the great Greek hero Achilles, and for his tragic death on the battlefield during the Trojan War.

According to legend, Patroclus was the son of Menoetius, one of the Argonauts. Patroclus was one of the many suitors who hoped to marry Helen, the most beautiful woman in the world. Her stepfather Tyndareos feared that the suitors who failed to win her hand might be resentful, so, at Odysseus's suggestion, he made them all swear to support whichever of them Helen chose, and to fight anyone who tried to harm the marriage. Eventually Helen chose a Greek prince named Menelaus. When Paris, son of the Trojan king Priam, later ran away with her, the Greeks, including Helen's suitors, went to attack Troy. So began the Trojan War.

Below: The slave girl Briseis is being passed to Agamemnon (seated) in this Roman painting from the first century CE. The figure between them is usually identified as Achilles.

By this time, Patroclus had another reason for going to Troy. He had killed a young man, Clitonymus, in a quarrel. He went into hiding in the house of Peleus, king of Phthia. There he struck up a close friendship with Achilles, the son of Peleus and the goddess Thetis. When the Trojan War began, Patroclus went to Troy to support Achilles, who was one of the Greeks' best fighters.

A sensible friend

Although Achilles was the higher born and better fighter of the two friends, Patroclus was older. Before they left, Peleus asked Patroclus to look after Achilles and to give him guidance and advice. Patroclus was perfectly suited to this task. He was kind, caring, and sensible, qualities that set him apart from the hotheaded and petulant Achilles. However, Achilles' childishness still caused trouble. In the 10th year of the war, he argued with Agamemnon, king of Mycenae and leader of the Greek forces, over a slave girl named Briseis, who lived with Achilles in his camp. This argument set in motion a chain of events that eventually led to Patroclus's death.

Agamemnon had been forced to give up his own slave girl, Chryseis, by the god Apollo. Angry at this loss, he decided to replace her with Briseis and sent his men to

Achilles' tent to fetch her. Patroclus had no choice but to hand her over to Agamemnon's men. The seizure of Briseis left Achilles furious. He was so angry that he refused to fight, or to let his men fight, for the Greek side. This was disastrous, because Achilles was a great soldier. With him off the battlefield, the Trojans soon gained the upper hand.

Nestor's plan

Achilles' petulance filled Patroclus with shame. Nestor, one of the oldest and wisest of the Greek leaders, suggested that if he could not persuade Achilles to change his mind, Patroclus might consider going into battle himself, disguised as Achilles, to scare the Trojans away. Patroclus agreed to go along with Nestor's plan.

By the time that Patroclus visited Achilles to implore him to fight, the Trojans had driven the Greeks so far back toward the sea that there was a danger they might set fire to the Greek ships. Achilles still refused to join in the battle himself. However, the danger was so great that he agreed to let Patroclus ride into battle disguised as him, but he told his friend that he must only chase the Trojans away from the ships, and then retreat. Patroclus put on Achilles' armor and led his men into battle. The ploy was a huge success. Many Trojans were killed, and the Trojan forces were forced back toward the walls of their city.

However, Patroclus did not heed Achilles' advice. Carried away with his success, Patroclus did not retreat, as Achilles had asked him to, but followed the Trojans across the battlefield. The god Apollo, who supported the Trojans in the war, knocked off Patroclus's helmet and tore his breastplate from his body, leaving him extremely vulnerable and revealing to the Trojans that it was not Achilles fighting but an imposter. First the Trojan Euphorbus struck him with a spear, weakening him considerably. Then Hector, the leader of the Trojan forces, killed him.

The horrified Greeks collected the body of Patroclus from the battlefield and took it to Achilles' camp. Achilles was overcome with grief. Desperate to avenge his dear friend's death, he returned to the battlefield and fought Hector in single combat, eventually killing him. Achilles' anger was still so great that for the next 12 days he drove his chariot around the walls of Troy, dragging Hector's body behind him. Later, when Achilles himself was killed by Paris, his ashes were mingled with those of Patroclus and placed in a golden urn made by Hephaestus, blacksmith of the gods. In this way, the two friends were united for eternity.

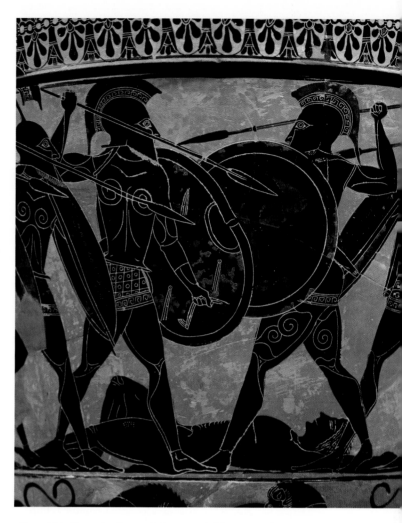

Above: This illustration from a sixth-century-BCE wine jar shows Greek and Trojan warriors fighting over the body of Patroclus.

Sources for Patroclus's story

The main source for the story of Patroclus is the *Iliad*, an epic poem about the last year of the Trojan War composed by Greek poet Homer (c. ninth–eighth century BCE). Many other ancient writers also referred to Patroclus. Among them were Apollodorus (third century BCE) and Pindar (c. 522–c. 438 BCE).

Although he was not the most famous of the heroes of the Trojan War, Patroclus played a central role in its story: his actions served as the catalyst that led to the deaths of Achilles and Hector. He also embodied many noble qualities, including courage, loyalty, and humility.

ANNA CLAYBOURNE

Bibliography

Homer, and Robert Fagles, trans. *The Iliad*. New York: Penguin, 2009.

SEE ALSO: Achilles; Agamemnon; Hector; Helen; Menelaus; Nestor; Paris; Peleus; Priam.

PELEUS

Peleus, a hero of ancient Greek myth, was the son of Aeacus, mythical king of Aegina, a Greek island southwest of Athens. His mother was Endeis. His siblings included his half brothers Telamon (father of the Trojan War hero Ajax) and Phocos. The distinguished hero Achilles was the son of Peleus and the sea goddess Thetis.

Aeacus banished Peleus and Telamon from Aegina after they had joined forces to kill their half brother Phocos. Peleus proceeded to Phthia in northern Greece, where he entered the service of a king in order to be "purified" for taking human life outside battle. Eurytion, king of Phthia, performed the purification, and Peleus married his daughter Antigone (not to be confused with Oedipus's daughter of the same name).

Peleus and Eurytion then went to the city of Calydon in Aetolia (a region in Greece) in order to aid some heroes who were seeking to rid the land of a ravenous wild boar. The boar had been sent by the goddess Artemis, who was angry at Oeneus, the local king, for omitting her in offerings to the gods. During the Calydonian boar hunt Peleus killed Eurytion with a miscast spear, was again driven into exile, and again sought purification. The killing may have been intentional—with his father-in-law out of the way, Peleus himself would have been able to gain control of Phthia.

The treachery of Astydameia

This time Peleus was purified by Acastus, king of the city of Iolcus in Thessaly in northeast Greece. Afterward Peleus competed in funeral games for Pelias, Acastus's father and predecessor, during which he wrestled the female warrior Atalanta, another veteran of the Calydonian boar hunt. Later, however, Acastus's wife, Astydameia, tried to seduce Peleus. When he resisted, she sent word to Antigone that he was going to marry her own daughter Sterope. Antigone, believing herself abandoned, committed suicide.

Astydameia then told Acastus that she had been raped by Peleus. Although desiring revenge, the king could not harm the man he had purified without violating religious law. So he took Peleus hunting on nearby Mount Pelion, stole his sword, and abandoned him while he slept, so that Peleus would become prey for centaurs, vicious half-man, half-horse creatures that inhabited the area. Peleus managed to save himself after being given a sword by the wise centaur Cheiron. In another version the gods gave him a sword.

Later Peleus gathered a force of soldiers, including the heroes Castor, Pollux, and Jason. With them he stormed Iolcus and killed Astydameia and, according to Greek scholar and historian Apollodorus (fl. 140 BCE), also Acastus.

Left: The Calydonian boar hunt is depicted in this second-century-BCE alabaster relief.

Right: In this painting Italian artist Pompeo Girolamo Batoni (1708–1787) depicts the centaur Cheiron teaching Achilles to play the lyre.

After other adventures, including service as an Argonaut, Peleus married Polydora, who was a Spartan princess. In another version Polydora was Peleus's daughter rather than his wife. Later Peleus married the sea goddess Thetis. She was the daughter of the sea god Nereus and was courted by the gods Zeus and Poseidon. It was revealed that her son would be more powerful than his father, however, so Zeus resolved to marry Thetis to a mortal in order to prevent the birth of a son who could challenge him.

The Judgment of Paris

Thetis had the power to change shape, so Peleus enlisted the help of the centaur Cheiron to capture her and make her his wife. The marriage, celebrated on Mount Pelion, was attended by all the gods except the goddess Eris (meaning "strife"), who was not invited. To cause trouble, she tossed a golden apple inscribed "To the Fairest" among the guests. Three goddesses, Hera, Athena, and Aphrodite, claimed the apple. Zeus arranged for Paris, son of the king of Troy, to judge.

Paris decided for Aphrodite, who promised him the most beautiful woman in the world. That woman was Helen, wife of Menelaus, king of Sparta in Greece. With Aphrodite's help, Paris took Helen to Troy, causing the Greeks to attack Troy and thus setting off the Trojan War. Through one of the distortions in chronology that occasionally occur in Greek mythology, the only son of Peleus and Thetis, Achilles, was old enough to fight at Troy, where Paris killed him.

Achilles and Cheiron

Thetis had hoped to immortalize Achilles and, as an infant, placed him in the hearth fire at night in order to burn away his mortal part. Peleus observed this and accused her of trying to kill their son. Thetis, enraged at Peleus's lack of faith, left and returned to the sea. Unable to raise Achilles alone, Peleus took him to Cheiron, who raised and instructed him in warfare. In the *Iliad*, an epic poem by Homer (c. ninth–eighth century BCE), Peleus was accompanied on this mission by two exiles then living at his court in Phthia, Phoenix and Patroclus. Patroclus remained with Achilles and Cheiron, while Peleus installed Phoenix as king of the Dolopians, a people who lived in Thessaly.

Peleus was elderly by the time the war broke out, and he stayed in Phthia. Taking advantage of the absence of most Greek warriors, the sons of Acastus attacked Phthia

and drove Peleus from power; soon after, according to the version by Apollodorus, he died in exile. According to another version, Achilles' son Neoptolemus, together with Thetis, intervened to save Peleus.

Many scenes from Peleus's life featured on ancient Greek vase paintings. The wedding of Peleus and Thetis is the main scene depicted on the François Vase (c. 570 BCE) by artist Kleitias, and Peleus is also pictured at the Calydonian boar hunt. Other scenes on black-figure amphorae (two-handled urns) include Peleus wrestling Atalanta and chasing Thetis.

JIM MARKS

Bibliography

Homer, and Robert Fagles, trans. *The Iliad*. New York: Penguin, 2009.

Howatson, M. C. *The Oxford Companion to Classical Literature*. New York: Oxford University Press, 2005.

SEE ALSO: Achilles; Atalanta; Castor and Pollux; Helen; Jason; Paris; Patroclus.

PELOPS

Pelops, a Greek hero, was the son of Tantalus, king of Argos (or in some versions king of Corinth or of Lydia). Pelops won a famous chariot race with the king Oenomaus to gain the hand in marriage of the king's beautiful daughter, Hippodameia.

Above: Pelops is depicted sitting on a throne in this marble relief, which adorns a Roman sarcophagus found in North Africa. His wife, Hippodameia, stands next to him.

When Tantalus invited the gods to a feast, they were glad to accept. Tantalus was said to be a son of Zeus, the king of the gods, and had often shared the gods' hospitality on Mount Olympus. The main course at the feast was a meat stew, well spiced and savory, but the gods felt that something about it was not quite right. Only the goddess Demeter, who was mourning the kidnap of her daughter Persephone by Hades, the god of the underworld, ate some of the stew. While she distractedly nibbled at a bone, the other gods demanded to know what the stew was made of. Tantalus laughed and told the gods that it was his own son, Pelops.

Tantalus had wanted to see whether the gods would realize that the stew contained human flesh, but the gods were disgusted at Tantalus's impiety. They brought Pelops back to life by boiling his bones in a magic cauldron, and Demeter gave him an ivory shoulder blade to replace the bone that she had chewed. Pelops emerged from the cauldron twice as handsome as he had been before.

The gods curse Tantalus

The gods became even more outraged with Tantalus when they later discovered that he had also stolen nectar and ambrosia from their own feasts to share with his human friends. They destroyed Tantalus's kingdom, and when he died and went to the underworld, they devised a special punishment for him.

Tantalus was suspended from the branches of a fruit tree laden with all kinds of luscious fruit, over the waters of a muddy lake. When he leaned down to drink, the waters of the lake retreated, so that he could never quench his thirst. When he tried to pluck some fruit to satisfy his hunger, the wind blew the branches out of his reach. In this way he was condemned to eternal thirst and hunger. The word *tantalize*, derived from his name, reminds us of his fate.

Meanwhile, Pelops and his followers gathered up the treasures of the realm and set out to found a new kingdom. One of the places they visited was Elis (a region in southern Greece), where Oenomaus was king.

Oenomaus had a beautiful daughter named Hippodameia. He guarded her very closely indeed because an oracle had told him that the man whom Hippodameia married would cause his death. Oenomaus challenged any

Right: This coastline forms part of the the Peloponnese. It is named after the ancient Greek hero Pelops and marks the territory he once controlled.

suitor who asked for his daughter's hand to a chariot race, after which the winner would be allowed to kill the loser. The stakes were so high because Oenomaus knew that he was nearly impossible to beat. The horses that were harnessed to his chariot had been given to him by his father, Ares, god of war, and could run faster even than the north wind. His charioteer, Myrtilus, was a son of Hermes, the speedy messenger god, and was famous throughout Greece for his driving skills.

In spite of the heavy odds against them, however, suitors continued to present themselves because Hippodameia was very beautiful and the kingdom of Elis was very rich. One by one, each of them lost the race, after which Oenomaus killed him and nailed his head to the palace gates.

The chariot race

Pelops was not deterred by the rows of heads facing him as he approached the palace. Poseidon, god of the sea, had given him a fast golden chariot that was able to race across water. When Hippodameia saw Pelops, she fell in love with him immediately.

She feared that he also would suffer the fate of the other suitors and decided to do her best to help him. Together with Pelops, she bribed her father's charioteer, Myrtilus, to sabotage Oenomaus's chariot by replacing the pins that held the wheels on the chariot's axles with wax plugs. Myrtilus's reward was to be half of the kingdom.

The race began. Oenomaus knew that Pelops would be harder to beat than the other suitors. He let Pelops get slightly ahead, and then he stood up and poised his spear to fling at Pelops to kill him. At that moment the wax pins melted completely, and Oenomaus's chariot crashed and killed him.

Pelops had won the race and the hand of Hippodameia, but he had no intention of keeping his side of the bargain with Myrtilus. He killed him by throwing him into the sea. Before Myrtilus drowned, however, he managed to curse Pelops and all his descendants.

Pelops and Hippodameia ruled Oenomaus's kingdom and extended it by conquering neighboring regions. Their rule covered a large part of Greece, and the southern peninsula of Greece is still known today as the Peloponnese, which means "Pelops's land."

As for the curse of Myrtilus, it hung over all Pelops's descendants, including his son Atreus, his grandsons Agamemnon and Menelaus, and his great-grandson Orestes.

A shrine to Pelops at Olympia, a city in Elis, was said to have been built by Heracles, one of Pelops's most renowned descendants. Artistic representations of Pelops include a sculpture on the temple of Zeus at Olympia, which shows the moment before the chariot race began. According to Greek travel writer Pausanias (143–176 CE), the race was also depicted on the seventh-century-BCE Chest of Cypselus.

PETER CONNOR

Bibliography

Bulfinch, Thomas. *Bulfinch's Mythology.* New York: Barnes & Noble, 2006.

Howatson, M. C. *The Oxford Companion to Classical Literature.* New York: Oxford University Press, 2005.

SEE ALSO: Agamemnon; Atreus; Heracles; Menelaus; Orestes; Philoctetes.

PENELOPE

Penelope was the wife of the Greek hero Odysseus. Even though her husband took 10 years to return home from the Trojan War, Penelope never gave up hope that he might come back. She thus came to be seen as the epitome of fidelity.

Penelope was the daughter of the Spartan prince Icarius and the nymph Periboea. Icarius's brother Tyndareos arranged Penelope's marriage to Odysseus in return for Odysseus's advice on the selection of a husband for his daughter Helen.

Following the wedding, Icarius pleaded with Penelope to stay. However, by drawing her veil over her face, Penelope signaled that her new life was with Odysseus. Icarius dedicated a statue to Modesty on the spot where she stood, and the newlyweds began their life together on the island of Ithaca.

Odysseus and Penelope had not been married long before the Trojan prince Paris's abduction of Helen incited the Greeks to go to war with Troy. The conflict lasted 10 years and only ended when the Greeks used trickery to breach the Trojans' walls. After their victory, the various Greek leaders sailed back to their respective cities. However, Odysseus's journey home was long and arduous—it was only after 10 more years and numerous adventures that he finally arrived back in Ithaca.

Penelope and the suitors

Penelope never gave up hope that her husband would return safely. However, most people assumed that he was dead and expected Penelope to remarry. In the months following the end of the Trojan War, more than 100 suitors from all over Greece traveled to Ithaca to seek Penelope's hand in marriage, setting up camp at Penelope's home. Try as she might, Penelope could not persuade them to leave. After six or seven years of being put off by Penelope, the suitors finally demanded that she select a husband. She announced that she must first complete a burial blanket for Odysseus's father. For three years Penelope wove her blanket during the day and secretly unwove her progress at night so that the work would never be completed. Finally, however, one of her handmaidens betrayed her to the suitors.

At this point Odysseus arrived back in Ithaca. When the goddess Athena warned him of the situation at his palace, Odysseus disguised himself as a beggar and visited Penelope, who did not recognize her husband. However, his assertion that he had met Odysseus on his travels filled her with new hope. Penelope told the beggar of her next diversionary tactic. She would announce that the suitor who could stretch Odysseus's bow and shoot an arrow through 12 ax handles set in a row would become her new husband. Penelope knew that no one but Odysseus himself could accomplish this feat.

All the suitors tried in vain. Odysseus, however, completed the task with ease. He then threw off his

---

Happy and Unhappy Endings

Our main source for the story of Odysseus and Penelope is the *Odyssey*, an epic poem written by Greek poet Homer. The work concludes with the joyous reunion of Penelope and Odysseus. However, other versions of Penelope's story end less happily. Apollodorus (fl. 140 BCE), a Greek prose writer, records several of these alternate endings. In one version of the story, Penelope was seduced by Antinous, the most unpleasant of the suitors, and returned by Odysseus to her father. In another version, Penelope surrendered to the sexual advances of Amphinomus, another suitor, and Odysseus killed her for being unfaithful. In other versions of the myth, the enchantress Circe, whom Odysseus met on his travels, bore him a son named Telegonus, who accidentally killed Odysseus in Ithaca. Penelope later married Telegonus, whereupon Circe granted the pair of them immortality. Some of these alternate endings paint Penelope in a morally questionable light. However, the most enduring image of Penelope is that of the steadfast wife and mother in Homer's *Odyssey*.

Above: *This fresco by Italian artist Pinturicchio (1454–1531) depicts Penelope being harassed by suitors while weaving at her loom. In the background a ship returns Odysseus to his home island.*

disguise and, with the help of his son Telemachus and some faithful servants, slaughtered all of the suitors. Odysseus then sent for Penelope. Still not believing that her husband had really returned, Penelope demanded that their bed be moved out of their bedroom. Odysseus protested that the bed, built with a living tree as one of the bedposts, could not be moved. Thus Odysseus passed Penelope's final test to prove his identity and the pair were happily reunited.

Penelope in art and literature

Penelope has been a popular subject in various artistic media. Vases and relief sculptures have borne her image since the fifth century BCE, and artists have painted scenes of her, Odysseus, and Telemachus since the 1500s. In the 20th century she appeared in the opera *Pénélope* by Gabriel Fauré (1845–1924) and the ballet *Odyssey* by George Couroupos (b. 1942).

The story of Penelope and Odysseus is told at greatest length by Greek poet Homer (c. ninth–eighth century BCE) in the *Odyssey*, an account of Odysseus's travels after the Trojan War. Historians are divided about the extent to which Homer's stories are based on real events and people. Pausanias, a Greek geographer living in the second century CE, claims to have visited the site of the statue to Modesty and the site of Penelope's tomb on his travels. It is more likely, however, that Penelope was created by Homer as the representation of a model Greek wife. No matter what the truth, Penelope's character is echoed throughout literature in portrayals of women whose faithfulness cannot be shaken.

DEBORAH THOMAS

Bibliography

Homer, and Robert Fagles, trans. *The Odyssey.* New York: Penguin, 2009.
Howatson, M. C. *The Oxford Companion to Classical Literature.* New York: Oxford University Press, 2005.

SEE ALSO: Circe; Helen; Odysseus.

PERSEUS

In Greek mythology, Perseus was famous above all for two great feats: slaying the Gorgon Medusa and rescuing the African princess Andromeda from a sea monster.

The story of Perseus is one of the most popular Greek legends. It has been retold many times, notably by Greek poets Homer (c. ninth–eighth century BCE) and Hesiod (fl. 800 BCE), and by Roman poet Ovid (43 BCE–17 CE). Because there are so many literary sources, there are numerous different versions, some of which are mutually contradictory. In outline, however, the story is as follows. Perseus was the son of Zeus and Danae, daughter of King Acrisius of Argos, a city of the Peloponnese peninsula in southern Greece. The Delphic oracle warned the king that he would be slain by his own grandson. At the time of the prophecy, Danae was not even pregnant. In an effort to prevent the inevitable, Acrisius locked up his daughter in an underground chamber made of brass or stone with only a single, tiny aperture for light and air. Her sole companion was a nurse. In later accounts, Danae's prison became a bronze tower. The earliest work in which this version appears is the *Odes* of Roman poet Horace (65–8 BCE).

Divine intervention

What the oracle had not mentioned, however, was that the father of Acrisius's grandchild would be Zeus, the most powerful of all Greek deities, against whom resistance was useless. When the time was ripe, the chief god came through the roof of Danae's cell in a shower of gold. The fruit of their union was Perseus. When Acrisius discovered the child, he tried to save himself by locking Danae and Perseus inside a chest, which he cast into the sea. Zeus, however, would not let his offspring drown. He watched over the chest until it drifted close to the shore of Seriphos, an island in the Aegean Sea. There it was noticed by a fisherman, Dictes. He caught the chest in his net,

released its occupants, and took them to his brother, Polydectes, king of the island. The monarch received the woman and her baby son hospitably and let them live in peace on his island.

Before long Polydectes fell in love with Danae, but his desire for her was inhibited by the fact that she already had a child. As Perseus grew up, there was increasing tension between him and his mother's suitor. In an effort to rid himself of Perseus, Polydectes hatched a complicated plot. He announced his marriage to Danae and demanded a wedding gift from all the warriors of the kingdom. He anticipated, correctly, that Perseus, who by this time had grown into a man, would want to bring the most lavish present of all to his mother's wedding. So when Perseus asked Polydectes if he had anything in mind as a gift, the king suggested the head of the Gorgon Medusa, a fearsome monster who could turn men to stone with a single look. Naturally Polydectes thought that such a task was impossible—the monster would kill Perseus, and he and Danae would be left alone together.

Polydectes, however, underestimated the determination and resourcefulness of his bride-to-be's son. Perseus went about his task with a will, first visiting the Graeae, sisters and guardians of the Gorgon. These three witches, who were the daughters of Phorcys and Ceto, were gray-haired from birth and shared only one eye and one tooth among them. Their names were Deino ("dread"), Enyo ("horror"), and Pemphredo ("alarm"). Perseus elicited from them the secret whereabouts of the Gorgon—thought by some writers to have been a cave in a remote part of northern Africa, in a land that is now part of Libya—by stealing their one eye, which he used as a bargaining tool. As he left the Graeae he also stole some magical aids that would prove vital to his quest—a helmet of darkness that rendered the wearer invisible, a pair of winged sandals, and a reflecting shield. (In other versions of the story, Perseus was given the helmet by Hades, the sandals by Hermes, and the shield by Athena.) Thus armed, Perseus tracked down the Gorgon and slew her while she slept. He took care not to look at Medusa directly—which would have been his death—but

Right: This ancient Roman fresco depicts Perseus freeing Andromeda from her chains in time to save her from Poseidon's sea monster.

approached her by walking backward and looking only at her image reflected in his highly polished bronze shield. He cut off her hideous, snake-covered head with a sickle and took it with him as a trophy.

African excursion

With Medusa's head in his possession, Perseus now had the power to turn anything to stone, and on his way home he used it to transform the giant Atlas into a mountain. (However, this contradicts another story in which Heracles—a descendant of Perseus—encounters the giant on his return from the garden of the Hesperides.) Continuing his journey flying over Ethiopia with his winged sandals, or, according to some accounts, on the winged horse Pegasus, Perseus noticed a maiden tied to a rock in the sea, naked except for her jewelry, while two anguished people watched her from the shore. Perseus landed beside the couple, Cepheus and Cassiopeia, who told him that they were sacrificing their daughter, Andromeda, to atone for Cassiopeia's sin of boasting that their only child was more beautiful

Pegasus

According to some versions of the legend, when Perseus cut off Medusa's head, the beautiful winged horse Pegasus sprang from the Gorgon's neck. In other accounts, the stallion was created by Poseidon from drops of Medusa's blood that had fallen into the realm of the sea god.

By all accounts, as soon as he was born, Pegasus flew across the Mediterranean Sea from northern Africa to Mount Helicon in Corinth on mainland Greece. There he struck the earth with his hoof and caused the Hippocrene fountain to flow. The waters of this spring came to be regarded as a source of artistic inspiration and were sacred to the Muses. As a result, Pegasus, too, was strongly linked with literary creativity. In other myths, the horse served Zeus faithfully as the carrier of his thunder and lightning; he also became the favorite mount of Apollo and the Muses.

Pegasus was eventually tamed by the hero Bellerophon, who broke the horse using a golden bridle given to him by Athena. When Bellerophon was sent to destroy the fire-breathing dragon Chimaera, which had been ravaging the Lycian countryside, he rode Pegasus above the dragon's reach and was able to kill her.

Early Corinthians inscribed some of their coins with the figure of Pegasus. To Romans, Pegasus was a symbol of immortality.

Left: This painting by British artist Frederick Leighton (1830–1896) shows Perseus riding Pegasus to the rescue of Andromeda.

than the Nereids, sea nymphs and daughters of Poseidon. Poseidon, angered by this affront, had sent first a flood to ravage the kingdom, and then a sea monster that fed on human flesh. Desperate, Cepheus and Cassiopeia consulted an oracle, who told them that the only way to appease the sea god was to sacrifice their daughter to his monster. They promised Perseus that he could marry the girl if he could only save her. No sooner had they finished speaking than the monster broke the surface of the waves and bore down on Andromeda. Perseus flew over to the rock and decapitated the monster with a single blow of his sickle. In some versions of the legend, Poseidon later turned the body of the monster into the sea's first coral.

Andromeda fell in love with her rescuer and wanted to marry him. However, she was already betrothed to another, Agenor. On the day of the wedding between Perseus and Andromeda, Agenor and his henchmen turned up uninvited, disrupting the ceremony and demanding that Andromeda be released from the bargain. Reneging on their earlier promise, Cepheus and Cassiopeia sided with Agenor because he was the son of a powerful neighboring king. When Perseus insisted that the wedding go ahead, Agenor tried to abduct Andromeda, while his friends attacked Perseus. Perseus took out Medusa's head from the bag in which he kept it and turned Agenor and his gang to stone. He also transformed Cepheus and Cassiopeia, so that Cassiopeia was punished for her sin of pride. Perseus flew off with Andromeda in his arms.

Unfinished business

When Perseus reached Seriphos, he discovered that, in his absence, Polydectes had mistreated his mother. The hostility between the couple seems to have arisen from Danae's desire to delay the wedding until her son's return; the king wanted to go ahead with the wedding because he knew— or thought he knew—that they would wait forever. Perseus confronted the king, and as they argued it dawned on the young man that the purpose of the Gorgon mission had been to kill him. Incensed, he held up the Gorgon's head: as soon as Polydectes set eyes on her face, he turned to stone. Perseus was reunited with Danae, and they decided to return to Argos. Before they left, Perseus gave Medusa's head to the goddess Athena, who placed it on her shield or breastplate.

Below: This ancient Roman statue of Perseus depicts the hero holding the head of the Gorgon Medusa.

Perseus in Art

The exploits of Perseus have been a popular theme for artists throughout the Common Era. Two of the most distinguished works on the subject are *Perseus Releases Andromeda* by Flemish master Peter Paul Rubens (1577–1640) and *The Arming of Perseus* by British painter Edward Burne-Jones (1833–1898). Both paintings adapt the Perseus legend to the artist's own purposes. Rubens depicts Perseus mounted on the winged horse Pegasus, even though most literary versions of the tale suggest that the hero flew with the aid of winged sandals. Burne-Jones, on the other hand, ignores the tradition that the Graeae were old and ugly. Instead, he portrays the three sisters as classic Pre-Raphaelite beauties.

Below: In Edward Burne-Jones's painting, Perseus does not steal the winged sandals but is given them by the Graeae, who are neither old nor ugly but young and beautiful.

Acrisius meets his fate

On their return to Argos, Perseus, Danae, and Andromeda were welcomed home by King Acrisius. The king had not forgotten about the oracle, but he was glad finally to have a male heir. He saw that Perseus was a fine young man and found it impossible to imagine him committing murder. Some time later, however, Perseus went to Larissa, a city in Thessaly in east-central Greece, to participate in a discus contest at some funeral games. One of his throws accidentally struck the head of a spectator and killed him—when Perseus went to try to help his victim, he discovered that it was Acrisius. The Delphic oracle's prophecy had been fulfilled. In other versions of the legend, on hearing of Perseus's imminent return, Acrisius fled to Thessaly to escape the fate prophesied by the oracle. Perseus followed him there, but had no hostility toward his grandfather: his death was still an accident. Given the manner of Acrisius's death, Perseus was uneasy about succeeding his grandfather, so he exchanged thrones with the king of Tiryns and Mycenae, two great Bronze Age cities of the Peloponnese. In later life, Perseus and Andromeda had seven children—six sons and a daughter, Gorgophone, who became infamous for refusing to follow the Greek custom of committing suicide after the death of her first husband. When Perseus died, he was placed by his grieving father Zeus in the night sky, where he became a constellation visible in winter to observers in the northern hemisphere. In it he appears with sword upraised and the head of the slain Gorgon Medusa on his outstretched hand.

KATHLEEN JENKS

Bibliography

Hesiod, and M. L. West, trans. *Theogony and Works and Days.* New York: Oxford University Press, 2008.

Howatson, M. C. *The Oxford Companion to Classical Literature.* New York: Oxford University Press, 2005.

SEE ALSO: Andromeda; Bellerophon; Danae; Gorgons; Heracles.

PHAETHON

In Greek mythology, Phaethon—whose name means "shining" or "radiant one"—was the son of the nymph Clymene. He did not know who his father was, and when he asked his mother, she told him that he was the child of Helios, the sun god.

Phaethon assumed that Clymene had told him the truth about his father's identity, but when his schoolfriend Epaphus mockingly doubted his paternity, he went back to his mother and demanded proof. She told him to go and ask Helios himself; she directed him to seek out his father in India, the land where the sun rises.

The answer and the promise

When Phaethon arrived at the sun god's palace, he stood amazed. Everything from the columns to the doors, which were engraved by Vulcan himself, was fashioned in gold, silver, bronze, and ivory. Helios was reclining on a throne of emeralds and surrounded by gods and goddesses who represented the passage of time. When Phaethon asked Helios whether he was his father, the sun god replied that not only was he the boy's father, but that he would also grant Phaethon whatever his heart desired. Phaethon thought for a moment before asking to drive his father's chariot, the vehicle that brought the sun to the world every morning at dawn.

Helios saw the danger and pleaded with Phaethon to change his mind. "Look at the worry in my face," he pleaded. "Hear the concern in my voice: they should be proof enough of my love for you." He went on to say that the horses were too difficult even for Zeus to control, and that the path through the sky was dangerous and filled with monsters such as the Scorpion, the Lion, the Bull, and the Crab. Helios begged Phaethon to ask for anything else, but Phaethon was determined to attempt the impossible. Helios realized that he must comply with his request because he had sworn by the Styx River to grant Phaethon's wish, and not even a god could break such a solemn promise.

Distraught, Helios gave Phaethon all the advice he could, then rubbed a magic ointment on his face to protect

Above: This 17th-century Italian oil painting depicts the fateful meeting between Phaethon and his long-lost father, Helios.

Celestial Science

Despite the moral lessons to be learned from Phaethon's tragedy, his story may have a deeper scientific significance. For example, scholars such as Diodorus Siculus (90–21 BCE) of Rome connected Phaethon's story with the creation of the Milky Way. The streak of stars was clearly visible in the dark skies of the ancient world, and the story helped to explain it.

Some scientists have also questioned whether the legend arose because of Earth's contact with a comet or meteor. Others have suggested that the myth might have resulted from a particularly dry period. Ancient people could have interpreted either phenomena as the consequence of the chariot of the sun coming too close to Earth. Stories from ancient Mesoamerica and China both suggest a dry period between 1200 and 1000 BCE. Whether a natural phenomenon lies at the root of this myth or not, one thing is certain: the effects of such an event were extremely troubling, especially in a world with limited understanding of meteorology.

him from the intensity of the sunlight. No sooner had Phaethon set off than the horses realized that their usual driver was not at the reins. When Phaethon passed the Scorpion in the sky, he was frightened and dropped the reins. The horses ran out of control, wildly galloping first high, then low, dragging the sun across mountaintops and valleys, setting fire to everything in their path. Not only did mountains and cities catch fire, but also rivers, springs, and fields of crops. According to Ovid (43 BCE–17 CE), the Latin poet who tells this story in its entirety in the *Metamorphoses*, Phaethon's chariot ride blackened the skin of Ethiopians, created the Libyan Desert, and caused the Nile River to hide its head in the sand.

When earth goddess Gaia could take no more of this destruction, she cried out to Zeus to intervene. The chief god struck the chariot with a bolt of lightning, and Phaethon plummeted to his death into a river, later said to

Below: The Fall of Phaethon *by Luca Giordano (1632-1705).*

Right: This 16th-century Italian painting depicts the moment when the Heliades, Phaethon's sisters, mourning his death, begin to turn into trees.

have been the Eridanus (the modern Po in northern Italy). Helios himself mourned for a day, during which the sun was not seen in the sky. According to Ovid, Helios shirked his light-bringing responsibility out of anger at Zeus, who, he asserted, could not have handled the chariot any better than Phaethon. It was only after other gods and goddesses interceded that Helios resumed his duties, but not before savagely beating his horses for their part in his son's death.

Meanwhile, nymphs in the service of Hesperus (the Evening Star) found and buried Phaethon's body. When they did so, two miraculous transformations took place. First, Cycnus was so distraught by the death of his friend Phaethon that the gods took pity on him and placed him in the stars as a swan (the constellation Cygnus). The second transformation was that of Phaethon's sisters, the Heliades. Having mourned their brother at his tomb on the banks of the river, the Heliades attempted to rise, but their bodies were no longer human. Where there had formerly been skin, bark grew. Their legs became rooted to the ground, their arms turned into boughs, and leaves sprouted from the tops of their heads. Clymene, their mother, attempted to tear the bark away, but the girls cried out in agony. As their bodies were changed into poplar trees, their tears turned to amber, a precious gemstone that was worn by Roman brides. In Ovid's account, the tomb of Phaethon was forever shaded by poplar trees:

"Here Phaethon lies, his father's charioteer—
Great was his fall, yet did he greatly dare."

Explanatory theories

Phaethon's story may have its origins in explanations of climatic or astronomical phenomena, such as those that are thought to occur when Earth passes through the tail of a comet. However, it can also be interpreted as a warning against the impulsiveness of youth. If it had not been for his stubbornness, insatiable curiosity, and refusal to heed his father's warnings, Phaethon might not have died in such violent and tragic circumstances. His relentless ambition served as a reminder of the need for humility, and of the fact that humans were subservient and inferior to the gods. This story, like that of Daedalus and Icarus, was used to illustrate what can happen to children who disobey their parents' wishes.

Later, scholars during the Renaissance also interpreted this story as a warning, but this time in a Christian context: the moral was that humans should not strive to be too

close to God, which was, after all, Lucifer's mistake. It was also during this period in Europe that Phaethon became an inspiration for artists, most notably in a work by Peter Paul Rubens (1577–1640). Phaethon's name has survived in modern English usage, where a phaeton is a four-wheeled, horse-drawn vehicle and, more recently, a model of Volkswagen automobile.

ANTHONY BULLOCH

Bibliography

Howatson, M. C. *The Oxford Companion to Classical Literature.* New York: Oxford University Press, 2005.

Ovid, and A. D. Melville, trans. *Metamorphoses.* New York: Oxford University Press, 2008.

SEE ALSO: Daedalus; Icarus.

PHILOCTETES

In Greek mythology, Philoctetes was the hero to whom Heracles entrusted his famous bow and poisoned arrows. He used these weapons to shoot Paris, whose death played a major part in the Greeks' final victory in the Trojan War.

Philoctetes was the son of Demonassa and Poeas, king of the Malians, a people who inhabited part of southern Thessaly, a region of mainland Greece near Mount Oeta, to the northwest of Athens between Epirus and the Aegean Sea. Etymologically, the name Philoctetes means "one who likes to acquire things," and as a young man he received one of the most famous gifts in Greek legend: the bow and arrows that had formerly belonged to Heracles, which in most versions the hero gave Philoctetes as a reward for lighting his funeral pyre.

When the Greeks under Agamemnon set sail from the mainland port of Aulis at the start of the Trojan War, they were warned by an oracle that, on their way across the Aegean Sea, they must stop on an island and sacrifice at the altar of a deity named Chryse. Only one of the sailors on board the flotilla knew where to find this shrine—Philoctetes, who in his youth had been present at a sacrifice offered there by Heracles.

The Greeks eventually landed on the island. As they approached the open-air altar, Philoctetes was bitten on the foot by a serpent. The wound would not heal, and Philoctetes' cries of pain made it impossible for the Greeks to perform the sacrifice, which needed to be carried out in silence. The odor of his wound was also offensive, so they took him to the neighboring island of Lemnos, put him ashore, and sailed for Troy.

Crucial comeback

In the ninth year of the Trojan War, the Trojans had the upper hand. Either Helenus or Calchas prophesied to the Greeks that Troy could be taken only if four conditions

The Death of Heracles

Heracles won Iole, daughter of King Eurytus of Oechalia by beating the king in an archery contest, but was not awarded his prize. He later avenged this injustice by killing the king and taking Iole as his concubine, although by then he was married to Deianeira. When he returned from Oechalia his jealous wife decided to try to win her husband back by using a love charm. What she thought was a love charm, however, was actually a deadly poison. Years before, the centaur Nessus had tried to rape her and was killed by one of Heracles' arrows. As he died, he gave Deianeira his bloodstained robe, telling her that it was an aphrodisiac. The blood on the robe had been poisoned by the venom from the Lernean Hydra, into which Heracles had dipped his arrows. Deianeira innocently gave Heracles the fatal garment. After putting it on, Heracles felt a searing pain. He tore the robe off, and his flesh came off with it. Thus trapped painfully between life and death, Heracles bravely opted for the latter. With his son Hyllus, Heracles built

a funeral pyre on top of Mount Oeta and clambered to the top of it. None of his friends and family, however, could bear to light the pyre. Philoctetes chanced upon this gathering and was persuaded by Heracles to light the pyre in exchange for his bow and arrows. The mortal part of Heracles burned away, and Philoctetes took possession of the magical weapons.

Like most Greek kings of the generation that lived through the Trojan War, Philoctetes is said in some versions to have vied for Helen's hand and swore to her father, Tyndareos, that he would support Helen's husband, whoever he was, in the event of any calamity involving her. After Helen was seized by Paris and taken to Troy, Tyndareos called in the oaths. Each of the former suitors arrived with reinforcements to help Helen's husband, Menelaus, recapture her. According to Homer, Philoctetes led seven ships from the Malians and Olizonians, although during the war he was afflicted with a terrible wound that necessitated his absence from battle.

were met: first, that Achilles' son Neoptolemus fight for the Greeks; second, that Pelops's bones be brought to Troy; third, that the Palladium (a small wooden statue of Pallas Athena that was supposed to safeguard Troy) be stolen from the city; and finally that Heracles's bow and arrows be used against Troy.

In order to satisfy the fourth requirement, Odysseus returned to Lemnos, where he found Philoctetes living in squalor and using the bow and arrow to hunt birds for food. Philoctetes had no desire to help the Greeks—after all, it was they who had marooned him there in the first place. So Odysseus persuaded his companion, Neoptolemus, whom Philoctetes had never met, to trick the castaway into giving up his weapons. The plan worked, but Neoptolemus then had a change of heart and insisted that they rescue Philoctetes. Odysseus was undecided, but Heracles, now a god, appeared and directed the outcome. Philoctetes accompanied the Greeks back to Troy, where he killed Paris.

Different sources give varying accounts of Philoctetes' fate after the Trojan War. According to Greek poet Homer (c. ninth–eighth century BCE), he returned to Thessaly; but according to Greek playwright Apollodorus (third century BCE) and Roman poet Virgil (70–19 BCE), he journeyed to southern Italy, where he founded the city of Petelia in Lucania. He is also said to have built a temple to Apollo the Wanderer, where he dedicated his magical bow and arrows. Most accounts agree, however, that Philoctetes was killed in battle.

Variant accounts

That is the bare outline of the story of Philoctetes. The details have been fleshed out by numerous writers since antiquity, thus giving rise to many variant versions. For example, according to some authors, it was not Philoctetes himself who lit Heracles' funeral pyre but his father, Poeas, who later bequeathed the bow and arrows to his son. Several writers—notably Roman epic poet Valerius Flaccus (first century CE)—state that Philoctetes was one of the sailors who accompanied Jason on his quest for the Golden Fleece. However, Apollonius of Rhodes (third century BCE), the traditional source of the story of the Argonauts, does not mention him aboard the *Argo*.

The Trojan War occurred a generation after Jason's voyage, and it was mainly the sons of the Argonauts who led the Greek forces to Troy. Philoctetes

Left: This statue by French sculptor Jean-Baptiste Carpeaux (1827–1875) shows Philoctetes as he is bitten by the serpent.

Philoctetes' Wound

There are several different accounts of the way in which Philoctetes acquired his festering wound. According to Proclus (c. 410–485 CE), Greek philosopher and author of a summary of the Trojan War, Philoctetes was bitten by a snake on the island of Tenedos while the Greeks were feasting there. Apollodorus (third century BCE) had previously stated that this happened during a sacrifice to Athena or Apollo. Sophocles instead locates this event at the temple of the nymph Chryse on an island of the same name that was said to have subsequently been submerged beneath the sea. Neither Sophocles nor any other writer gave a precise location for the island, but it was generally assumed to have been near Lemnos. The wound never healed, causing Philoctetes immense pain and altering his whole life. Henceforth he was driven psychologically into a middle ground between life and death—his fate is thus similar to that of Heracles after he had come into contact with the Hydra's venom.

In the account of the life of Philoctetes given by Servius Tullius (578–534 BCE), Philoctetes had promised Heracles that he would never tell anyone where to find his grave. When pressed for the information, however, Philoctetes marked the place by stamping his foot. While he was doing this one of the deadly arrows fell loose of the quiver, pricking his foot. The wound putrefied, and eventually Philoctetes' comrades could no longer bear to hear his continual moaning. They marooned him on nearby Lemnos, a place also associated with other smelly things in mythology—the divine blacksmith Hephaestus and the Lemnian women, who were cursed with a strange body odor.

Below: The adder or viper is thought to have been the poisonous serpent that bit Philoctetes on the foot.

was the only hero who is said to have taken part in both expeditions. In some versions of the legend, he is even said to have been one of the early suitors of Helen of Troy.

Many of the great ancient Greek dramatists are known to have written about the story of Philoctetes, but the only one of their works that survives is *Philoctetes* by Sophocles (c. 496–406 BCE). The speech in which the hero expresses his anguish at having been betrayed by those he regarded as his friends, and the scene in which he has contact with humans for the first time in almost a decade, make this play one of the most powerful in Western literature.

Although the story of Philoctetes is heroic and full of great achievements, the legendary figure became most famous for his suffering. This illustrates a common tendency in Greek mythology to balance great glory with great suffering in the lives of its heroes. The character of Philoctetes has become an archetype of the misunderstood and abused genius whose assistance becomes essential to the survival of his people in times of adversity.

KATHRYN CHEW

Bibliography
Bulfinch, Thomas. *Bulfinch's Mythology.* New York: Barnes & Noble, 2006.
Graves, Robert. *The Greek Myths.* New York: Penguin, 1993.
Homer, and Robert Fagles, trans. *The Iliad.* New York: Penguin, 2009.
Sophocles, and Carl Phillips, trans. *Philoctetes.* New York: Oxford University Press, 2003.

SEE ALSO: Achilles; Helen; Heracles; Jason; Odysseus; Paris.

PLEIADES

In Greek mythology the Pleiades were the seven daughters of the Titan Atlas and the oceanid Pleione. According to legend, the sisters were immortalized by Zeus as a cluster of stars. One version said their half sisters made up the Hyades group of stars.

The Pleiades are a Y-shaped group of seven stars that are part of the constellation Taurus (the Bull). They are best seen in dark skies and are often almost invisible in cities because of light pollution. In the northern and southern hemispheres, the Pleiades, also known as the Seven Sisters, are located above Orion.

Although the names of the female characters involved in the Pleiades myth changed over time, the male characters generally remained the same. In one version of the myth the giant Orion, who was a hunter, became infatuated with the seven sisters and pursued them relentlessly. According to Greek mythographer Apollodorus (fl.140 BCE), the sisters were walking in Boeotia (a region of Greece) with their mother when the hunter spotted by them. He pursued all the Pleiades until the gods decided to intervene. In some of the very early versions of the myth, it was Pleione rather than her daughters who was chased by Orion.

Zeus, the king of the gods, first turned the Pleiades into rock doves and then into stars. Some ancient authors wrote that the transformation of the women into stars began with their grief at Zeus's punishment of their father—Atlas was forced to carry the weight of the sky on his shoulders.

One story included the Hyades—five half sisters and a half brother, Hyas. Hyas died after being bitten by a snake, and the Hyades died of grief for him. The Pleiades died from mourning their half sisters. Out of pity, Zeus transformed them all—Hyades and Pleiades—into stars.

Below: The Pleiades are part of a larger cluster made up by hundreds of thousands of stars. The seven stars that constitute the Pleiades are the brightest of all of these stars.

The Pleiades in Literature

Mention of the Pleiades as stars appeared much earlier than details of the myth. The cluster is mentioned in the epics of Greek poet Homer (c. ninth–eighth century BCE), the *Iliad* and the *Odyssey*, and in the epic *Works and Days* by Greek poet Hesiod (fl. 800 BCE). Hesiod also called the grouping of stars the Atlageneis and said that their appearance signaled the beginning of the harvest.

The first text to give the individual stars names was a mere fragment of a poem that probably dates from the time of Hesiod. The individual stars were called Taygete, Electra, Alcyone, Sterope (or Asterope), Celaeno, Maia, and Merope. As a group they were called the Pleiades by the mythical singer Musaeus who quoted the poem and said that they were the daughters of Atlas.

Daughters of Pleione

In Greek myths, similar collective names were often given to members of a family. The ending *-ides* means "daughter of" and was added to the name of either the father (which was more common) or the mother. Thus in ancient Greek the daughters of Atlas would usually be called the Atlantides. There was, in fact, another group of minor goddesses by this name who appeared later in Greek mythology. They are said to be the daughters of Atlas and Hesperia and are sometimes called the Hesperides. Ancient collectors of myths explained the name Pleiades as meaning "daughters of Pleione."

In other versions a different goddess and even a mortal woman have been identified as the mother of the Pleiades.

Aethra, also a daughter of Oceanus, was called mother of the Pleiades in one source. Greek poet and scholar Callimachus (c. 305–c. 240 BCE) suggested that the Pleiades were daughters of an unnamed queen of the Amazons. He listed their names as Coccymo, Plaucia, Protis, Parthenia, Maia, Stonychia, and Lampatho. He also credited them with introducing nighttime festivals and choral dances to Greece. Later on, other authors felt free to list different goddesses as members of the Pleiades and to change details of the story. The names Dione, Asteria, and Calypso were included in the names of Pleiades at one time or another. The commonly accepted names are Maia, Electra, Taygete, Alcyone, Celaeno, Sterope, and Merope.

Lovers, husbands, and children

Although one version of the myth claimed that the Pleiades fled Orion because they were followers of the goddess Artemis (the virgin huntress) and had vowed to remain unmarried, most versions gave them husbands or lovers. Sterope (sometimes called Asterope) married Oenomaus, a son of the war god Ares and king of the Greek city of Pisa in Elis. Oenomaus and Sterope had a son named Leucippus and two daughters, Hippodameia and Alcippe. Leucippus was killed when he fell in love with a nymph named Daphne, who was a follower of Artemis. He disguised himself as female to be near her and was killed by the other nymphs when they discovered that he was actually a man.

Below: Remains of the ruined ancient city of Troezen still stand in Greece. According to mythology the city was built by Anthas and Hyperes, sons of the deity Poseidon and the Pleiad Alcyone.

Above: Two of the Pleiades are depicted descending from the sky in this 19th-century painting by English artist Henry Howard (1769–1847).

Hippodameia became famous for her beauty and was widely sought after, not only because of her looks but also because she was the heiress to the throne of Pisa. After Leucippus's death, whoever married Hippodameia would become king. Her father did not want her to marry, since an oracle had foretold that he would die by the hand of his daughter's husband. Oenomaus killed many of Hippodameia's suitors in chariot races until the hero Pelops rigged the race and killed the king.

Merope is the dimmest of all the Pleiades. The ancient Greeks explained this as being caused by her embarrassment because she was the only sister to marry a mortal. She married Sisyphus, son of Aeolus. When Sisyphus lay dying, he asked Merope not to bury him. When he got to Hades, however, he complained that his wife had neglected to bury him and asked for permission to return so that he could punish her. Once back among the living, he refused to return and was forcibly carried back to the underworld by the messenger god Hermes. There he was punished for this and other crimes by being set the endless task of rolling a huge stone to the top of a hill, only to have it roll back down each time.

Celaeno was the mother of two sons, Lycus and Chimareus, by either the sea god Poseidon or the Titan Prometheus. Alcyone, who was also called a lover of Poseidon, had several children by the god: one daughter, Aethusa, and four sons, Hyrieus, Hyperenor, Hyperes, and Anthas. Hyrieus is regarded as the founder of the royal dynasty at Thebes (a city in Boeotia), and Hyperes and Anthas built twin cities that would later unite to become the more famous city of Troezen (in southeast Greece).

Taygete, Maia, and Electra all had affairs with Zeus and had children by him. Taygete was reluctant at first and fled Zeus. The goddess Artemis attempted to help her by turning her into a cow (or a deer), but Zeus made love to her anyway—we are not told whether it was in animal form or not. In gratitude, Taygete gave Artemis the Ceryneian Hind, a deer with golden antlers. Heracles would later capture this deer as one of his labors. Taygete's son was Lacedaemon, mythical ancestor of the Spartans. He ruled a region that was named after him.

Maia gave birth to the god Hermes after Zeus visited her in a cave in Arcadia (in southern Greece). Electra had two sons by Zeus, Dardanus and Iasion, and became the ancestor of the Trojan royal house. One version said that when Troy fell, she left her sister stars and became a comet, although there is no evidence that this myth reflected an actual astronomical event.

LYN GREEN

Bibliography

Bulfinch, Thomas. *Bulfinch's Mythology.* New York: Barnes & Noble, 2006.

Hesiod, and M. L. West, trans. *Theogony* and *Works and Days.* New York: Oxford University Press, 2008.

Homer, and Robert Fagles, trans. *The Iliad.* New York: Penguin, 2009.

SEE ALSO: Calypso; Daphne; Heracles; Hesperides; Orion; Pelops.

PRIAM

Priam was the king of Troy, a city in western Asia, during the Trojan War against the Greeks. Priam lost all 50 of his sons during the siege. Because of this, he came to personify the suffering of the Trojan people.

Priam came from a famous family. One of his ancestors, Dardanus, founded the city of Troy, and its ruling dynasty, the Dardanids, was named for him. Priam's father, Laomedon, was a king of Troy known for his untrustworthiness. This trait was illustrated by two instances in which he reneged on his word, episodes that would have serious implications for Priam.

For a year Laomedon was served by the gods Apollo and Poseidon, who were disguised as mortals. Their period of servitude was a punishment imposed by Zeus, the king of the gods, after they rebelled against him. Poseidon helped to build the walls of Troy, while Apollo tended the king's cattle. However, once their work was done, Laomedon refused to pay them. The two gods reacted angrily. Apollo sent a plague upon the Trojans, while Poseidon ordered a sea monster to attack them.

An oracle revealed that the gods would only be appeased by the sacrifice of Laomedon's daughter, Hesione, to the sea monster. Laomedon did as the oracle commanded, but Hesione was saved at the last minute by Greek hero Heracles. Heracles had agreed to carry out this feat in return for two divine horses that Laomedon owned. However, despite advice to the contrary from his young son Podarces, Laomedon snubbed Heracles. Furious at the king's behavior, Heracles later returned to Troy with an army, killing Laomedon and all but one of his sons. Heracles spared Podarces because he had advised Laomedon to be true to his word. Hesione then bought her brother's freedom by giving Heracles her veil. From this moment on, Podarces was known as Priam, from the

Greek verb *priamai*, meaning "to purchase." As the only surviving male member of the royal family, Priam became king of Troy.

Priam went on to father 50 sons and 12 daughters, although not all his children were by the same partner. Priam's first wife was Arisbe, the daughter of Merops, a famous seer. The pair had a son called Aesacus, who had remarkable gifts of foresight and could interpret dreams, a skill that was shared by his half sister Cassandra. However, Priam's most renowned union was with his second wife, Hecuba, with whom he had a large number of children. Several of them played major roles in the Trojan War; indeed, one of them instigated it.

When Hecuba was pregnant with her second child, she dreamed that she was carrying in her womb a blazing firebrand that set light to both the city of Troy and the forests on Mount Ida and burned them to the ground. Priam and Hecuba asked Aesacus (or in some accounts Cassandra) to interpret the dream and were told that the baby was destined to bring about the destruction of Troy. When the child was born, Priam decided to kill him, but he could not bear to do so with his own hands. Instead he ordered that the child be left on Mount Ida to die. However, like many mythical babies condemned to the fate of exposure, the boy survived. The newborn infant was rescued by shepherds, who named him Paris and brought him up as if he were their own child.

As a young man, Paris ventured from the mountains to Troy at a time when games were being held. During the games he succeeded in defeating all the other contestants. In doing so he enraged his brother Deiphobus and was forced to take refuge at the altar of Zeus. At this point, the seeress Cassandra recognized Paris as the son of Priam. The king immediately welcomed him back into his family, an act that was to have tragic consequences both for Priam personally and for the city of Troy as a whole.

Achilles and the sons of Priam

Paris's subsequent abduction of Helen, wife of King Menelaus of Sparta, led the Greeks to attack Troy. During the Greeks' 10-year siege of the city, Priam had to endure the loss of all of his sons. Most of them died at the hands of Greek hero Achilles. For example, Priam's youngest son, Troilus, was killed after Achilles lured him into an ambush at a fountain outside the walls of Troy. In most accounts he was decapitated or otherwise mutilated. Another of Priam's sons, Lycaon, had the misfortune to encounter Achilles twice. The first time the pair met, Lycaon was in an orchard outside the city, cutting branches from a fig tree to make rails for his chariot. Achilles captured the Trojan prince and ransomed him. The second time the pair met, Achilles showed less mercy. In the intervening period Achilles' great friend Patroclus had been killed in battle, and his death had filled Achilles with an unquenchable lust for Trojan blood. Lycaon pleaded desperately for his life, but Achilles ignored his protestations and killed him with his sword.

However, Achilles' greatest anger was reserved for another of Priam's sons, Hector, who had been personally responsible for the death of Patroclus. The eldest son of Priam and Hecuba, Hector had led the Trojan resistance for nine years before he chose to confront Achilles outside the walls of Troy. Priam desperately tried to persuade his son to withdraw to the safety of the city, but Hector refused. Priam could only watch as Achilles first killed his son and then tied his corpse to his chariot and dragged it around the city walls. Eventually Priam was forced to go to Achilles' tent and beg for the return of Hector's body (see box).

The death of Priam

After the death of Hector, the Greeks tricked their way into the city of Troy and began to lay waste to the city. Among those to die in the carnage was Priam himself. Despite his age and great frailty, Priam prepared to

The Meeting of Priam and Achilles

The episode that began with the death of Hector did not come to a conclusion until the elderly Priam made a secret nighttime journey into the Greek encampment to visit Achilles. Priam was guided to the tent by Hermes, messenger of the gods, and took with him gifts to appease the Greek warrior. Once he arrived at the tent, Priam begged Achilles to show pity and return the body of his son for a formal burial. Priam told Achilles of the great suffering that he had already endured due to the deaths of most of his 50 sons, and reminded Achilles that his own father, Peleus, was also old and would soon know what it was like to lose a son. Achilles was deeply affected by Priam's pleas and agreed to an 11-day truce so that Hector might receive a proper funeral. The account of Priam's petitioning Achilles is recorded in Homer's *Iliad*. Their momentary reconciliation and the transcendence of their enmity is one of the most famous and most moving sequences in the whole poem.

Below: This plaster relief by Antonio Giaccarelli (1799–1838) depicts a kneeling Priam begging Achilles for his son's body.

Above: The Death of Priam *by Pietro Benvenuti (1769–1844)*
depicts Neoptolemus, son of Achilles, about to slaughter the Trojan king on
the altar of Zeus.

join the defense of the city, until Hecuba persuaded him
to take refuge at the altar of Zeus inside the royal palace.
However, Neoptolemus, son of Achilles, ignored the
sacred nature of the sanctuary and killed the king at
the altar. Before he died, Priam was fated to witness one
last tragedy—the death of Astyanax, the infant son
of Hector and the last possible inheritor of the Trojan
throne. Like his grandfather, Astyanax was cruelly killed
by Neoptolemus.

Priam in art and literature

The most important source for the story of Priam is the
Iliad, the account of the Trojan war by Greek epic poet
Homer (c. ninth–eighth century BCE). Priam also appears
in the *Aeneid* by Roman poet Virgil (70–19 BCE) and the
works of Greek travel writer Pausanias (143–176 CE).
Priam is widely represented in ancient Greek art. His death
at the altar of Zeus was a particularly popular subject and

was depicted in Greek and Etruscan vase paintings, relief
sculptures on temples, and wall paintings. The deaths of
Priam's sons, and the events leading up to them, are also
frequently depicted in classical art. The Trojan king is often
shown as a passive and helpless observer in the background.

Priam is also depicted with the body of Hector or
petitioning Achilles for the return of his dead son's corpse.
His story is also represented in European paintings from
the 18th century, in 18th- and 19th-century drama, and in
19th-century opera. More recently, Priam's story inspired
English composer Michael Tippett (1905–1998) to write a
full-scale opera, *King Priam* (1962). It has become well
established in the operatic repertoire.

ANTHONY BULLOCH

Bibliography

Homer, and Robert Fagles, trans. *The Iliad.* New York: Penguin,
2009.
Virgil, and Robert Fagles, trans. *The Aeneid.* New York: Penguin,
2009.

SEE ALSO: Achilles; Aeneas; Hector; Hecuba; Heracles; Laomedon;
Menelaus; Paris.

PSYCHE

Psyche, whose name means "soul" in Greek, was a beautiful young woman who became the lover of Cupid, the divine son of Venus, the Roman goddess of love. Before Psyche could win Cupid, however, she was forced to undergo many trials and seemingly impossible challenges.

The main source for the story of Psyche is Roman writer Lucius Apuleius (c. 124–c. 170 CE), who lived in northern Africa, then part of the Roman Empire. His most famous work is *Metamorphoses* (also known as *The Golden Ass*), which concerns the adventures of a young man who is changed into an ass by a witch and then wanders about looking for a cure for his metamorphosis. In the course of his adventures, the young man overhears a story told to a young woman who has been abducted on the day of her wedding by robbers and is being held hostage by them. The story is intended to encourage the woman not to give up hope. It concerns two young lovers—Cupid and Psyche—who, against all odds, succeed in coming together and living happily ever after.

The story of Cupid and Psyche may have been well

Right: Psyche Abandoned (1790) by French sculptor Augustin Pajou. The statue depicts Psyche just after she has been deserted by her lover, Cupid.

known in the Greek-speaking world before the time of Apuleius, but no one knows for sure. The tale is very unusual in the field of Greek myth in that the version told by the later Roman writer is the only one to have survived from antiquity. There are no other independent accounts or even casual references to the story before this time, and the only other version that survives was written by Christian allegorist Fulgentius, who lived over 300 years after Apuleius. Historians believe that an earlier Greek writer did produce a long account of the story, but this version is completely lost and no one knows when it was written. However, elsewhere in *Metamorphoses*, Apuleius drew on earlier Greek sources for his material, and it is likely that he also did so in the case of the story of Cupid and Psyche.

Because of the comparative lack of ancient sources, some modern scholars have suggested that the story of Cupid and Psyche somehow belongs in a different category from other Greek myths and have labeled it as a fairy tale or popular legend. Others, however, dismiss this claim. They argue that, while the story certainly has many traditional fairy-tale components, the same is true of many of the myths from ancient Greece.

According to Apuleius, Psyche was the youngest of three princesses. All three were very beautiful, but Psyche's beauty far exceeded that of the other two, and she came to be regarded, first by her own people and then throughout the world, as being more lovely even than Venus herself. People traveled on pilgrimages from other lands in order to catch sight of her, and the traditional centers of Venus's worship began to be ignored.

The theme of mortal beauty becoming excessively regarded is widespread in Greek myth, and it almost always resulted in severe punishment, with some sort of dramatic or horrific reversal imposed by Venus. So it was with Psyche. Even though neither Psyche nor her parents claimed that she rivaled Venus (as was the case in most such instances of this theme), the goddess of love acted to put Psyche in her place. She instructed her son Cupid to make Psyche fall in love with the lowest and most wretched of all mortals.

The oracle of Apollo

Psyche's beauty was so extraordinary that suitors were too shy to woo her, and unlike her sisters, she remained unmarried. Psyche thus found herself living in loneliness. In distress, her father consulted the oracle of Apollo at Miletus in search of a remedy. Apollo's reply was that Psyche should be exposed on a mountaintop to await her future husband, a hideous monster. The king duly followed

Below: In The Legend of Cupid and Psyche *by Swiss painter Angelica Kauffmann (1741–1807), Psyche is depicted with her two sisters. The winged figure of Cupid looks on.*

the oracle's instructions. This part of the story also echoes elements of other Greek myths: kings often sacrificed their daughters to monsters or dragons. The best known example is that of Greek princess Andromeda, who was chained to a rock as an offering to a sea monster but then rescued from her fate by the hero Perseus.

Psyche's rescuer was Zephyrus, the west wind, who carried the princess off to a magical kingdom. There she dwelled in a luxurious palace located in a forest paradise. Psyche was waited on by invisible servants who continually replenished her food. She found herself visited every night by a mysterious and passionate lover. However, he used the darkness to conceal his identity, always leaving before daybreak. He also insisted that Psyche should never try to find out who he was and warned her that if she ever set eyes on him or learned his identity, she would lose him forever.

After a while, Psyche arranged for her sisters to visit her in her magical palace. However, the sisters were jealous of Psyche's new life and tried to play on her doubts and worries. They suggested that Psyche's mysterious lover might be the terrible monster to whom she should have been exposed on the mountain. Psyche's lover had warned

Below: This painting by
Italian artist Egisto Ferroni
(1835–1912) depicts
Psyche being carried
off by Zephyrus, the
west wind.

her about the
envious nature of her
sisters, but she was still
swayed by their arguments. Psyche
eventually allowed her doubts to win her over.

One night Psyche took a lamp to her bedroom so that
she could see her lover's face. She also took a knife with
her so that she could cut off his head if he really was the
fearsome creature that her sisters had warned her about.
However, when she lit the lamp, what she saw was not a
monster, but an extraordinarily beautiful young man.
Psyche's lover was Cupid himself, who had fallen in love
with the girl while carrying out the mission his mother
had given him to destroy her.

While gazing on the features of her lover, Psyche idly
fingered Cupid's bow and arrows, which were lying at the
foot of the bed, accidentally pricking her finger. This

caused her to fall
hopelessly in love with
Cupid. However, at that very
moment, a drop of hot oil fell from
Psyche's lamp onto Cupid's shoulder. Cupid
awoke immediately and fled from the building, returning to
his mother. Furious at his betrayal, Venus locked him up in
her palace.

Disconsolate, Psyche began to wander the world in
search of her lost love. She became so dejected that at one
point she even tried to drown herself. However, the god
Pan found her and urged her to be resolute instead. Psyche
sought help from the goddesses Ceres and Juno, the
patronesses, respectively, of motherhood and marriage.
However, both were unwilling to risk offending Venus and
refused to help her. Psyche finally decided to appeal to the
goddess of love herself.

Parallels with Other Myths

The story of Psyche echoes those of a number of other Greek myths. For example, the idea of a hero who ignores a warning and then is punished for his or her contrariness is common. Just as Psyche could not stop herself from looking at her lover's face, the mythical singer Orpheus could not resist one quick glance at his wife, Eurydice, whom he had just rescued from the underworld. Hades had allowed Eurydice to return to the land of the living on the condition that Orpheus not look at her before he reached the surface. Like Psyche, Orpheus was punished severely for his foolishness; his wife slid back to the depths of the underworld, never to return. Unlike Psyche, Orpheus received no reprieve. He wandered the countryside in grief until he was finally torn limb from limb.

This part of Psyche's story also has parallels with the story of Erichthonius, a mythical king of Athens. Erichthonius was the son of Hephaestus and Athena. When he was a baby, Athena put him in a chest and entrusted him to the daughters of Greek king Cecrops. Athena instructed them not to look into the chest under any circumstances. However, the princesses could not resist peeking inside. What they saw was a creature that was half-human and half-snake. Driven mad with terror, they threw themselves to their deaths from the top of the Acropolis, the highest hill in Athens.

Venus reacted angrily to Psyche's pleas. However, in a move that has parallels with the actions of a number of other figures in Greek myth, Venus did not reject Psyche outright. Instead, she set her a number of seemingly impossible tasks to perform. First, Venus presented Psyche with a great heap of thousands of mixed seeds to be sorted out by nightfall. Then she demanded that Psyche collect wool from a flock of wild sheep. Unexpectedly, Psyche succeeded in performing both labors. In the first test, she was helped by a colony of ants. In the second, a river god warned her that the sheep ate human flesh and advised her that, rather than approach the sheep directly, she should collect the loose pieces of wool attached to nearby bushes. Venus then demanded that Psyche bring her water from the waterfall that flowed into the Styx itself. The Styx, the river that flowed through the underworld, was guarded by terrible dragons. Again Psyche received miraculous assistance, this time from the eagle of Jupiter.

Finally, Venus demanded that Psyche enter the land of the dead and bring back in a box a little of the beauty of Persephone, queen of the underworld. At this last request, Psyche went to a high tower in despair, once again intending to commit suicide. However, the tower itself told her how she could enter the underworld, instructing her how to pass by Cerberus, the monstrous dog that guarded the entrance to the land of the dead, and persuade the ferryman Charon to take her across the Styx. The tower also warned her not to look into the box that Persephone would give her. By following the tower's instructions, Psyche managed to complete the task. However, like many Greek heroines before her (see box), she could not resist peeking into the box, just as before she had not been able to resist taking a glimpse at the sleeping Cupid. She was immediately overcome by the sleep of death that the box contained.

By this time Cupid had found out that he was unable to live without his beloved Psyche. He awoke his lover by pricking her with the tip of one of his divine arrows. Cupid then pleaded with Jupiter to make Psyche immortal

Left: Cupid and Psyche *by Italian sculptor Antonio Canova is one of the most famous depictions of the couple.*

Above: Charon and Psyche *by English Pre-Raphaelite painter John Roddam Spencer Stanhope (1829–1908) depicts Psyche preparing to cross the Styx River.*

so that she could become his bride. Jupiter was so enchanted by the young Cupid that he granted his request, then he reconciled Venus to her son's love. Cupid and Psyche were married in a grand wedding attended by all the gods, and in due course the pregnant Psyche gave birth to a child, Voluptas (Pleasure). Reunited after overcoming seemingly impossible challenges and long separations, the young couple were rewarded with a long and happy marriage. The Soul, to read the story symbolically, as many subsequently did, was ultimately reunited with Love, after suffering many tribulations.

Psyche and Cupid in art

Although there are no references to Psyche in Greek literature, and only two by subsequent Roman writers, she was depicted relatively frequently in classical art. Psyche was especially popular in the art of ancient Rome and appeared in paintings, bronze and terra-cotta statuettes, and relief sculptures on sarcophagi. Sometimes she appeared by herself, but more often she was paired with Cupid. Some representations are clearly illustrations of scenes from Apuleius's story, while others simply depict the two lovers

together. The lovers continued to be a popular subject in later years. Painters who depicted Psyche and Cupid—often at the moment when Psyche sees her sleeping lover by lamplight for the first time—include Raphael (1483–1520), Giorgio Vasari (1511–1574), and Lo Schiavone (1522–1563) in the 16th century; Peter Paul Rubens (1577–1640), Anthony van Dyck (1599–1641), and Luca Giordano (1632–1705) in the 17th century; and numerous French and English artists in the 18th and 19th centuries. Two famous statues of Psyche are located in the Louvre in Paris, one by French sculptor Augustin Pajou (1730–1809), the other by Italian sculptor Antonio Canova (1757–1822). Psyche's story also inspired works by English poets John Keats (1795–1821) and William Morris (1834–1896), and various musical compositions, including the symphonic poem *Psyche* by French composer César Franck (1822–1890) and several operas.

ANTHONY BULLOCH

Bibliography

Apuleius, and Joel C. Relihan, ed. *The Tale of Cupid and Psyche.* Indianapolis, IN: Hackett, 2009.

Bulfinch, Thomas. *Bulfinch's Mythology.* New York: Barnes & Noble, 2006.

SEE ALSO: Andromeda; Erichthonius; Orpheus.

PYGMALION

In Greek mythology, Pygmalion was a king of Cyprus who fell in love with a statue. Far from being a hopeless case, his love was so great that finally his wish was granted, and his beautiful statue became a real woman.

Although in most versions of the story Pygmalion is king of Cyprus, the legends do not include his family background. Cyprus is an island in the Mediterranean Sea, southeast of Greece, and for much of ancient history it was populated by Greeks. However, it is unclear whether the mythical Pygmalion was based on a real person. There could have been a real King Pygmalion at some point in history, but the magical story by which we remember him is a work of fiction.

Right: The moment at which the statue comes to life is masterfully captured in Jean-Léon Gérôme's Pygmalion and Galatea *(1890).*

Right: In this painting by Bronzino (1503–1572), Pygmalion sacrifices a bull to Aphrodite in front of his beloved statue.

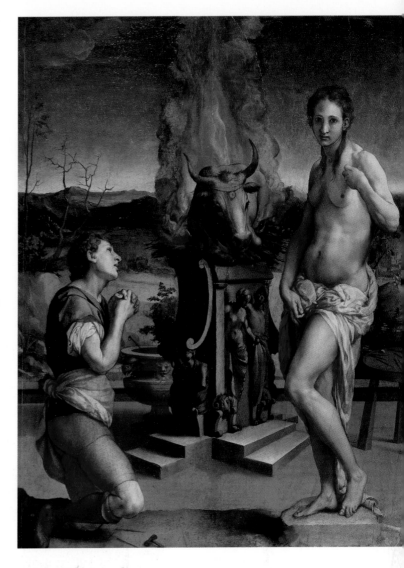

According to legend, Pygmalion found real women rude, sinful, and full of terrible faults. This was partly as a result of his unhappy experience with the Propoetides, a group of women from the city of Amathus on Cyprus. They refused to worship the goddess of love, Aphrodite, who was also patroness of Cyprus. Pygmalion was shocked by their wickedness and eventually decided that he had so little time for women that he would not marry at all. He resolved to be a lifelong bachelor.

Beautiful statue

As well as being king, Pygmalion was famous for his remarkable skill as a sculptor. When he stopped looking for a wife, he had little else to occupy his spare time. So he devoted himself to his carving and created a stunningly beautiful ivory statue of a young woman. She was perfect in every way, and lovelier than any real woman. Yet the statue was so lifelike that at first glance anyone would have thought it was a real person.

Pygmalion spent many hours gazing in wonder at his achievement, and before long he grew obsessed with the statue. He could not stop himself from stroking its cold surface and kissing its lips. He began to imagine that the statue loved him too. In fact, he became so deluded that he even took care to touch the statue gently, in case he bruised it.

As time went on, Pygmalion treated the statue more and more like a girlfriend. He spoke to it, making passionate declarations of his feelings. He brought it flowers and gifts of amber and seashells. He put rings on its fingers, and pearl earrings in its ears, and precious necklaces around its neck. He dressed it in expensive gowns and robes. Finally, he took to laying the statue down in a soft bed at night, with its head resting on feathered pillows, so that it would be warm and comfortable. To Pygmalion the statue was real and could feel its surroundings.

Aphrodite finds out

According to legend, Aphrodite, Greek goddess of love, could always sense immediately when humans fell under her spell, no matter where they were. She suddenly felt the presence of love in the palace of Pygmalion—no ordinary love, but the greatest she had ever known. She went to investigate and saw Pygmalion talking to and kissing his beloved statue. Instead of laughing at him, Aphrodite was impressed by the strength of his feelings.

The time came for the festival of Aphrodite—a lavish occasion when the people of Cyprus sacrificed white cattle, burned incense in her temple, and prayed to their goddess. As king, it was Pygmalion's duty to lead the celebrations. When he had made his offerings in the temple, he went to the altar to pray. He was very shy and hardly dared to ask for what he really wanted. He longed for the statue to be his wife, but he knew it was impossible and would sound stupid. So instead he asked that he might marry a woman who was something like his ivory maiden.

The goddess Aphrodite, who knew all about love and how it worked, understood the true meaning in Pygmalion's heart, and she decided to help him. The fire in the temple flared up three times—a sign from the gods that Pygmalion's prayer had been heard.

Pygmalion went home to his statue. This time, when he touched it, it felt warm. Its skin became soft, and it breathed and came to life. Pygmalion could not believe it, but it was true—the statue had become a living woman.

Shaw's Pygmalion

Irish writer George Bernard Shaw's play *Pygmalion* is now more famous than the Greek legend on which it was based. It tells the story of Henry Higgins, a scientist who studies phonetics, or speech sounds. To win a bet, he trains a young working-class flower seller named Eliza Doolittle to drop her strong cockney (lower-class London) accent, and to speak and behave like an aristocratic lady. He succeeds at first, managing to pass Eliza off as a society lady at upper-class parties, but eventually she rebels against his training.

The plot of Shaw's play is not strictly based on the original story. Instead, Shaw used the title to describe a man who tries to shape and control a woman to make her just the way he wants her to be, as the original Pygmalion did when he created his statue. Henry Higgins is trying to mold Eliza's personality, speech, and behavior, not her physical shape, and since she already has a mind of her own, she does not stand for it.

In 1956 Shaw's *Pygmalion* was turned into a successful musical, *My Fair Lady*, with music by Frederick Loewe and lyrics by Alan Jay Lerner. Among the featured songs were "On the Street Where You Live," and "I Could Have Danced All Night." In 1964 a film version of the musical was released, directed by George Cukor (1899–1983).

Left: The film version of My Fair Lady *stars Audrey Hepburn as Eliza Doolittle and Rex Harrison as Professor Henry Higgins.*

Pygmalion gave thanks to Aphrodite with all his heart and kissed the maiden. When she opened her eyes, Pygmalion was the first thing she saw, and she fell in love with him at once. They were married, and Aphrodite herself attended the wedding. Although in the earliest versions of this legend Pygmalion's wife had no name, later she was conventionally identified as Galatea. Pygmalion and Galatea had two children: their son was Paphos, for whom a coastal town in southwest Cyprus was named.

Artistic inspiration

The story of Pygmalion was originally a minor myth that received little prominence and appeared only a few times in ancient writings. Athenian writer Apollodorus (fl. 140 BCE) included it in his collection of myths and legends. It was also recounted by Roman poet Ovid (43 BCE–17 CE) in *Metamorphoses*, and mentioned in the work of Greek writer Nonnus (fl. c. 450–470 CE). The legend was popularized much later by a range of artists in the Common Era, for whom it represented a wide range of truths, including the power of creativity, the strong

bond between art and love, and the longing of some humans to mold their loved ones into a desired image. The most famous version of all is the 1913 play *Pygmalion* by Irish author George Bernard Shaw (1856–1950) (see box), which inspired the musical *My Fair Lady* (1956). The story has also inspired other musical works, such as the operetta *Die Schöne Galathée* (The Beautiful Galatea) written in 1865 by Austrian composer Franz von Suppé (1819–1895). Among the many paintings and drawings that depict the moment when the statue comes to life are works by Spanish artist Francisco Goya (1746–1828) and French painter Jean-Léon Gérôme (1824–1904) (see page 268).

Anna Claybourne

Bibliography

Howatson, M. C. *The Oxford Companion to Classical Literature.* New York: Oxford University Press, 2005.

Ovid, and A. D. Melville, trans. *Metamorphoses.* New York: Oxford University Press, 2008.

See also: Galatea.

RHEA SILVIA

Rhea Silvia, also known as Rea Silvia and sometimes as Ilia, was the mother of Romulus and Remus in Roman mythology. According to Latin poet Ennuis (239–169 BCE), she was the daughter of Aeneas—the Trojan hero who led the survivors of the defeated city of Troy to Italy.

Ennuis recounts that after the death of Aeneas, Ilia had a dream that foretold that Mars, the god of war, would visit her. Aeneas appeared to Ilia in the dream and assured her that, following a period of hardship and suffering after her encounter with Mars, her fortunes would change and would "rise out of a river." The reference was to the salvation of Romulus and Remus, the twin sons of Ilia and Mars, from the Tiber River in Rome. Servius, who commented on the myth of Aeneas given by Virgil (70–19 BCE) in the *Aeneid*, confirms that Ennius and Naevius (c. 270–c. 199 BCE) affirmed that Romulus was the founder of Rome and that he was the grandson of Aeneas through his daughter Ilia.

According to Greek biographer Plutarch (c. 46–120 CE), Roman tradition continued to honor Romulus and Remus as the city's founders, but by the first century BCE there had been a major change within the tradition. In the intervening years, ancient scholars had debated the foundation date of the city of Rome. It was no longer set in the years immediately following the Trojan War, but in the period of the eighth century BCE. To bridge the gap between the end of the war and the city's foundation, and to accommodate an alternative tradition which stated that the first Romans had come from Alba Longa—a city in the mountainous region outside Rome (and not from Lavinium where Aeneas had settled)—the ancients invented a long series of Alban kings. These rulers had supposedly descended from Aeneas through his son Ascanius (also known as Iulus). The first of these mythical kings was Silvius ("he of the forest"), whose child was Aeneas Silvius; this Aeneas in turn was the father of Latinus Silvius. The cognomen (last name) of Silvius was borne by successive generations of kings who followed Aeneas Silvius on the Alban throne. The name of Rhea Silvia reflects the feminine form of *Silvius*.

Origins of Rhea's name

Later writers continued to refer to Rhea Silvia poetically as Ilia, formed from Ilion, an ancient name for Troy, but her full name is more common. The personal name Rhea is of uncertain origin. It is not found among any of her forebears in the Roman tradition. While some scholars have supposed that it might be related to the name Remus (or even to Reate, the Sabines' capital city), it is more likely an imaginative borrowing from Greek myth, in which Rhea was the sister and wife of the Titan Cronus. Cronus and Rhea were the parents of Zeus, Hera, Hestia, Poseidon, Demeter, and Hades—the Olympian gods—but *Rhea* (or *Rea*), by its association with the Greek

Left: Italian artist Jacopo della Quercia (1374–1438) portrayed Rhea Silvia with her twins, Romulus and Remus, in this sculpture.

Above: Soldiers lead Rhea Silvia to her execution in this fresco at the Trinci Palace, Foligno, Italy. Amulius, King of Alba Longa, who was also her uncle, ordered her death after she gave birth to the twins Romulus and Remus. She was spared, but only at the pleading of Amulius's daughter.

deity of the same name, enhances the status of the mother of Romulus and Remus. The founder of Rome, by implication, was greater than ordinary heroes, and was from the beginning destined to achieve divine status.

Rhea Silvia's father was Numitor, a king of Alba Longa. Dionysius of Halicarnassus (first century BCE) and Livy (59 BCE–17 CE) recount how Amulius, Numitor's younger brother, deprived Numitor of his rightful kingship at Alba Longa. To be certain that there would be no offspring of Numitor who might one day rise up and avenge their ancestor, Amulius took the drastic step of forcing Rhea Silvia to become a vestal virgin. As a priestesses of the hearth goddess Vesta, she was consecrated to divine service and barred from marriage, but one duty of these virgin priestesses was to draw water from a sacred well for ritual use in Vesta's sanctuary. In fulfiling this task, Rhea entered a grove of the war god Mars, where there

was such a well. Mars was attracted to the virgin priestess and revealed himself to her, eventually becoming the father of the twins Romulus and Remus. When the twins' birth was reported to Amulius, he imprisoned Rhea Silvia on the grounds that she had broken the vows that she had been forced to take to become a vestal virgin, and he exposed the twins in a small chest on the Tiber River. The twins were saved when their vessel, set adrift on the river, reached the shore of the future city of Rome. Romulus and Remus were nursed by a she-wolf, the sacred animal of Mars, and then found by the herdsman Faustulus. Many years later, Rhea Silvia was set free when Amulius was deposed at the hands of her sons.

DANIEL P. HARMON

Bibliography

Gardner, Jane F. *Roman Myths*. Austin, TX: University of Texas Press, 1993.

Turcan, Robert, and Antonia Nevill, trans. *The Gods of Ancient Rome: Religion in Everyday Life from Archaic to Imperial Times*. New York: Routledge, 2001.

SEE ALSO: Aeneas; Romulus and Remus.

ROMULUS AND REMUS

The twins Romulus and Remus were the mythical founders of Rome. According to legend, they were the sons of the god Mars. Left to die as infants, they survived after being suckled by a she-wolf.

The legend of Romulus and Remus has been in existence at least since the time of Roman historian Fabius Pictor, who lived in the late third century BCE. Fabius wrote a history of Rome that included an account of its founding. Scholars believe that Fabius based his work on that of Greek historian Diocles of Peparethos, who probably also lived in the third century BCE. Earlier Greek historians had referred to Rhomos, a son or brother of Aeneas—or even to Rhomulos and Rhomos—in their accounts of the founding of Rome. A character called Rhome, described either as Aeneas's daughter, a Trojan captive of the Greeks, or a Trojan refugee, also features in some Greek versions. It is difficult to tell when, and under what circumstances, the brothers Rhomulos and Rhomus might have become the twins Romulus and Remus of classical legend. However, we do know that the legend was well established by the end of the third century BCE, since a statue of a wolf nurturing the twins was erected in Rome in 206 BCE.

Fabius Pictor's work is now lost. However, his version of events was recounted by two later writers, Dionysius of Halicarnassus (first century BCE) and Livy (59 BCE–17 CE). The version of the story of Romulus and Remus that is familiar today is largely drawn from the work of these two writers. The story tells of an Italian noble named Amulius, who lived in Alba Longa, a settlement in the mountains near the present-day site of Rome. Amulius gave his older brother Numitor the choice between the family's wealth and the Alban kingship. Numitor chose the kingship, but Amulius later deposed Numitor and killed Numitor's son. Amulius also forced Numitor's daughter, Rhea Silvia, to become a vestal virgin. The vestal virgins were priestesses of Vesta, goddess of the hearth, who vowed to remain chaste all their lives. Amulius wanted to ensure that Rhea would never produce offspring who could one day avenge their grandfather.

Sons of Mars

Four years after her consecration as a vestal virgin, Rhea was carrying out her duty of fetching water from a sacred spring when she entered a grove that was sacred to Mars. Darkness came over the sky, and Mars revealed himself to Rhea and raped her. She became pregnant with twin sons. When Amulius heard of the twins' birth, he imprisoned Rhea Silvia on the charge that she had violated her vow of virginity and insisted that her illegitimate twins be thrown into the Tiber. The infants were carried in a small wooden chest to the river. They were set adrift on the Tiber, which was swollen from heavy rainfall. The little ark floated down river, finally reaching the shore below the Palatine Hill, the future site of Rome.

The twin brothers were saved from certain death when a she-wolf found them and nursed them. In some versions they were fed food by a woodpecker. They were the recipients of another piece of good fortune when a herdsman named Faustulus chanced upon them. Because the herdsman had been present in Alba when the twins were set adrift, he knew their identity. Faustulus and his wife Acca Larentia brought up the children as their own in their cottage on the Palatine, without revealing who they were, and named them Romulus and Remus.

The capture of Remus

The twins grew up to become leaders of a band of young herdsmen and warriors. Never idle, they passed their time exercising and hunting with their friends, driving away robbers, and capturing thieves. When the twins were about 18 years old, they came into conflict with the herdsmen of Numitor over rights to pasturage in the meadowland between the Aventine and Palatine hills. One day the herdsmen of Numitor ambushed Remus and a number of his band and easily captured them. The prisoners were then taken before the king in Alba Longa.

When he learned of his brother's capture, Romulus was eager to follow in hot pursuit. However, Faustulus advised him to wait. His foster father took Romulus aside in

Above: This marble relief depicts the heads of the twin brothers Romulus and Remus.

private and revealed to him the circumstances of the twins' birth. Romulus and Faustulus decided that it was time for the twins to take their revenge against Amulius.

In preparation, Romulus called together the men of the village, instructing them to go in small groups to Alba Longa and, without causing any suspicion, to gather around the marketplace, where they would await orders. Meanwhile, the captors took Remus to Amulius. The Alban king made a judgment against Remus and then turned him over to Numitor, who was present at the hearing, for determination of punishment, because the matter

concerned Numitor's herds. However, Numitor was so impressed by Remus's bearing and courage that he was overcome by curiosity and spoke privately with the youth, inquiring about his life and origins. Remus told him all that he knew, which was little. Numitor agreed to spare Remus's life if he would assist in a plan to take revenge against Amulius for the wrongs inflicted upon the house of Numitor—the deprivation of his kingdom, the

Above: Now located in the Palazzo dei Conservatori, Rome, this bronze Etruscan statue of a she-wolf dates from around 500 BCE. The statues of the infants Romulus and Remus were added around 2,000 years later.

imprisonment of his daughter, and the destruction of his family. Remus embraced the plan enthusiastically. Numitor told him they must bide their time but that he should send a message to his brother Romulus, summoning him to come as soon as possible.

When he arrived before Numitor, Romulus informed him of the twins' true identity. Meanwhile Faustulus had been apprehended at the gate of Alba, with the ark in which the twins had been exposed concealed beneath his garment. He had brought the little box to prove the identity of his foster sons. However, the guard at the gate discovered the concealed ark and, suspicious because Faustulus was hiding such an apparently harmless object, seized him. Other guards crowded around. As fate would have it, one of these men had carried the infants to the river 18 years earlier. He immediately recognized the curious object that Faustulus was carrying. When the true nature of the little receptacle was revealed, Faustulus was sent to be interrogated by Amulius himself.

Faustulus was forced to admit to the Alban king that the twins were still alive. However, he also told him that they were tending their flocks far from the city. He had brought the ark, he insisted, only to show Rhea Silvia. Amulius sent the herdsman away with a guard to find and bring back the twins. However, the guard was overcome with sympathy for Faustulus and the twins and betrayed the king by revealing the developing situation to Numitor. Numitor, in turn, advised Romulus and Remus to take quick action. The combined force of the Albans loyal to Numitor and the twins' Palatine villagers lurking in the marketplace quickly overwhelmed Amulius's soldiers and killed the king. Numitor, restored to his rightful kingship, gave Romulus and Remus authority to found a new city.

The founding of Rome

Romulus wanted to found their new city on the Palatine Hill, while Remus favored another hill, the Remoria. When Romulus and Remus put the question of which hill they should choose for their new city to Numitor, he advised them to leave that choice, as well as the decision as to which of the two would rule, to the gods. Numitor said that the twins would be able to discover the will of the gods through augury. Augury was a way of interpreting divine will by observing the behavior of animals. Numitor told the twins that the gods' decision would be revealed through the appearance of an unusual formation of birds—the twin who saw the birds first would be the one favored by the gods.

Romulus took up a position on the Palatine Hill, while Remus stood on the Remoria (see box). Romulus boastfully claimed to have seen the birds right away and sent messengers to summon Remus. In the meantime, Remus saw six vultures flying from the right. When Remus arrived on the Palatine, he asked Romulus about the birds he had seen. Romulus hesitated in answering; during this pause, 12 vultures suddenly appeared. Romulus then replied that what had happened some time before was not as important as the birds he could see for himself at that very moment. Remus had seen only six; Romulus, twelve. They argued over the fact that Remus had seen the vultures first but the larger number of birds had appeared to Romulus. Numitor ruled that the decisive factor was who saw the birds first. However, he ruled that Romulus's initial sighting was the most important. The implication, in Dionysius's

Below: The Founding of Rome by Romulus *by Italian artist Giuseppe Cesari (c. 1568–1640). Romulus (right) oversees the digging of the ramparts.*

The Remoria

Scholars are divided about the exact location of the Remoria, the hill on which Remus stood while waiting for omens from the gods. Roman writer Sextus Pompeius Festus (second or third century CE) suggested that it was the Aventine Hill in Rome. However, this identification does not fit the evidence well. Dionysius of Halicarnassus said that the hill was "quite suitable for a city, not far from the Tiber, about 30 stades [5 miles or 8 km] from Rome." Some present-day scholars have suggested that the most likely location for the Remoria is in Magliana at the fifth milestone of the Via Campana, where the grove of the Roman fertility goddess Dea Dia stood. The sanctuary of the goddess was on the slopes of a hill now called the Colle delle Piche, "the Hill of Magpies." The hill stands close to the Tiber, about 5 miles from Rome, just as Dionysius described. Significantly, magpies were birds that often featured in auguries.

Above: In this illustration Romulus stands over the body of his brother, Remus. In the best known version of the myth, Romulus killed Remus after he mocked Rome's fortifications.

account at least, is that Romulus won the contest through dishonesty, having summoned Remus before he had actually seen any birds at all.

There are various accounts of what happened next. In one a fight broke out between the twins, with each supported by his own followers. Faustulus, in an attempt to end the battle, stepped between the two and was killed in the fray. Remus also perished. As a sign of remorse, Romulus buried him at his brother's beloved Remoria before building the new city on the Palatine.

In another version of the story, Remus conceded the kingship to Romulus. However, when the foundations of Rome were laid, Remus mocked Romulus by leaping over the low wall, proclaiming that an enemy could overcome the new city's defenses just as easily. According to Livy, Romulus then killed his brother in anger. Other sources say that Remus was killed by a foreman named Celer, who was standing on the walls supervising the construction.

Whoever was responsible for Remus's death, Romulus went on to become king of Rome. The city grew as fugitives from other cities came to live there. In order to procure wives for the many men living there, Romulus invited the Sabines, a neighboring tribe, to the city for a festival, and then captured their women.

Romulus ruled his people for 40 years, but then vanished mysteriously. While he was gathering his troops at the Campus Martius (Field of Mars), a thunderstorm blew up. Romulus was enveloped in a cloud and disappeared completely. His soldiers then hailed him as a god, believing that he had been taken up to heaven. Historically, Romulus was identified with the god Quirinus.

DANIEL P. HARMON

Bibliography

Gardner, Jane F. *Roman Myths.* Austin, TX: University of Texas Press, 1993.

Scheid, John, and Janet Lloyd, trans. *An Introduction to Roman Religion.* Bloomington IN: Indiana University Press, 2003.

Wiseman, Timothy Peter. *Remus: A Roman Myth.* New York: Cambridge University Press, 1995.

SEE ALSO: Rhea Silvia.

SATYRS

In ancient Greek mythology satyrs were half-human, half-animal creatures who followed Dionysus, god of wine, and did his bidding. They spent most of their time drinking alcohol, dancing, and chasing women.

Satyrs are usually depicted with human torsos, the legs and feet of goats, and animal-like horns on their heads. Alternatively they might have fur all over their bodies and the tails of horses. In some stories, rather than being partly animal, they were wholly human in form and wore animal skins. Like wild animals, satyrs were associated with woods, hills, and pastures and were rarely seen in towns or cities. The Roman equivalents of satyrs were fauns. Fauns also had goats' feet and lived in woods, but were generally gentler and less rowdy than their Greek counterparts.

All satyrs were male: female followers of Dionysus were known as maenads. Some tales say the satyrs' home was in Ethiopia, or on various islands in the Mediterranean Sea. According to most stories, however, they had no fixed abode and simply followed Dionysus wherever he went.

Party animals

Satyrs loved wine, laughter, singing, dancing, and all sorts of music. In fact, they loved noise of any kind. They were also famed for their lust for women. They were especially avid in their pursuit of nymphs—young, beautiful female nature spirits, most of whom were daughters of gods.

When not behaving in a debauched manner, satyrs were usually fast asleep, snoring loudly. Except for serving Dionysus, they rarely worked or helped anyone and were interested only in their own pleasure. Along with usually being drunk, they were scruffy, mischievous, and coarse.

Right: This statue from the second century BCE shows a classic satyr, with goat's legs and horns, and a human torso and head.

Yet they were capable of being charming, too, and knew how to flatter and delight women. They could also play beautiful music on their flutes.

Master of the revelers

Dionysus, whom the satyrs followed, was generally regarded as the god who created wine and first gave it to humans. He was associated with all kinds of self-indulgent pleasures and with various altered states of awareness, such as drunkenness and euphoria. Satyrs were usually depicted dancing around the god, playing music, drinking, and enjoying themselves.

Dionysus was said to have gone to war to conquer India. Many of his satyrs went with him and joined him in battle. They also helped the Olympians (the main family of Greek gods) fight the Giants, a monstrous race that threatened to overthrow them. According to legend, satyrs rode into battle on the backs of asses, and the braying of their mounts frightened the Giants, helping the Olympians to a famous victory.

Leading satyrs

Several of the satyrs had individual names and adventures. Among the generals in Dionysus's army in India were Astraeus, Gemon, and Lamis. Another famous satyr was Marsyas. He found a magical flute that the goddess Athena had made, but had thrown away because she thought that playing it made her look ugly. At the time, she said that anyone who picked up the flute would be punished. Marsyas, however, defied the divine will, and learned to play the instrument brilliantly. One day he met Apollo, god of music, in the town of Nysa, and challenged him to a music competition. Apollo played his lyre, a harplike instrument; Marsyas played his flute. Apollo was judged the winner, but, not content with his victory, was furious with Marsyas for having dared to challenge him in the first place. He punished the satyr harshly, hanging him up in a tree and skinning him alive. The satyr's blood (or, in some versions, the tears of the other satyrs as they mourned him) became the Marsyas River. Later Apollo

was so stricken with remorse for what he had done that he broke some of the strings of his own lyre in anguish.

Silenus was, strictly speaking, not a satyr, but one of the sileni. Sileni were similar to satyrs but older, and they always had horses' ears. However, they were often seen as merely a type of satyr. Silenus was very old and fat, and he loved wine above all else; but he was also kind and wise. He was said to have cared for Dionysus when he was a baby, and he acted as his closest friend and adviser.

Pan is often mistaken for a satyr because he looked like one, with a human head, chest, and arms, and a goat's legs, horns, and ears. In fact, however, Pan was a deity—the god

Right: This bust of a satyr was found at Herculaneum, a Roman town destroyed in 79 CE by a volcanic eruption of Mount Vesuvius.

Satyr Plays

In ancient Greece, satyr plays were short, often rude, comedies performed at the end of festivals held to honor Dionysus, god of wine. They rounded off afternoons of dramatic entertainment that traditionally consisted of three tragedies, each of which was written by a different playwright—the three playwrights were in competition with one another.

As light relief after the sadness and seriousness of the main dramas, satyr plays provided fairly frivolous interpretations of ancient myths, and they often featured a legendary hero who had been a character in the preceding trilogy. The genre took its name from the chorus—12 actors dressed in animal skins with tails, representing 11 cowardly, lecherous, wine-loving satyrs and their leader, Silenus, foster father of Dionysus himself. Their speeches on stage set the scene and offer an ironic commentary on events as they unfold.

Dating from the sixth century BCE, satyr plays are the world's earliest known form of dramatic comedy, and they influenced the development of later Greek, and hence Western, comedy. Although at the height of ancient Greek civilization there was a huge body of work of this type, only one complete example has survived: *Cyclops* by Euripides (c. 486–c. 406 BCE). After an introductory speech by Silenus, the greater part of this short work—running time no more than 30 minutes—is an exchange between the one-eyed monster Polyphemus and the hero Odysseus, who has been shipwrecked at the foot of Mount Etna, Sicily. Euripides adds Silenus and the chorus, but otherwise leaves the story much as it appeared in his source, Book Nine of the *Odyssey* by Homer (c. ninth–eighth century BCE).

Left: This painting by English artist Anthony Van Dyck (1599–1641) depicts the fateful moment when satyr Marsyas picks up the flute discarded by the goddess Athena.

of shepherds and flocks, wildlife, forests, and fertility. Sometimes Pan was attended by satyrs, and in Roman mythology he became Faunus, leader of the fauns.

What satyrs symbolized

Satyrs represented the wilderness, and the part of being human that involves animal instincts, impulses, and desires. This is symbolized by their part-animal bodies and by their love of food, drink, music, and sex—things that indulge the body and the senses. As well as being part of mythological stories, satyrs appeared as a chorus in many ancient Greek plays, known as satyr plays (see box).

In modern English the word *satyr* can mean a lecherous man. Satyrs have also been represented many times in paintings, sculptures, and other forms of art, right up to the present day.

ANNA CLAYBOURNE

Bibliography

Euripides, and P. Burian and A. Shapiro, eds. *The Complete Euripides.* New York: Oxford University Press, 2009–2010.

Homer, and Robert Fagles, trans. *The Odyssey.* New York: Penguin, 2009.

SEE ALSO: Maenads; Silenus.

SIBYL

In ancient Greece and Rome, a Sibyl was a prophetess inspired by a god, usually Apollo. She was often associated with a particular shrine, most notably the temple at Delphi. Her prophecies were unintelligible when she uttered them, but they were interpreted by attendant priests.

Below: This painting on an Athenian vase shows Aegeus, king of Athens, consulting the oracle at Delphi.

According to tradition, Apollo loved a woman named Sibylla, who was a prophetess in Asia Minor (part of modern Turkey). When he offered her any gift she wanted, she asked for a life "as long as the grains in a handful of sand." Apollo granted her wish. Sibylla forgot, however, to ask for everlasting youth. The years passed and Sibylla lived on. At last she became so shriveled that her tiny body was hung in a jar, where she everlastingly repeated, "I want to die."

Twelve prophetesses

In time, any prophetic priestess of Apollo became known as a Sibyl. Sibyls were believed to live 900 to 1,000 years. Some could interpret dreams; others could make their voices heard after death. Their predictions were taken down in writing by priests, often in the form of Greek hexameter verse. By the fourth century BCE there may have been as many as 12 Sibyls around the Greco-Roman world. The earliest is thought to have been the Sibyl who lived in a cave on Mount Cuma, near Cumae, a Greek colony in southern Italy. The most famous was Apollo's priestess at Delphi (a Greek city-state in Phocis on the southern slopes of Mount Parnassus); she was better known as the Pythia, and was called Herophile. Further Sibyls were found at Erythrae, on a gulf near Chios, due west of Izmir on the coast of modern Turkey; at Samos, the most easterly of the Greek Sporades islands; at Sardis in Turkey about 6 miles (10 km) from the coast of the Aegean Sea at the base of Mount Tmolus; and at Tibur (modern Tivoli, northeast of Rome, Italy). The Trojan or Hellespontine Sibyl was based near the ancient city of Troy on the shores of the Hellespont (now known as the Dardanelles), the strait connecting the Sea of Marmara with the Aegean Sea. Four other Sibyls, including the Persian Sibyl (see box, page 283),

Left: The cave of the Cumaean Sibyl near Puzzuoli, Italy, is a modern tourist attraction.

Tarquinius again refused to pay, she burned three more. At this point the king realized his error and paid for the last three books the price she had originally asked. The Sibylline texts were carefully guarded in the temple of Capitoline Jupiter in Rome. In times of national crisis, a board of specially appointed state leaders would consult the oracles, seeking advice about the correct plan of action after natural calamities such as pestilence or earthquake or to explain how an evil portent was to be appeased. The Sibylline books were not consulted, however, as a guide to the future.

When the books were accidentally burned in a temple fire in 83 BCE, senate envoys were sent to collect replacement oracular sayings from other shrines of Apollo. These new texts were moved in 12 BCE by Emperor Augustus (ruled 27 BCE–14 CE) to the Temple of Apollo, on the Palatine Hill in Rome. There they remained, safe and intact, until about 405 CE. The priests authorized to interpret the Sibylline texts had no other public duties because the job entailed considerable work. They were responsible for keeping the books safe, and for interpreting the texts whenever directed to do so by the senate. They were also in charge of implementing any measures suggested by their reading of the texts.

In the *Aeneid*, the epic poem by Virgil (70–19 BCE), the Cumaean Sibyl guides the hero Aeneas on his journey to the underworld. She directs him to look in a forest for the Golden Bough, a branch that will serve as his passport to the realm of the dead. Sibyl calmed the barking of the three-headed guard dog Cerberus, and negotiated with the infernal boatman Charon for Aeneas to cross the Styx River. Sibyl led Aeneas through the murky realm of Hades, pointing out the places of torment and showing him the heroes in the Elysian Fields. She then told him how to return to the land of the living through gates of horn and ivory. The Cumaean Sibyl's caves and the underground cavern still exist. Speaking tubes cut through the rock and skillfully arranged sounding boards make it seem as if the prophetic voice is issuing from the center of the earth and speaking from every side, just as it is described by Virgil.

This same prophetess is, in some accounts, the original Sibyl who journeyed to Cumae from Erythrae. According to Roman writer Petronius (d. 66 CE), the very first Sibyl was still hanging in a bottle during his lifetime, begging to die. Greek geographer Pausanias (143–176 CE) claims to have seen a stone jar at Cumae containing the bones of the dead Sibyl.

practiced in Babylon (part of modern Iraq), Egypt, Libya, and Phrygia (part of Anatolia, a region of modern Turkey). Their exact locations are uncertain. Even less is known of the Cimmerian Sibyl. The Cimmerians were an ancient people who were driven out of the Crimea in the Black Sea region by Scythians in the eighth century BCE. They migrated to Anatolia, destroying the kingdom of Phrygia, and invading Lydia in the seventh century BCE. The Cimmerian Sibyl is thought to have been established on the Bosporus coast, near modern Istanbul, although she may have moved with her people.

Cumaean Sibyl

The Cumaean Sibyl was especially important in Roman belief. According to legend, she offered the last king of Rome, Tarquinius Superbus (ruled 534–510 BCE), nine books of prophecy, but at a tremendous price. He refused to pay, so the Sibyl burned three of the nine books and offered him the remaining six for the same amount. When

Sibyl at Delphi

The oracle of Apollo at Delphi is generally regarded as a Sibyl, even though she was known as the Pythia. The extent of the link is unclear, partly through lack of archaeological evidence, and partly because the rites were performed there for more than a thousand years, during which time they were described and depicted in a wide range of often conflicting ways by numerous writers and artists. The first reference to an oracle at Pytho, the older and ritual name of Delphi, is in Book Eight of the *Odyssey* by Homer (c. ninth–eighth century BCE).

The Delphic priestess was originally a young maiden, but in later times every holder of the office was an old woman. She presided over a ceremony of consultation on the seventh day of nine months of the year. At these times anyone could question her directly to seek an answer sent from Apollo himself through the medium of his priestess. The Pythia is generally held to have sat on a throne in the shape of a tripod in the innermost sanctuary of Apollo's temple. From there she spoke enigmatic prophecies that were almost always considered to be accurate. If her words did not correspond to subsequent events, reconsideration of

Michelangelo's Sibyls

While the Sibyl and her utterances were important parts of the ancient cult of Apollo, her appeal did not cease with the end of the classical period. Sibyls can also be found in Christian art. In the fine black-and-white basilica at Siena, Italy, for instance, a series of Sibyls is represented in the floor mosaics. Five Sibyls feature on the ceiling of the Vatican's Sistine Chapel, the masterwork of Italian artist Michelangelo (1475–1564):

the Cumaean, Delphic, Erythraean, Libyan, and Persian Sybils. Each one is portrayed differently. The Persian Sibyl, for example, consults an ancient text, while the Delphic Sibyl—a beautiful young woman—looks at the world with an expression of wonder and fear.

Below: This detail from the ceiling of the Sistine Chapel shows the Persian Sibyl consulting holy writings.

A Natural Explanation of the Delphic Oracle

Nearly all ancient accounts of the oracle at Delphi agree that the words Apollo inspired the priestess to utter were initially unintelligible, and that their prophetic significance had to be interpreted by priests. For hundreds of years it was unclear whether this was a literal or metaphorical description of what went on inside the temple. In 1998, however, geologists discovered beneath the sacred site intersecting fault lines that emitted ethylene from a chasm deep inside the earth. This sweet-smelling gas was used by doctors until the 1970s in general anesthesia; in mild doses it has hallucinatory power. Thus it appeared that the ancient writers' descriptions of the priestesses' behavior were factual rather than figurative. At last, 1,600 years after the oracle was closed down, we have a convincing explanation for the utterances of the Pythia: natural vapors induced the priestesses into trancelike states.

Below: The gorge at Delphi. This is where ancient peoples left offerings for Apollo in order to obtain the god's guidance.

what she had said would invariably conclude that it was the questioner's interpretation, rather than the divine message, that was at fault. The importance of the Delphic oracle declined during the Roman domination of Greece. Roman general Sulla (138–78 BCE) stripped it of many treasures, and Emperor Nero (ruled 54–68 CE) is said to have stolen 500 bronze statues. In 390 CE, Emperor Theodosius I (ruled 379–395 CE) closed the oracle in the name of Christianity; it never reopened.

Adaptability

Although Sibyls were strongly connected with particular places, they could make their prophecies anywhere, not just within the confines of their own temples. They were principally conduits of the word of Apollo, but they could also act on behalf of supplicants whose previous appeals to other deities had gone unanswered. Despite their influence throughout the Greco-Roman world, little is known about the exact nature of the Sibyls' rituals, and nothing is known about how new priestesses were chosen.

KARELISA HARTIGAN

Bibliography

Homer, and Robert Fagles, trans. *The Odyssey*. New York: Penguin, 2009.

Pausanias, and Peter Levi, trans. *Guide to Greece*. New York: Penguin, 1979.

Virgil, and Robert Fagles, trans. *The Aeneid*. New York: Penguin, 2009.

SEE ALSO: Aeneas.

SILENUS

Fat, ugly, constantly drinking wine, and sporting a tail and a pair of horses' ears, Silenus was the guardian and best friend of Dionysus, the Greek god of wine and intoxication. He proved to be a wise and caring companion.

Silenus was a satyr, one of a race of wild male creatures, half human, half animal, who attended Dionysus. The younger satyrs had human heads and chests, with goats' legs, tails, and horns. The older satyrs known as sileni, were more likely to have horses' legs, tails, and ears in addition to human upper bodies. In some stories there were many sileni; in others, Silenus was the only one.

There are various accounts of Silenus's origins. Some relate that he was the son of Pan, god of shepherds and fertility, while other versions say that he was a son of Hermes, messenger of the gods, or Gaia, the ancient earth goddess. Silenus himself was the father of two of the younger satyrs, Astraeus and Maron, and also of a centaur—a creature who was half human, half horse—named Pholus.

Silenus was more powerful than the younger satyrs and was sometimes regarded as a kind of god, although in his appearance and fondness for overindulging he was more like a human. He was usually depicted as a smiling, bald old man with a huge belly, a beard, and a short, stubby nose. He always carried wine with him and was almost always drunk. He often rode a donkey.

Right: This is a classical bust of Silenus. The satyr was famed for his disreputable behavior but also for his wisdom and kindliness.

He was also, however, very wise, and he possessed the ability to predict the future. Yet Silenus was reluctant to act as a seer and was much happier simply enjoying himself. If humans wished the satyr to share his knowledge with them, they had to catch him while he was drunk and tie him up with flowers.

Another aspect of Silenus's character was his caring nature, which he demonstrated in his relationship with Dionysus. Dionysus was the son of Zeus and the mortal Semele. Semele died while pregnant with Dionysus. Zeus snatched the baby from her womb and concealed him in his thigh before giving birth to Dionysus himself. Hera, Zeus's wife, was jealous of her husband's affair and consequently hated the baby. Silenus claimed that he had rescued Dionysus and looked after him so as to protect him from Hera's anger. Later, the satyr became Dionysus's tutor. He taught him how to make wine from grapes and how to keep bees. When the god grew up, Silenus became his most trusted companion. Along with the other satyrs, he rode into battle with Dionysus when the Olympian gods went to war against the Giants.

Myths about Silenus

The best-known myth about Silenus involved Midas, a king of Phrygia in western Asia. According to one version, the drunken Silenus lost his way and became separated from Dionysus and the other satyrs. He came to the beautiful gardens of King Midas, who invited him to stay and threw a great feast in his honor. When Dionysus found Silenus, he was so grateful to the king that he granted him his wish: he wanted to be able to turn anything into gold by touching it—Midas's famous "golden touch." However, in another version, Midas

Above: The Drunken Silenus *by French artist Honoré Daumier (1808–1879). This charcoal drawing depicts Silenus as an inebriated and overweight old man, supported by other satyrs and his donkey.*

trapped the satyr by filling a spring in his garden with wine. Silenus was tempted by this bait, and Midas caught him. Forced to reveal his wisdom in exchange for his freedom, Silenus told Midas that humans are happiest if they are never born, and if they are born, happiest if they die young.

In *Cyclops*, a play by Greek dramatist Euripides (c. 486–c. 406 BCE), Silenus is portrayed as a servant of the Cyclops Polyphemus, the one-eyed giant whom Odysseus encountered on his journey home from the Trojan War. Euripides explained that while pursuing robbers who had kidnapped Dionysus, the ship carrying Silenus and his sons was blown off course in the direction of Polyphemus's island, where they were captured by the Cyclops, and made to serve him. *Cyclops* is a type of play known as a satyr, a comedy that includes a chorus—characters who chant, dance, and comment on the action—of satyrs.

Interpreting Silenus

Like all the satyrs, Silenus represented sensual pleasure and self-indulgence. However, he was a satyr with a difference: he was the only one to be named, and he was older and wiser than the rest of his kind. As a result, despite his drunkenness and ugly appearance, the ancient Greeks regarded him with love and respect. He appeared in a number of satyr plays, as well as in carvings and vase paintings. In ancient Athens people used storage boxes carved into the shape of Silenus. Some Greeks believed that the satyr had invented the flute, or even music itself.

The Greeks also linked Silenus with Athenian philosopher Socrates (c. 470–399 BCE). Like Silenus, Socrates was renowned for an outer ugliness that concealed great inner wisdom. Because of this connection, pictures of Socrates and Silenus often look similar.

The character of a drunken but lovable old man has featured in many works of literature throughout history. One of the most famous examples is Falstaff, a fat, drunken, yet much-loved character who appears in several plays by William Shakespeare. Some scholars think that Shakespeare, who often looked to the classical era for his source material, may have based his character on Silenus.

ANNA CLAYBOURNE

Bibliography

Euripides, and P. Burian and A. Shapiro, eds. *The Complete Euripides.* New York: Oxford University Press, 2009–2010.

Homer, and Robert Fagles, trans. *The Odyssey.* New York: Penguin, 2009.

Howatson, M. C. *The Oxford Companion to Classical Literature.* New York: Oxford University Press, 2005.

SEE ALSO: Cyclopes; Midas; Odysseus; Satyrs.

SISYPHUS

In Greek mythology, Sisyphus was known as the most cunning of men. He ruled the great city of Corinth, but was also guilty of many crimes, for which he was punished after death by a never-ending torment.

Sisyphus was the son of Aeolus and his wife Enarete. In some versions this was the same Aeolus who was the god of the winds; in others, Sisyphus's father was a different Aeolus, the king of Thessaly in northeast Greece.

Sisyphus was a complex character. He was renowned for his cunning and wisdom, and was a successful leader who founded the Isthmian Games, an athletics festival held every two years near Corinth. Yet many of the tales about Sisyphus reveal a selfish and unpleasant person—a thief and a trickster who raped or seduced women and attacked and murdered travelers.

Violent affairs

Sisyphus's wife Merope was one of the Pleiades, the seven daughters of the Titan Atlas who were later turned into stars. The giant hunter Orion had wanted to marry Merope, but instead she chose Sisyphus. Some accounts tell how Merope was humiliated to be the only one of her sisters who had married a mortal and that, as a result, her star was the dullest of all the Pleiades since she hid her face in shame. With Merope, Sisyphus had four sons, including Glaucus, who became the father of the hero Bellerophon.

Sisyphus had affairs with a number of other women. One affair was with his niece Tyro, the daughter of his brother Salmoneus, whom he hated. Sisyphus learned from an oracle that if Tyro bore him children, they would kill Salmoneus. In some versions of the story Sisyphus married

his niece; in others, he raped her. Either way, Tyro and Sisyphus had two sons. To stop the prophecy from coming true Tyro killed her children, but her act was in vain: Zeus, angry at Salmoneus for considering himself the god's equal, struck him dead with a thunderbolt.

Another story about Sisyphus tells how his cattle were stolen by Autolycus, a famous thief. The cunning Sisyphus aimed to catch the culprit red-handed: he fastened lead tablets, imprinted with the words "stolen by Autolycus," to his beasts' hooves, and then followed their tracks when they went missing. In revenge he seduced—or in some versions raped—Autolycus's daughter Anticlia. Anticlia later gave birth to the hero Odysseus, whom many believed was the son of Sisyphus, and not of Anticlia's husband Laertes. This alternative account of Odysseus's parentage would help explain the Greek hero's own cunning and ruthless nature.

Right: Sisyphus *by Italian artist Titian (c. 1488–1576). The painting depicts Sisyphus pushing a heavy boulder up a steep hill— a never-ending task set as a punishment by the gods, since the boulder always rolled back down to the bottom again.*

Above: The ruins of Corinth, including this Temple of Apollo, date to the sixth century BCE. Sisyphus was believed to have founded the city.

Founding a city and cheating death

Corinth, on the Greek mainland near Athens, was a powerful city in ancient Greece whose ruins can still be seen today. Some sources relate how Sisyphus founded a great city called Ephyra, later renamed Corinth. Other accounts mention that the enchantress Medea gave Corinth to Sisyphus, who became its king.

One myth tells how Sisyphus gained a source of clean water for his city by making a deal with the river god Asopus. In return for information about Asopus's daughter Aegina, whom Sisyphus had witnessed being abducted by Zeus, the river deity granted him a freshwater spring. Zeus was furious when he learned of this tale-telling and sent Thanatos, the personification of death, to take Sisyphus's life. However, Sisyphus managed to trap Thanatos and imprison him in a dungeon. This imprisonment had a dramatic effect: death could not come for anyone, and so people stopped dying. In response, the gods dispatched Ares, god of war, to rescue Thanatos, who was once again sent to claim Sisyphus. This time, Sisyphus did die, but first he told Merope not to bury him properly. The lack of correct funeral procedure so appalled Hades, lord of the underworld, that he made Sisyphus return to the living to ensure that things were done properly. Once again, Sisyphus had proved his cunning: he refused to go back to the underworld and lived for many more years on earth.

When Sisyphus finally died, Zeus and the other gods devised a terrible punishment for his trickery. He had to push an enormous boulder up a high, steep hill. Every time he neared the top, the boulder rolled down, and Sisyphus had to start again. This torment, the best-known aspect of the Sisyphus myth, was to continue for all eternity.

Symbolism and art

Some scholars have suggested that Sisyphus's punishment has a symbolic meaning. One interpretation is that the boulder represents the sun as it rises and falls each day; another is that it symbolizes humanity's struggle in the endless pursuit of knowledge. Today, the word *sisyphean* describes something that is endless, repetitive, or pointless.

Sisyphus's task captured the imagination of ancient Greek artists, who often depicted it on vases. It has also inspired modern artists, as well as the French writer Albert Camus (1913–1960), whose essay "The Myth of Sisyphus" interpreted the punishment as a symbol for the absurdity of life. Camus concluded that humans can achieve happiness by recognizing this absurdity and rising above it.

ANNA CLAYBOURNE

Bibliography

Camus, Albert, and Justin O'Brien, trans. *The Myth of Sisyphus.* London: Penguin, 2000.

Homer, and Robert Fagles, trans. *The Odyssey.* New York: Penguin, 2009.

SEE ALSO: Bellerophon; Odysseus; Pleiades.

TANTALUS

Tantalus is famous for spending eternity reaching for tempting fruit that always moved away from his grasp at the last moment. This was his punishment for a series of crimes that offended the gods.

Tantalus was the son of Zeus and the Oceanid Pluto (not to be confused with the Roman god of the dead, who was also known as Pluto). Tantalus was a king, but different versions of the story disagree about where he ruled. Some say he lived at Sipylus and ruled the kingdom of Lydia (in modern Turkey); others say he was king of Phrygia or Paphlagonia (also in modern Turkey). Ancient Greek geographer Pausanias (143–176 CE) reported that Tantalus's tomb was on Mount Sipylus, and modern archaeologists have identified various sites that might correspond to it. However, the myth of Tantalus does not reveal enough to connect the mythical Tantalus to a historical person.

According to the myth, Tantalus married twice and had several children. His daughter Niobe insulted the gods by claiming that her own children were more beautiful and worthy of praise than them. To punish her, the gods Leto, Apollo, and Artemis killed the children, and Niobe was turned into a stone that stood on Mount Sipylus.

Tragedy continued down Tantalus's family line. His grandsons included Atreus and Thyestes, who feuded bitterly over the throne of Mycenae. This feud continued into the next generation when Aegisthus, son of Thyestes, murdered Agamemnon, son of Atreus. (Agamemnon was the commander of the Greek army that besieged the city of Troy.)

Tantalus also upset the gods in various ways. As a son of Zeus, he was welcomed by the gods, who invited him to eat with them on Mount Olympus. At dinner, his table manners were terrible and offended the gods, and he could not resist stealing some of their food—nectar and ambrosia—and taking it to share with his human friends. He also gave away secrets that the gods had discussed over the meal.

Another of Tantalus's crimes was described by some writers as being more serious. He held a feast for the gods—some claim to apologize for his earlier behavior—but he also decided to test whether the gods were as all-knowing as people reputed them to be. He killed his own son, Pelops, then cooked him in a stew and served it up at

Right: The myth of Tantalus was a common source for ancient artists. King Tantalus is depicted reaching for fruit in this fourth-century-BCE vase painting.

Left: French artist Bernard Picart (1673–1733) engraved Tantalus enduring the punishment Zeus set him. Tantalus was sent to Tartarus, in the underworld, where he could not quench his thirst from water in which he stood or feed his hunger with fruit that was just out of reach.

In Tartarus, the part of the underworld where sinners were punished, Tantalus was forced to stand up to his chin in a pool of fresh water, but whenever he tried to lower his mouth to the water to drink, the water level dropped and he could not reach it. Hanging above the pool were tree branches laden with delicious ripe fruit; but when Tantalus tried to reach for some, the wind blew the branches aside so that he could never quite touch them. According to some versions, Zeus also balanced a massive boulder above Tantalus so that as well as suffering from eternal hunger and thirst, he was constantly nervous about the boulder crushing him.

Tantalus's fate served as an example to others, warning them not to upset the gods, and many ancient Greek and Roman writers retold his story. In the *Odyssey* by Homer (c. ninth–eighth century BCE), for example, the hero Odysseus recounts the sight of Tantalus suffering when he visited the land of the dead, and describes the "pear-trees and pomegranates, apple-trees with their glossy burden, sweet figs and luxuriant olives" that were tormenting Tantalus. Other writers who recorded the story of Tantalus include Apollodorus (third century BCE), Hyginus (first century BCE), Ovid (43 BCE–17 CE), and Plutarch (c. 46–120 CE).

Because it makes such a striking visual image, Tantalus's punishment has appeared countless times in art from ancient to modern times.

Tantalus today

Today the details of Tantalus's life are not well known, but his punishment in the underworld is famous and has become a part of modern language. His name came to form the common word *tantalize,* which means to tempt someone, usually with something they cannot have. A tantalus is also a kind of cabinet that shows its contents but locks so that a key is needed to access the items.

ANNA CLAYBOURNE

Bibliography

Homer, and Robert Fagles, trans. *The Odyssey.* New York: Penguin, 2009.

Ovid, and A. D. Melville, trans. *Metamorphoses.* New York: Oxford University Press, 2008.

SEE ALSO: Agamemnon; Pelops.

the feast to see if the gods would notice. The gods did indeed know what had happened, and most of them refused to eat the stew. However, Demeter, goddess of crops, was in mourning for her daughter Persephone, who had been stolen away to the underworld. She absent-mindedly ate Pelops's shoulder. The gods managed to bring the boy back to life, giving him an ivory shoulder to replace the one that had been eaten; but they never forgave Tantalus for his deceptive evil act.

The golden dog

Tantalus was also said to have stolen a golden dog belonging to Zeus—or to have persuaded a man named Pandareos to steal it for him. When challenged, Tantalus swore in the name of his father Zeus that he knew nothing about the dog. Zeus was so angry about the lie that he used a huge rock from Mount Sipylus to crush Tantalus to death. The king was carried off to the underworld, where an even worse fate awaited him.

THESEUS

Theseus, the greatest Athenian hero, was born to Aethra in Troezen, Greece. Aethra's father, Pittheus, claimed that Aegeus, king of Athens, was Theseus's father; but Aethra herself said that it was the sea god Poseidon. Whichever story was true, Theseus inherited characteristics from both his mortal and his immortal father.

Above: In this 17th-century painting by French artist Laurent de La Hire (1606–1656), Theseus lifts a rock while his mother, Aethra, points toward the sandals and sword that the boy's father, Aegeus, hid for his son.

King Aegeus was troubled that his two marriages had produced no children, so he consulted the Delphic Oracle. At a loss to understand the Oracle's advice, Aegeus went to Troezen's king, Pittheus, for guidance. There he drank so much that he was compelled by Pittheus to sleep with Aethra, the king's daughter. Before Aegeus left Troezen, he placed a sword and a pair of sandals beneath a heavy rock and told Aethra that when her son could lift the stone, he should take the tokens and make his way to Athens. When Theseus was a young man he retrieved the sword and sandals and made his way north along the Gulf of Corinth toward his father's city.

The journey to Athens

During his journey, Theseus encountered a series of local brigands who preyed upon travelers. One of them, Periphetes, beat passersby with a bronze club. When Theseus came upon him, he seized the club and killed Periphetes. He kept the club as a token of his first heroic deed. The young hero next encountered Sinis, the Pine Bender. Sinis's method of killing travelers was to tie his victims to two pine trees that he had bent and secured to the ground. Then he would release the trees, tearing the person in two. Theseus overpowered Sinis and used his method against him. Near the city of Megara, Theseus came across a robber, Sciron, who stopped travelers and made them wash his feet, whereupon he kicked them over

a cliff into the sea, where a giant turtle would devour the body. When Theseus bent down to Sciron's feet, he grabbed the villain and hurled him over the cliff into the waters below. Theseus next came to the city of Eleusis. There he encountered Procrustes, who forced anyone he captured to lie in a special bed, which he then stretched or chopped his victim to fit. Theseus took Procrustes and fastened him to the torturous bed, then killed him in the same way that his victims had died. (Today philosophers use the phrase *Procrustean bed* to describe an argument that is forced to suit a favorite theory.)

When Theseus reached Athens, people had already received news of his deeds and he was hailed as a hero. Once there he went immediately to king Aegeus's palace. The king did not recognize him, but the sorceress Medea, who had fled to Athens from Corinth and was married to the king, suspected the young man's identity and became jealous. She devised a plan to cause Theseus's death: she declared that in order to prove his heroism, he should kill a wild bull that was ravaging the Plain of Marathon. Theseus captured the bull and sacrificed it to Apollo, god

The Origins of the Minotaur

Poseidon sent to King Minos a beautiful white bull as proof of his right to rule Crete, and in return for the god's support, the king was supposed to sacrifice the bull to the sea god. Minos could not bear to kill such a beautiful animal and offered another bull to Poseidon. As punishment the god afflicted Poseidon's wife, Pasiphae, with a passion for the white bull. With the aid of the palace engineer Daedalus, the queen mated with the bull and later gave birth to Asterios, otherwise known as the Minotaur—a beast that was part man and part bull. Minos ordered Daedalus to create a maze at the palace at Knossos in which to hide the monster. The Minotaur fed on human flesh from seven boys and seven girls whom Minos claimed as a tribute from the Athenians each year, or every nine years. He blamed the Athenians for the death of his son, Androgeos.

Although the Cretan Minotaur is a mythological figure, archaeologists have confirmed that Cretans used bulls in ceremonies, and that labyrinthian parts of the palace did exist.

Left: In this 19th-century watercolor painting, king Minos's daughter Ariadne holds a ball of thread. Theseus used the thread to return from the Labyrinth, shown in the background.

of divination. Upon his return to the palace, Medea, who had also raised suspicion about Theseus in Aegeus's mind, persuaded the king to offer Theseus a cup of poisoned wine. As the hero was lifting the drink to his lips, however, King Aegeus recognized Theseus's sword and sandals as his own, and he dashed the cup to the ground. Aegeus welcomed Thesesus as his son and as heir to the throne. Medea fled before she could be brought to justice.

Theseus and the Minotaur

Minos, king of Crete, whose son Androgeos had been insulted (or killed) in Athens, was demanding an annual gift from the Athenians in recompense. Each year seven boys and seven girls traveled to the island of Crete to try to escape from the Labyrinth at Knossos in which roamed the Minotaur, a terrifying monster that was part man and part bull. No one had ever returned alive from the Labyrinth. One year Theseus volunteered (or was specially chosen) to

lead the expedition to Crete. He set sail for the island on the same ship as Minos.

During the journey to Crete, Minos tossed a ring overboard and dared Theseus to retrieve it. Minos believed that this would test rumors that Poseidon was Theseus's father. Theseus accepted the challenge and leaped into the sea. In its depths he was welcomed by the sea goddess Amphitrite and other sea nymphs. They gave him a magnificent crimson cloak and a shining crown adorned with dark roses. Everyone on board the ship was amazed when dolphins carried Theseus back to the surface, wearing the gleaming crown and holding Minos's ring. Although it was clear to Minos that Theseus had been protected by Poseidon, he was sure that the Minotaur would kill Theseus.

At Knossos, Theseus won the attention of Minos's daughter, Princess Ariadne. When he set off to face the Minotaur, she gave him a ball of thread to unwind as he

Minoans and Mycenaeans in Crete

Theseus's liberation of Athens from paying tribute to Crete by killing the Minotaur is a mythical event. However, there is a historical parallel: the Mycenaeans, Greek-speaking people inhabiting the area we now know as Greece, overthrew the Minoan civilization on Crete in about 1400 BCE. Perhaps the historical event lies behind the story of Theseus's killing of the Minotaur.

Archaeologists who have examined ruins of the Minoan civilization on Crete, including ancient records of trade transactions between Cretans and other Mediterranean nations, speculate that there were a number of causes for the downfall of the Minoans. One popular explanation is that there was an enormous volcanic eruption on a nearby island around 1600 BCE that led to widespread devastation in the area. Tidal waves apparently traveled from the center of the eruption to northern Crete, where they demolished many palaces, including Knossos itself.

After the catastrophe some Minoan survivors migrated to mainland Greece, and those that stayed were later subjugated by invading Mycenaeans. Archaeologists and historians suggest that evidence of an invasion of Crete is indicated by the existence of two different languages on many ancient Cretan trade documents. They argue that Minoan scribes were recording transactions in a Minoan form and in another language that their new rulers, the Mycenaeans, could understand.

Right: Although most of the palace of Knossos was devastated around 1500 BCE, some parts still stand, including the northwest portico, pictured here.

made his way through the Labyrinth so that he would not get lost. Eventually Theseus confronted the Minotaur and, using a sword, club, or his hands, killed it. Then, retracing his steps using the thread, Theseus and the others made their way safely out of the Labyrinth. Theseus then set sail for Athens, taking Ariadne with him.

However, Theseus abandoned Ariadne on the first island they came to—some say it was the little island of Dia, but a more common myth claims it was Naxos. Before leaving Ariadne, Theseus gave to her the crown that he had received from Amphitrite. Dionysus, god of wine, saw the lonely princess and rescued her. According to one version of the myth, he put the crown into the sky, and it is now known as the constellation Corona, the Crown.

When Theseus had left Athens, he had told his father that he would change the sails of his ship from a dark color to white if his expedition was successful, but

Theseus forgot his promise. From his position on a cliff top, Aegeus saw Theseus's ship return but saw that its sails were dark. Believing that his son was dead, he threw himself into the sea. Legend has it that this is how the Aegean Sea received its name.

Following Aegeus's death, Theseus became king of Athens. He made the city strong and prosperous, and he became known for his wisdom and compassion. Various myths say that Theseus greatly improved the lives of the citizens. Developments were credited to him that were in fact instituted over several hundred years. Various legends claim that he united all of the small villages around Athens into a single political unit, over which he ruled. Theseus also supposedly instituted the Panathenaia, the all-Athens festival that Athenians celebrated each year in honor of Athena, goddess of war. In many legends about Theseus, he is not only revered as a great hero but also remembered as a great political leader.

Above: In this painting Venetian artist Vittore Carpaccio (c. 1460–1526) depicts an Amazon embassy meeting with an Athenian court to demand the return of their queen, whom Theseus had taken as his wife.

Other myths

According to one myth, Theseus accompanied Heracles on his ninth labor to retrieve the belt of Hippolyte, queen of the Amazons. (In different versions Hippolyte is known as Antiope.) In one account Theseus carried off the queen to be his bride; an Amazon army attempted to retrieve her and attacked Athens. Under Theseus's leadership the Amazons were conquered in a violent conflict. The Amazon queen stayed with Theseus and in due time bore him a son, whom he named Hippolytus.

Later Theseus abandoned the Amazon queen and married Phaedra, daughter of Minos and sister of Ariadne. By this time Hippolytus had grown into a handsome young man and was devoted to the goddess Artemis. However, Aphrodite, goddess of erotic love, was angry that Hippolytus did not worship her. In her jealousy she caused Phaedra to fall in love with her stepson. He, of course, rejected her advances. Shameful of her passion and fearing that Hippolytus would tell her husband, Phaedra wrote a letter falsely accusing Hippolytus of raping her, and then took her own life. Theseus read the letter and, despite Hippolytus's protests of innocence, prayed to Poseidon for his own son's death. Theseus learned the truth too late and Hippolytus died.

Another myth recounts Theseus's adventures with his companion Peirithous. They decided to find their ideal wives together and went to Sparta to abduct the princess Helen, who was renowned for her beauty. They drew lots to decide who would marry Helen, and Theseus won. However, Helen was too young to marry, and Theseus left her with his mother, Aethra, in Troezen. Next the two friends set off to find a partner for Peirithous, who wanted to make Persephone, queen of Hades, his wife.

When the travelers arrived in the underworld, Hades welcomed them and offered them seats. They accepted his invitation, but the chairs in which they sat would not release them. In one version, the chairs induced forgetfulness: anyone who sat in them could not remember how to leave Hades' realm. While the two friends were stuck in their seats, Helen's brothers Castor and Pollux rescued their sister from Aethra. Theseus and Peirithous remained captive until Heracles arrived in the underworld to complete his last labor many years later. Heracles had to bring Cerberus, the three-headed hound of Hades, back to Eurystheus, king of Mycenae. Heracles was able to prize Theseus from his seat, but he failed to release Peirithous, who remained trapped for eternity.

When Theseus returned to Athens, he discovered that he had lost the kingship to Menestheus, a descendant of an earlier Athenian king. Theseus went into exile on the island of Scyros. There his host Lycomedes, who was a supporter of Menestheus, hurled him to his death from a cliff.

Theseus did not lie in an unmarked grave, however. In 475 BCE Athenian general Cimon (c. 510–c. 451 BCE) found a skeleton on Scyros with huge bones that had been buried with a bronze club. He concluded that the body belonged to Theseus. Legend has it that the burial spot was revealed to Cimon by an eagle that scratched the ground above the grave. He returned to Athens with the skeleton and the club and buried the bones in the center of the city. Athenians were delighted that relics of their greatest hero were returned home. Since Theseus was considered by many as protector of the poor, a sanctuary was made around Theseus's tomb where slaves and poor people could find refuge.

Theseus in drama

In early classical dramas that were largely about other Greek heroes, Theseus's character represented virtues that Athenians believed him to exemplify: generosity, justice, and compassion. In *Heracles* by Euripides (c. 486–c. 406 BCE), Theseus supports Heracles on his deathbed; he promises his friend to uphold his name after his death. In *Suppliant Women*, Euripides again casts Theseus as a

Below: In this 18th-century sculpture by Italian artist Antonio Canova, Theseus is portrayed sitting on the body of the Minotaur.

compassionate hero. In the play Theseus insists that the laws of the gods be respected, and he compels the citizens of Thebes to return the bodies of slain enemies for burial. In *Oedipus at Colonus,* the second play in the trilogy that includes *Oedipus Tyrannus* and *Antigone,* but the last one that Sophocles (c. 496–406 BCE) wrote, Theseus welcomes the aged outcast Oedipus to Athens and restores his abducted daughters to him. At the close of the play, Oedipus leads Theseus to the place where Oedipus will die and entrusts the care of the site to the Athenian leader. According to Sophocles' play, Oedipus becomes a guardian hero of Athens and Theseus becomes a protector of Oedipus's tomb.

Theseus also appears in postclassical literature, most notably in *A Midsummer Night's Dream* by British dramatist William Shakespeare (1564–1616). Although the main action of Shakespeare's play takes place in an enchanted forest outside Athens, the final marriage between Theseus and Hippolyte, the Amazon queen, takes place in Theseus's Athenian palace.

Theseus's myth is a popular subject in ancient and modern art. Depictions of his conquest of the Minotaur adorn many ancient Greek vases and Roman frescoes. Spanish artist Pablo Picasso (1881–1973) had a lifelong interest in bulls as well as in mythology—he painted many versions of the encounter between Theseus and the Minotaur. Italian sculptor Antonio Canova (1757–1822) included a statue of Theseus looking down upon the vanquished Minotaur in his classical collection; the contest also appears in the statuary copies of ancient works in the Tuileries Gardens, Paris.

In ancient Greece, Theseus's exploits were represented on the Treasury of the Athenians in Delphi and on the Hephaesteion in Athens. This temple still overlooks the ancient Agora and was once thought to be dedicated to Theseus; it is now known to have been dedicated to the smith god Hephaestus. To this day a subway stop in Athens is called Theseion for the great Athenian hero.

KARELISA HARTIGAN

Bibliography

Cotterell, Arthur. *Oxford Dictionary of World Mythology.* Oxford: Oxford University Press, 1986.

Euripides, and P. Burian and A. Shapiro, eds. *The Complete Euripides.* New York: Oxford University Press, 2009–2010.

Howatson, M. C. *The Oxford Companion to Classical Literature.* New York: Oxford University Press, 2005.

SEE ALSO: Amazons; Ariadne; Daedalus; Heracles; Hippolytus; Minos; Pasiphae.

TIRESIAS

In Greek mythology, Tiresias was a soothsayer—someone who could predict the future. He was famous around ancient Greece, and people would often travel great distances to seek his advice. He was known for being blind, living to a great age, and repeatedly changing his gender.

Tiresias was the son of Everes, a shepherd, and the nymph Chariclo. He is said to have had three daughters: Manto, Historis, and Daphne. Tiresias lived in Thebes, a great city near Athens. Part human and part divine, he lived to a much greater age than any normal human being. Some sources say he lived for seven generations, which would total more than 150 years. Others say that he lived for nine generations, or up to 200 years.

Tiresias's blindness

There are several different accounts of the cause of Tiresias's blindness. Some say that Tiresias was such a skilled soothsayer that he was able to give away all the gods' plans and secrets to humans, and that the gods blinded him as a punishment. In another version, he was blinded after accidentally seeing the goddess Athena taking a bath. In some accounts Athena blinded him; in others it was the work of the Titan Cronus, who inflicted blindness on any mortal who looked upon a deity without the god's consent. Tiresias's mother, Chariclo, begged Athena to give her son back his sight, but Athena was unable to do this, so she gave Tiresias a different kind of vision—the gift of prophecy. She also granted him the power to understand

Right: In this fifth-century-BCE vase painting, Greek hero Odysseus consults the standing soothsayer, Tiresias. In Greek mythology Odysseus sought Tiresias's advice to help him return to his home and to his wife.

the language of birds, guaranteed him a long life, and said that he would still be able to predict the future after his death, when he went to the underworld.

Changing gender

According to a different myth about Tiresias, one day he came across two snakes mating. He hit them with a stick, killing the female snake. At that moment he was transformed into a woman. Tiresias remained a woman for the next seven years, during which time he got married. At the end of the seven years, he again saw two snakes mating and hit them with a stick. This time the male snake died, and Tiresias became a man again.

Sometime after this, Zeus, the chief Greek god, quarreled with his wife, Hera, about the joys of love and

whether they were better for a man or for a woman. Hera said they must be better for men, which was why Zeus had so many affairs. Zeus said that women had a better time. Since Tiresias had experienced life as a man and as a woman, Zeus and Hera asked him to settle the dispute. Tiresias declared that Zeus was correct, saying that women experience nine or 10 times the amount of pleasure making love than men do. Hera was so furious about losing the argument that she struck Tiresias blind, but Zeus rewarded him by giving him the power to see into the future.

Tiresias and Thebes

Tiresias often helped and advised the people of Thebes. Most famously of all, he revealed to Oedipus, king of Thebes, that he had unknowingly killed his own father and married his own mother. Horrified at the news,

Below: Tiresias, the blind soothsayer, is depicted with a helpful boy in this 18th-century illustration by British artist John Flaxman (1755–1826).

Oedipus blinded himself and ran away from Thebes in despair, leaving the city in trouble. The citizens were suffering from a deadly plague, Oedipus's sons were fighting for the throne, and the city was under attack by invaders. Tiresias declared that the end of the plague would come when a Theban man sacrificed himself. Menoeceus, Oedipus's cousin, killed himself to fulfill the prophecy. However, the city was still plagued, and Tiresias said that the citizens should flee. They did so, eventually coming to a cold spring called Tilphussa. Tiresias is reported to have died after drinking from the waters of the spring.

In the underworld

In the *Odyssey* by Homer (c. ninth–eighth century BCE)—the tale of Odysseus's long journey home from the Trojan War—the enchantress Circe tells Odysseus that he must visit Tiresias in the Land of the Dead and ask him about the future. In the underworld, Tiresias tells Odysseus that he will find the Island of the Sun, and that if he wants to get home quickly he must not harm the magical sheep and cattle that graze there, since they belong to the sun god Helios. However, Odysseus's ships become stranded at the island, and his men cannot resist killing some of the animals to eat. As Tiresias had predicted, Odysseus arrives home 10 years late and alone, after all his men had been killed and his ships wrecked.

Enduring appeal

Tiresias was a well-known character in the ancient world. He was considered to be the greatest and wisest of all soothsayers. Ancient writers who recalled Tiresias's life included Aeschylus (525–456 BCE), Pindar (c. 522–c. 438 BCE), Sophocles (c. 496–406 BCE), Euripides (c. 486–c. 406 BCE), Apollodorus (third century BCE), Hyginus (first century BCE), and Ovid (43 BCE–17 CE). Since then, Tiresias has continued to appear in literature and art. Victorian poets Alfred Lord Tennyson (1809–1892) and A. C. Swinburne (1837–1909) both wrote poems about him, and more famously he appeared as a character in the epic poem *The Waste Land* by T. S. Eliot (1888–1965).

ANNA CLAYBOURNE

Bibliography

Homer, and Robert Fagles, trans. *The Odyssey.* New York: Penguin, 2009.

Ovid, and A. D. Melville, trans. *Metamorphoses.* New York: Oxford University Press, 2008.

SEE ALSO: Daphne; Odysseus; Oedipus.

TITHONUS

In Greek mythology, Tithonus was
the beautiful son of Laomedon and
Strymo, daughter of the Scamander
River. His brother was Priam, king of
Troy. He was beloved by Eos, goddess
of dawn. It was through her that
Tithonus achieved immortality, but not
eternal youth. Thus, he withered as he
grew old and was eventually turned
into a cicada, a loud chirping insect.

In his youth, Tithonus was so good-looking that he
attracted the amorous attentions of Eos, goddess of
dawn, and she carried him off to be her lover.
He fathered two children by her—Memnon and
Emathion. The abduction of mortals by deities for
sexual purposes is a common theme in Greek
mythology. Usually, the gods have their way with
the humans and then abandon them immediately. Eos
herself, for example, had other liaisons at various times
with the humans Cleitos and Orion, and she
attempted another with Cephalus, but these were no
more than brief encounters. The goddess's love for
Tithonus was more enduring than any of the others.
It survived until Tithonus grew old and his hair
turned white. At this point, Eos finally left him, but
even then she let him remain in her palace. There he
continued to feed on ambrosia (the food of the gods)
and wear celestial clothing. At length, however, Tithonus
lost the use of his limbs, and Eos then shut him up in his
bedchamber, from which his feeble voice could still be
heard from time to time.

Ill-chosen words

If nature had been left to take its course, Tithonus would
have died. While he was shut away, however, Eos had
carried off another mortal, the beautiful boy Ganymede.
Zeus wanted this youth for himself, to serve as cupbearer
to the gods on Mount Olympus. Although Eos had to
submit to the chief god's will, she was entitled to ask him
to compensate her for the loss of Ganymede. Her request
was that Tithonus be made immortal. Zeus granted her
wish to the letter, but unfortunately she had phrased it
badly. Eos had demanded only that her lover be given
eternal life; she had not said anything about eternal youth,
or even about arresting the rate of his physical decay.
Thus Tithonus was trapped forever in his disintegrating
body. He became more and more decrepit and wizened
until Eos finally took pity on him and turned him into a
cicada. The insect endlessly croaked his one remaining
desire—to be allowed to die. This story is one of the oldest
in Greek mythology—parts of it were recounted by poet

*Left: The painting on
this amphora from the
second century BCE
shows Eos weeping
over the body of her
son, Memnon.*

Above: To ancient Greeks, dawn was the goddess Eos. Her consort was Tithonus, a mortal to whom she gave the unwanted gift of immortality.

Homer (c. ninth–eighth century BCE). The chirruping noise made by Tithonus after he was turned into a cicada is thought to have been the "unquenched voice" referred to in the "Homeric Hymn to Aphrodite," a poem from the sixth century BCE.

Children of Tithonus

Memnon grew up to become king of the Ethiopians. He dwelled in Africa until the start of the Trojan War, when he promptly answered the call to assist his father's kinsmen. His uncle, King Priam, received him with great honors, and listened attentively as Memnon recounted a series of vivid stories about life in Ethiopia. Only a day

after his arrival, however, Memnon grew tired of reminiscence, became impatient for action, and led his troops into the field. He slew Antilochus, son of Nestor, and the Greek forces broke up in disarray until their champion, Achilles, entered the fray and faced Memnon in single combat. The battle between the two men was long and hard, but eventually the Greek prevailed and Memnon was killed. The Trojans fled the scene. Eos, who had looked on helplessly from the heavens as her son was slain, then sent winds to carry his body to the banks of the Esepus River in Paphlagonia, an ancient region of northern Anatolia (part of modern Turkey). In the evening the goddess traveled there and mourned her son. In another version of the story, Memnon's body was wafted back to Ethiopia, where mourners raised his tomb in the grove of the nymphs near a stream. Zeus then turned the sparks and

Right: This engraving by French artist Bernard Picart (1673–1733) depicts Tithonus turning into a cicada. His lover, Eos, looks on helplessly—she condemned him to eternal life.

cinders of Memnon's funeral pyre into birds. The creatures divided into two flocks that fought each other for the pile of ashes until they fell into the flames and were burned as sacrificial victims. Every year thereafter, on the anniversary of Memnon's death, other flocks of birds returned to the scene and fought to their deaths.

Eos was inconsolable over the loss of her son. Her endless tears could be seen early in the morning in the form of dewdrops on the grass. At a certain location on the banks of the Nile River in Egypt stood a great statue of Memnon. According to legend, when the first rays of the rising sun fell on this effigy, it emitted a mournful sound like the snapping of a harp string.

Emathion, the other son of Tithonus and Eos, became king of Arabia. He was killed by Heracles during the hero's 11th labor, the recovery of the golden apples from the garden of the Hesperides. Emathion's offspring became rulers of Macedon, so he was thus one of the mythical ancestors of Alexander the Great (356–323 BCE).

Literary links

The story of Tithonus has inspired many artists and writers since classical antiquity. Of the ancient authors who covered the topic, the most famous was Roman poet Ovid (47 BCE–17 CE) in the *Metamorphoses*. One of the best-known quotations in English literature—"And after many a summer dies the swan"—comes from the poem "Tithonus" by Alfred Lord Tennyson (1809–1892). In this work the eponymous hero laments his fate, saying sadly of himself: "Me only cruel immortality consumes."

JAMES M. REDFIELD

Bibliography

Bulfinch, Thomas. *Bulfinch's Mythology.* New York: Barnes & Noble, 2006.

Homer, and Robert Fagles, trans. *The Iliad.* New York: Penguin, 2009.

Howatson, M. C. *The Oxford Companion to Classical Literature.* New York: Oxford University Press, 2005.

Ovid, and A. D. Melville, trans. *Metamorphoses.* New York: Oxford University Press, 2008.

Tennyson, Alfred, and Christopher Ricks, ed. *A Collection of Poems by Alfred Tennyson.* Garden City, NY: International Collectors Library, 1972.

SEE ALSO: Achilles; Ganymede; Heracles; Laomedon; Memnon; Priam.

TROILUS

The role of the Trojan prince Troilus in the Trojan War varied according to different authors. In some accounts he was a great warrior, in others a defenseless boy. All versions agree, however, that Troilus was killed by the Greek hero Achilles—it was prophesied that Troy would never fall if the youth reached the age of 20.

According to most sources Troilus was the son of Priam and Hecuba, king and queen of Troy. In a version provided by Greek dramatist Apollodorus (third century BCE), however, the youth's father was Apollo, god of light and prophecy. Some authors regarded Troilus as a relatively unimportant character in the Trojan War: Greek poet Homer (c. ninth–eighth century BCE), for instance, referred only to his death in the epic the *Iliad*—perhaps because Homer felt that Troilus was too young to take part in the fighting. However, much later works, such as those believed to be by Dictys of Crete and Dares the Phrygian, which were translated into Latin around the fourth and fifth centuries CE, respectively, portray Troilus as one of the great heroes of Troy. According to the work by Dares, Troilus was a large and handsome boy who was strong for his age, brave, and eager for glory. He was a fierce fighter who wreaked havoc among the Greeks, especially after the death of his brother Hector at the hands of Achilles. In this version of events, the Greek warriors Diomedes and Odysseus both considered Troilus to be the bravest of men and the equal of Hector.

The death of Troilus

Most accounts agree on the manner of Troilus's death: he was ambushed outside the city of Troy by Achilles, who killed him with his spear in a sanctuary of Apollo. There are, however, differences in the details of Troilus's death. The best-known version comes not from a text but from a vase painting. The sixth-century-BCE François Krater (a vessel used for diluting wine with water) depicts a variety of scenes connected with the murder. In one, Achilles hides while Troilus, on horseback, accompanies his sister Polyxena as she draws water from a fountain. In another, Achilles runs after Troilus, who attempts to flee on his horse. In yet another scene Achilles, who has captured the youth, kills him on Apollo's altar. In the epic *Aeneid* by Roman poet Virgil (70–19 BCE), Troilus flees from Achilles in a chariot, only to become entangled in his horses' reins.

Troilus and Criseyde: a medieval romance

The story with which Troilus is most famously associated comes not from the Graeco-Roman era but the medieval one. The biggest influence on this story was the Latin translations of Dictys and Dares. Until the Renaissance in the 15th and 16th centuries CE, the art of reading ancient Greek was largely lost in the Western world. Consequently the most important sources of Greek mythology—such as Homer's epics—were not available to medieval authors, who had to rely on existing Latin versions of the story of the Trojan War. Although scholars argue that the literary value of the works by Dictys and Dares is limited, it is thought that they constituted an important source of information and inspiration for the medieval romances involving Troilus.

English poet Geoffrey Chaucer's (c. 1342–1400) *Troilus and Criseyde* begins with the narrator sketching the background. Calchas, a Trojan priest, foresees that Troy will fall and therefore defects to the Greek camp, leaving his daughter Criseyde behind in the city. Troilus, a handsome and valiant Trojan prince, falls in love with Criseyde but has no idea how to pursue her. Meanwhile Criseyde, as a young widow, is concerned to maintain her chaste reputation. With the help of Criseyde's uncle Pandarus, who is a good friend of Troilus and more than happy to act as a go-between, Troilus manages to visit Criseyde and win her heart. Their happiness, however, is short-lived: the Trojans lose a battle, and one of their elders, Antenor, is captured. In the Greek camp, Calchas reminds the Greeks that Troy will soon fall and asks them to ensure that his daughter will be reunited with him. The Greeks agree to trade Antenor for Criseyde. In the city, the news

Above: This fresco (c. 550–c. 520 BCE) depicts Troilus on horseback. The fresco comes from the Tomb of the Bulls in Tarquinia, Italy.

comes as a devastating blow to the lovers, who are forced to remain silent about their affair: to reveal it would destroy Criseyde's reputation. The exchange takes place and the pair separate, but only after Criseyde has promised that she will return within 10 days. Soon, however, Criseyde's love for Troilus proves untrue. She accepts the advances of her Greek escort, Diomedes, and betrays Troilus for fear of being left without a protector. Not long afterward, Troilus is killed in battle. Chaucer, however, refuses to put all the blame on Criseyde, whom he considers equally with Troilus to be a victim of love and fortune: "I cannot find it in my heart to chide this hapless woman more than the story will; her name, alas, is punished far and wide, and that should be sufficient for the ill she did; I would excuse her for it still."

Different Versions of Troilus and Criseyde

Chaucer's *Troilus and Criseyde* was one of several versions of the story in the medieval period and later. Chaucer's lengthy poem, composed around 1385, was an adaptation of the work by Italian poet Giovanni Boccaccio (1313–1375), *Il filostrato* (The Love Struck). In turn, Boccaccio's poem was influenced by the 12th-century French poem *Roman de Troie* by Benoît de Sainte-Maure. This poem, which contains the earliest known version of the Troilus and Criseyde story, was a reworking of Homer's *Iliad* based on the works attributed to Dares the Phrygian and Dictys of Crete; it was also heavily influenced by the medieval society in which Benoît de Sainte-Maure lived.

In the late 15th century, at the end of the medieval period, Scottish poet Robert Henryson (c. 1425–c. 1508) took up the theme of the two lovers in *The Testament of Cresseid*, which forms a continuation of Chaucer's story. In Henryson's poem, after Cresseid (Criseyde) betrays Troilus, she is punished by the gods with leprosy. When Troilus finally meets her again he fails to recognize her in her diseased state. Shakespeare (1564–1616) also wrote a version of the story, *Troilus and Cressida*. While some scholars have compared this play unfavorably to his other works, others argue that it should be regarded as a clever alternative to, rather than a flawed example of, a classical tragedy.

Left: A 19th-century engraving depicting Cressida from Shakespeare's Troilus and Cressida. *The medieval character Cressida, or Criseyde, was based on the classical figure of Chryseis, who was captured by the Greeks. The revenge of her father, Chryses, had severe repercussions for the Greeks.*

The love story of Troilus and Criseyde was a medieval invention. While the accounts by Chaucer and other writers (see box) were presented as an ancient tale, with characters' names taken from the legend of Troy, the passions of those characters and their interrelationships were very different from the Greek versions. For example, Criseyde can be identified as Chryseis, the daughter of the Trojan priest Chryses, but in the medieval story her father was a much more famous priest named Calchas. The fact that Calchas was actually a Greek priest seems not to have bothered the medieval audience—if they were even aware of such discrepancies. The Trojan War served merely as a setting for a typical medieval story in which everything revolved around the courtly love of the main characters. Although the Trojan heroes were valiant in battle, they put their romantic interests ahead of their exploits on the battlefield, and love became the main focus of the story.

FEYO SCHUDDEBOOM

Bibliography

Apollodorus, and Robin Hard, trans. *The Library of Greek Mythology.* New York: Oxford University Press, 2008.

Chaucer, and Nevill Coghill, trans. *Troilus and Criseyde.* London: Penguin, 1971.

Hamilton, Edith. *Mythology.* New York: Grand Central, 2011.

Homer, and Robert Fagles, trans. *The Iliad.* New York: Penguin, 2009.

SEE ALSO: Achilles; Hector; Hecuba; Priam.

PRONUNCIATION GUIDE

Using the Pronunciation Guide

A syllable rendered in large capital letters indicates that the syllable should be stressed. Where two syllables are stressed in a single word, large capital letters indicate where the main emphasis should fall, while small capital letters indicate the position of the secondary emphasis.

Achelous	AK-e-LOW-us
Achilles	a-KIL-eez
Actaeon	ak-TEE-on
Adonis	a-DON-nis
Aegir	A-jeer
Aeneas	ee-NEE-ass
Agamemnon	ag-uh-MEM-non
Ajax	AY-jaks
Alcestis	al-SES-tis
Andromeda	AN-DROM-eh-da
Anemoi	a-NEE-moy
Antigone	an-TIG-o-nee
Aphrodite	af-ro-DIE-tee
Apollo	a-POL-o
Arachne	a-RAK-nee
Ares	AIR-eez
Ariadne	ar-i-AD-nee
Artemis	AHR-te-mis
Asclepius	as-KLEP-ee-us
Astarte	as-TAR-tay
Atalanta	at-a-LAN-tuh
Ate	AY-tee
Athena	a-THEE-na
Atlas	AT-las
Atreus	AY-tree-us
Attis	AT-is
Bacchus	BAK-us
Bellerophon	bell-AIR-o-fon
Britomartis	brit-O-mar-tis
Cadmus	KAD-mus
Callisto	ka-LIS-toe
Calypso	ka-LIP-so
Cassandra	ka-SAN-dra
Castor	KAS-ter
Circe	SIR-see
Clytemnestra	kly-tem-NES-tra
Cronus	KRO-nus
Cupid	KEW-pid
Cyclops	SI-klops
Daedalus	DED-a-lus
Danae	DAY-nigh
Daphne	DAF-nee
Demeter	dem-MEE-ter
Deucalion	dew-KAY-lee-on
Diana	die-AN-a
Diomedes	die-oh-MEE-deez
Dionysus	die-oh-NIGH-sus
Dis	DIS
Dryads	DRY-adz
Electra	ee-LEK-tra
Endymion	en-DIM-ay-on
Eos	EE-os
Erichthonius	er-IK-tho-nee-us
Eros	EER-os
Europa	you-RO-pa
Faunus	FAW-nus
Gaia	GUY-er
Galatea	gal-a-TEE-a
Ganymede	GAN-ee-meed
Hades	HAY-deez
Hebe	HEE-bee
Hecate	HEK-a-tee
Hecuba	HEK-u-ba
Helios	HE-lee-os
Hephaestus	hef-EYE-stus
Hera	HER-a
Heracles	HER-a-kleez
Hermaphroditus	her-maf-ro-DI-tus
Hermes	HUR-meez
Hero	HE-ro
Hesperides	hes-PER-e-deez
Hestia	HES-ti-a
Hippolyte	hip-POL-i-tee
Hippolytus	hip-POL-i-tus
Hypnos	HIP-nos
Icarus	IK-a-rus

The House of Troy

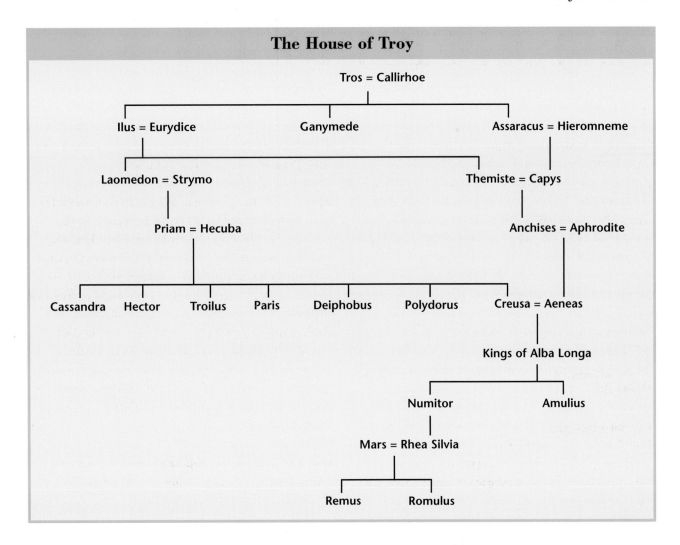

Tros = Callirhoe

Ilus = Eurydice   Ganymede   Assaracus = Hieromneme

Laomedon = Strymo   Themiste = Capys

Priam = Hecuba   Anchises = Aphrodite

Cassandra   Hector   Troilus   Paris   Deiphobus   Polydorus   Creusa = Aeneas

Kings of Alba Longa

Numitor   Amulius

Mars = Rhea Silvia

Remus   Romulus

---

undoing. Advised not to fight Achilles, he did so anyway and was killed.

Menelaus: son of Atreus and Aerope and brother of Agamemnon. He was married to Helen of Sparta, who was considered to be the most beautiful woman in the world. Menelaus fought her abductor, Paris, in a duel and the latter was only saved by the intervention of Aphrodite.

Neoptolemus: son of Achilles who was considered to be a ruthless fighter. He was among the Greek soldiers who hid in the wooden horse. He killed Priam, king of Troy.

Odysseus: king of Ithaca whose great cunning was a key factor in the Greeks' success. The 10-year journey home that he endured after the war was the subject of the *Odyssey* by Homer (c. ninth–eighth century BCE).

Paris: son of Priam and Hecuba. His abduction of Helen, queen of Sparta, was the catalyst for the Trojan War. A great

archer, Paris killed Achilles with an arrow that hit the Greek warrior's one weak spot—his heel.

Patroclus: son of Menoetius and the comrade of Achilles. When Achilles refused to fight, Patroclus dressed in his friend's armor and took to the battlefield in his place. Many Trojans died at Patroclus's hands, but he was finally killed by Hector.

Philoctetes: son of Poeas and holder of Heracles' great bow, the arrows of which never missed their target. He killed Paris and returned safely after the war to either Greece or Italy.

OTHER MORTALS

Arachne: daughter of Idmon of Colophon. She was renowned for her talent for weaving, but was turned into a spider after beating the goddess Athena in a contest to see who could weave the best tapestry.

Cassandra: seer daughter of King Priam and Hecuba who was cursed so that no one would believe her prophesies. After the end of the Trojan War she was taken as a concubine by Agamemnon. She was killed by his wife Clytemnestra on the couple's return to Mycenae.

Clytemnestra: daughter of Tyndareos and Leda; sister of Castor, Helen, and Pollux; and wife of Agamemnon. She was angered by Agamemnon's sacrifice of their daughter Iphigeneia, and jealous of the relationship between Agamemnon and Cassandra. She murdered the lovers when they returned from the Trojan War.

Heracles: the greatest Greek hero. He was the son of Zeus and Alcmene. Heracles was most famous for the 12 labors he was set by Eurystheus as purification for killing his wife, Megara, and their two children. He aided the gods in their successful battle against the Giants, and for his deeds and heroics was immortalized among the gods and had a constellation named for him by Zeus.

Iole: beautiful daughter of Eurytus, king of Oechalia. She was offered in marriage by her father to the winner of an archery contest. It was won by Heracles, but Eurytus did not keep his word. Iole was later taken as a concubine by Heracles. On his death she married Hyllus.

Iphigeneia: daughter of Agamemnon and Clytemnestra and the sister of Electra, Orestes, and Chrysothemis. She was sacrificed by Agamemnon in order to summon a wind that would take the Greek fleet to Troy.

Leda: daughter of the Aetolian king Thestius, and wife of Tyndareos. She was seduced by Zeus in the shape of a swan. Leda subsequently gave birth to two sets of twins— Castor and Pollux, and Helen and Clytemnestra.

Narcissus: beautiful son of the river god Cephissus and the nymph Liriope. Known for his vanity, Narcissus fell in love with his own reflection while gazing into a pool of water.

Niobe: daughter of Tantalus, and wife of Amphion, king of Thebes, by whom she had many children. Niobe's boasts about her fertility angered the goddess Leto, who sent her son Apollo and daughter Artemis to kill Niobe's children.

In her grief Niobe was turned into a rock on Mount Sipylus, where water ran down her face like tears.

Oedipus: son of Laius, king of Thebes, and Jocasta. He unwittingly killed his father and married his mother. By Jocasta he had four children: Antigone, Eteocles, Ismene, and Polyneices.

Orestes: son of Agamemnon and Clytemnestra, and the brother of Electra, Iphigeneia, and Chrysothemis. Orestes killed his mother and her lover, Aegisthus, after they murdered Agamemnon. Orestes was then pursued by the Furies, who wanted to punish him. However, he was saved by the intervention of Apollo.

Orpheus: the most gifted singer and musician in the Greek world, he outsang the sirens while traveling with the Argonauts. Orpheus visited the underworld in a failed attempt to retrieve his dead wife, Eurydice. He then wandered the land mourning her until he was torn to pieces by Thracian women.

Peleus: son of Aeacus, king of Aegina, and Endeis, and brother of Telamon. He was a great warrior and was rewarded with a rare opportunity to marry a goddess, Thetis, by whom he fathered Achilles.

Pelops: son of Tantalus, king of Lydia. He was killed as a child then cooked and served by his father to the gods, who brought him back to life. Pelops eventually became ruler of most of southern Greece. He married Hippodameia, with whom he had many children.

Penelope: daughter of Icarius and the nymph Periboea; wife of Odysseus and mother of Telemachus. For 10 years Penelope waited patiently for Odysseus to return from the Trojan War.

Perseus: son of Zeus and Danae. He killed the Gorgon, Medusa; rescued Andromeda from a sea monster; and founded the city of Mycenae. He and Andromeda married and had a son, Perses.

Psyche: lover of Cupid. With Zeus's permission they were married and Psyche became immortal.

Semele: daughter of Cadmus and Harmonia, and by Zeus the mother of Dionysus. Semele demanded that Zeus appear to her in all his splendor, which he did, burning her to death. Zeus snatched her unborn baby and sewed it into his thigh, from which Dionysus was born.

Sisyphus: wily son of Aeolus, king of Thessaly, and Enarete. He founded Ephyra, which was later called Corinth. He cheated death twice, and when he finally died of old age he was condemned in the underworld to perpetually roll a boulder up a hill only for it to roll back down again.

Tantalus: father of Pelops, Broteas, and Niobe. He was punished by the gods for serving them the flesh of his son, Pelops. His sentence was to stand in water that disappeared when he was thirsty, and within arm's reach of plentiful fruit that moved away from each of his hungry lunges.

Theseus: son of either Poseidon or Aegeus, king of Athens, and Aethra. By the Amazon Antiope, he fathered Hippolytus; later he married Phaedra. Theseus accomplished many heroic deeds, including slaying the Minotaur, a monster with the body of a man and the head of a bull. Theseus was eventually killed by Lycomedes, king of Scyros.

Tyndareos: king of Sparta, husband of Leda, and the father of Castor, Clytemnestra, Pollux, and Helen. On the advice of Odysseus, Tyndareos proposed an oath be taken by Helen's many suitors that bound them to protect her choice of husband. The oath led to the Trojan War.

Nymphs

Callisto: mountain nymph who was raped by Zeus. Hera turned her into a bear when she discovered her husband's infidelity. Callisto's son, Arcas, was ignorant of her identity and nearly hunted her down. However, Zeus took pity on Callisto and transformed her into a constellation called Ursa Major (great bear).

Calypso: daughter of the Oceanid Perse. Her powers of seduction were enough to keep Odysseus on her island and away from his home for seven years.

Daphne: mountain nymph who was pursued by the god Apollo after he had been struck by one of Eros's arrows.

Daphne rejected his advances and was transformed into a laurel tree by her father, the river-god Peneius.

Echo: mountain nymph and a servant of Hera. She agreed to Zeus's plea for her to distract Hera, but was discovered and punished. She lost her ability to speak her thoughts and was only able to repeat what others had already said. Unable to articulate her love for the beautiful Narcissus, she pined away until only her voice remained.

Eurydice: wife of the singer and musician Orpheus. She died twice, first from a snake bite and later when her husband narrowly failed in his attempt to rescue her from the underworld.

Harmonia: mother by the war god Ares of a race of warrior women called the Amazons.

Hesperides: four Naiads named Aegle, Arethusa, Erytheia, and Hesperia who lived in a garden at the edge of the world. There they guarded the golden apple tree that Gaia had given to Hera.

Liriope: lover of the river god Cephissus and mother of the beautiful but conceited Narcissus.

Melite: water nymph who had a liaison with Heracles and gave birth to Hyllus. Hyllus avenged Heracles' death on his father's old enemy Eurystheus.

Perse: Oceanid who was mother of four famous mythological characters: Calypso, who fell in love with Odysseus and kept him on her island for seven years; Aeetes, a fierce king who set a dragon to guard the Golden Fleece; Circe, who detained Odysseus for a year on her island; and Pasiphae, mother of the monstrous Minotaur.

Pleione: Oceanid who was mother of the seven Pleiades. They were immortalized in the night sky as a cluster of seven stars.

Pomona: Dryad who, despite her efforts to remain chaste, was seduced by Vertumnus, the Roman god of the changing seasons.

Rhode: Oceanid for whom the Greek island of Rhodes was named.

FURTHER READING AND RESOURCES

Aeschylus, and A. Shapiro and P. Burian, eds. *The Oresteia.* New York: Oxford University Press, 2010.

Apollodorus, and Robin Hard, trans. *The Library of Greek Mythology.* New York: Oxford University Press, 2008.

Apollonius Rhodius, and R. Hunter, trans. *Jason and the Golden Fleece.* New York: Oxford University Press, 2009.

Bulfinch, Thomas. *Bulfinch's Mythology.* New York: Barnes & Noble, 2006.

Calame, Claude, and Daniel W. Berman, trans. *Myth and History in Ancient Greece.* Princeton, NJ: Princeton University Press, 2003.

Crudden, Michael, trans. *The Homeric Hymns.* New York: Oxford University Press, 2002.

Euripides, and Peter Burian and Alan Shapiro, eds. *The Complete Euripides,* 5 vols. New York: Oxford University Press, 2009–2010.

Finley, M. I. *The World of Odysseus.* New York: New York Review of Books, 2002.

Hamilton, Edith. *Mythology: Timeless Tales of Gods and Heroes.* New York: Grand Central, 2011.

Homer, and Robert Fagles, trans. *The Iliad.* New York: Penguin, 2009.

Homer, and Robert Fagles, trans. *The Odyssey.* New York: Penguin, 2009.

Macgillivray, Joseph Alexander. *Minotaur: Sir Arthur Evans and the Archaeology of the Minoan Myth.* New York: Hill and Wang, 2000.

Ovid, and A. D. Melville, trans. *Metamorphoses.* New York: Oxford University Press, 2008.

Rose, Carol. *Giants, Monsters, and Dragons.* New York: Norton, 2000.

Rosenberg, Donna. *World Mythology: An Anthology of the Great Myths and Epics.* New York: McGraw-Hill, 2001.

Sophocles, and Robert Fitzgerald, trans. *The Oedipus Cycle: Oedipus Rex, Oedipus at Colonus, Antigone.* San Diego, CA: Harcourt, 2002.

Virgil, and Robert Fagles, trans. *The Aeneid.* New York: Penguin, 2009.

West, Martin L., ed. *Homeric Myths, Homeric Apocrypha, Lives of Homer.* Cambridge, MA: Loeb Classical Library, 2003.

FOR YOUNGER READERS

Bolton, Lesley. *The Everything Classical Mythology Book.* Avon, MA: Adams Media Corporation, 2002.

Colum, Padraic. *The Children's Homer: The Adventures of Odysseus and the Tale of Troy.* Mineola, NY: Dover Books, 2004.

Colum, Padraic. *The Golden Fleece and the Heroes Who Lived before Achilles.* New York: Random House, 2010.

Fleischman, Paul. *Dateline: Troy.* Cambridge, MA: Candlewick Press, 2006.

Green, Jen. *Ancient Greek Myths.* New York: Gareth Stevens, 2010.

Innes, Brian. *Myths of Ancient Rome.* Austin, TX: Raintree Steck-Vaughn, 2001.

Lively, Penelope. *In Search of the Homeland: The Story of the Aeneid.* New York: Delacorte Press, 2001.

Schomp, Virginia. *Myths of the World: The Ancient Greeks.* New York: Benchmark, 2008.

Schomp, Virginia. *Myths of the World: The Ancient Romans.* New York: Benchmark, 2009.

INTERNET RESOURCES

The Age of Fable: Thomas Bulfinch

Electronic version of the 1913 edition of Bulfinch's compilation of myths, including Greek and Roman myths.

www.bartleby.com/bulfinch

Digital Librarian: Mythology

A collection of links to sites that are useful to students of mythology.

www.digital-librarian.com/mythology.html

Encyclopedia Mythica

Encyclopedia of mythology, folklore, and legends from around the world. The site is divided geographically, with Greece and Rome included in the section for Europe.

www.pantheon.org

Etymological Dictionary of Classical Mythology

A site that lists modern words and terms derived from figures or episodes from classical mythology.

http://library.oakland.edu/information/people/personal/kraemer/edcm/contents.html

Forum Romanum

The site, dedicated to Roman literature, contains works by a vast number of Roman authors in the form of both original Latin texts and English translations.

www.forumromanum.org

God Checker

Aimed largely at younger users, this humorous site contains descriptions of the gods of a variety of ancient civilizations, including Greece and Rome.

www.godchecker.com

Gods, Heroes, and Myth

This general site for world mythology contains particularly comprehensive lists of Greek and Roman mythology.

www.gods-heros-myth.com

The Golden Bough: A Study in Magic and Religion

Electronic version of the 1922 edition of James Frazer's *The Golden Bough*, a study in comparative mythology.

www.bartleby.com/196

Greek Mythology Link

Extensive site that includes maps, timelines, and biographies of all the major characters in Greek mythology.

www.maicar.com/GML

Internet Classics Archive

Collection of English translations for ancient texts, primarily works written by Greek and Roman authors such as Apollodorus, Pausanias, and Ovid.

http://classics.mit.edu/index.html

The Mystica

This site that provides information on world mythology features sections on Greek mythology, Roman mythology, and Greco-Roman mythology.

www.themystica.org/mythical-folk/info/topics.html

MythHome

Comprehensive site that covers all the major pantheons, including ancient Greece and Rome, with material organized by culture, time, and theme.

www.mythome.org/mythhome.htm

Mythography

This site is dedicated to Greek, Roman, and Celtic mythology and includes extensive links to other relevant print and online resources.

www.loggia.com/myth/myth.html

Mythweb

Aimed primarily at younger users, this site provides a basic introduction to Greek mythology, including the Olympian deities and the major myths.

www.mythweb.com

Olga's Gallery: Ancient Greek and Roman Myths

This catalog of paintings that depict scenes from classical mythology allows the user to select a Greek deity or hero and then view a selection of paintings that feature him or her.

www.abcgallery.com/mythindex.html

Theoi Project: A Guide to Greek Gods, Spirits, and Monsters

This comprehensive site features extensive lists of Greek mythological figures and explores Greek mythology in classical literature and art.

www.theoi.com

Windows to the Universe

This site, aimed at younger users, includes information about the relationships between space and mythology. Material related to Greece and Rome is included in the Classical Mythology section.

www.windows2universe.org/mythology/mythology.html

INDEX

Page numbers in **boldface** type refer to main articles. Page numbers in *italic* type indicate illustrations.

PICTURE CREDITS

COVER
Pandora (front top): Photos.com
Perseus (front bottom): Photos.com
Medusa (back): Shutterstock, Clara Natoli

FRONT MATTER
Trojan Horse (p. 1): Photos.com
Icarus (p. 4): Shutterstock, Thor Jorgen Udvang
Medusa (p. 6): Shutterstock, Clara Natoli

ARTICLES
AKG: 47, 61, 76, 84–85, 90, 95, 116, 121, 125, 144, 230, 252, 274, 280; Cameraphoto 113, 148, 231, 261; Erich Lessing 38, 41, 58, 67, 68, 69, 70, 72, 74, 82, 96, 101, 106, 111, 122, 123, 141, 166, 192, 200, 206, 210, 211, 287, 289, 296; Gilles Mermet 54, 135; Joseph Martin 156; Nimatallah 137, 140; Rabatti 130; Rabatti-Domingie 107, 150, 269; S. Domingie 80.
Art Archive: Archaeological Museum, Ferrara/Dagli Orti 193; Archaeological Museum, Naples/Dagli Orti 30; Archaeological Museum, Sparta/Dagli Orti 174; Archaeological Museum, Tipasa/Dagli Orti 242; Bardo Museum, Tunis/Dagli Orti 182; Bodleian Library, Oxford 216; Chateau de Chambord/Dagli Orti 59; Dagli Orti 164, 175, 302; Heraklion Museum/Dagli Orti 26; Jan Vinchon Numismatist, Paris/Dagli Orti 196; Louvre, Paris/Dagli Orti 105, 109, 139, 152, 232; Musee des Beaux-Arts, Besancon/Dagli Orti 279; Musee des Beaux-Arts, Orleans/Dagli Orti 209; Museo Civico, Allessandria/Dagli Orti 265; Museo Nazionale Taranto/Dagli Orti 29; Museo Nazionale Terme, Rome/Dagli Orti 195; National Archaeological Museum, Athens/Dagli Orti 239; Palazzo Pitti, Florence/Dagli Orti 27; Royal Palace, Caserta/Dagli Orti 11.
Ashmolean Museum, Oxford: 87.
Boston Museum of Fine Arts: 51.
Bridgeman Art Library: Alinari 264; Art Gallery and Museum, Kelvingrove, Glasgow 78; Ashmolean Museum, Oxford 227; Birmingham Museums and Art Gallery 167; Bolton Museum and Art Gallery 205; British Museum 131; Courtauld Institute Gallery, Somerset House, London 187; Faringdon Collection, Buscot, Oxon, UK 228; Ferena Art Gallery, Hull City Museums and Art Galleries 93; Fine Art Society, London, UK 66; Fitzwilliam Museum, Cambridge 142; Galleria degli Uffizi, Florence 42, 251; Hermitage, St. Petersburg, Russia 17; Leicester City Museum Service 248; Louvre, Paris/Giraudon 46, 217; Musee des Beaux-Arts, Calais 286; Musee des Beaux-Arts, Rouens/Giraudon 45; Museum of Fine Arts, Budapest 291; National Museum Wales 21; Palazzo Ducale, Mantua 118, 198; Palazzo Vecchio, Florence 138, 253, 259; Peter Willi 234–235; Rafael Valls Gallery, London 219; Rijksmuseum Kroller-Muller, Otterlo, Netherlands 103; Roy Miles Fina Paintings 267; Southampton City Art Gallery, UK 250; Staatliche Museen, Berlin 281; Victoria and Albert Museum, London 295; Worcester Art Museum, Massachusetts 94; York Museums Trust 297.
Brown Reference Group: 32, 278.
Corbis: Alexander Burkatovski 71; Alinari Archives 19, 183, 283; Araldo de Luca 22, 44, 89, 97, 104, 129, 197; Archivo Iconografico SA 10, 43, 88, 102, 151, 157, 236, 276; Arte & Immagini srl 13, 132, 161, 241; Bettmann 24; Chris Hellier 179, 218; Christie's Images 136, 225, 268; Corcoran Gallery of Art 33; Dave G. Houser 288; David Lees 81; Francis G. Mayer 8, 100, 178; Gail Mooney 112; George McCarthy 256; Gian Berto Vanni 258; Gianni Dagli Orti 25, 50; Historical Picture Archive 110, 300, 303; Jason Hawkes 77; Michael Nicholson 181; Mimmo Jodice 14, 64, 143, 149, 247, 266; National Gallery Collection 168, 233, 245; North Carolina Museum of Art 31; Paul Almasy 115; Roger Wood 180; Ruggero Vanni 237; Sandro Vannini 12, 272; Stapleton Collection 39, 160; Todd A. Gipstein 128; Yann Arthus-Bertrand 48.
Eye Ubiquitous: G. Betts 184.
Getty Images: Hulton Archive 203.
Jim Steinhart: 172.
Karelisa Hartigan: 235.
Kobal Collection: Warner Bros. 270.
Lebrecht Collection: Interfoto, Munich 20, 37, 65, 79, 159, 190, 199, 207, 223, 224, 285; Rue des Archives 23, 188, 201.
Mary Evans Picture Library: 62, 86, 108, 145, 155, 158, 169, 171, 176, 186, 202, 213, 214, 215, 229, 277, 290; Arthur Rackham Collection 177, 226.
Photos.com: 191, 299.
Photos12.com: 263; ARJ 16, 92, 220, 221, 222; Oasis 255.
Rene Seindal: 127, 154, 249, 275.
Scala Archives: Corsini Collection, Florence 262; Galleria Sabauda, Turin 194; Gregorian Museum of Etruscan Art, Vatican 298; Ministero Beni e Att. Culturi 126; Musee Jacquemart-Andre, Paris 294; Museo Archeologico, Ferrera 63; Museo delle Ceramiche, Florence 55; Museo Etrusco Guarnacci, Volterra 240; Museo Gregoriano Profano, Vatican 212; Museo Nazionale, Naples 238; Museo Pio-Clementino, Vatican 173; Padua, Palazzo Papafava 114; Palazzo Poggi, Bologna 73; Palazzo Pubblico, Siena 271; Rovigo Pinacoteca dell' Accademia dei Concordi 60.
Topham: 53; British Library/HIP 146; British Museum/HIP 34, 170, 208, 292; Charles Walker 52, 57, 195; Photri 257.
Travel Ink: Richard Rawlingson 243.
Werner Forman Archive: 282, 284; Private Collection 35.
World Art Kiosk: John P. Ross 165; University of California/Kathleen Cohen 9, 28, 293.